Faulkner and the Artist

FAULKNER AND YOKNAPATAWPHA

1993

Faulkner and the Artist

FAULKNER AND YOKNAPATAWPHA, 1993

EDITED BY
DONALD M. KARTIGANER
AND
ANN J. ABADIE

UNIVERSITY PRESS OF MISSISSIPPI
JACKSON

PS
3511
.A86
Z 783 1157
1996

99 98 97 96   4 3 2 1

The paper in this book meets the guidelines for permanence and durability of the
Committee on Production Guidelines for Book Longevity of the
Council on Library Resources.

Library of Congress Cataloging-in-Publication Data

Faulkner and the artist / edited by Donald M. Kartiganer and Ann J.
Abadie.
    p.   cm. — (Faulkner and Yoknapatawpha, 1993)
Includes index.
    ISBN 0-87805-849-4 (cloth : alk. paper). — ISBN 0-87805-848-6
(pbk. : alk. paper)
    1. Faulkner, William, 1897–1962—Characters—Artists. 2. Art and
literature—Southern States—History—20th century. 3. Artists in
literature. I. Kartiganer, Donald M., 1937– . II. Abadie, Ann
J. III. Series: Faulkner and Yoknapatawpha series.
PS3511.A86Z78311265   1996
813'.52—dc20   95-41964
                                                           CIP

British Library Cataloging-in-Publication data available

To
Evans Harrington
Director
Faulkner and Yoknapatawpha Conference
1974–1993

Contents

Introduction

1

"Faulkner and the Artist"—from the outset the topic seemed anachronistic, even quaint. It emerged, in part, in response to the fact that 1993 was the twentieth anniversary of the Faulkner and Yoknapatawpha Conference, and thus a suitable moment to emphasize precisely that quality in Faulkner and his work that led to the conference's original founding, but which has been minimized in recent years. Clearly, the "art" of the writer, his power to render into a unique language and vision the world around him, has given way in current literary criticism to the power of the external world itself: the contextual forces of history and culture, of race, class, and gender, of prior uses of language from sources high and low. Together they comprise a set of preexistent pressures inscribing themselves within the work to which the single artist—William Faulkner—signed his name, but from which, in large part, he has been removed.

To be sure, the topic "Faulkner and the Artist" does not in itself necessarily violate the critical movement toward context, as this volume certainly demonstrates. Here are essays analyzing the impact of the visual arts on Faulkner; the presence in his texts of his giant precursor *Ulysses*; the capacity of social narrative, the "already told," to determine Faulkner's own telling.

Yet, everywhere in the volume is at least the implicit idea of Faulkner the maker, taking hold of myriad influences, compelling them to yield place to his own re-creation. Despite the awareness these writers have of how much the world made him, "Faulkner and the Artist" cannot help but remind us of how much Faulkner remade the world, converting even its most secretly powerful determinants, its multiple ideologies, into an imagery distinctively his own.

It is a matter of outrageous irony, perhaps, but in literature the great social clashes of history no less than the painful experience of

ix

the individual are secondary to the meaning which they take on through the skill, the talent, the imagination and personal vision of the writer who transforms them into art. Here they are reduced to more manageable proportions; here they are imbued with humane values; here, injustice and catastrophe become less important in themselves than what the writer makes of them.[1]

This is Ralph Ellison, writing in 1964, making the case—very close to the beginning of that period in literary study in which the case would have to be made—for what we have come to call, and frequently dismiss as, "literary heroism." It is an argument I will attempt neither to amplify nor contest here, although obviously it is far closer to the attitude of William Faulkner than that of the majority of his most astute critics today. Rather, before properly introducing the essays that follow, I want to say something about how much Faulkner— perhaps to a unique degree—was an artist, and nothing but an artist. That is to say, regardless of whether one sees his work as the result of his culture or the revision of it, one has the sense that he was a writer whose life outside writing not only has never truly come clear to us, but in a strange way never existed. It is as if, pace Foucault, it is not the author who disappeared but the man.

A common, indeed nearly unanimous, observation among Faulkner's biographers is his habit of role-playing, a habit so persistent as ultimately to create an impenetrable barrier to the revelation of his personality. The biographical consensus is as well a confession that, whatever the exhaustive accounts of what he did and said and wrote, the subject remains an enigma. Joel Williamson states the problem candidly. Among writers of Faulkner's generation, he writes, "none was so deeply unknowable. . . . Virtually no one, it seems, ever knew the real Faulkner." Tracing the long history of poses and posturing—the wounded World War I pilot, the bohemian artist, the town bum, the tough-guy bootlegger, the romantic suitor, the farmer, the gentleman rider—Williamson summarizes, by way of measuring the greatness of the writer and the elusiveness of the man: "One of his gifts, perhaps his greatest gift, was that there was no certain Faulkner, nor even a given sequence of Faulkners. It was endless Faulkner. He could be almost anything, take almost any view within the compass afforded him by his culture. In successive phases of his life, he tried very nearly all of them."[2]

This sense of the various faces of Faulkner hiding the real man is not merely the conclusion of his major biographers, only one of whom—Joseph Blotner—actually knew him. In an interview with Judith Sensibar in 1986, his daughter, Jill Faulkner Summers, said: "Pappy always—it would be hard for me to say that I could look at him at one point and say, 'this is who he really is,' because, almost always he was playing a part."[3] In life and in death, to his contemporaries and to his biographers, the prevailing theme of his character is its mystery.

Combined with the vividness of Faulkner's poses are the remoteness, the silences, the capacity to withdraw in social situations, that add not only to his unknowableness, but to the suspicion that he was determined to maintain it. In *William Faulkner of Oxford*, a collection of over forty accounts by people who knew him, many of them over a period of years, there is constant reiteration of this remoteness: "You might speak to him all day long and he wouldn't recognize the fact that you were around. Sometimes he didn't greet his best friends on the street. He didn't mean to be rude—just preoccupied. His friends understood him and knew that he was in no mood to talk. They accepted that fact."[4]

His daughter Jill may have accepted it less easily, yet came to regard it as a given in their relationship: "There was no such thing as the library ever being off-limits. I spent much of my childhood reading on the couch while he was working. I could even talk at him, make comments and such; but I wasn't supposed to ask direct questions, and I wasn't to *expect* an answer. When Pappy was really concentrating, he didn't hear anything anyway. Nothing could bother him."[5]

Some interpreted that "preoccupiedness" as indifference,

possibly even a form of contempt. Albert I. Bezzerides, a screenwriter and friend of Faulkner in Hollywood in the 1940s, recalls: "there was always a kind of distance between us. He always managed to keep himself separate. If he sat with people in the living room, you always had a feeling he was not really there; he was in his head somewhere. He was off thinking about what he was doing. I think we probably bored him to death because he participated very little in conversation or anything." When Bezzerides would occasionally take Faulkner on long drives, "I always talked because he never said a thing; he never said one word. I found the silence a little difficult to stand, so to fill the silence, I would talk about hunting or trucking trips I had made out of Fresno in my youth. Once, during one of my transitions or pauses, Bill said, 'Bud,' and I said, 'Yeah, what is it, Bill?' He said, 'Bud, you're an animal, but I'm just a vegetable.' "[6]

A vegetable because he had nothing to say? because he required the most attentive cultivation? or because, among animals at least, he was of another species entirely?

The corollary of his aloofness, for his more sympathetic acquaintances, was that in detaching himself from them he was inhabiting profounder spheres of thought and observation. If he did not seem to see the face before him, it might be because, as Emily Whitehurst Stone said, "his eyes . . . burned through the flesh and bone of everybody in front of him." Missed by those around him, even when he was ostensibly there, he himself missed nothing—nothing at least of what he believed he needed to see. He once surprised Emily by commenting on some changes she had made in the furnishings of her home.

"You surprise me," I said. "Phil says you never see anything."
"I see everything," he said.[7]

There were those who claimed close friendship with Faulkner, yet recognized, and observed, the inviolable borders he erected. Dr. Felix Linder knew Faulkner since boyhood: "I've been around him every which way you can imagine. I've known him in my practice. I've been hunting with him. I've been fishing with him. I've been on the place with him: he's got a farm out here on Highway 30 East. . . . [But] William never did talk about his writing. Never even spoke to me about it. Never said a word about it to me. I didn't want to ask him."[8]

Dr. Linder was not, of course, the only one. Except when he was asking for advances from his publishers, laying out the plots and time frames of future work, Faulkner—once he was past the apprentice years with Phil Stone—did not discuss his writing with anyone. And yet, what was the friendship made of in which the largest part of a character was utterly off limits? Phil "Moon" Mullen put it succinctly: "Bill Faulkner and I were not what you would call intimate friends. I doubt if he had any."[9]

From these quite representative recollections an image emerges analagous to an iceberg: on the surface a self character-ized either by remoteness or by masquerade; beneath, the 90 percent mass, a private, undisclosed being. What was it the masks protected? Was there a self he dared not reveal, or one he did not know and wished in his "preoccupation" to discover? Was it, as Williamson writes, that Faulkner "could never imag-ine that [the world] would take him as he was"?[10] Or was it, in ways that defy any kind of biographical or psychological evi-dence, that Faulkner was only, and supremely, an artist? Per-haps it was not only a plea for privacy but a declaration of identity when he wrote to Malcolm Cowley that "the sum and history of my life" should simply read: "He made the books and he died."[11]

When I first visited Oxford, at the 1987 Faulkner conference, I heard a story, several versions of which I have heard since— not, as it turns out, describing the same incident, but referring to an incident which happened more than once. A woman at the conference, who had grown up in Oxford but since moved away, remembered how as a four- or five-year old in the 1950s she had encountered the famous writer. She was playing on the sidewalk outside her home, probably on South Lamar, when she noticed a man walking toward her—tweed jacket, khaki trousers, pipe—

headed for the Square. As he came abreast, she said, "Good morning." The man kept on walking without saying a word. She burst into tears and dashed into the house. Upon questioning by her mother, she explained what had happened; the description of the man (and possibly his behavior) left no doubt in the mother's mind as to his identity. Immediately she was on the phone to Maude Falkner. "Miss Maude, this is ————; you have *got* to do something about that son of yours! He just walked past my little girl in the street without so much as a hello, and she's standing here crying her heart out!"

"That son of yours" was, of course, over fifty years old at the time, and the recipient of the most prestigious literary honor in the world. The tone of Maude's reply, however, at once conciliatory and resigned, indicated this was not the first such phone call she had received. She would indeed talk to Billy, but she urged the mother to tell her daughter that he meant no harm. "He just didn't see her," Maude insisted, "he was writing."

Writing, of course, is what writers do. If Faulkner seems a unique example of that activity, it is owing, on the one hand, to his enigmatic character, his remarkable inaccessibility even to those closest to him, and, on the other hand, to the quality and enormous output of his writing. During the fifteen-year period 1928–1942 Faulkner wrote nine or ten novels (depending on how one regards *Go Down, Moses*), and wrote or revised over seventy short stories. Six or seven of the novels, a score of the stories, are among the indisputably major works of American literature, and virtually all the writing is of compelling interest. As the example of a single writer's sustained excellence, there is nothing to equal it in the twentieth century.

Behind the quantity and the quality is Faulkner's overwhelming tenacity and dedication. During these years, he was forced, because of financial difficulties, to do eight different tours of duty, of varying length, as a screenwriter in Hollywood. He lost his first child shortly after her premature birth and his youngest brother Dean in a plane crash. His marriage to Estelle was enduring yet unhappy, and it led him into a number of love affairs, which created their own turmoil. Yet, the fact is that nothing could stop him. In 1931, the year that his daughter died, he published sixteen stories and began *Light in August*, which he completed six months later. Following the death of his brother, while staying with his widowed sister-in-law and mother, he finished the final chapters of *Absalom, Absalom!* The financial problems, the marital problems, his need to assume, in his middle thirties, responsibility as the head of his family and the support at times of over a dozen people—none of this seemed to stand in his way, whatever his frequent complaints. It is as if all this life, which occasionally drove him to despair, could merge for him into the material within which he acted, and yet outside of which he truly lived: striding the world a foot above it, absorbing all of it as, oblivious, he passed it by: "he was writing."

2

Joel Williamson's "A Historian Looks at Faulkner the Artist" is at once a personal essay on the condition of being a historian— and a historian of William Faulkner in particular—as well as an account of a crucial occurrence in the life of Faulkner's great-grandfather, William C. Falkner. Or, to put it more accurately—given Williamson's acute awareness of the different responsibilities and methods of the writer of fiction and the writer of history—a historian's calculated guess as to the facts of that occurrence. Shortly before the conference on "Faulkner and the Artist" began, Williamson's *William Faulkner and Southern History* was published, which includes a carefully argued and plausibly, if not definitively, documented claim that Faulkner's great-grandfather, the "Old Colonel," fathered a daughter with a mulatto slave around 1864, beginning a mulatto line of Falkners that continues to the present. Williamson's essay is both the story of Falkner's "shadow family" and the story of Williamson's discovery of it: the story of Emeline Lacy Falkner and her children, Delia, Hellen, Arthur, and—very possibly the daughter of William C. Falkner—Fannie Forrest Falkner. The process of discovery leads Williamson, like a real-life incarnation of Faulker's Ike McCaslin, from census records to the Ripley cemetery, from the home of Emeline's great-granddaughter Elizabeth to Rust College in Holly Springs, from which Fannie Forrest Falkner was graduated "near or at the top of her class." Williamson the historian cannot refrain from admitting that the story may not be true: "I never found the document in which the Colonel said Fannie is my daughter." Yet he argues for its likelihood, as well as for the fact that "the implications of this for William Faulkner's life and work are myriad and profound."

What these implications are, Williamson does not spell out, but they are obvious enough. One of the great moral issues of Faulkner's fiction—central to *Absalom, Absalom!* and *Go Down, Moses*—is the white man's denial of the black man or woman who is his kin. Did Faulkner have black kin of his own, of whom he knew and refused to acknowledge? And did he write these two novels in self-serving forgetfulness of his own knowledge, or as self-indictment in the only expression that truly mattered to him—his fiction?

As the indispensable biographer of Faulkner, and as the author of a soon to be published biography of Robert Penn Warren, Joseph Blotner approaches Faulkner the artist by comparing his life and writing to Warren's—beginning with the extraordinary fact that a Nobel Prize winner and America's first Poet Laureate were born eight years apart in two small Southern towns, New Albany, Mississippi, and Guthrie, Kentucky, within two hundred miles of each other. Although they seem to have met only once, brought together by their mutual editor Albert Erskine in 1952, they shared not only a general Southern heritage (whatever the differences between the Middle South and the Deep South), but a common ancestry from the British Isles. More striking are the romantic frustrations of their youth: seeing the objects of their affection marry "taller, better-looking men"; missing the opportunity to participate in either World

War I or World War II—"they both missed the war and lost the girl." Ultimately, of course, their careers moved in very different directions: Faulkner the high school dropout, supremely devoted to the single genre of the novel; Warren superbly educated, a master in virtually all the literary genres, as well as an editor, critic, and teacher. Yet their work reveals common concerns and qualities, perhaps above all, the recognition of humanity "bound by something like Original Sin yet capable of redemptive action if not salvation."

In "Faulkner, Home, and the Ocean," Michel Gresset explores the biographical and aesthetic implications of "homecoming" in Faulkner: of a life spent largely in Oxford and of a fiction "in which, literally or symbolically, homecoming is enacted again and again." Interestingly enough, Gresset finds this preoccupation with homecoming first adumbrated in a Faulkner letter of 1921 to his mother, describing the Atlantic Ocean and a feeling inspired by it of having recovered something forgotten: "as if I could close my eyes, knowing that I had found again someone who loved me years and years ago." This theme of return, of remembering, of home, quickly shifts to its more dominant physical manifestation—the hill—in a story the following year; yet both ocean and hill retain in Faulkner's fiction their significance as part of a "set of fantasies," a controlling imagery, a way of articulating both the sense of the foreign and the well-known, curiously exemplified, in his first great novel, by the alien individual—months from suicide—still moved by a familiar figure: "like a sign put there saying You are home again."

The next three essays move from biographical concerns to Faulkner's relationship to the fine arts: those of his native South, particularly as practiced by female artists; the revolutionary world of early twentieth-century painting; and the architecture of Oxford and Lafayette County.

In "Cracked Urns: Faulkner, Gender, and Art in the South," Susan Donaldson examines Faulkner and his work in terms of his response to the shifting definitions of male and female roles in the early twentieth century. Seeing himself in a somewhat embattled position—disturbed by the emergence of the New Woman on the national scene as well as by the long tradition of female prominence in Southern visual and literary art— Faulkner fashions a model of manhood in which success is measured by the male capacity to "contain" women both as artist and as man: "creating art implicitly defining the artist as male and the object of artistic desire and creation as female." Yet his uneasiness over the difficulty and complexity of such containment—or perhaps the inherent uneasiness of a fictional vision that constantly refuses the clarity of all boundaries—leads not only to the creation of comically ineffectual artist figures like Elmer and Horace Benbow, but to a series of novels—*The Sound and the Fury, As I Lay Dying, Sanctuary, Light in August*, and *Absalom, Absalom!*—in which women characters somehow escape, at least partially, the desperate efforts of males to confine them within strict demarcations. Complicating a characteristically high modernist sense of the male as spectator and the female as object of the gaze is "the barely suppressed fear that woman could not, after all, be successfully contained, that the boundaries lying between woman as the object of art and desire and man as artist and creator were distressingly subject to violation."

For Panthea Reid, Faulkner was an incipient visual artist— much encouraged by his mother Maude, herself a painter— whose gradual familiarity with Post-Impressionist art forced him to recognize his own limits as a painter, yet provided him with a theory and method that he would eventually import into his radically innovative prose fiction. In the work of Cezanne, Seurat, Gauguin, Van Gogh, Matisse, and Picasso, Faulkner discovered a visual modernism that "posited a whole new rela- tion between the artist and the world," abandoning representa- tionalism, the idea of painting as a vehicle for conveying a world external to itself, and instead emphasizing the art's own "internal values," its own medium of expression. Turning to manuscript and typescript evidence, Reid argues that Faulkner's different methods of revising his poetry and his prose reveal his

attempt to duplicate in his fiction an artistic process of "breaking
and bending and reassembling planes" that he found in modern
painting. Having "failed" as painter and poet, Faulkner suc-
ceeded in fiction because it was only in that form that he could
enact the great lesson of modern painting: "that the work of art
is the creation of the artist who is free to use the medium as she
or he pleases."

While readers of Faulkner are invariably aware of the natural
world of his fiction—the woods, the rivers, the land from which
tenant farmers eke a meager living or which country people
tediously travel—they have been much less conscious of what
Thomas Hines calls "the built environment" of that fiction: the
human-made structures that in fact are far more prominent than
the natural ones. In "William Faulkner and the Meaning of
Architecture: The Greek Revival of Yoknapatawpha," Hines
points to Faulkner's fictive architecture as a "tangible past," a
visible documentation of the continuation of time, sometimes
over generations. Central to most of Faulkner's Yoknapatawpha
novels is a significant architectural presence: the houses of
Sartoris or Compson or Sutpen, the old Frenchman's Place, the
courthouse. The style of these structures, reflecting the taste of
the nineteenth-century South, is the neoclassic expression of
the Greek Revival—a style which, Hines demonstrates in great
detail, characterizes many of those public and private buildings
of Lafayette County and Oxford which became the models for
the buildings of Yoknapatawpha and Jefferson.

The second half of the volume takes up more purely literary
issues: intertextuality both within Faulkner's texts and between
those texts and their various precursors; artist figures in the
fiction; the ultimate separation of art from life.

In "Recovering the Teller in the Tale: An Unfinished Project,"
Wesley Morris at once recognizes the postmodernist deconstruction of the artist—the myth of the godlike genius calmly
aloof from his creation—and seeks to reinstate him, not as a
specific individual but as "story" itself, or "the forces that
produce stories." Implicit to those forces is a relationship be-

tween teller and listener, a set of exchanges, a dialogue, that is "fundamentally ethical and political." Morris is acutely sensitive to the way in which social narratives produce "reality," generating meaning and value from "facts." Facts, he writes, have dual allegiances: to the material world and to narrative: "A fact is matter phrased or narrated. Narration gives meaning, creates interest, envisions consequences, and judges guilt and innocence." The great potential of literature and the artist—which postmodernism, in its insistence on the absolute absence of that which is before or after textuality, has been unable to account for—is the capacity to represent an alternative to the "reality" created by the dominant, often repressive, social narrative. The suggestion Morris offers—tentatively enough to render this project "unfinished" yet enormously provocative—is that the "peculiar genius of the imaginative storyteller is in hearing the already told and in envisioning how it may be retold in order to foreground the ethical and political." The possibility of such artistry is what the postmodern needs to consider if it is to "address the material needs of life."

In " 'Paradoxical and Outrageous Discrepancy': Transgression, Auto-Intertextuality, and Faulkner's Yoknapatawpha," Martin Kreiswirth addresses the intertextuality that characterizes Faulkner's fictional practice—not the relations between Faulkner's texts and those of other writers, but the relations among Faulkner's own texts, the "auto-intertextuality" so prominent in a corpus whose creation of a world, a Yoknapatawpha cosmos, has seemed to many readers its most significant achievement. Of particular concern to Kreiswirth is the tendency of critics to stress those intertextual connections that "project comprehensiveness, totality, unity, and monologism," while ignoring those that project "discontinuity, heterogeneity, dialogism, and contingency." Borrowing from the work of Michel Foucault, Kreiswirth argues that a "transgressive textual activity" is central to Faulkner's art, a strategy of "subversions and incongruities" that militates against closure. Although citing numerous examples of discrepancy *between* texts, Kreiswirth concludes his argument by focusing on the gaps *within Absalom, Absalom!* that open between the various appendices—the chronology, genealogy, and map—and the novel proper. These inconsistencies "produce and indeed model precisely the transgressive activity that underwrites the whole of Yoknapatawphan intertextuality itself." It is an activity, Kreiswirth claims, that readers must not ignore or stabilize, but acknowledge as a "self-contradictory plenitude that denies ultimate coherence."

Michael Zeitlin describes a more conventional kind of intertextuality, that between Faulkner's *Pylon* and Joyce's *Ulysses.* Fundamental to "*Pylon*, Joyce, and Faulkner's Imagination" is his desire to restore the artist's presence, his role as a conscious "dominant player" in the analysis of the relationship between literary texts. Zeitlin is sensitive to the current argument of "intertextuality," the notion that authors are less the deliberate speakers of their discourse than ambiguous figures "dispersed" into it, and that intertextual dynamics are a dialogue of units of language rather than individual authors in quest of a distinctive voice. Yet he insists that traditional notions of influence cannot be ignored, that Faulkner "read, rewrote, and 'cathected' other texts" in ways that can be incorporated into the study of the "wider 'nets' of interconnecting cultural discourses." Focusing on *Pylon*, the novel Faulkner wrote while "in trouble" with *Absalom, Absalom!*, Zeitlin analyzes Faulkner's engagement with another text—Joyce's *Ulysses*—which he imitated and revised "in order to solve a whole range of narrative problems uniquely relevant to [his] predicament as both an artist and historical subject in the year 1934."

For Candace Waid, one of the most fascinating aspects of Faulkner's fictional accounts of the artist at work is his tendency to employ the imagery of sexuality. In "The Signifying Eye: Faulkner's Artists and the Engendering of Art," Waid focuses on the early fiction up to *The Sound and the Fury*, as well as *The Wild Palms*, in which specific concern with "the conception, genesis, and orgins of a work of art" reveals a series of male artist figures who are at once sensitive to the traditional connection between creation and procreation and "haunted and lured by the troubling presence of the female body." Faulkner's artists participate in a process that seems to try to duplicate female procreation even as it denies female sexuality; the work of art is idealized as the virgin female body, yet it implies the act of birth as "a terrifying creation from a female abyss," the womb as both the ultimate creator and the signifier of nothing. In detailed readings of the "Wild Palms" section of *The Wild Palms* and *The Sound and the Fury*, Waid describes the sexual drama of Charlotte and Wilbourne, culminating in the death of the female visual artist at the hands of the male writer, and the crisis in *The Sound and the Fury* of the male narrators, whose words crumble in their attempts to articulate the "absent" yet visually figured female force of Caddy.

While critics have often commented on the various artist figures in Faulkner—the sculptor Gordon of *Mosquitoes*, the glassblower Horace Benbow of *Flags in the Dust*, the lyrical narrator Darl of *As I Lay Dying*—Michael Lahey points to Faulkner's many lawyers as artist figures, generally of a corrupt nature. In "The Complex Art of Justice," Lahey summarizes Faulkner's own art as "a social, creative, healing practice that explores the productions, extensions, and applications of law as a social, narrowly creative, never healing practice." In novels such as *Sanctuary*, *The Wild Palms*, *Go Down, Moses*, and *The Town*, Faulkner presents several versions of the law as (in its practitioners' hands) an institution that "invents itself for its own ends," creating not only its own rules and regulations but even "that fictional sense of order and place that law justifies itself as existing to serve and protect." In other words, it creates itself in order to create the world—not so much in response to its subjects and their changing needs but in the service of its own virtually autonomous and mechanistic operation.

In " 'Longer than Anything': Faulkner's 'Grand Design' in *Absalom, Absalom!*," Robert Hamblin identifies a division in the novel between the "design" of Thomas Sutpen and that of his creator, primarily as a means of exploring Faulkner's understanding of the function and power of art. Hamblin argues that Faulkner's development from *The Marble Faun* to *Absalom, Absalom!* manifests a gradual shift from an emphasis on the superiority of life over art to its reversal. By the mid-1930s Faulkner's increased pessimism—owing to the arrival of middle age, frustration over his inability to achieve critical or financial success, his unhappy marriage, and his continuing alcoholism— led him in *Absalom* to tell a story demonstrating the fundamental, necessary predetermined tragedy of history. Over against that necessary tragedy, however, stands the artist's imagination, the creative power that makes a "mark," a "scratch," the endurance of which becomes Faulkner's representation of the artist's capacity "to defeat time and death." From the novel's very title to the map that constitutes its true ending, Faulkner lifts the material of the novel from fact to myth, from "the inevitable, downward spiral of history" to the "evocation of an order and harmony." The result is a novel, and a Faulknerian aesthetic, that transforms a history of "futility and failure" into a "celebration of the superiority of art over life."

Although famous for his obsession with his privacy, Faulkner was the subject of numerous photographs, many of them through his own arrangement. In "The Ephemeral Instant: William Faulkner and the Photographic Image," Thomas Rankin describes the writer's response to the art of photography as practiced on him: its power "to reinforce existing truths and create new realities," its susceptibility to control by the subject as well as its power to distort that subject. Rankin is primarily concerned with three groups of photos—those taken by the Cofields (Colonel J. R. and his son, Jack), Martin Dain, and Alain Desvergne—and the different images of Faulkner they produce, ranging from at least the appearance of informality and intimacy to the carefully staged.

The volume concludes with a short story, "Uncle High Lonesome," and an homage to Faulkner and Samuel Beckett, which the novelist and short story writer, Barry Hannah, delivered during the conference. Neither summary nor quotation are necessary here, except to say that it is reassuring to be reminded that splendid American prose did not die with the subject of the conference. Faulkner's contributions to our literature are not simply his own art products and his example of dedicated artistry, but the artists who have followed: uplifted, inspired by him.

Donald M. Kartiganer
The University of Mississippi
Oxford, Mississippi

NOTES

1. Ralph Ellison, *Shadow and Act* (New York: The New American Library, 1966), 148–49.

2. Joel Williamson, *William Faulkner and Southern History* (New York: Oxford University Press, 1993), 5, 332.

3. Judith Sensibar, " 'Drowsing Maidenhead Symbol's Self': Faulkner and the Fictions of Love," in *Faulkner and the Craft of Fiction: Faulkner and Yoknapatawpha, 1987*, ed. Doreen Fowler and Ann J. Abadie (Jackson: University Press of Mississippi, 1989), 139.

4. J. W. (Bill) Harmon, "Hometown Actor," in *William Faulkner of Oxford*, ed. James W. Webb and A. Wigfall Green (Baton Rouge: Louisiana State University Press, 1965), 93.

5. *Faulkner and the Craft of Fiction*, 132.

6. Louis Daniel Brodsky, *William Faulkner: Life Glimpses* (Austin: University of Texas Press, 1990), 61, 65.

7. Emily Whitehurst Stone, "Some Arts of Self-Defense," in *William Faulkner of Oxford*, 96, 98.

8. Felix Linder, "A Gentleman of the First Order," in *William Faulkner of Oxford*, 172–73.

9. Phillip E. Mullen, "The Fame and the Publicity," in *William Faulkner of Oxford*, 162.

10. *William Faulkner and Southern History*, 328.

11. *The Faulkner-Cowley File: Letters and Memories, 1944–1962*, ed. Malcolm Cowley (New York: The Viking Press, 1966), 126.

A Note on the Conference

The Twentieth Annual Faulkner and Yoknapatawpha Conference sponsored by the University of Mississippi in Oxford took place August 1–6, 1993, with nearly three hundred of the author's admirers from thirty-five states and twenty-one countries in attendance. The conference brought together eminent critics and historians to examine the topic "Faulkner and the Artist" and to share the latest findings in Faulkner research. Lectures presented at the conference are collected in this volume. Brief mention is made here of other activities that took place during the week.

The conference opened on Sunday, August 1, with a variety of events. First, the University Museums hosted a reception for conference participants and offered a special viewing of *Glennray Tutor's Mississippi: Night and Day Paintings*. The artist, whose illustrations have appeared on six Faulkner and Yoknapatawpha posters, was on hand to greet guests and talk about his work.

At the opening session, after Chancellor R. Gerald Turner welcomed participants, Patrick McCarthy of Hattiesburg and Lakeysha Greer of Magnolia received the 1993 Eudora Welty Awards in Creative Writing. Presenting the awards, selected annually through a competition held in high schools throughout Mississippi, were author Joan Williams and William Ferris, director of the Center for the Study of Southern Culture.

Conferees were then treated to an Opera Memphis production of two Faulkner novels set to music by Nashville songwriters David Olney, Tom House, Karren Pell, and Tommy Goldsmith. None of the composers had had operatic experience before Michael Ching, artistic director of Opera Memphis, enlisted them to work with his company's National Center for the Development of American Opera. The collaboration produced the two works presented at the conference, a series of songs based on *As I Lay Dying* and a one-act operatic version of the first chapter of *Light in August*. Singing lead roles in the performance of *Light in August* were Nancy Hornback, resident artist with Opera Memphis, as Lena Grove, and Dale Morehouse, then director of the University of Mississippi Opera Theatre, as Henry Armstid. The composers themselves performed the *As I Lay Dying* selections, delighting the audience with their music and with comments about their first encounters with opera and with Faulkner.

Faulkner's home, Rowan Oak, was the site of the awards ceremony for the fourth Faux Faulkner Contest, sponsored by American Airlines' *American Way* magazine, Yoknapatawpha Press and its *Faulkner Newsletter*, and the University of Mississippi. At this year's ceremony special guest Jack Hemingway, son of Ernest, and *American Way* publisher George W. Lodge joined Dean Faulkner Wells, organizer of the contest, in congratulating the winner, Peter Stoicheff, a professor at the University of Saskatchewan.

After a buffet supper, held on the lawn of Dr. and Mrs. M. B. Howorth, Jr., and sponsored by *American Way*, Gloria Baxter of Memphis State University presented her stage adaptation of *As I Lay Dying*. Originally performed at the Museum of Modern Art in Paris, the production features the central presence of Addie Bundren and attempts to capture in live performance "the thunder and the music of the prose" that, for the spellbound reader of Faulkner's great novel, "take place in silence." Appearing in the conference performance were Memphis State students and faculty and, in the role of Addie, Shira Malkin Baker of Rhodes College. The day's program ended with an autograph party at Square Books.

Monday's program consisted of four lectures and the presentation "Knowing William Faulkner," during which J. M. Faulkner, through slides and stories, provided unique insight into the personality of his famous uncle. Other highlights of the conference included panel discussions by local residents and the "Teaching Faulkner" sessions conducted by visiting scholars James B. Carothers, Robert W. Hamblin, Arlie Herron, and Charles A. Peek. Chester A. McLarty was moderator for "Oxford Women Remember Faulkner," a panel discussion featuring Mary McClain Hall, Anna Keirsey McLean, and Bessie Sumners. Howard Duvall, Xandra Williams Jenkins, and Patricia Young served as panelists for the "Faulkner in Oxford" session M. C. Falkner moderated.

The week was filled with lectures, discussions, performances, and other activities as well. On Tuesday, conference participants toured various locales—Lafayette County, Holly Springs, New Albany and Ripley, Pontotoc, the Mississippi Delta, and Bruce, Calhoun City, and Vardaman. Before going off to another lecture, the pilgrims were refreshed at a party at Tyler Place given by Ruthie and Chuck Noyes, Sarah and Allie Smith, and Colby Kullman. The annual picnic at Rowan Oak was rained out this year, but plenty of fried chicken was served up, with bluegrass music, in Johnson Commons on campus.

Rain also caused the closing party to be moved from Ammadelle, home of Mrs. John Tatum and her family, to St. Peter's Episcopal Church. There a fond farewell was bid to Evans Harrington, director of the conference for twenty years. Dan Williams, acting chair of the University's English Department, and many others commended Harrington for his patience, gentle guidance, and generosity over the years. He was presented with a bronze statue of Temple Drake, sculpted by the accomplished local artist Bill Beckwith of Taylor, Mississippi.

The conference planners are grateful to all the individuals and organizations who support the Faulkner and Yoknapatawpha Conference annually and especially to those mentioned herein. In addition, we offer thanks to Mrs. Jack Cofield, Dr. William E. Strickland, Mr. Richard Howorth of Square Books, Mr. James Rice of Holiday Inn/Oxford, the City of Oxford, the Oxford Tourism Council, the Southern Arts Federation, the National Endowment for the Arts, the Lila Wallace-Reader's

Digest Fund's Opera for a New America Program, and the Plough Foundation.

Finally, our deepest thanks go to Evans Harrington, to whom this volume is dedicated.

Faulkner and the Artist

FAULKNER AND YOKNAPATAWPHA

1993

A Historian Looks at Faulkner the Artist

JOEL WILLIAMSON

I want to thank the Department of English and the Center for the Study of Southern Culture for this opportunity to take a look back at a book that I finished writing a year and a half ago, but saw for the first time two days ago here in Oxford. The book, *William Faulkner and Southern History*,[1] seemingly miraculously, appeared at Square Books last Saturday (July 24, 1993). It was supposed to appear everywhere Thursday, but it didn't, and, judging from previous experiences in the publishing world, I was hoping it would surface some time before the first snow next winter. But lo and behold, Saturday it *was* published in Oxford. We don't know about the rest of the world, but it showed up here. And, of course, Oxford is the one place in the world where it ought to appear.

You can't help but compare the first appearance of a book with the birthing of a baby. This book was previously scheduled to be published on May 6th, and I felt very full, ready to deliver. But it didn't come. A month goes by and I feel larger, more pregnant, and even more nervous. Then comes June 6th and I'm getting more anxious. A ten-month baby? Then comes July 6th and I'm even more anxious. Now it's approaching August 6th and I'm getting very large and exceedingly anxious. What does a twelve month baby look like, I began to ask myself. Will it already have teeth and talk?

Now that the book is out, I feel like sending Oxford University Press a telegram like the one Dorothy Parker sent to a woman friend after she had delivered her baby. Dorothy Parker had a mind that was very quick. She was fond of one-liners. So

3

when her friend had her baby, Dorothy sent her a telegram. "Congratulations," it said, "I knew you had it in you." I knew Oxford had the book in it, and I am glad to see it delivered.

It is appropriate, today, that I talk about Faulkner as an artist and myself as a historian because we do share one large thing. We were both failures in our first major ambition in life. Faulkner failed as a poet and became a writer of fiction; I failed as a writer of fiction and became a writer of history. For him prose fiction seemed to be second best and for me writing history is second best, too. So that leaves me looking at Faulkner, indeed looking at artists generally, with envy and desire.

I first came to Faulkner only in my forties after nearly twenty years of studying Southern culture. In particular, I had been studying black/white relations in the South. Then, in the process of offering a new course, I had to read *Intruder in the Dust*, and I was hooked immediately. I read all of Faulkner in one fell swoop—if you can say that you can read all of Faulkner in one fell swoop. I came out with great envy of him.

I had just finished the first draft of a book on race relations. It came to be called *The Crucible of Race: Black-White Relations in the American South Since Emancipation*.[2] To complete that book, I had done several years of really intensive research. The mode was day by day, week by week, all by myself for months at a time, on the road from archive to archive, all the way from Cambridge, Massachusetts, to Austin, Texas, and all points in between. When I read Faulkner, I found that he had somehow intuited what I had so laboriously learned. He already knew what I had learned, not just about race relations, but about the essentials of Southern culture. He had not made his rounds through the archives.

Also he had not sweated and paid his scholarly dues. He had not had twenty-four semesters of college and university education, a fact of my own life that I noted with dismay just before I left graduate school at Berkeley. Each semester, students indicated on a registration sheet how many semesters he or she had been in school. So a freshman would enter one as he or she registered for the second semester, and postgraduate students would get up into the teens and twenties. I recall the last one I filled out declared that I had spent twenty-three semesters of my life in school.

The contrast with Bill Faulkner is glaring. Here was this man who was a self-confessed defector from the academic process after the seventh grade, and he knew what I knew; in fact, he knew more than I knew, and he expressed it more movingly. He had not endured—suffered rather—the academic process, and yet he too found that Southern culture is peculiarly marked by race, sex, and violence with a little bit of "class" thrown in. Class is not the right word, I think. Social hierarchy in the South, yes, but class lines, no. That's a Northern and European idea that people keep trying to impose on the South without much success. But race, sex, and violence get you very, very close to the Southern essence. Faulkner got there, and got there, it seemed, by less tedious means than mine. There was one last insult, he got there in his thirties, and I only got there in my forties. It is akin to the situation with professors of mathematics, who all seem to bloom at twenty-three while most of the rest of us only start at thirty-five. Comparatively, we seem retarded.

Envy was one of two emotions, twin emotions. There was also desire—the desire to gain some of that power and imagination that he had, and to fold those into what I was doing as a scholar.

One way to get at the nature of the tension involved here is to talk about *The Caine Mutiny*. *The Caine Mutiny* is a novel by Herman Wouk that was published in 1951. It is about a very minor warship, the *Caine*, which served in the Pacific during World War II. The commanding officer of the *Caine* is Captain Queeg. Captain Queeg is a coward and a tyrant. In combat, in the face of the enemy and under fire, he is about to pull the *Caine* out of the line of battle. His officers relieve him of command—always an exceedingly serious, very dangerous proceeding for naval officers. There is a court martial that finally vindicates Queeg's accusers.

I was in the Navy when *The Caine Mutiny* came out. There was a great turmoil among the Navy's officer corp about this book. They said that no Captain Queeg had ever existed among them. He was not a real person. It was a slander. "I've never known a naval officer like Captain Queeg," they insisted. This kind of criticism hit the national media. Finally, I read something that resolved the question for me. There was one senior officer somewhere who said he had never met a Captain Queeg in all his years in the Navy, but if he took all the bad qualities of all the officers he had ever known and put them together, they would be Captain Queeg.

For me, this captures the essence of the tension between fiction and history. In fiction, you can create a character out of qualities that you know exist in the broad spectrum of humanity. In history, purely and simply, you only inherit the character. The characters are there in the form dictated by the evidence at hand, and you have to deal with that evidence. In fiction, you can create a character that suits your imagination. There may be a price to pay. The reader reads the character, and he or she says either it does work or it does not work. In fiction, you use your imagination and take your chance. There may well be a bill to pay if you are a bad artist, a bad writer.

In the historical profession we are trained not to take chances, to invite no bills. We are trained to collect and revere hard evidence that leads to solid conclusions and to fear the use of imagination in presentation that might lead merely to suggestions. Imagination is necessarily bridled by the training that one gets in graduate school in history in America. This was more true in decades past than now. Only recently have there been signs that we might be moving away from this. But it is by no means smooth sailing for the adventurously imaginative graduate student today. The professionally wise student follows the route well charted by older sailors.

The best illustration of the intensity of that training that I can think of actually involved a rebellion against it by a very contrary historian who had a fantastic imagination. I don't recall this man's name, but he came out of one of the large universities in the Midwest. He reached the dissertation stage in his doctoral program. He went to the Library of Congress in Washington and spent weeks, perhaps months there. Everyone saw him diligently copying down notes. He went back home and wrote his dissertation. He defended it, got a job and began teaching somewhere. Then after a couple of years, somebody wanted to work on an allied topic. He did what historians often do—get somebody's work that's close to your interest, chase the footnotes down, spread out, and start over by building on work already done. This researcher secured a copy of the dissertation, went to the Library of Congress, and began the chase. He took one footnote, looked for the information and found that it wasn't there. He took another footnote, went back, looked for the information and found that it wasn't there. He ran a whole sequence, and none of it was there. This man had imagined all of his footnotes. There was no basis for his dissertation. He just wrote it. It was a story, a plausible story, and even experts in the field believed it. God only knows why he did that. It probably would have been easier to research and write the dissertation in the usual way. But it was undeniably a brilliant display of imagination. He was defrocked, of course. Defrocked historians always drive taxis. I don't know why that is, but he is probably driving a taxi somewhere today. My guess is Milwaukee.

We do not want to abolish evidence. And we are certainly not going to plead that we should abolish historians. What we want to do is make a plea for tolerance in the historical profession in relation to presentation; for differing styles of presentation; for alternative ways of offering the truth the scholar is trying to find in deep research. To begin to explain my meaning, I want to tell you about a section in *William Faulkner and Southern History*—a section we can call the "Emeline Story." I want to talk about how history works in that story, and about how the book tests the tolerance of my profession for the use of imagination in the presentation of the material I found.

First let me fill in the background about how I came to begin this book, and then talk about the "Emeline Story." First off, why did I come to Faulkner so late—only in my forties? In truth, I was about seventeen when I first saw a page of Faulkner fiction. I was a freshman at the University of South Carolina. I had grown up in a little town in upstate South Carolina that had a great library. During my early teens, I would go into the library and, metaphorically, run my finger along the stacks. I would encounter an author with six inches of books, nine inches of books, twelve inches of books, and I would start reading that author. I had only the vaguest idea about who these writers were. Thomas Wolfe was about two feet—big, big books. I read all that—just going down the line. I would get very sad toward the end of a run because I was losing—leaving—that author's universe. I would have to go trolling through the stacks again. But Wolfe, Dos Passos, Hemingway, everybody was there . . . except William Faulkner.

This began about 1943. Then I went to the University of South Carolina as a freshman in September, 1946. I went to the library and into the fiction section. I was trolling with my finger again, and there was Faulkner. I had a vague idea that if you were really intelligent and if you aspired to say you were educated, you were supposed to have read Faulkner. So I pulled out a volume at random, and opened to the first page. I read that one, and the next, growing more confused. I couldn't make heads or tails of it. It didn't make sense. You're making the right guess—these were the first pages of *The Sound and the Fury*. I said to myself, you must be dumb, Joel. You can't even understand the first pages of this book. I looked both ways to make sure no one saw me, closed the book, and slid it back in the stacks.

I didn't touch Faulkner again until I was a professor giving an undergraduate seminar—"Race Relations Through Litera-ture"—in the early 1970s. I decided I needed to include a Faulkner book in the course. I asked a literary scholar which one I should use. He said *Intruder in the Dust*. That triggered me. I read it, and, as they say, "it blew me away." I just could not believe that man knew so much about the essences of Southern culture—especially race relations—and had not been where I had been in universities and archives. But he did. And he presented it so vividly and powerfully through fiction. Of course, as a historian, I was debarred from writing anything like that. But the next time around, a year later, the "Race Relations Through Literature" seminar became "William Faulkner and Southern History." It still is. As the students read and discussed seven Faulkner novels during the first eight weeks, I lectured on Southern culture and Faulkner biography. At first, for the biography, I pirated Michael Millgate unconscionably, and then I pirated Joseph Blotner unconscionably.

I offered that seminar for several years, and then I accepted an invitation to go to Harvard in the fall of 1981 to be a partial replacement for David Donald, another notable Mississippian and one of the great American historians. Being a guest, I was able to choose my courses. I asked to give the lectures that I usually do in Chapel Hill on "White Culture and Race Relations in the American South," and my Faulkner undergraduate seminar. At Harvard students did not sign up for their classes beforehand. They simply attended classes first and registered later. The Faulkner seminar had space for fifteen students, but seventy-five appeared for the first meeting. It was a mob scene. Faulkner had not been offered at Harvard during living memory, and they all wanted to get into the Faulkner seminar. Harvard students are always aggressive, bumptious and bright, so they raised Cain. "I want this class," everyone demanded. Then the battle line broadened. "Why doesn't the English Department teach Faulkner?" they asked. Authorities, officially, made no response. Weeks later, I was at an academic gathering, drinking the sherry that I learned was mandatory in the scholarly process at Harvard, when a professor of literature came to me. Somehow, he felt he had to explain what had happened. "Well, Mr. Williamson," he said after we had passed the preliminaries, "it's not that we have anything against Mr. Faulk-

ner. And it's not that we have anything against the South."
Then, with a slight shrug of the shoulders, he added, "We just
don't do anything in the twentieth century." That was it. No
Faulkner at Harvard it seems. Not Faulkner's fault. Not even
the fault of the South.

The semester passed quickly. Next April I mailed off the
typescript for *The Crucible of Race*. I mailed it off on Friday
and actually on Monday I intended to start another book that
was tentatively titled *The Souls of White Folk*. It was to be a
large study of twentieth-century Southern white culture. I got
out of bed and sat down to write. I couldn't begin, so I started
writing Faulkner. I started writing the book that day, making
myself put one word down and then the next. That was 1982. It
took two more years for *Crucible* to find print. Then during
another two years I did an abridgment called *A Rage for Order*.[3]

Faulkner was on the back burner until the summer of 1986,
and then I began to dig and dig earnestly. I came to Mississippi
prepared to do whatever I had to do to find him wherever he
was. I was led first to look at the ancestry. The idea here was to
use the ancestry to educe the culture that produced the artist
who produced the art. By this time, I had a scheme going for
the book in which I would use the ancestors as part one to set
up the culture. Thus real people would carry themes of race,
sex, violence, and social hierarchy. At the same time I would
use their lives to lay down patterns of economics, politics,
religion, and ideas. So, first I would establish the broad cultural
context and then swing into the life as part two and end with
the writing as part three. That's essentially the way I was
teaching this undergraduate seminar.

I came to Mississippi to stay a while. I went to Ripley, the
original Falkner homeplace. I hate to confess my ignorance, but
I had loosely concluded that Faulkner's great grandfather, the
"Old Colonel," was a great slaveholding planter who happened
to live in town. He was not. He was, essentially, a town-
dwelling business person and sometime lawyer. There was no
plantation and never a large number of slaves. I began to make

the ordinary moves a historian would make. I went to the public library, where happily that brilliant archivist Tommy Covington had already gathered and processed a mass of material on both local history and the Falkners.

One of the first things I did was look at the census of 1850, which was the first fully detailed census conducted in the United States. I found the Old Colonel right away. He lived in Ripley. He had a two-year-old child. He was living with a middle-aged widow and the remainder of her family. I knew that his first wife had recently died. So he had made a household for himself and his son by bringing in the widow—not unusual at all in those years when early death and fragmented families were common. Then I looked at the slave schedule. There were five slaves that belonged to William Falkner. They lived in his yard, in his household. These five slaves were two young adults, male and female; two teenagers, boy and girl; and one infant about a year old. As a historian, I knew what this profile most likely meant. These five slaves, particularly the four older ones, were taken out of a larger holding. This is a dowry, as it were, for a wife. That turned out to be the case. They had belonged to Holland Pearce, Falkner's deceased wife.

Next, I perused the 1860 census. In 1860 Falkner had six slaves in his yard: two adults and four children. But there had been a striking change. All of those first five in 1850 were described as "black" and all of those in 1860 as "mulatto." Census takers did not do family trees. They looked at the faces. Signs of white blood got "M" for mulatto. So the census taker came to Falkner's house, and he found a mulatto woman twenty-seven years old. Also in the yard was a mulatto man aged twenty-one, and four mulatto children who were eight, six, four, and one. Again the historian says this was the usual 1800s birthing pattern. A woman would have a child soon after mating, and then she would have a child at two year intervals after that for four years. After three children, there was often a hiatus. There might be another flight of three, or birthing became sporadic. You really couldn't tell. It had to do with the way a woman's body naturally recovered after delivery. There would be an interval during which she could not conceive again.

In 1980 I had published a book on miscegenation called *New People: Miscegenation and Mulattos in the United States*[4] in which I studied interracial mating and the children that resulted. I found a pattern in antebellum slaveholding that I called the "shadow family." In this situation the man in the white household, the slaveholder, had a white family in the front of the house while he had a mulatto family in the back of the house. The slave mother was almost always a domestic. She was almost always a mulatto. Very often she was a very light mulatto. She would begin to have children. There would be three in a row spaced about two years apart. Then would follow a hiatus and scattered birthing.

Falkner is an obvious suspect as the father of these children. There was no smoking gun as yet, just the pattern. Over the next four years, before I found the smoking gun—or rather *a* smoking gun—I carried that possibility in my mind. I watched for the usual signs. Often the master favored his children. Sometimes there would be conspicuous favoritism in his will. Sometimes the will provided for the emancipation of certain slaves, for their education as carpenters, domestics, or other occupations, and resettlement in free territory. Early on, I found the Old Colonel's will—nothing. But he wrote it in 1889, only weeks before he died. The children in the census of 1860 would already be well into adulthood, already taken care of, so there was not much to conclude from their absence from his will.

Meanwhile, I easily found the mulatto family of 1860 in subsequent censuses. The two older males were not related, but the older female was mother to the three younger children. It happened that there were only two sets of Falkners in Tippah County. There were the white Falkners and there were the mulatto Falkners. I quickly found the mulatto family in the census of 1870. There was Emeline Falkner, the mother. She was thirty-three in 1870 and forty-three in 1880, not thirty-seven and forty-seven, hence the twenty-seven in 1860 should have been twenty-three. In 1870 there was a fourth child. In that year Emeline's daughter Fannie was six years old, also mulatto, and lived with her mother. Emeline was "keeping house" amongst the gentry in Ripley. So here was Emeline Falkner. I knew her name now, her age, her "color," and the general profile of her life. Then in the census I found the first child, Delia, and the second child, Hellen. They were both working as domestic servants for the gentry in Ripley. Then I found the little boy who was one year old in 1860, Arthur. In 1870, he was, in essence, put out as an apprentice to a farmer. I ran their names on through the census of 1910. All were still alive in Ripley. Soon I found marriage and other relevant records in the courthouse. I knew fairly well where they were and what they were doing over the years.

And then one day I was browsing in the Ripley town cemetery and behold, there they were. All in a row. Falkner Edgerton here, Hellen's son and grandson to Emeline. Then there was Hellen on one side of a tombstone and Delia on the other side. The tombstone on the middle grave was mossed over so that I could not read it. After a day or so, I confessed my dilemma to Tommy Covington, the local librarian. He pulled out a sheet of paper, some tape, and a crayon. He told me how to make a rubbing. I did so, and it read, "Mrs. Emeline Lacy Falkner." It gave her birthdate and death date under a dedication, "Sacred to the Memory of Our Mother," and over a benediction, "Blessed Are the Pure in Heart for They Shall See God." There was Emeline. She died October 17, 1898.

So evidence began to build. Meanwhile, I was working on all kinds of other things relating to Faulkner's ancestry—going to the courthouse, going to the Chancery Clerk's office and pulling down those giant old record books, antebellum, postbellum, looking for anything the Old Colonel was doing—what was he buying, what was he selling. He bought and sold slaves fairly often, I noted, but he held only several at any given time.

I was scanning those pages when I saw that in 1881 Emeline bought a lot from Richard J. Thurmond. Richard Thurmond was the man who shot and killed the Old Colonel in 1889. I had already been shocked to find in the census of 1880 that Emeline and Fannie were working as domestics in Thurmond's house. In 1880, amazingly, the woman who used to live in Falkner's yard was working in the house and living in the yard, along with her teenage daughter, of the man who would kill the Old Colonel in 1889. The mystery got thicker and more interesting. I identified the lot Emeline bought. It was just north of "the African Church." I was able to find it on the maps that surveyors used and to identify the street. Just at that time I had to drive to Memphis to give a talk to the West Tennessee Historical Society. I had to leave Ripley, but I thought I would just drive by that piece of property. I drove by and there were three houses on Emeline's lot. An African American woman was sitting on the porch of one house. I so much wanted to stop and open a conversation, but I didn't feel that I had time.

I went on to Memphis, gave the talk on Friday, and returned Monday morning. I went to the courthouse again. Plowing through the transaction books, I found Emeline's story. Emeline was originally owned by a man from Virginia named Benjamin E. W. Harris. Ben had brought Emeline and her two children, Delia and Hellen, to Waverly, Tennessee, sometime before 1856. He "pawned" those slaves to a lender for $400. Early in 1857 he had to come up with that $400 or else lose the slaves and something like another $500, considering the approximately $900 they were worth in that time and place. Harris was taking advantage of the economic realities of cotton slavery. In the 1850s, the price of cotton was going up and the price of slaves doubled in the decade. The further west you went—into newly developed cotton lands—the more valuable slaves were. All Ben Harris had was Emeline and those two children. These two children would turn out to be his by Emeline. He was borrowing money on his own two daughters and their mother. In Tennessee in 1857, he found that he could not pay back the $400. He had an uncle down in Tippah County, of which Ripley was the county seat. Ben wrote him. The uncle arrived with $400 and enough money to get them back down to Tippah County. Now the uncle had a bill of sale for these slaves that actually covered a loan.

They all came to Tippah County. One imagines that Harris and Emeline and those children were in some tortured way a family. Soon Harris's uncle sold Emeline and her children to his son. By now she had given birth to a male child. She and her three children were worth about $2000 by estimates made in Tippah County. The uncle sold Harris's family to his son, and the son put those folks in a buggy and drove to Helena, Arkansas. There he and his father, who followed by rail and boat, tried to sell them for $2200. But buyers were not buying. Finally, they gave up and returned to Tippah County.

Meanwhile, Harris hurried to Helena looking for Emeline and his children, but he couldn't find them. Back in Ripley, he went to court. His lawyer was John Wesley Thompson, the Old Colonel's uncle. The clerk of court was Richard Thurmond, the man who would shoot and kill the Old Colonel. Thurmond issued an order saying, "Hold these slaves until we get some bond to insure against their sale." The slaves were then sequestered by the sheriff, who was, incidentally, John Young Murry, William Faulkner's other Ripley great-grandfather. The affair went on for a couple of years very slowly. The uncle and his son died, both suddenly. Unbridled imagination says that Emeline was not totally innocent, and poison came into play. Or, perhaps, they died natural deaths. They certainly *should* have died some kind of early death.

Finally, Harris engaged another lawyer. His new lawyer was William Falkner. In the summer of 1859, the case suddenly accelerated. Now affidavits were taken. Court was held, and the judge decided that Harris could have his slaves back if he paid the estates of these deceased relatives $525. He did that by "pawning" his slaves again—this time to Falkner. Falkner loaned Harris $900 on Emeline and her children. You can imagine that $525 went for the debt, a lot of money for Falkner's fee as attorney, and a little for Ben Harris. Thus, these mulatto slaves came to be in Falkner's yard in 1860.

At this point in the research, I was saying to myself, so that was it. The mystery was solved. Benjamin E. W. Harris was the father. Emeline was the mother and these were their children. Those two mulatto males, ages twenty-one and eight, in the Falkner household in 1860 were simply inventory in the slave trade. Harris was the father of Delia, Hellen, Arthur, and, presumably, Fannie.

That afternoon, I drove over to Emeline's lot. Fortunately, the woman was sitting on her front porch again. She could not help me, she said, but referred me to her neighbor. That neighbor was, marvelously, Emeline's great-granddaughter, Elizabeth, Hellen's granddaughter. She is a gracious lady, and we soon fell into an easy and eager exchange of information. There came a time in our conversation when I felt I needed to confirm that Harris was the father of Emeline's children—to close that family circle with testimony from the family itself. "So," I said, making a question of the statement, "Ben E. W. Harris was the father of Delia, Hellen, Arthur, and Fannie?"

"No," Elizabeth responded, "the Colonel was Fannie's father."

Needless to say, I was astounded. Harris was, indeed, the father of the older children, but Fannie was the *Colonel's* daughter! Elizabeth went on to tell me about Falkner and Fannie. The Colonel always took care of Fannie, acting as her protector in the town—where, for example, some people thought she dressed too well—and, finally, sending her off to Rust College in nearby Holly Springs. He would go visit her, Elizabeth said, and when he did, he brought flowers. This was precisely the stuff of the "shadow family." The Colonel was committed to his child, and he exhibited his love regardless of the disapproval of the white community. Fannie did her part well also. She was bright, finishing Rust near or at the top of her class. At graduation she made a speech glorifying the achievements of women in history. She was also good at voice, and at commencement sang a solo, "On the Heights." One can see her, in the catalogue at Rust College: Fannie Forrest Falkner. The family says that Falkner chose her given names. The Forrest in her name derived from the Old Colonel's admiration for Nathan Bedford Forrest. The Fannie came from the Colonel's favorite sister. In truth, Falkner's youngest sister, "baby sister," was called Fannie.

The oral history fits well with known facts. Colonel Falkner really wanted to be a general. Indeed, he wanted to be another Nathan Bedford Forrest, but he kept getting rejected by his superiors and by his men. His men died in battle in unseemly numbers. In the fall of 1863, at the age of thirty-eight, the Colonel dropped out of the war and, literally, out of sight. Confederate records suggest that he was suffering from bleeding ulcers at the time of his resignation from command. It may be—and I suggest this in the book—that Emeline became the woman in his life in that period of great frustration and depression, that he took refuge with her behind the lines, and that Fannie was the child of that union. If her ages recorded in the censuses of 1870 and 1880 are correct, Fannie was born about July, 1864. After the war, however, the Colonel returned to Ripley and his white wife and sired several children by her, all the while recognizing Fannie in special ways.

Fannie finished Rust and married Matthew Dogan, the brightest boy in the college. Matthew became a professor, and then, for more than forty years, the President of Wiley College in Marshall, Texas. Like Rust, Wiley was a school for African Americans sponsored by Northern white Methodists. Matthew and Fannie had several children, all of whom married into the mulatto elite in America. One daughter, Blanche, married a leading African American lawyer in Baltimore who was himself the son of a Methodist bishop. Their children became a part of the mulatto gentry, if I may use that term, in Baltimore. One of the photographs in the book is of their daughter, Faulkner Hughes. Faulkner (spelled with a "u") was Queen of the Me-Do-So Cotillion in Baltimore in 1956. It is a very elegant proceeding, the coming out of a beautiful young woman, as it were. Ironically, it happened just at the time that William Faulkner the writer was withdrawing in disappointment and depression from the civil rights movement.

To conclude: What emerges is somewhat redemptive for my profession. Working as a historian in the traditional mode did get me onto the track. I could never have conceived of the Emeline story out of my imagination. Once I began to make the ordinary moves in historical research, the story began to unfold. At this point, today, I have a plausible story. But it may not be true. I never found the document in which the Colonel said "Fannie Forest Falkner is my daughter." Family histories are often terribly confused. Such was certainly the case with the white Falkners. Perhaps Emeline's descendants have been mistaken, and the Colonel was not Fannie's father. Who, after all, is my father? Friends and relatives always remarked on the fact that I did not look like anyone in my family. All we have in my case is circumstantial evidence, my mother, perhaps, being the best witness as to the facts. I know what Emeline's descendants tell me. What they tell me is impressively consistent. Presumably, their primary source is Emeline. The family story is fairly consistent within itself, and, most of all, it is highly consistent with the documentary evidence I have found. I rather think that it is true. As a historian, however, I cannot pronounce it true; I can only say that it is very likely that Colonel Falkner mated with Emeline and fathered Fannie, and that the three of them did these various things. Undeniably, the implications of this for William Faulkner's life and work are myriad and profound.

I could easily write this story in fictional form. I can imagine scenes. I can even imagine dialogue between Fannie and her father: The Old Colonel—sixty and gray of hair—riding the train to Holly Springs, buying the flowers, the hack spinning from town out to the college grounds, the meeting, the large, frock-coated man standing, hat in hand, bowing to hear the slight, light young woman in Victorian frill, people watching them discreetly from the distance.

"Well, Fannie. . . ," he says.

But the discipline of history does not allow me to write descriptions that I can imagine, even though these might be— William Faulkner would say—more true than facts. The art of writing history rubs roughly against the art of writing fiction; it grates . . . and stops.

The discipline also limits plot. Imagine that the Colonel sent his daughter off to college to get her away from Dick Thurmond, his partner in business and a man old enough to be her grandfather. What if Thurmond really did love Fannie, married and white though he was? What if he shot the Colonel down in the streets of Ripley for taking his love away? An adventurous hypothesis, but one that might go far toward explaining what has never been very well explained: How Thurmond could walk up to the Colonel, put a pistol in his face with no clear provocation, and when the Colonel cried: "What do you mean, Dick?" shoot him in the mouth.

I could not close the circle of the Colonel and Emeline and Fannie with imagination, but in this book, I could do, did do, and attempted to do other things to test the tolerance of my profession for alternative modes of presentation. One idea was simply to have no "front matter" at all in the book. As usual, page 1 would carry the title and page 2 would be blank. Page 3 would simply begin the text—as a work of Faulkner's fiction might begin without fanfare. The publishers objected, but assented to moving the introduction, preface, and acknowledgments to follow the text at the end of the book. However, they balked at either omitting the table of contents altogether or moving it to the rear with the other "front matter." Perhaps, they feared that if they yielded on that I would next want to move the title page to the rear also, or even to do without a title entirely. I confess, both thoughts did enter my mind. I concluded instantly that moving the title page to the rear would be silly; erasing the title, however, deserves more thought. What would you make of a book without a title? The ruling idea, of course, was: Why not simply tell the story? If the story does not stand by itself, why should it be made seemingly to stand by preliminary trumpeting? Ultimately, we did cut the table of contents to a single page with very spare wording and large spaces between and around words—minimalism, an artist would say.

Much more innovative in the book is the appropriation of Faulkner's fiction for presentation as history. I could not create characters—for example, a Captain Queeg—but I could use Faulkner's characters, including their very own words in quotes. In the book I recognized Faulkner characters as real. I offered them as though they were historical. Like my own historical characters, they acted in past tense. Thus: "Joe Christmas went," rather than "Joe Christmas goes." I used their voices to break the monophonic, history-speak, faceless sound of my own voice. I used their points of view to circle subjects and amelio-rate my necessarily stand-still Monophysitic gaze. More simply, I included Faulkner's characters in my draft of the index on a par with my historical characters. The professional indexer would not, could not, allow such a transgression; fictional char-acters must shoulder quotes. How else, she said, can one tell that they are not real? How, indeed?

I will not attempt to catalogue all of my efforts at innovation in this book, efforts that reflect my desire to write history as an artist might paint. However, let me close with a confession that makes my salient point. There is one paragraph in the book that is carefully constructed fiction. The scene I describe could not have happened in just that way, as I well know. Even so, the violation of history, though deliberate and premeditated, is trivial, a misdemeanor rather than a felony. Further, the crime is confessed even as it is committed by switching the tense from the simple past that history prefers to the literary present of fiction. I trust that the paragraph carries the narrative effectively forward and thus earns legitimacy. It is, I believe, the way the particular story deserves to be told; it puts a reading on the occasion, an appreciation of the human condition that transcends facts. I hope the paragraph rings so true to readers that none will ever pause to question its form. And if one does question this rendering, I hope that he or she will allow me, yet once more, to appropriate and alter Faulkner by saying: I do care about facts, and I care more about truth.

NOTES

1. *William Faulkner and Southern History* (New York: Oxford University Press, 1993).

2. *The Crucible of Race: Black-White Relations in the American South Since Emancipation* (New York: Oxford University Press, 1984).

3. *A Rage for Order* (New York: Oxford University Press, 1986).

4. *New People: Miscegenation and Mulattos in the United States* (New York: The Free Press, 1980).

William Faulkner and Robert Penn Warren as Literary Artists

JOSEPH BLOTNER

One of the indisputable facts of modern literature is the world-wide influence of William Faulkner's work, which has been studied intensively in essays, books, and conferences, both national and international. It is fascinating to see this influence, transmuted into other languages and enriched with other cultures. What I want to do here is to narrow the focus to our own literature and culture and to juxtapose his life and work with that of another writer. Born only eight years apart, William Faulkner and Robert Penn Warren were both members of two different generations, separated by the differing extent of their immersion in what Warren once called the watershed experience of the First World War. The comparison and contrast will be instructive: in showing the common heritage on which they both drew, in identifying what one gained from the other—if only in the greater awareness of possibilities for art—and in the similar personal elements in their lives.

It should also be useful to examine the differing talents which drove these lives and careers. Beyond this, I hope that the several parallels will illuminate patterns to be seen in other Southern writers and possibly in a particular kind of writer as well. Perhaps we can also speculate about this unusual phenomenon of a Nobel Laureate and America's first Poet Laureate (more about that office later) being born in two small towns not many miles apart. In these times we are likely to factor in the soil, the water, and even electric power transmission when we try to understand the elements which make people what they are. What sort of elements helped to make them what they were? Faulkner said he did not understand the source of his gift: "I dont know where it came from," he wrote Joan Williams. "I dont know why God or gods or whoever it was, selected me to be the vessel." Railing with angry hyperbole against an intrusion upon his privacy, he said that it had not come from Oxford. He wrote that, in order to protect himself, he had "deliberately buried myself in this little lost almost illiterate town."[1] But Oxford and Lafayette County as sources for his art are clear in countless pages. And in "Mississippi Hills," a poem he may have written as a kind of epitaph, he wrote that, in death, that soil would find him breath, rooted in it as he was like a tree.[2] As for Robert Penn Warren, he said that Guthrie, Kentucky, was "a place to be from" and asserted with some exaggeration that he never lived at home again after he went off to college at sixteen. Yet a poem such as "Old-Time Childhood in Kentucky" and a novel such as *Night Rider* both show how deep were his roots there.[3] But I am getting ahead of the story.

Often when outsiders speak about the South, one is tempted to ask, which South do you mean? These two writers were born in different states, Warren two hundred miles northeast of Faulkner's birthplace in the land the Indians called "the dark and bloody ground." The main cash crop in Kentucky was tobacco. It was the Middle South. Louisiana, where Warren went to teach, was a different country, almost tropical by comparison. He and his student and editor-to-be, Tennessean Albert Erskine, luxuriating in its warmth, energetically planted a garden one March. Sunburned from their efforts, they arose the next morning to find that their crop had been killed by frost. And though Faulkner grew up in hill country rather than the flat, rich, alluvial lands of the Delta or the sandy plains of the coast, North Mississippi was still, in comparison with middle Tennessee, the Deep South. (And at this conference, one not used to the generous heat and humidity might well ask, if this little postage stamp of native soil doesn't qualify as part of the

Deep South, what does?) Faulkner always called it "my country," a usage Warren understood. It was a feeling for place he
shared when he looked back on his lost job at Vanderbilt
University and said he had wanted to spend his life in the
beautiful country of middle Tennessee. And if he had been able
to do so, he would have remained there, a sort of neighbor of
William Faulkner, half a state away. In a certain sense, however,
for both of them, "my country" meant the South in general.

They shared a common heritage, but beyond that, a particular
one as well. Their people came from the British Isles, Warren's
an undiluted English strain, and Faulkner's a mix of Scottish
and Scotch-Irish, but also, probably some English and perhaps
even some Welsh, though he preferred, romantically, to say the
four main ancestral families were all Scotch. The Falkners and
the Murrys, like the Penns and the Warrens, followed a common migratory pattern from the southeast Atlantic coast,
through Virginia, then along various routes that carried them
across the Appalachians to the frontiers of the then Southwest.
They helped in the forging of the new nation, two of the Falkner
brothers fighting at Cowpens and King's Mountain. One Warren
was wounded at Cowpens and another, according to tradition,
lost his life at Bunker Hill. A matter of military record, however,
is the service of Colonel Abram Penn, Robert Penn Warren's
great-great-grandfather, at the head of his regiment in two
Revolutionary War battles and in the line of review on the
day at Yorktown when the band played "The World Turned
Upside Down."

Like most other writers of the Southern Literary Renaissance,
these two had kinsmen in the Civil War. (Their fathers would
have called it The War Between the States.) But Warren was
one generation closer to his soldier kinsmen than Faulkner was.
Colonel Penn's grandson, Gabriel Thomas Penn, was Robert
Penn Warren's grandfather. A captain of cavalry, he fought not
only against the Federals at Shiloh but also against bushwhackers. William Faulkner's great-grandfather had more of both
glory and disaster, first at the head of his infantry regiment at

First Manassas and then on horseback, like Captain Penn, until the disintegration of Colonel William C. Falkner's First Partisan Rangers sent him into private life and the contraband business too. Some of the differences between these two soldiers exemplified divisions in the Southern mind. No advocate of slavery, Captain Penn saw the institution of slavery as doomed and fatal. And he hated to see the coming of the war. "This will break up the country," he said, "and my people helped make it." Even if the South were to win, victory would leave the country, in his word, "balkanized."[4]

But he was entrapped like most of the others who shared this view, and when the time came, he took up the saber that would later repose in the attic with the other mementos. You fought, he said, because "you went with your people."[5] And in the latter darkening days of the war he raised his own company to prolong the stubborn resistance. Colonel Falkner, eager for glory and cheated of it in the Mexican War, led one regiment and raised another. Both men survived, but though Captain Penn went on to become for a time a successful tobacco farmer and landowner, his most dramatic days were past. For Colonel Falkner, others lay ahead—the highs and the lows just as precipitous and profound as they had been earlier. And as for the violence and danger of those times, even though Captain Penn did not, like Colonel Falkner, meet his death at the hand of an enemy, he had to wait until long past the war's end before he could return home for fear of reprisals from the kin of men he and his troopers had hanged as bushwhackers.

So these lives, in fact and legend, were a major part of their descendants' legacies. And it is no wonder that they laid hold of these imaginations as those of their fathers—too close in a far less dramatic time—could not do. There was no war for the fathers to fight, and so they went into business and farming, meeting sometimes with substantial success and at other times with palpable failure. The military heroism of the grandfather and the great-grandfather went in time directly into fiction and poetry—Captain Warren's into grimly realistic poetry and

Colonel Falkner's into vividly romantic prose. But the fathers could at least help to provide an entry for the sons into the world of books. Even though Murry Falkner was not much for books, he could pass on those his father had provided amply—Shakespeare, Balzac, Hugo, and Conrad among numerous others. Robert Franklin Warren kept his old Greek textbook, a testimonial to the passion for learning that had driven him to hire tutors out of his modest clerk's salary. And at Grandpa Penn's farm in Cerulean Springs, Robert Penn found the volumes from which the old man often read to him under the old cedar tree on the long summer afternoons: history and tales and poems too, stirring ones like those from the old man's favorite, Lord Byron. And the two writers had another legacy as well from Grandpa Penn and Grandfather John Wesley Thompson Falkner: oral history, reinforced by the stories of the other old people, stories of the events of the war and their sequels in the forty years before the two boys were born.

But there was one curious thing, common to both writers, in their usages of the past. Each would draw for material upon one side of the family to the exclusion of the other. It is not surprising that the stories of Grandpa Penn—illustrated with battle maps scratched in the dust—should have been ready to hand for the mature writer. And there was a maiden aunt who supplied the Penn genealogy, going back to William Penn the Quaker and even (according to her) to the Penns at Agincourt. As for the Warrens, when young Robert Penn asked his father about them, he would reply curtly, "There is nothing to be known." The truth is that there was much to be known, none of it discreditable and much of it shared with many of the people of that region and that time. (It may be that a sense of personal failure led to that expunging of the past.) William Faulkner's literary debts to the Falkners and the Murrys are well known. But curiously enough, he drew almost nothing from his mother's family, the Butlers. One set of circumstances provides a likely cause. His maternal grandfather, Charles Butler, was prominent in the community—a peace officer and tax assessor and collector. He had also earned a degree of notoriety, as had the Old Colonel, by a homicide—only one though as compared with the Colonel's three. And it was committed, Butler maintained, in the performance of his duties as town marshal. But he could leave no direct and immediate impress on his grandson's memory because he left town ten years before Faulkner was born, under circumstances the town was convinced were scandalous and probably criminal, and never returned.

There were other skeletons in the closet too. There existed at that time in Oxford a local version of what historians sometimes call a "shadow family," a mother and her mulatto children replicating the appearance of the children of a neighboring white family, often those living in the big house on the same property. The existence of this social phenomenon must have contributed to the imaginative process which brought to life tragic characters such as Joe Christmas and L. Q. C. McCaslin's nameless great-great-great-granddaughter in "Delta Autumn," as well as, probably, to others such as Elnora, the mulatto woman who works in Bayard Sartoris's kitchen and in whose features can be seen those of the Sartoris line.[6]

One basic familial correspondence should not be forgotten: the gene pools. They produced writers: Faulkner's great-grandfather, father, two brothers, and daughter all worked at writing books, from fiction to travel writing to autobiography. Warren's father, sister, and daughter all wrote poetry. (Parenthetically, both fathers were shy about their efforts, Murry Falkner writing a cowboy story in a ledger in the office where he was Secretary of the University of Mississippi, and Robert Franklin Warren attempting to conceal a vanity volume in which he had published a poem.) Murry's mother-in-law, Lelia Swift Butler, was a serious artist who was offered a scholarship to study sculpture in Rome. Ruth Penn Warren was a devoted teacher who held classes in the Guthrie schools and in her own home. The two sons showed marks of genius in their early schooling. Each skipped three grades and demonstrated talent with the pen and brush as well as the textbook. Ruth Penn Warren carefully kept a watercolor which had won a prize for her son at the state fair. He painted landscapes, particularly the western scenes he loved, all his life. Faulkner went from boyish sketches in hymn books during church to meticulous and imaginative illustrations for the books he wrote, hand-printed, and bound. He too, from time to time, would again take up the pen and the brush in the latter decades of his life. But both paid a price for being precocious and different. Warren was threatened and once, it appears, dangerously abused by grade school classmates who decided to teach him something about the consequences of making straight A's. Faulkner, of course, became the butt of ridicule to those who thought he was putting on airs, as in fact he was, when he wore the full dress suit which helped to earn him the sobriquet "Count No 'count."

Both mothers were apparently dominant in their marriages and exerted a strong command over their sons' affections. Both boys were first in the birth order, and like their parents and their siblings in their turn, had black "nurses," Callie Barr and Seeley Bradshaw. The children's participation in family religious activity—orthodox Methodism for both—lapsed not long after childhood. Each son experienced some degree of distance or estrangement from his father. Each had a more congenial, vigorous, and outgoing younger brother who would be much more warmly remembered in their hometowns even after the older brother's success. But one significant difference should be noted. So much was Robert Penn doted on that his siblings felt he had been substantially favored—in education and in other ways. Billy Falkner, however, was the despair of his father, who could not quite accept his son's success even when it was manifested in a concrete way with a whopping Hollywood salary check. On the other hand, Maud Falkner, like Ruth Penn Warren, never stopped believing in her son's gifts or glorying in his successes.

Setting them apart further from the others was the factor—enormously important in youth—of physical appearance. And it was not just size, both of them being shorter and smaller than most of their fellows. Thin-lipped Billy Falkner's most prominent feature was the heroic nose he would later be able to feature in self-caricatures. At age sixteen, Robert Penn suffered the physical and psychological trauma which would be lifelong: the accident which would cost him the sight of his left eye and the career he had dreamed of. He had wanted to take up his appointment to Annapolis and become an Admiral of the Pacific Fleet. Bill Falkner had wanted to become an ace in aerial combat on the Western Front. He did manage to enlist as an aviation cadet but never got off the ground. Robert Penn read about the war in the papers, and his brief experience was not naval but military when he soldiered one summer as a college sophomore in the Civilian Military Training Camp. Theirs were dreams to be realized vicariously or imaginatively in the creation of experience they never knew at first hand. (As late as the next World War both of them—clearly unqualified for the military—would attempt to enter the service.)

There were other unfulfilled ambitions in the late adolescent years. Both had participated in the front porch courtships of that time, but both lost the objects of their affection to taller, better-looking men, Falkner to a lawyer, Warren to a psychologist. (Later both would make spectacularly unhappy marriages.) So they missed the war and lost the girl. The results included an early cynicism expressed most fully in the medium which not only provided an outlet for the frustration but also offered a way of life, in fact as well as appearance. It was poetry.

By their midteens they were both in thrall to it. It was Swinburne, Faulkner said, who had sprung upon him "like a highwayman," and after him Housman, who "filled his inner life." Warren, in the bitterness of his shattered hopes, had gone to Vanderbilt intending to become a chemical engineer. (Both boys, confounding the stereotype, were good at science.) But an early predisposition to poetry was there. Warren—called "Red" for his shock of bright hair—had not manifested it the way Billy Falkner had done, even in grade school, when he said, "I want to be a writer like my great-granddaddy." As a small boy Robert Penn asked his father to read "Horatius at the Bridge" so many times that his father finally told him to learn to read so that he could do it himself. Then, as a sixteen-year-old freshman, he came under the influence of a fine teacher and poet-to-be, John Crowe Ransom. From that time on, he said, "for me it was poetry or death."[7]

So they both wrote poetry, in an amount that is hard to imagine until one has seen it, in their unpublished papers as well as those that saw print. Like most beginners they took models, and the dominating one for both—exposed to him as they had been by a brilliant older friend, Phil Stone, on the one hand, and Ransom on the other—was T. S. Eliot. But though they paid him the compliment of imitation (Faulkner did a long version of "The Love Song of J. Alfred Prufrock" and Warren would recite *The Waste Land* passionately from memory), they experimented with other forms and masters too: the ballad and the elegy, the metaphysical poets and e.e. cummings.

Nor was their work carried out in a solitary apprenticeship like Milton's or Hawthorne's. Though Faulkner would have to wait until he was nearly thirty to see the cafés of the Left Bank, where so many of his contemporaries had written their work, he had in Oxford the tutorials of Phil Stone, and in New Orleans in the offices of a new magazine called the *Double Dealer* he could sit on the floor nursing his bottle and hearing literature, art, and criticism debated. There in that congenial city he also enjoyed the society of an avuncular Sherwood Anderson and the company of literary journalists as they discussed writing in the speakeasies of the *Vieux Carré*.

Nashville was a far cry from New Orleans, but when Warren arrived as a Vanderbilt freshman he found what was arguably the best English Department in an American university. As a seventeen-year-old, Red Warren was accepted as an equal in the give-and-take of a group of devotees who called themselves The Fugitives and collaborated to produce what many would call, excepting only Eliot's *Criterion*, the best literary magazine in English. At their meetings Ransom, Allen Tate, Donald

Davidson, and the others would bring their new poems for dissection. Warren had his first Left Bank literary experience just a few years after Faulkner, when, during a vacation from his work as a Rhodes scholar, he sat in the company of Allen Tate, John Peale Bishop, and F. Scott Fitzgerald. For both him and Faulkner, their strenuous apprenticeship was soon followed by frequent trial by print.

Their publishing careers took different shapes, though there were certain similarities. Faulkner's first book was the collection of poems, *The Marble Faun*, of 1924, and Warren's second was also a collection, *Thirty-Six Poems*, in 1935, after his biography, *John Brown: The Making of a Martyr*, six years before. Both had their major popular successes—Faulkner's *Intruder in the Dust* and Warren's *All the King's Men*—within a few years of each other in the 1940s. Warren went on to publish a total of half the number of novels Faulkner wrote, and published no more in the last decade of his career. Faulkner's only other book of verse to appear in his lifetime was *A Green Bough*, which came not much beyond the midpoint of his life. But to its end, he would give voice to the urge to which Warren gave full rein, when, like Thomas Hardy in his later years, he devoted his creative energies to poetry rather than prose fiction. Faulkner would say he regarded himself as "a failed poet," that the writer ideally wanted to put his emotions and thoughts into fourteen lines, but when he couldn't, he took two thousand words and tried in the short story, the next most "severe" medium, and if he couldn't do that, he took two hundred thousand words and wrote a novel. Poetry for him was "some moving, passionate moment of the human condition distilled to its absolute essence."[8]

Warren would say that his encounter with the poetry of John Crowe Ransom and Donald Davidson in 1921 constituted a transforming experience in demonstrating the use of native materials for poetry. He relived this experience with fiction in 1929 at Oxford University when John Gould Fletcher gave him a copy of *Soldiers' Pay*. It made a "profound and undefinable impression" on him. He would write, "What happened to me was what happened to almost all the book-reading Southerners I knew. They found dramatized in Faulkner's work some truth about the South and their own Southernness that had been lying unvoiced in their experience. Even landscapes and objects took on a new depth of meaning, and the human face, stance, and gesture took on a new dignity. There was the thrill of seeing how a life that you yourself observed and were part of might move into the dimension of art. There was, most personally, the thrill of discovering your own relation to time and place, to life as you were destined to live it."[9] This introduction came at a crucial time, for though Warren's work on *John Brown* was biography, he was trying out in it techniques in dialogue and scene-staging plus an exploration of themes which would profit him when in just a few years he would begin writing extended prose fiction.

During the rest of his life Warren worked to gain readers for Faulkner both through writing and word-of-mouth. He reviewed *These 13,* Faulkner's first book of stories when it appeared in 1932 and after that two novels and a collection of poems. Then, in 1946, he wrote an important review of a crucial book, Malcolm Cowley's *The Portable Faulkner.* Cowley had persuaded the Viking Press to put together this representative sampling of his work not only out of admiration, but also out of a kind of indignation that all but a few of Faulkner's books were out of print at a time when he was working as a scriptwriter in Hollywood to stay solvent and save his home. "The study of Faulkner," Warren wrote, "is the most challenging single task in contemporary literature for criticism to undertake. Here is a novelist who, in mass of work, in scope of material, in range of effect, in reportorial accuracy and symbolic subtlety, in philosophical weight, can be put beside the masters of our own past literature." Cowley's book, he concluded, "would be valuable at any time. But it is especially valuable at this time. Perhaps it can mark a turning point in Faulkner's reputation. That will be of slight service to Faulkner, who, as much as any writer of our place and time, can rest in confidence. He can afford to wait. But can we?"[10] The review helped to achieve the hoped-for revival. Five years later Warren delivered a lecture entitled "Faulkner and His South"—perhaps the best single essay on Faulkner ever published—which he included later in a wide-ranging collection of essays he edited on Faulkner's work.[11] Few novelists ever served a fellow novelist better.

What did Warren learn from Faulkner's artistry? A great deal, for he was not only an acute reader but a professional critic whose talents in several genres, particularly in combination with those of Cleanth Brooks, gave aid and comfort to generations of teachers. Warren knew enough to learn from Faulkner, and I think it is fair to say that he learned not to use too much. Flannery O'Connor remarked, "The presence alone of Faulkner in our midst makes a great difference in what a writer can and cannot permit himself to do. Nobody wants his mule and wagon stalled on the same track the Dixie Limited is roaring down."[12] Nonetheless, Warren's fiction shows a resonance with Faulkner's on several counts.

Here are some of them. Seven of Warren's ten novels are set entirely in the South, the other three principally there. Southern history is the staple of most of them, and Southernness is central to such major poems as *Brother to Dragons*, "Audubon: A Vision," and "The Ballad of Billie Potts." As with Faulkner's works, these are grounded in the local and particular but move toward the general and universal. Like their mutual ancestor, Mark Twain, Faulkner and Warren used the regional and the colloquial, the vulgar and also the mythic. And of course they used themselves—quite naturally, in disguise. The nameless reporter in *Pylon* was born from Faulkner's experiences with newspaper friends at the time of the dedication of New Orleans' Shushan Airport. Jack Burden in *All the King's Men* similarly gained a good deal from Warren's friendship with Nashville newspapermen who participated in events which have their counterpart in his earlier novel, *At Heaven's Gate*. As to the question of influence, there is the indisputable fact that Warren did not publish his first novel until ten years after he had read Faulkner. But rather than positing specific resemblances such as those between *The Sound and the Fury* and William Styron's *Lie Down in Darkness*, it should be more useful to consider larger patterns.

To mention a few, there is the prose saturated with poetic imagery and symbolic patterns. These are, of course, employed by many other novelists. So is the presence of violence, but—to many reviewers at least—it is endemic in the work of both these novelists. (Warren once told me, "violence is always there beneath the surface of Southern life." Faulkner had something of the same thing in mind when he would say, in Virginia, "my country was frontier not too long ago.") Deaths occur in all but two of Faulkner's novels, by homicide in eight of them and by suicide in three. (And this is by no means the total body count.) There are homicides in all ten of Warren's novels and suicides in three of them. Is this a personal predilection for violence, or a result of the fact that both novelists wrote in societies where violence was endemic as well as traditional? There are other correspondences. To name just one more, the relationships of protagonists to their fathers are characterized by conflict, distance, and absence or by the presence of ineffectual father-surrogates. In Faulkner's nineteen novels I count only one major father-son relationship which is predominantly loving. There, in *The Unvanquished*, the father is a soldier who turns murderer. (I'm not sure how to characterize the very different relationship in the penultimate novel, *The Mansion*, by which point in the Snopes saga Chick Mallison has begun to treat his uncle and father-surrogate, Gavin Stevens, with something like avuncular concern and affection—a situation not unknown, I suspect, to other fathers.) In two Faulkner novels the grandfather is the recipient of filial love from a grandson. In nine of Warren's ten novels the father or father surrogate is a failure or a betrayer. What are we to make of this pattern? Does it represent a conviction about the nature of the father-son relationship, or is it the manifestation of an essentially personal and particular situation?

To return to the personal in a different aspect, I have quoted Warren on Faulkner. What did Faulkner have to say about Warren? Before the publication of *All the King's Men*, Warren's editor sent Faulkner a set of proofs in the hope of a promotional quote. Faulkner's reply was disappointing. "The Cass Mastern story is a beautiful and moving piece," he wrote. "That was his novel. The rest of it I would throw away."[13] Unknowingly returning the compliment, as it were, Warren wrote to Albert Erskine about a review of *Requiem for a Nun* he had promised. "I finished the Faulkner last night," he told him, "with very mixed feelings. The narrative stuff is the true Faulknerian voice, the play stuff is damned near junk in large [order?]."[14] (At several points in his struggle to complete the play version of the work, Faulkner came close to expressing the same opinion himself.) Warren too went through prolonged struggles in dramatizing *All the King's Men*. Both writers declared that they were not playwrights and sought the help of experienced dramatists in this uncongenial form.

What of the personal in the conventional sense? Did they ever meet? Their editor, Albert Erskine, brought them together once. The three had a companionable dinner during which Faulkner began to talk about the *fact* of a thing as compared with the *truth* of a thing. As an example, he began to talk about a particular short story. Then he found another example in a novel. He did not name the author, and only gradually did Warren realize that both examples came from his own work, particularly his much admired story, "Blackberry Winter."

What gifts did they share? Several. Apart from the intellectual power of genius, prodigious amounts of energy and extraordinary reservoirs of memory. The ability to combine narrative drive and poetic statement. The capacity for tireless experimentation (for Warren, this trait chiefly in the poetry) and painstaking revision. A sweeping historical consciousness. ("Time spreads and is the important thing, the terrible thing," Warren told Ralph Ellison, seeing one of his own constant concerns in Faulkner's work. "A tremendous flux is there, things flowing away in all directions."[15]) An overarching view of man bound by something like Original Sin yet capable of redemptive action if not salvation. A great richness of native materials and the ability to invest them with transcendent meanings. The ability to enjoy the good things of life, including Jack Daniel's Old Time Quality Tennessee Sour Mash Whiskey.

Faulkner and Warren had the great advantages of sureness of regional identity as well as secure devotion to their art. They were Southerners with a capital S. In the midst of the civil rights crisis of the 1950s, Faulkner said of the South, "It's my country, my native land, and I love it"—in spite of its faults.[16] Warren, from the 1940s to the end of his life, was an expatriate living in the midwest and New England. As late as the mid-1950s he drove through Tennessee and Kentucky farmland looking for a place to buy so that his children could absorb in their childhood something he had known in his own. As for sureness of their vocation, they took other work when they had to—teaching for Warren and scriptwriting for Faulkner. (Faulkner's servitude in Hollywood totaled several years, whereas Warren scored the way Faulkner always wanted to, with the sale of film rights. There was something of irony there, however, in the fact that when Columbia Pictures bought *All the King's Men* for $200,000, Harcourt Brace got half of it and insisted that it all be paid in one year, so that even after the agent's commission Warren paid more in taxes than he received in salary that year from his teaching job.) There was no doubt of their true metier. In an apprentice story Faulkner put the phrase in the mouth of a fictional surrogate: "words are my meat and bread and drink."[17] A fellow writer, speaking to Warren of the reluctance with which he sometimes approached his work, once asked if Warren felt the same anguish. Warren looked at him as if he were speaking in an unknown tongue. "It's what I do," he said. Warren and Faulkner both admired Robert Frost, and they could have endorsed the poet's words in "Two Tramps in Mud Time": "My object in living is to unite/ My avocation and my vocation/ As my two eyes make one in sight."

How did they differ? In many ways and many circumstances. With characteristic embroidery upon the truth, Faulkner liked to call himself "the world's oldest living sixth-grader." A high school dropout, he got most of his education outside the classroom. And for most of his life he stayed at home, enmeshed in a network of family relationships and the fabric of the past as well as the present. Warren was a learned diplomate of three universities, a polymath who read Dante with unflagging devotion for sixty years of his long life. He was an innovative editor, a first-rate critic, and an influential teacher. (One marked difference between the two: Warren not only analyzed Faulkner's work in print, he also taught it in the classroom. Another: Warren did extensive research for at least two novels, *At Heaven's Gate* and *World Enough and Time*, whereas Faulkner looked at source material for one, *A Fable*.) Warren wrote with distinction in all of the major literary genres and produced masterpieces in at least two of them.

Younger than Faulkner by more than the actual chronological span of eight years, born in a significantly different political milieu, Warren lived longer and came to occupy a more liberal position on the race question than Faulkner did. He unenthusiastically wrote an early essay espousing the Separate but Equal doctrine as his assigned contribution to *I'll Take My Stand*, the so-called manifesto of the Nashville Agrarians. (When he submitted his manuscript, however, it seemed so liberal that Allen Tate reacted with shocked disapproval and Donald Davidson could hardly believe that Warren had actually written it.) Later he repudiated it with two of the most comprehensive books by a white artist on the American civil rights crisis: *Segregation: The Inner Conflict in the South* and *Who Speaks for the Negro?* Faulkner, attacked as racist and then as a gradualist, tried to establish a middle position for Deep South moderates, and as an artist he explored the ancient injustices which produced profoundly tragic consequences. A fellow crafts-

man told Warren, "I see certain parallels between the development of your work and its movement from *I'll Take My Stand*
to *Band of Angels* and *Segregation*, and Faulkner's Lucas Beauchamp," who "appears first as an aged and lecherous
coachman. . . . Then in his final metamorphosis he is an
estimable symbol of human courage."[18] The writer was Ralph
Ellison, whose classic novel, *Invisible Man*, is, to my mind, the
finest depiction of the black experience in America, a work
whose relevance transcends the black-white formulation.

The rewards came to both of them: seats in the National
Institute and the American Academy, the Pulitzers and National
Book Awards, the medals and the ribbons. The outcry in some
quarters against Faulkner's Nobel Prize was bitter to him, and
the trip to Stockholm was for the most part an ordeal. When the
bill was introduced in Congress to create a Poet Laureateship
for the United States, Warren called it "idiocy." The Laureateship was a British institution, he said, whose literary results
varied "from ludicrous to distinguished." He could not write
poems to order, he said. (One of his eventual successors,
Richard Wilbur, said, "Robert Penn Warren will not write an
ode on Ronald Reagan's horse.") When the office was rendered
"harmless" (Warren's word)—made a one-year sequel to the
post of Consultant in Poetry to the Library of Congress—he
consented to serve in it as long as his failing health would
allow. Both men paid their dues, Faulkner in the inspirational
speeches he felt he had to give, Warren on the endless commit-
tees and boards. And both answered the call to serve as cultural
ambassadors for their country.

Their differences were apparent in their later years. Warren
gladly left off prose fiction to return exclusively to poetry with
such passion and virtuosity that it became a commonplace not
just to say that he was the dominant American poet of his time,
but one comparable to Yeats in his magisterial last years, as well
as America's premier man of letters. Faulkner, a sometime poet,
short story writer, essayist, and dramatist, was faithful to his
metier, a novelist to the end. Creating the great overarching

construct of his apocryphal Yoknapatawpha County, he also remained the dazzling experimentalist and innovator.

What more is there to say? We have said some things about the elements which link them, and some which separate them, but nothing really about the soil or climate which nurtured them. What nurtured their genius was their capacity to absorb, understand, and use their general inheritance: the literary art to which in time they made their contribution—a mark, Faulkner said, on the wall of oblivion, a view of man's striving and also man's fate, with which Warren would have agreed.[19] Two Southerners, they shared a loyalty to their land and to their art, with a passionate devotion expressed by a novelist they both revered, Joseph Conrad, whose narrator says of the hero of *Lord Jim* that he persevered in his destiny as he conceived it, *usque ad finem*, thus to the end. And so did they.

NOTES

1. *Selected Letters of William Faulkner*, ed. Joseph Blotner (New York: Random House, 1977), 348, 319.

2. XLIV, *The Marble Faun* and *A Green Bough* (New York: Random House, 1965), 67

3. Robert Penn Warren, *New and Selected Poems: 1923–1985* (New York: Random House, 1985), 45–46; *Night Rider* (Boston: Houghton Mifflin, 1939).

4. Robert Penn Warren, *Jefferson Davis Gets His Citizenship Back* (Lexington: University Press of Kentucky, 1980), 3–5, 8–10.

5. Ibid.

6. Joel Williamson, *William Faulkner and Southern History* (New York: Oxford University Press, 1993), 64–71.

7. William Faulkner, "Verse Old and Nascent," *Early Prose and Poetry*, ed. Carvel Collins (Boston: Little Brown, 1962), 114–18; Robert Penn Warren, *Portrait of a Father* (Lexington: University Press of Kentucky, 1988), 16; *Talking with Robert Penn Warren: Interviews, 1950–1978*, ed. Floyd T. Watkins and John T. Hiers (New York: Random House, 1980), 28; unpublished interview by Joseph Blotner.

8. *Faulkner in the University*, ed. Frederick L. Gwynn and Joseph L. Blotner (Charlottesville: University of Virginia Press 1959), 4, 22, and 202.

9. "Introduction: Faulkner Past and Present," *Faulkner: A Collection of Critical Essays*, ed. Robert Penn Warren (Englewood Cliffs, N.J.: Prentice Hall, 1966), 1.

10. Robert Penn Warren, "Cowley's Father," *The New Republic* 115 (August 12, 1946): 176–80; August 26, 1946: 234–37.

11. See note 9.

12. Flannery O'Connor, *Mystery and Manners: Occasional Prose*, selected and edited by Sally and Robert Fitzgerald (New York: Farrar, Straus & Giroux, 1969), 45.

13. *Selected Letters*, 239.

14. RPW to Albert Erskine, probably September 30, 1951, courtesy of Random House.

15. *Talking with Robert Penn Warren*, 39.

16. *Faulkner in the University*, 83.

17. "Out of Nazareth," *New Orleans Sketches*, ed. Carvel Collins (New York: Random House, 1958), 110.

18. *Talking with Robert Penn Warren*, 48.

19. Christopher Waldrep has suggested a fundamental difference on one of the eternal questions: "This dichotomy is manifested in the opposing views of the southern court system. . . . While both writers recognized the appearance of injustice in southern courts, Faulkner agreed with those who found that criminals almost always met their just desserts—as defined by the community—at the hands of the law. In Faulkner's view, the community's role is crucial. He believed courts sometimes maintained order more effectively by appeasing the lower classes than by rigidly punishing every transgression. It was not always in the best interest of the community, or even fundamentally fair, Faulkner thought, for courts to punish every guilty defendant or acquit every technically innocent defendant." See "William Faulkner, Robert Penn Warren, and the Law," *Southern Studies: An Interdisciplinary Journal of the South*, n.s. 2 (Spring 1991): 39–50. Jeanette Chaplin has suggested a similarity in attitudes and fictional materials: "Both 'Prime Leaf' and 'Barn Burning' are effective narratives representing the historical South and are charged with the emotional impact provided by the difficult choices facing the protagonist. Warren and Faulkner both present the internal conflict and realistically depict the uneasy father-son relationship without sacrificing the message that moral decisions must be based on established principles regardless of the resulting personal consequences." See "Burning Barns in Warren and Faulkner," in *"To Love So Well the World": A Festschrift in Honor of Robert Penn Warren*, ed. Dennis L. Weeks (New York: Peter Lang, 1992), 226–27.

Faulkner, Home, and the Ocean

MICHEL GRESSET

I would like to begin with two remarks. The first is about the title of this conference, which is ambiguous—deliberately and rightly so: "Faulkner and the Artist" is neither "Faulkner and the Artists," nor is it "Faulkner the Artist," and in dealing with it I have kept in mind that the title I originally submitted was "Faulkner's Self-Portraits as an Artist in His Correspondence"—a title which is still the frame of the present paper, now called "Faulkner, Home, and the Ocean," though I have also kept in mind that my original interest in Faulkner was *How did Faulkner become Faulkner*, which, to my mind, is another way—a psychological way—of dealing with the problem raised here. The second remark is about my using several articles I have already written and published: this is one more proof that repetition is to the point, particularly when the point does not seem to have been made.

As James Watson put it in Faulkner's letters to his parents which he edited in 1992 under the title *Thinking of Home*[1] (fourteen years after Joseph Blotner's *Selected Letters*),[2] "the letters are not self-consciously literary in themselves."[3] But why should one insist on self-consciousness—why should a budding artist be necessarily self-conscious, if not because *we* cannot think otherwise, because for us the proof of an artist lies in the fact that he describes himself as such, through the use of words or through other means? It is as if the question *How did Faulkner become Faulkner* could only take place in the all too glaring light of self-consciousness, when in fact what actually took place was probably the opposite. The development of a set

41

of fantasies that were to last for the whole of Faulkner's fictional career was achieved not at all in the full (shall I add: theoretical?) light of self-consciousness, but in the semi-obscurity (the shadows) of experience.

One of these fantasies, perhaps formed very early, was undoubtedly associated with the ocean. Of course, one cannot say when: which, for example, was the first beach to be trodden by young Faulkner: was it by the Gulf of Mexico? Why did the much less tropical Atlantic, found in Connecticut, appeal so much to him? And why was he so impressed by his voyage to Europe on the *West Ivis* as to describe the ocean at length at the beginning of "Elmer"? Indeed in his very first letter to his mother from New Haven, dated October 6, 1921, one finds such a remarkable description that I regard it as no less than the possible beginning (or inception) of Faulkner's prose:

> There's only one sensation to be compared with seeing mountains, and that's seeing the ocean again. Coming up along the sound yesterday I was looking for it all the time; there's a strange feeling in the air: you pass through tight little New England villages built around plots of grass they call greens. The sky toward the sea is pale, about the color of salt, against which the inevitable white church spires are drawn clearer and whiter still. Every where the trees are turning—fall has already come here—ferns, and gum trees, all the underbrush is yellow and red, and over the whole thing is a queer feeling, an awareness of the slow magnificent ocean, *like something you have heard or smelled, and forgotten.* Then, suddenly, you see it, a blue hill going up and up, beyond the borders of the world, to the salt colored sky, and white whirling necklaces of gulls, and, if you look long enough, a great vague ship solemnly going some where. *I can't express how it makes me feel to see it again, there is a feeling of the most utter relief, as if I could close my eyes, knowing that I had found again someone who loved me years and years ago.* (145, emphasis mine.)

About the last sentence, one can only be struck by the fact that what is expressed in spite of the apparent difficulty ("I cant express how it makes me feel to see it again") is no less than a cluster of rare fantasies to be found in the novels and stories later, sometimes much later: the association of the ocean not with space but with time ("slow") and beauty ("magnificent"), and therefore with some impression made in youth, its recall through the two lesser senses, hearing and smelling, and its final equation with forgetting, which is exactly what it is all about, since seeing the ocean is like finding oneself in the presence of something or someone long lost. In other words, there is nothing visual, nothing pictorial about the ocean until it is *seen again*. But even then one comes across a paradox, because it is "as if I could close my eyes": the ocean thus becomes an objective correlative of affective memory, in whose presence, as in the presence of someone loved who has been lost for a long time, one can rest from everyday toil.

At this stage I can only admire Roland Barthes for saying two things that are very much to the point here. 1. A literary description is always the repetition of something already seen and therefore (and often visually) *framed* by memory (in other words, there is something Proustian in all literature). 2. What distinguishes Sade is "not at all the crimes and perversions described in his discourse, but the discourse itself as founded upon his own repetitions (not those of others)."[4] Not only is time always involved in writing, and the past a necessary, if untold, figure in it; Southern writers know this well, as Willie Morris reminds us in his essay "Coming on Back" and as Eudora Welty knows even better: "Time is very important to us because it has dealt with us."[5] Repetition (therefore time as well as one's own personal set of fantasies) is also involved here: it may even be at the root of all writing.

As I hope to show, this is precisely what happened with Faulkner, who can therefore be described as a paradigm of the artist in fiction. This is also to say that I find myself agreeing with Watson, not when he writes about the necessary "self-consciousness" of the artist, but when he writes that in New Orleans, in 1925, "[Faulkner] was unconsciously gathering and storing the material of fictions he subsequently would write"

(43)—beginning with the well-known *New Orleans Sketches*, particularly with the seminal piece entitled "The Liar."[6]

In 1975 I wrote a short article entitled "Faulkner et l'océan"[7]—half jokingly since there was no allusion to the ocean whatsoever in the course of the article. The article described the circumstances in which I read Faulkner for the first time when, in a single year, 1952 (which was also the year of Faulkner's triumph in Paris at the *"Festival des Oeuvres du XX siècle"*), there appeared translations of no less than three of his books: *Knight's Gambit, The Wild Palms,* and *Intruder in the Dust.* Maybe the ocean of the title was the Atlantic, between America and Europe. What my title suggested was simply my intuition that the sea ought to be a key metaphor in the writing of this great inland writer: seldom, except perhaps with such continental writers as Balzac and Flaubert, have there been literary works so devoted to the earth as Faulkner's. And yet with him the ocean has always remained a powerful metaphor (indeed the key metaphor) of experience, including sexual experience. In *The Wild Palms*, Faulkner's only novel about love, the sea is hardly more than a smell, but in *Go Down, Moses*, one can read specifically about young Isaac McCaslin, "after he had grown to a man, and had seen the sea."[8]

Usually, however, the sea is a metaphor of more general experience. In *The Hamlet* (published in 1940 but begun in 1925 or so), one finds a passage about Mink Snopes after the murder of Jack Houston, which is all the more to the point as it harkens back, almost twenty years after the event, to the early, October 1921 letter of Faulkner to his mother. At that time, Faulkner had just turned twenty-four. Here is the passage from the novel:

> He was seeking the sea. He was twenty-three then, that young. He had never seen it; he did not know certainly just where it was, except that it was to the south. He had never thought of it before and he could not have said why he wanted to go to it—what of repudiation of the land, the earth, where his body or intellect had faulted somehow to the cold undeviation of his will to do—seeking

what of that iodinic proffer of space and oblivion of which he had no intention of availing himself, would never avail himself, as if, by deliberately refusing to cut the wires of remembering, to punish that body and intellect which had failed him. Perhaps he was seeking only the proffer of this illimitable space and irremediable forgetting along the edge of which the contemptible teeming of his own earth-kind timidly seethed and recoiled, not to accept the proffer but merely to bury himself in the myriad anonymity beside the impregnable haven of all the drowned intact golden galleons and the unattainable deathless seamaids.[9]

From a narrative point of view, the passage consists of the author's discourse on the applicability of the sea metaphor to the strange case of Mink Snopes, that "damned little murdering bastard," that "wasp," as his wife calls him when he meets her again at the Varner house after the murder. Then Mink is reminded of the time when he first saw his wife at the lumber camp. For this poor white character, the sea is equated with whatever is strange or foreign or outlandish (or exotic) in his experience. What is familiar to him is the earth and one's burial into the "myriad anonymity"; what he is unfamiliar with is "the impregnable haven" of all drowned riches and of all unattainable, deathless nymphs. As in the early sketch entitled "Nympholepsy" (and as in the moving scene between Quentin and Caddy at the branch in *The Sound and the Fury*), water is the symbol of the association of desire and death.

It is not only Eliot in *The Waste Land* who made water an objective correlative of the desire to end all desires. Estelle Oldham herself had written a beautiful page of fiction when, in July 1929, "in one of her gorgeous silk dresses" she walked down to the beach where she and Faulkner had been honeymooning in Pascagoula, and was about to drown herself when she was rescued by her husband and a friend. "Was it a serious attempt at suicide or a kind of gesture?" Joseph Blotner asks.[10] Whatever its nature, what is so striking about the episode is that it was a kind of "acting out" of the writer's most secret fantasies. I am not saying that Faulkner wanted his new bride to die by drowning—nor did he wish that his younger brother

Dean die in a "dying fall" when his own plane crashed in 1935, after he had written and even published *Pylon*, in which the fall to death is described. I am only saying that it was characteristic of a writer's life that behind those scenes were fantasies, the one involving the sea very much as in Baudelaire, the other involving the sky very much as in Mallarmé.

When in October 1921 Faulkner wrote that "there is a feeling of utter relief [in the ocean], as if I could close my eyes, knowing that I had found again someone who loved me years and years ago," anecdotally he was probably expressing the recognition of the affective importance of his mother's presence during his youth. Symbolically, however (as he could not have known), he was already speaking in the terms he would use much later in 1957, for the engineering students of the University of Virginia, in order to describe a country which he visited only late in his life, when he was a kind of "roving ambassador" of the U.S. in the world. He was asked about his trip to Greece, and he responded in this way, which tells us as much about himself and his own fantasies as about Greece:

It was a strange experience in that that was the only country that looked exactly like we had—I mean, the background, the educational background of the Anglo-Saxon had taught him to expect to look. And sure enough there was the Hellenic light that I had heard of, had read about. And I saw Homer's wine-dark sea too. And there was a—the only place I was in where there was a sense of a very distant past but there was nothing inimical in it. In the other parts of the Old World there is a sense of the past but there is something Gothic and in a sense a little terrifying. . . . The people seem to function against that past that for all its remoteness in time it was still inherent in the light, the resurgence of spring, you didn't expect to see the ghost of the old Greeks, or expect to see the actual figures of the gods, but you had a sense that they were near and they were still powerful, not inimical, just powerful. That they themselves had reached and were enjoying a kind of nirvana, they existed, but they were free of man's folly and trouble, of having to involve themselves in man's problem. That *they at last had the time to watch what man did without having to be involved in it.* Yes, it was very interesting.[11] (Emphasis mine.)

The account given in New Haven of a visit to the seaside in 1921 also ends with the onlooker being allowed to close his eyes, and therefore to be at rest, or at least to cease to be involved. This tells a lot about sight, by far the primary, the most urgent sense for Faulkner (as for many other writers—so much so that it was described as the outrageously privileged sense in modern writing), and the one always associated with tragedy: one need only think of the beginning of *Sanctuary*. In the description of the sea in 1921 and that of Greece in 1957, one looks at the same phenomenon from two different perspectives. Serenity lies in the suspension of watching (and being watched)—or, if watching must go on, it lies in the watcher no longer having to feel involved in what is being watched.

The truth about the ocean may have been told by Faulkner when, on July 16, 1927, he wrote to the book editor of *The Chicago Tribune* about *Moby Dick*. In Melville's masterpiece the narrative unrolled, he said, "all against the grave and tragic rhythm of the earth in its most timeless phase: the sea."[12] To Faulkner, the sea was therefore a "phase" of the earth; only it was the most "timeless" one. With Faulkner, the sea is not the medium of departure; it is part of an inner landscape. The medium of departure, for him, is clearly the air—as shown in *The Wild Palms*.

I once published, in the now defunct Japanese Faulkner review, an article entitled "Home and Homelessness in Faulkner's Works and Life" because I wanted to show that the same value that ruled Faulkner's life afterwards could be seen at work in his writings from the very beginning—in particular in the truly inaugural sketch entitled "The Hill" (published in 1922), in which (I am now quoting from this article of mine) "years before he 'discovered that [his] own little postage stamp of native soil was worth writing about,' he made a triple hit with the description of a privileged character in a privileged landscape at a privileged time: 'The hamlet slept, wrapped in peace and quiet beneath the evening sun, as it had slept for a century. . . . [B]efore him lay the hamlet which was home to him, the tieless casual. . . .' " [13] This "tieless casual," I continued (in whose denomination one can see a double definition of homelessness), "happens to be the prototype of so many typical Faulkner heroes to come, all of them young males, and all deeply idealistic, that it is impossible to overrate his importance in the dynamics of Faulkner's literary creation."[14]

It is precisely within "the dynamics of Faulkner's literary creation" that I would now like to concentrate on the title chosen by James Watson for the volume of letters to his mother and father. "Thinking of Home" is taken from Darl's well-known thought, at the end of one of his most beautiful monologues, the sixth one in *As I Lay Dying*: "How often have I lain beneath rain on a strange roof, thinking of home." But the phrase, or a quite similar one, occurs in the course of one of Faulkner's last letters to his mother, postmarked in Pascagoula, June 25, 1925:

> I am sorry I slipped up about writing, But when you spend most of your time writing words, as long as you are all right you want to take it out in thinking about home—writing letters is like the postman taking a long walk on his day off, or the street car motorman taking a car ride. (212)

This is one more example of the life and the works using the same language: in either case, "thinking of [or about] home" means primarily being unable to take one's mind away from home while one is away, while one is therefore more or less willingly (as with Faulkner in Pascagoula) alienated (Hawthorne would have said "estranged"), and feeling a nostalgia, a longing to go back, to return, some would even say to regress, toward "home," or where one belongs. Naturally the question is what does it mean to "belong" somewhere. If one follows American ideology from well before Faulkner to after Willie Morris, "Home is where the heart is." But where is the heart (metaphorically, of course)—and *what* exactly is the heart? From my point of view here, it will not do to associate it only with the emotional functions; it has to cover the functions of the mind as well. What I think one ought to associate Faulkner's home with is a landscape, and in this landscape the main, dominating feature is undoubtedly not the ocean, but the hills. "Gosh, I'm homesick for the hills today," he writes at the end of a letter to his parents from New Orleans, March 11, 1925. As the narrator puts it about Horace in chapter 2 of *Sanctuary*, "It was that country. Flat and rich and foul. . . . That Delta. Five thousand square miles, without any hill save the bumps of dirt the Indians made to stand on when the River overflowed."[15] This demonstrates that the hills were not only or merely a realistic feature of the land in North Mississippi, but also a feature of Faulkner's make-up, both affective and mental—as he showed by titling one of his very first prose pieces, and a fundamental one to boot, "The Hill."[16]

As is rather well-documented in this collection of letters, Faulkner's heart could only have been where his literary creation took him, and, as everyone knows, at least in terms of locale, this was almost always to the country around here—even, as I hope to have shown, too, when the "realistic" landscape was French. To me, however, Faulkner's fiction lies between two poles, neither of them having to do with realism. One is represented, indeed, by Darl's pathetic confession about how often he had "lain beneath rain on a strange roof, thinking of home," and the other by Quentin's phrase when the southbound train stops in Virginia and when, raising the window, he finds out that "[T]he car was blocking a road crossing" and there was a Negro on a mule, "waiting for the train to move." What follows was a manuscript addition to the typescript of the novel: "as if they had been built there with the fence and the road, or with the hill, carved out of the hill itself, like a sign put there saying You are home again."[17]

In both cases, going away and coming back ("Going la maison," as the Creoles of Louisiana put it in a translation of "going home" that I wish we could use in metropolitan French), what one attends might well be called a poetics of return, and where the heart is, in Faulkner's case, is simply where the fantasies are. The best proof is the little self-portrait he drew at the end of one of his letters to his mother from Paris in 1925: clearly, he represented himself as a faun.[18]

NOTES

1. *Thinking of Home: William Faulkner's Letters to His Mother and Father, 1918–1925*, ed. James G. Watson (New York: Norton, 1992).

2. *Selected Letters of William Faulkner*, ed. Joseph Blotner (New York: Random House, 1978).

3. *Thinking of Home*, 44. Further quotations are given in the text.

4. Quoted by Philippe Sollers in *"Vérité de Barthes," Le Monde* (July 16, 1994): 26.

5. Quoted by Willie Morris in *Terrains of the Heart and Other Essays on Home* (Oxford, Mississippi: Yoknapatawpha Press, 1981), 9.

6. *William Faulkner: New Orleans Sketches*, ed. Carvel Collins (New York: Random House, 1958; repr. 1968).

7. *Faulkner, Sud* (Marseille), 14/15 (1975): 185–89.

8. William Faulkner, *Go Down, Moses* (New York: Random House, 1942), 195.

9. William Faulkner, *The Hamlet* (New York: Random House, 1940) 270.

10. Joseph Blotner, *Faulkner: A Biography*, one-volume edition (New York: Random House, 1984), 245.

11. *Faulkner in the University*, ed. Frederick L. Gwynn and Joseph L. Blotner (Charlottesville: University Press of Virginia, 1959), 129–30.

12. William Faulkner, *Essays, Speeches, and Public Letters*, ed. James B. Meriwether (New York: Random House, 1965), 197.

13. William Faulkner, *Early Prose and Poetry*, ed. Carvel Collins (Boston: Little, Brown & Co., 1962), 91–92.

14. Michel Gresset, "Home and Homelessness in Faulkner's Works and Life," *William Faulkner: Materials, Studies, and Criticism* (Kyoto: Yamaguchi), 5 (May, 1983): 30.

15. William Faulkner, *Sanctuary* (New York: Jonathan Cape & Harrison Smith, 1931), 16.

16. See my "Faulkner's 'The Hill,' " *Southern Literary Journal* 6 (Spring 1968): 3–18.

17. William Faulkner, *The Sound and the Fury* (New York: Jonathan Cape & Harrison Smith, 1929), 106.

18. The self-portrait, originally drawn at the end of a letter to his mother dated September 6, 1925 (*Selected Letters*, 17–18), was first reproduced by Joseph Blotner in *Faulkner: A Biography* (New York: Random House, 1974), 461. In 1975, it was used as a tailpiece at the end of each article in *Sud*, 14/15. It was used again in 1984 as the illustration on the cover of Judith L. Sensibar's book, *The Origins of Faulkner's Art* (Austin: University of Texas Press, 1984).

Cracked Urns: Faulkner, Gender, and Art in the South

SUSAN V. DONALDSON

In 1935 Mississippi painter John McCrady produced a painting offering a witty commentary on the relationship between artist and audience and, inadvertently, upon the gender politics of art as well (figure 1). Titled *Political Rally*, the painting portrays a speaker trying to whip up enthusiasm for Mississippi politician Theodore "The Man" Bilbo—but with only partial success. For the crowd the speaker exhorts is not particularly attentive; indeed, the "audience" seems to boast as many counterspeakers

Figure 1. John McCrady, *Political Rally* (1935). Courtesy of Mr. and Mrs. Jack M. McLarty, Jackson, Mississippi.

51

and private arguments as it does listeners, and, as if to under-score the tenuous nature of the audience, children oblivious to the crowd *and* the speaker frolic in the foreground. More to the point, the painting also includes an elusive, pipe-smoking figure in the right foreground who, significantly enough, stands apart from the crowd and its boisterous activity and who represents, according to John McCrady himself, none other than William Faulkner.[1]

In true Faulknerian style, the writer's figure is conspicuous by virtue of his ostentatious effort to look inconspicuous, and the more we look upon that diminutive and hooded figure, the more pronounced and droll becomes the contrast between Faulkner and the rabble-rouser with his crowd. For in the painting Faulkner emerges as everything that the speaker and his crowd are not—meditative, skeptical, measured, and what's more, shrewdly attentive. And unlike the speaker, the painting slyly hints, the artist possesses the power to capture and trans-form the crowd into obedient and pliable vassals subject to the artist's commands in future works of the imagination.

Perhaps not quite so immediately noticeable is the largely male character of the scene, even though the crowd of listeners does include a few women and even a little girl or two. Set in the public town square, the gathering is implicitly a masculine affair of politics, speeches, tobacco smoke, and rowdiness. Even the witty counterpoint presented by the figure of Faulkner, the artist who stands apart, weighs, and gathers material for future novels and short stories, underscores the masculine air of the event. For the fiction that he will create from this particular event will still bear something of its male imprint—and, for that matter, the stamp of its pipe-smoking, hat-wearing, tweedy creator.

But can we be so sure that Southern art is so resolutely masculine? For the curious thing about this painting is the way it represses the gender politics of Southern art and literature. Both John McCrady and William Faulkner were heirs to a regional artistic legacy that had been identified as largely feminine by the early twentieth century, and Faulkner's own comments about Southern art being nothing more than "a polite painting of china by gentlewomen" testified to the strength of that inheritance.[2] By the first two decades of the twentieth century white Southern women in particular had achieved prominence in portraiture and in fiction, had found places for themselves among the book reviewing pages of local newspapers, and had taken up key positions in organizations focusing on arts, literary activities, and historic preservation. So prominent was the traditional position of women in Southern art and literature that Faulkner apparently felt compelled to tell his correspondent Malcolm Cowley that art in the South "was really no manly business."[3] Indeed, Faulkner even went as far as to suggest in one of his aborted introductions to *The Sound and the Fury* that the male artist in the South was "forced to choose, lady and tiger fashion, between being an artist and being a man."[4]

Faulkner's own quarrel with Southern art reveals not just how deeply engendered his view of Southern literature and painting was but how profoundly implicated his work was in the crisis of masculinity characterizing early twentieth-century American culture. Like many high male modernists of the late nineteenth century and early twentieth century, Faulkner responded to that crisis and his own regional artistic legacy by creating art implicitly defining the artist as male and the object of artistic desire and creation as female.[5] And nowhere was this demarcation between male artist and female object of art more apparently discernible than in Faulkner's obsessive use of urns, vases, and images of containment to define not just woman but art in general. For Faulkner, urns suggested the possibility of containing and confining women within the realm of a rigorously masculine art. But those figures of containment and confinement also signalled something of Faulkner's own entrapment—in narrowing definitions of twentieth-century masculinity and in a regional heritage of painting and literature defined in part by women.

If the identity of Southern artist was profoundly ambiguous and disturbing for Faulkner, it is because so much of his artistic inheritance was one of gender battles—in the South and in high modernism. Southern literary history has traditionally set its sights on a male lineage of writers going all the way back to John Pendleton Kennedy and the 1832 publication of *Swallow Barn*, generally hailed as the beginning of the plantation tradition. But the truth of the matter is that white women played a large role in Southern letters beginning with the publication of Caroline Gilman's *Recollections of a Southern Matron* in 1838.[6] A good many white women, like E. D. E. N. Southworth, who was abandoned by her husband in the late 1840s, resorted to the pen for financial support, and though Southworth observed that it was in the "darkest days of my *woman's* life, that my *author's* life commenced," her author's life turned out to be highly successful.[7] Southworth, who eventually produced approximately fifty novels, was, according to Nina Baym, "probably the most widely read novelist in the nineteenth century."[8] Nearly as popular was Alabama novelist Augusta J. Evans, who first found fame with the 1859 novel *Beulah* and then produced a few years later the best-selling novel of the Confederacy, a volume called *Macaria; or Altars of Sacrifice*. Evans won the most fame, though, for her 1866 novel *St. Elmo*, tracing the trials and tribulations of her spunky, ambitious, pious heroine Edna Earl. So popular was this novel that the name St. Elmo was eventually appropriated, historian Mary Kelley tells us, "as the name for objects as disparate as female academies, a cigar, a Southern punch, steamboats, and thirteen towns stretching from New York to California."[9]

Other women writers in the South may have achieved less spectacular success than Evans and Southworth, but white women writers nonetheless took on a new prominence during the Civil War, when, as Drew Gilpin Faust has observed, "women . . . became acknowledged creators and custodians of public as well as domestic culture in the wartime South."[10] By the 1870s women writers in the South were ubiquitous enough to prompt South Carolina poet Paul Hamilton Hayne to complain about what he called "the fungous school" of Southern literature, "the worst enemies," he declared, "of the intellectual achievement and repute of their section." And even more appalling than the writers, he asserted, were their readers, reviewers, and patrons:

> By means primarily of local influence and patronage, of the *claquement* of friends and allies, and the blatant commendation of the press (generally the provincial press)—in brief, by the blowing of an orchestra of brazen trumpets, all set to the one tune of indiscriminate adulation, the unlucky masses are stunned, if not into admiration, at least into acquiescence. They find it is "quite the thing" to have read Mrs. Duck-a-love's "pathetic and passionate romance, that marvellous revelation of a woman's famishing heart," or Mrs. General Aristotle Brown's "profound philosophic novel."[11]

White women painters were slower to achieve public notice although there were notable exceptions, like Irish-born Henrietta Johnston, who managed to support her family in early eighteenth-century Charleston painting pastel portraits of the city's elite (figure 2).[12] But then painting and drawing, as Faulkner observed with such bitterness, were indeed considered "a fashionable accomplishment" for ladies of the antebellum South more intent upon ornamenting parlors than pursuing professional careers.[13] By the late nineteenth century, though, amateur women painters could be found throughout the urban South in academies and in local art associations. New Orleans in particular became something of a center for women artists, first with the establishment in 1887 of what became known as the Newcomb Art School—that is, the art department at Sophie Newcomb College, the women's affiliate of Tulane University—and later the Newcomb Pottery, famous for its Art Nouveau botanical designs up until the 1940s (figure 3).[14] There china painting was a particularly important part of the curriculum—a fact that we would do well to keep in mind if we remember Faulkner's own remark about china painting in the South—and it was generally viewed as an occupation peculiarly suited for

Figure 2. Henrietta Johnston, *Henriette C. Chastaigner* (1711). Courtesy of Carolina Art Association, Gibbes Art Museum, Charleston, South Carolina.

Figure 3. Newcomb Pottery (c. 1903). Covered jar designed by Marie de Hoa LeBlanc. Courtesy of Dr. and Mrs. S. A. Cronan. Chrysanthemum vase designed by Harriet Joor and on loan to Newcomb College. Courtesy of Harley Howcott. Vase designed by Marie de Hoa LeBlanc. Courtesy of Mr. and Mrs. Charles B. Murphy.

women students, in part because the task of throwing and firing the pots was reserved for professional male potters.[15] And though the management of the pottery was largely male, women were in charge of china decoration, which at the Newcomb Pottery became closely associated with self-consciously Southern imagery, what art historian Jessie Poesch calls "the oak, moss, and moon motif" (figure 4).[16] Elsewhere at the turn of the century New Women, Southern style, like Anne Goldthwaite of Montgomery, Alabama, and Alice Ravenel Huger Smith of Charleston, were vigorously pursuing artistic careers rather than fashionable accomplishments fitting them for marriage.[17] Like many other women artists at the time, they were to find a home of sorts in the Southern States Art League, a regional arts organization founded in 1921 and boasting more than 500

Figure 4. Newcomb Pottery lamp base (c. 1927). Thrown by Joseph Meyer and decorated by Sadie Irvine. Courtesy of the Department of Art, Newcomb College, Tulane University.

members by the late 1920s.[18] Presided over for years by the irascible Ellsworth Woodward, founder of the Newcomb Art School, the organization sponsored annual conventions and exhibitions throughout the South and also supervised smaller circuit exhibitions at art clubs, public libraries, colleges, museums, and art galleries. The League's avowed purpose, in Woodward's words, was to "make it possible for Southern artists to interpret the spirit and tradition of the South," and accordingly, the artists who participated in the League's competitions and exhibitions, like Goldthwaite and Smith, as well as John McCrady, Lamar Dodd, Elizabeth O'Neill Verner, Marie Hull, J. Kelly Fitzpatrick, and Ella Sophonsiba Hergesheimer, specialized in images traditionally associated with the region—"picturesque" views of African Americans, rural scenes, and the inevitable magnolia.[19] In an organization that prided itself on annual prizes given for the loveliest Southern subjects, little room seemed to be available for the sort of abstraction and experimentation characterizing European painting since the turn of the century.

There seemed to be plenty of room, though, for women as artists and as organizers despite Ellsworth Woodward's dominating presence. Women's clubs and garden clubs played a significant role in organizing exhibitions and designating special awards for competitions, and so, for that matter, did individual members like Ethel Hutson, the league's long-term secretary treasurer, who was largely responsible for the day-to-day operations of the organization.[20] In fact, the art league had a distinctly feminine character despite its sequence of male presidents. Art historian Amy Kirschke notes that in 1933, 65 percent of the art league's 425 artist-members were women.[21]

This was a world that Faulkner, whose mother and grandmother were painters, must have known intimately.[22] Indeed, as Michael Grimwood tells us, despite the literary model proffered by the Old Colonel, Faulkner's great-grandfather, any sort of artistic vocation "was unmistakably a feminine rather than a masculine pursuit in the Faulkner household."[23] His mother was the one who encouraged him to write and to paint, and in many respects, if his early letters are any indication, she served as his earliest and perhaps most critical reader.[24] It is also a world that Faulkner would have known as an habitué of artistic circles in bohemian New Orleans, a milieu that one of his characters in his second novel *Mosquitoes* describes, tellingly enough, as "an endless gabbling of esthetic foster sisters of both sexes."[25]

A quick perusal of Faulkner's early letters, in fact, reveals that Faulkner was acutely aware of the ubiquitous presence of women in Southern arts and letters. A negative review of *The Marble Faun* by a woman writing for the *Memphis Commercial-Appeal*, the first reviewer that Faulkner mentions in his correspondence, prompts him to say half in jest and half in anger: "That lady she taken that book and run it through her typewriter any old dam way, didn't she. That's the kind of review I want—to find what is wrong with the stuff."[26] Faulkner also found himself the cynosure of book discussions by local women's clubs and even a few mash notes.[27] "I have had two more letters from strange females who saw my photo in the paper," he told his mother after an article on *The Marble Faun* appeared in the New Orleans *Times-Picayune*. "One about 40, gushing, you know; and the other about 14—on pink paper and terrible spelling."[28]

A few of Faulkner's early stories, like "Black Music" and "Carcassonne," also tell us something about the apprentice writer's highly ambivalent feelings about women readers and lady patrons of the arts. The former tells the tale of Wilfred Midgleston, a longtime resident in a Latin American city who once suffered the curious fate of being turned into a faun for the purpose of disrupting a wealthy woman's ambitious plans for transforming part of the Virginia mountains into an arts complex resembling a combination of the Acropolis and the Coliseum. And the one discordant note in the dazzling vision of poetic creation pondered by an unnamed artist in "Carcassonne" is the looming presence of the owner of the garret and darkness inhabited by the artist. Mrs. Widdrington, we are told, who is married to the owner of the Standard Oil Company, would "make a poet of you too, if you did not work anywhere."[29]

Most devastating of all, though, is Faulkner's savage portrait in *Mosquitoes* of the wealthy Mrs. Maurier, whose passion for collecting artists is matched only by her silliness and her penchant for platitudes about Art with a capital A. As a form of revenge the sculptor Gordon captures her likeness in clay, and the result, emphasizing her multiple chins, the "dead familiar astonishment of her face," the "empty sockets" of her eyes, and "something that exposed her face for the mask it was, and still more, a mask unaware," suggests nothing so much as the untenability of Mrs. Maurier's position in the realm of art. From Gordon's angry, purist perspective, she has purchased entry simply on the basis of her money (322).

But Gordon's form of revenge is more than simply an angry gesture made toward the power of lady patrons of the arts. His sculpture serves as a means of capturing and confining woman in an era when roles for women seemed to be expanding and gender boundaries appeared to be in distinct danger of blurring and disappearing altogether, especially in arts and letters, where women had indeed achieved prominence. This was, after all, the era of the New Woman, who had rejected the cloistered domesticity of her mother, eagerly sought higher education in the second half of the nineteenth century, made her presence felt in the marketplace and in turn-of-the-century reform movements, and even insisted upon redefining marriage as a partnership. Perhaps even more to the point as far as male modernist artists like Faulkner were concerned, femininity, in the form of the New Woman, seemed less and less subject to the tyranny of gender boundaries. Indeed, the flapper of the twenties was famed for her boyish figure and androgynous appeal, and it was precisely that androgynous quality, according to Carroll Smith-Rosenberg, that worried so many physicians and sexologists who tended to associate the New Woman with lesbianism.[30]

In this context, then, Gordon's strategy of capturing woman

within the confines of art takes on a special resonance, and if we have any doubt that the sculptor does indeed resort to art as a means of containing woman, we have only to look at his sculpture of a female torso, described at length at the beginning of *Mosquitoes*. It is, we are told, "motionless and passionately eternal—the virginal breastless torso of a girl, headless, armless, legless, in marble temporarily caught and hushed yet passionate still for escape, passionate and simple and eternal in the equivocal derisive darkness of the world" (11). Like Cyrano, who "locked" his love up "in a book," Gordon is able to prevent her escape by confining her within the boundaries of art (270). And there she exists, bound and motionless, as his "feminine ideal: a virgin with no legs to leave me, no arms to hold me, no head to talk to me" (26).

This bitter little passage, of course, says a good deal about Faulkner's own romantic troubles in the teens and twenties. Like Ernest Talliaferro, the young writer feared that he "had never had the power to stir women, that he had been always a firearm unloaded and unaware of it," and his early poetry and fiction is replete with elusive, darting women just out of reach of the male figures who obsessively pursue them (346). It is to be expected, then, that so many of these women, like the Beardsleyesque femmes fatales that Faulkner drew in his youth, resonate with glamour and danger, like the little sister Death revealed as the goal of Sir Galwyn's quest in *Mayday*.

But Gordon's words also speak volumes about the fearful consequences awaiting male artists in Faulkner's work who do not resort to this strategy of incarcerating woman, who fail to recognize that women have traditionally served both as signifiers of the boundaries lying between masculinity and femininity and, in the words of political historian Carole Pateman, as "potential disrupters of masculine boundary systems of all sorts."[31] For Gordon, *Mosquitoes* hints, is both a man and an artist, unlike so many of the would-be artists and would-be men in the novel, precisely because he has successfully captured woman within the confines of art, thereby designating in an androgynous age the boundaries between male and female, artist and the object of art. To fail at this crucial task, the novel suggests, is to be a failure not just as an artist but as a "man," as Ernest Talliaferro is a failure throughout *Mosquitoes*.

Nowhere did Faulkner explore this possibility of failure more explicitly than in his abandoned second novel "Elmer," a work that he later admitted was "too nearly autobiographical."[32] As David Minter shrewdly observes, " 'Elmer' is a portrait of the artist Faulkner did *not* wish to become."[33] Faulkner's own summary of the manuscript is perhaps just as revealing. "Elmer is quite a boy," he wrote his mother from Paris. "He is tall and almost handsome and he wants to paint pictures. He gets everything a man could want—money, a European title, marries the girl he wants—and she gives away his paint box."[34]

As telling as that last detail is the fact that it is a woman, his beloved, androgynous sister Jo-Addie, who gives Elmer his first box of paints and whose absence provokes in him a good deal of his yearning to create, as the manuscript says, "that vague shape somewhere back in his mind, trying to reconcile what is, with what might be." But unlike Gordon in *Mosquitoes*, Elmer never succeeds in capturing that shape within the boundaries of art, just as he never succeeds in capturing his two love interests. Eventually, Elmer is driven half in despair and half in romantic dreams to Europe, but he never quite manages to apply himself to his painting, and he certainly never manages to grasp any of the women—first Jo-Addie, then Ethel, then Myrtle—who slip deftly out of his grasp. What he is left with are simply the unused tools of his art, the brand-new paint tubes "virgin yet at the same time pregnant" in which "was yet wombed his heart's desire, the world itself—thick-bodied and female and at the same time phallic: hermaphroditic." No other passage in "Elmer" signals quite so emphatically his failure to transform the raw materials of art into a masculine vision that clearly defines the boundaries between male and female.[35]

Faulkner clearly meant "Elmer" to be a comic portrait of the would-be artist, but the underlying anguish that can be detected

in this abandoned novel, in Elmer's bewilderment and aimless-
ness, also reveals how deeply implicated Faulkner was in the
"complex renegotiations of gender" that historians like Barbara
Melosh see characterizing the period between the world wars.[36]
Implicit in "Elmer" is the unspoken assumption that the title
character never achieves full manhood or artistry, in part because the women about him remain so utterly elusive and in
part because masculinity itself appears to be diminished and
tenuous. Therein lies Faulkner's own complicated response to a
world of shifting gender boundaries. For it is important to keep
in mind that Faulkner grew up and came of age in a period
when definitions of white middle-class manhood were indeed
undergoing significant reformulation in response to the rise
of the New Woman and the emergence of a bureaucratic,
industrialized economic order.

Historian Clyde Griffen, for one, has expressed skepticism
that "a crisis of masculinity" did indeed exist in the early years
of the twentieth century. Fears about a crisis in manhood, he
notes, have been voiced for a hundred and fifty years and were
fervently reiterated in the 1950s by figures as notable as Arthur
Schlesinger, Jr. But like other historians of masculinity, Griffen
agrees that the increasing visibility of women in the world of
work, the growing tendency of men and women to mix socially
in public, and the transition from a rural-based economy to a
tightly organized national marketplace "softened the boundaries
between the gender spheres" and required extensive renegotiations in the way that white middle-class manhood and womanhood were defined.[37]

In particular, Griffen argues that at the turn of the century, a
new unifying norm of masculinity, finding its sharpest articula-
tion in mass magazines and bridging regional, occupational, and
class differences, considerably narrowed the broad range of
masculine cultural scripts available to nineteenth-century white
men. Before the Civil War, Griffen contends, "markedly divergent conceptions and styles of masculinity coexisted, not only
between social classes but within them." There were, for in-

stance, the rough-and-ready subculture of backcountry Southern males who often resorted to brutal combat to assert their
honor and a similar honor-bound and violence-prone world
encompassing working-class men in northern cities. But the
early nineteenth century also spawned the stately and stylized
code of honor lying at the heart of elite white Southern manhood, along with the sober, self-disciplined notion of working-
class manhood counselled by evangelical culture, the image of
the powerful, middle-class patriarch, and the open sentimental-
ism cultivated by northern male abolitionists.[38]

By the time, though, that the young Faulkner was avidly
reading his monthly copy of *American Boy*, one of those mass
magazines crucially important in the reformulation of white
masculinity, those various options for defining masculinity had
shrunk considerably.[39] Even in the turn-of-the-century South,
historian John Starrett Hughes concludes, the kind of honor-
obsessed masculinity defining, for instance, Faulkner's great-
grandfather, was becoming increasingly untenable.[40] Emerging
to replace this diversity of manly styles, Griffen asserts, was a
new, standardized notion of manhood combining virility, a
strong orientation toward the family and home, and an endless
appetite for consumerism. It was a notion, Griffen adds, potentially much more difficult actually to meet and fulfill because it
was fissured with potential contradictions. The new man was
supposed to be both a member of the new "bureaucratized
society" and an independent tough guy, a willing team worker
subsuming himself in the organization and a rugged individual
bristling with virility, a figure whose identity was defined simultaneously by his work and by his devotion to family.[41]

Just as important, perhaps, to this new ideal of manhood was
the idea of partnership with woman, one that encompassed a
celebration of companionate marriage and mutual sexual fulfillment. For an apprentice male artist like Faulkner, though,
coming of age at a time when notions of manhood were indeed
narrowing, that notion of partnership took on highly ambiguous
connotations. His early drawings reveal as nothing else does a

half-strangling, half-tenuous union between the New Woman and the aspiring male artist, who often takes the form, as Judith Sensibar has argued, of Pierrot, a highly ambiguous figure in his own right (figure 5).[42]

Throughout the whole of Faulkner's career, Sensibar argues, Pierrot, the clownish figure that Faulkner inherited from French Symbolist poetry, was to serve as Faulkner's "nemesis," the very "embodiment of failure in art and life, his other self, the dark double."[43] And if Pierrot served as an emblem of failed art and masculinity, it was precisely because he was forever bound to women whose androgyny and ambiguity signified freedom in opposition to the inertia and entrapment defining Pierrot in Faulkner's 1920 Symbolist play *The Marionettes* (figure 6). "For Faulkner's Pierrot," Sensibar observes, "the

Figure 5. Personae. From William Faulkner's *The Marionettes* (1920). Courtesy of Jill Faulkner Summers and the William Faulkner Collection (Acc. No. 6271aj), University of Virginia Library.

Figure 6. Marietta and Pierrot. From *The Marionettes* (1920). Courtesy of Jill Faulkner Summers and the William Faulkner Collection
(Acc. No. 6271aj), University of Virginia Library.

enemy is most often, and paradoxically, the ideal woman, whose
perfection and/or filial relation make her unattainable."[44] Hence
in *The Marionettes* and throughout Faulkner's early poetry, we
see Pierrot defeated again and again at the hands of Woman,
whose ability to take many forms, from shy virgin to raging
succubus, enables her to elude Pierrot's grasp and even, in the
case of the poem "Fifty Years After," to "ensnare" her pursuer
(figure 7).[45]

In *The Marionettes* the drunken and motionless Pierrot is
able to grasp his quarry Marietta only briefly, and then only
within the realm of dreams and in the form of a shade who
entices Marietta with his song and then abandons her. But the
lesson that Pierrot learns in Faulkner's dream play points the
way to the narrative strategies characterizing the novels to
come. It is through art that Pierrot is able to capture Marietta

Figure 7. Marietta. From *The Marionettes* (1920). Courtesy of Jill Faulkner Summers and the William Faulkner Collection (Acc. No. 6271aj), University of Virginia Library.

and to achieve the sort of nimble elusiveness that usually characterizes the figure of Woman in Faulkner's early work (figure 8). And it is through art, the last drawing of *The Marionettes* suggests, that Pierrot is able to construct an image of himself in the mirror he surveys, positioned, significantly enough, over the motionless body of Marietta (figure 9). Through art, this last drawing tells us, the male artist is able to construct a sense of self that is both male and artist, but he is able to do so only over the supine form of Woman finally captured and contained.

This was the lesson that Faulkner the aspiring artist also learned from his eager forays into high modernism—the early poetry of Conrad Aiken and T. S. Eliot and the paintings of Impressionism, Post-Impressionism, Futurism, and Vorticism.[46] From Aiken in particular the young Faulkner inherited the

Figure 8. Pierrot Singing. From *The Marionettes* (1920). Courtesy of Jill Faulkner Summers and the William Faulkner Collection (Acc. No. 6271aj), University of Virginia Library.

motif of "nympholepsy," which Aiken himself defined as "that impulse which sends man from one dream, or ideal, to another, always disillusioned and therefore always inventing new fictions."[47] And from modernist painting, which Faulkner explored with excitement during his 1925 sojourn in Paris, he acquired the strategy of positioning woman as the object of desire and art and man as creator and artist. Indeed, art historian Griselda Pollack argues that to a striking degree modernist French painting—from Edouard Manet's notorious *Olympia* to Picasso's *Les Demoiselles d'Avignon*—is preoccupied with the commercial exchange of sexuality. "The encounters pictured and imagined," she observes, "are those between men who have the freedom to take their pleasures in many urban spaces and women from a class subject to them who have to work in those spaces often selling their bodies to clients, or to artists." In such encounters,

Figure 9. Pierrot in the Mirror. From *The Marionettes* (1920). Courtesy of Jill Faulkner Summers and the William Faulkner Collection (Acc. No. 6271aj), University of Virginia Library.

she adds, "the territory of modernism" is often defined as "a way of dealing with masculine sexuality and its sign, the bodies of women."[48]

Above all, modernist literature and art situate the male artist in the position of spectator and *flâneur*, the man about town who enjoys the sights about him, and the woman as the object of the gaze. Baudelaire makes the engendering of those two positions quite clear in his famous essay "The painter of modern life":

> Woman is for the artist in general . . . far more than just the female of man. Rather she is divinity, a star . . . a glittering conglomeration of all the graces of nature, condensed into a single being; an object of keenest admiration and curiosity that the picture of life can offer to its contemplator. She is an idol, stupid perhaps, but dazzling and bewitching. . . . Everything that adorns women that serves to show off her beauty is part of herself.
>
> No doubt woman is sometimes a light, a glance, an invitation to happiness, sometimes she is just a word.[49]

What more of an invitation could the young Faulkner need to transform woman into word and to claim the two fold identity of artist and man? In the highly engendered inflections of male modernist art, the young poet found the means for reinscribing the boundaries between masculinity and femininity that appeared so blurred in the modern world, and in Keats, oddly enough, he also found the means for appropriating art from the domain of "polite painting of china by gentlewomen." Indeed, Faulkner's description of his discovery of Keats reveals not just his delight in a spiritually attuned precursor but palpable relief that art—and perhaps china painting in particular—could be retrieved from the encroaching presence of the feminine:

> I read "Thou still unravished bride of quietness" and found a still water withal strong and potent, quiet with its own strength, and satisfying as bread. That beautiful awareness, so sure of its own power that it is not necessary to create the illusion of force by frenzy and motion. Take the odes to a nightingale, to a Grecian urn, "Music to hear," etc.; here is the spiritual beauty which the moderns strive vainly for with trickery, and yet beneath it one knows are entrails; masculinity.[50]

In a word, Faulkner found his own notion of masculinity, one offering an alternative to the uneasy compromise between domesticity and virility in the turn-of-the-century ideal of manhood he had inherited. That notion was premised on the containment of woman, embodied for Faulkner as nothing else in the imagery of urns and vases haunting the whole of his work—urns that allude as much to the much despised china painting of gentlewomen as they do to Keats's own Grecian urn. As early as 1918 Faulkner had resorted to vase imagery to describe an attractive woman to his mother, and by the late 1920s that image had come to embody in his correspondence both the beauty and the emptiness that Baudelaire saw defining Woman.[51] And by the time Faulkner began writing his early novels, images of vases and urns had begun to recur with startling regularity—in "Elmer," *Mosquitoes*, *Flags in the Dust*, and even in a book review or two. Those images in turn, as David Minter and Gail Mortimer have eloquently argued, took on a host of disturbing and contradictory associations—profound male ambivalence about women and their bodies, protected sanctuaries, embodied artistic inspiration, and the defining fragility and elusiveness of that inspiration.[52]

Preeminent among these associations, though, is the figure of the male artist creating the perfect, beloved, implicitly feminine work of art. At times, as with Horace Benbow in *Flags in the Dust*, this figure takes on a distinctly comic and self-mocking air and even in many respects evokes the specter of Elmer, the failed male artist. There is indeed something precious and ineffectual about Benbow's glassblowing and his painstaking production of a clear amber vase that he keeps on his night table and calls by his sister's name. But Faulkner nonetheless found that image of creation compelling enough to describe himself at the outset of writing the novel closest to his heart, *The Sound and the Fury*. Besieged by personal problems and disappointed with Liveright's initial rejection of *Flags in the Dust*, he wrote in one of the novel's abandoned introductions:

> I said to myself, Now I can write. Now I can make myself a vase like that which the old Roman kept at his bedside and wore the rim slowly away with kissing it. So I, who had never had a sister and was fated to lose my daughter in infancy, set out to make myself a beautiful and tragic little girl.[53]

As Minter points out, this passage and similar ones conflate the very heart and center of *The Sound and the Fury*, the doomed Caddy Compson, with the novel and the image of the vase.[54] But the story of Caddy Compson is of course one that is conspicuously not her own. She is, to borrow Teresa de Lauretis's apt phrase, a figure "in someone else's story," a story told by her three brothers, Benjy, Quentin, and Jason, and by the implicitly male narrator of the last section, but never by herself, as numerous commentators have already pointed out.[55] In *The Sound and the Fury* we see Caddy only through the eyes of others. Indeed, the novel had its origins, Faulkner once declared, in the image of Caddy as a child looking in the window at the funeral of her grandmother, while she and her muddy drawers are looked upon by her three brothers.[56] And what the

gaze of her brothers tells us—here and throughout the novel—is
their passionate desire to hold the elusive Caddy fast within the
mirror that Benjy loves, "out of the loud world" in Quentin's
private fantasy of hell, and in Jason's tidy, devastating pro-
nouncement, "Once a bitch always a bitch."[57]

It was a strategy of containing woman that Faulkner would
explore repeatedly in the great works that followed—in *As I Lay
Dying*, which literally confines Addie Bundren in a much abused
coffin and figuratively imprisons her voice within a cacophony
of other voices, and in *Absalom, Absalom!*, in which Judith
Sutpen, caught between her brother Henry and her lover
Charles Bon, is described as "the blank shape, the empty vessel
in which each of them strove to preserve, not the illusion of
himself nor his illusion of the other but what each conceived the
other to believe him to be."[58] Always suffusing these narratives
of containment, however, is the barely suppressed fear that
woman could not, after all, be successfully contained, that the
boundaries lying between woman as the object of art and desire
and man as artist and creator were distressingly subject to
violation. Somehow Caddy Compson always lies just out of the
reach of the eager grasp of her brothers and even, for that
matter, of her creator William Faulkner, who repeats the story
of the Compsons again and again throughout *The Sound and the
Fury* just to catch a fleeting glimpse of his "heart's darling."
And although Addie Bundren may be quite conspicuously dead
throughout most of *As I Lay Dying*, the very title of the book
and her haunting, angry monologue encased within monologues
nonetheless testify to her endless capacity for slipping off her
bonds and eluding her captors.

That urns, vases, and narrative strategies of containment
might be subject to cracking and releasing the genie within,
Faulkner at times revealed almost in spite of himself. One such
inadvertent revelation, a poem from *The Green Bough*, is worth
quoting in its entirety:

> The race's splendor lifts her lip, exposes
> Amid her scarlet smile her little teeth;

The years are sand the wind plays with; beneath,
The prisoned music of her deathless roses.

Within frostbitten rock she's fixed and glassed;
Now man may look upon her without fear.
But her contemptuous eyes back through him stare
And shear his fatuous sheep when he has passed.

Lilith she is dead and safely tombed
And man may plant and prune with naught to bruit
His heired and ancient lot to which he's doomed,
For quiet drowse the flocks when wolf is mute—
Ay, Lilith she is dead, and she is wombed,
And breaks his vine, and slowly eats the fruit.[59]

If Lilith's mere glance suggests how gossamer her bonds are, Temple Drake in the original version of *Sanctuary* reveals the fearful prospect of looking too closely within those cherished, well-wrought urns. For Temple, who knows the real story of what happened at the Old Frenchman's place, whose rape lies at the heart of the novel, is the lure drawing Horace Benbow, who seeks those secrets for Lee Goodwin's defense, deep within the confines of *Sanctuary*'s narrative, into her room at Miss Reba's in Memphis. And once he ventures inside, he learns to his peril the price to be paid for looking too closely within the perfectly formed borders of sanctuaries, temples, urns, and vases. Inside her prison Temple moves with impunity, agility, and power, writhing, bedding Red, taunting Popeye, exploring her sexuality with a ferocity that evokes a glimpse of the Medusa, the horrifying, snaky female genitalia the very sight of which, Freud declares, promises castration for the male viewer.[60] True enough, Horace Benbow would reply, for after slipping inside Temple's prison and hearing her story, Horace finds the borders between himself and Temple blurring with dizzying speed. Returning home, he vomits, and as Noel Polk has argued, her rape becomes his rape, her story, his story.[61] Striking the lavatory, he "leaned upon his braced arms while the shucks set up a terrific uproar beneath her thighs. Lying with her head lifted slightly, her chin depressed like a figure lifted down from a crucifix, she watched something black and furious go roaring out of her pale body."[62]

The reversal that Horace experiences, from listener to teller, from bystander to victim, from man to woman, above all, from the urn's spectator to its inhabitant, points to the underlying suspicion marking so much of Faulkner's work that it may, after all, be the male artist, not the female object of desire, who is confined within cracked urns—and by implication within "the polite painting of china by gentlewomen." For if that revealing sculpture by the artist Gordon in *Mosquitoes* indicates the earnest desire to capture woman forever within the confines of art, it also says something about the male artist's own incarceration within shrinking definitions of masculinity forever bound to definitions of femininity, and within a regional art largely defined by women—like those women, for instance, so closely associated with the Newcomb Pottery in New Orleans. And if vases and urns had early on evoked femininity and art for Faulkner, so too had the figure of the Marble Faun, the defining trope of the writer's first book, revealed all too nakedly his own private image of masculinity, art, and "enthralled impotence."[63]

It is in *Light in August*, though, that Faulkner most directly confronts the possibility of his own incarceration, and the result is a text that reverses, with startling force, the strategies of narrative containment toward which he had so painstakingly worked in the twenties. As compelling and powerful a critique of race and racism as *Light in August* is, the novel is also an anguished meditation upon masculinity and femininity and upon Faulkner's own reluctant but inevitable indebtedness to Southern art defined by women. And in that meditation the novel itself—and by implication Faulkner's art in general—emerges as cracked urn, a trope of the male artist's failure to contain woman and an everlasting reminder of his own imprisonment within the confines of art defined all too often by women.

That ultimate failure is perhaps all the more poignant because

Light in August is filled with male characters yearning for the sort of absolute male autonomy and freedom from women that Faulkner undoubtedly saw characterizing his great-grandfather William C. Falkner, a man who could fight duels and wars, build railroads, and write novels in a world where women were apparently safely relegated to the domestic sphere. It is this sort of autonomy and freedom that Byron Bunch yearns for once he finds himself enslaved with love for Lena Grove, that Joe Christmas seeks down that long, lonely road of years in flight from nothing so much as Woman herself, that Lucas Burch runs to whenever Lena Grove comes into view, that Doc Hines defines as a refuge from bitchery and sin implicitly figured as female, that Percy Grimm, the would-be soldier, revels in as a member of the National Guard.

Oddly enough, it is also that ideal of utter male solitude and independence that defines Gail Hightower's dreams and stories of Civil War pomp and glory. Cuckolded, defrocked, and forced to resort to art lessons and card decorations for financial support—an occupation perilously close to china painting—Gail Hightower nonetheless finds relief of sorts in his twilight visions of military splendor, of wild cavalrymen galloping in and out of fire and smoke. For him those cavalrymen forever take the shape of boys on the verge of manhood in the defining male experience of his grandfather's generation—as World War I was the defining male experience for Faulkner's own generation, but not quite, of course, for Faulkner himself. "I tell you, they were not men after spoils and glory," Hightower remembers exulting to his silent wife; "they were boys riding the sheer tremendous tidal wave of desperate living. Boys. Because this. This is beautiful. Listen. Try to see it. Here is that fine shape of eternal youth and virginal desire which makes heroes."[64] To him the beauty of the moment is the emergence of manhood, a moment that he seeks to relive again and again each twilight. And in that moment, of course, there is no room for Hightower's wife, a fact that he finally recognizes toward the end. Indeed, there is hardly room for Hightower himself, for he eventually acknowledges that the glare of his visions of male glory has nearly eclipsed his own sense of self: "And I know," he tells himself, "that for fifty years I have not even been clay: I have been a single instant of darkness in which a horse galloped and a gun crashed" (542).

The curious thing about Hightower's vision of male apotheosis, though, is that it is largely bestowed upon him by a woman, his black nurse Cinthy, who, from his earliest childhood, fills him with tales of his grandfather's days of glory. Her storytelling quite simply makes Hightower's dreams of male glory possible, and for Faulkner that debt resonates with irony and anguish. No matter how deeply his male characters yearn for a world apart from women, no matter how desperately they flee that "lightless hot wet primogenitive Female" that Joe Christmas flees (126), the men of *Light in August* find themselves forever bound to women whose very presence apparently threatens the putative boundaries between male and female—and by implication the purity and autonomy of male art. Preceding Hightower's own tales of Civil War glory are Cinthy's stories— woman's art—just as Lena Grove's story, in a sense, precedes and succeeds all the male stories within *Light in August*, and just as the painting of china at Newcomb Pottery in New Orleans preceded Faulkner's own work. Opening and closing the novel, Lena evokes "something moving forever and without progress across an urn," but far from being contained by that urn imagery, Lena is herself something of a creator of urns and containers. Her story frames all the other stories told in *Light in August*, and inside the bounds cast by her tale, significantly enough, lie not woman but man and his deluded stories of male autonomy, story after story of men—Gail Hightower, Joe Christmas, Byron Bunch, Doc Hines, and Percy Grimm— desperately seeking and never finding freedom from woman.

Above all, though, there lies within the serene urn created by Lena Grove's story the broken pottery of Faulkner's own cherished strategies of containment. The terrifying vision of tainted femininity that Joe Christmas as a youth ponders is also

Faulkner's own anguished meditation upon the remnants of his art: "In the notseeing and the hardknowing as though in a cave he seemed to see a diminishing row of suavely shaped urns in moonlight, blanched. And not one was perfect. Each one was cracked and from each crack there issued something liquid, deathcolored, and foul" (208–9). In this image, I think, Faulkner acknowledges with devastating clarity and self-knowledge the failure of his art to contain woman, and in this respect, his own story is as much at one with Joe Christmas as it is of course with Gail Hightower, a dark avatar of the male Southern artist pondering the mysteries of his past. Joe Christmas's fate in the end, castrated at the hands of Percy Grimm and issuing forth black blood like nothing so much as those cracked and tainted urns, is in a manner of speaking Faulkner's fate as well. Like Joe's blood and Joe's story, slipping out of the cracks of the serene urn that is Lena Grove's tale, Faulkner is himself contained, trapped by ever-narrowing notions of manhood that made the ideal of male autonomy increasingly elusive, that insisted upon the interdependence of male and female, that denied in the end that woman could ever be finally captured and contained. And like Hightower he is trapped as well by an artistic legacy that he himself tended to see as largely female, a legacy defined as much by women like Cinthy and Rosa Coldfield in *Absalom, Absalom!* as by Hightower himself. No wonder, then, that Joe's blood, like the black fluid issuing from those horrifying cracked urns, provides so apt an emblem for Faulkner's own art, blurring boundaries between male and female, rendering those boundaries fluid, in spite of his own best efforts. If Joe in the end becomes that which he feared the most—"womanshenegro"—so too does *Light in August* itself reveal all too nakedly that its contours are also the contours of the polite painting of china by gentlewomen.[65]

NOTES

1. For discussions of the painting, see Keith Marshall, *John McCrady, 1911–1968* (New Orleans: New Orleans Museum of Art, 1975), 53; and Rick Stewart, "Toward a

New South: The Regionalist Approach, 1900–1950," *Painting in the South: 1564–1980*, ed. Ella-Prince Knox and David S. Bundy (Richmond: Virginia Museum of Fine Arts, 1983), 121, 123; see also catalog entry, *Painting in the South*, 290. I should note here my thanks to Noel Polk and Anne Goodwyn Jones for reading and commenting on this essay.

2. William Faulkner to Malcolm Cowley [January 1946], *The Faulkner-Cowley File: Letters and Memories, 1944–1962*, ed. Malcolm Cowley (London: Chatto & Windus, 1966), 78.

3. Ibid.

4. William Faulkner, "Introduction to *The Sound and the Fury*, 1933," *William Faulkner's "The Sound and the Fury:" A Critical Casebook*, ed. André Bleikasten (New York: Garland, 1982), 11.

5. See in general two excellent collections of essays on Faulkner and his representation of women: *Faulkner and Women: Faulkner and Yoknapatawpha, 1985*, ed. Doreen Fowler and Ann J. Abadie (Jackson: University Press of Mississippi, 1986); and "Faulkner and Feminisms," ed. John T. Matthews and Judith Bryant Wittenberg, *Faulkner Journal* 4 (1988–89): 1–187. See also Minrose C. Gwin, *The Feminine and Faulkner: Reading (Beyond) Sexual Difference* (Knoxville: University of Tennessee Press, 1990); and Anne Goodwyn Jones, " 'The Kotex Age': Women, Popular Culture, and *The Wild Palms*," *Faulkner and Popular Culture: Faulkner and Yoknapatawpha, 1988*, ed. Doreen Fowler and Ann J. Abadie (Jackson: University Press of Mississippi, 1990), 142–62. For general background on gender wars in modernism, see Marianne DeKoven, *Rich and Strange: Gender, History, Modernism* (Princeton: Princeton University Press, 1991); and Sandra M. Gilbert and Susan Gubar's two volumes, *No Man's Land: The Place of the Woman Writer in the Twentieth Century—The War of the Words* (New Haven: Yale University Press, 1987); and *No Man's Land: The Place of the Woman Writer in the Twentieth Century—Sexchanges* (New Haven: Yale University Press, 1989).

6. See, for example, Elizabeth Moss's discussion in *Domestic Novelists of the Old South: Defenders of Southern Culture* (Baton Rouge: Louisiana State University Press, 1992), 38–41; and Thadious Davis, "Women's Art and Authorship in the Southern Region: Connections," *The Female Tradition in Southern Literature*, ed. Carol S. Manning (Urbana: University of Illinois Press, 1993), 22–23. For an overview of gender biases in the writing of Southern literary history, see "On Defining Themes and (Mis)Placing Women Writers" and "The Real Beginning of the Southern Renaissance," Manning, 1–12 and 37–56. See also Anne Firor Scott, "Women in the South: History as Fiction, Fiction as History," and my article, "Gender and the Profession of Letters in the South," *Rewriting the South: History and Fiction*, ed. Lothar Hönnighausen and Valeria Gennaro Lerda (Tübingen: Francke Verlag, 1993), 22–34, 35–46.

7. Quoted in Mary Kelley, *Private Woman, Public Stage: Literary Domesticity in Nineteenth-Century America* (New York: Oxford University Press, 1984), 159.

8. Nina Baym, "Melodramas of Beset Manhood: How Theories of American Fiction Exclude Women Authors," *American Quarterly* 33 (1981): 124.

9. Kelley, 27.

10. Drew Gilpin Faust, "Altars of Sacrifice: Confederate Women and the Narratives of War," *Southern Stories: Slaveholders in Peace and War* (Columbia: University of Missouri Press, 1993), 120.

11. Paul Hamilton Hayne, "Literature at the South: The Fungous School," *Southern Magazine* 14 (1874): 651–52.

12. See Carolyn J. Weekley, "The Early Years, 1564–1790," *Painting in the South*, 10–12.

13. James C. Kelly, "Portrait Painting in Tennessee," Special Issue of *Tennessee Historical Quarterly*, 46 (1987): 201.

14. Alberta Collier, "The Art Scene in New Orleans—Past and Present," *The Past as Prelude: New Orleans, 1718–1968*, ed. Hodding Carter et al. (New Orleans: Pelican Publishing House for Tulane University, 1968), 162.

15. Jessie Poesch, *Newcomb Pottery: An Enterprise for Southern Women, 1895–1940* (Exton: Schiffer Publishing, 1984), 7, 9, 13–14, 17.

16. Ibid., 56, 66.

17. See, for example, Don Doyle's discussion of the increasing role of women in the arts in Nashville of the late nineteenth and early twentieth centuries, *New Men, New Cities, New South: Atlanta, Nashville, Charleston, Mobile, 1866–1910* (Chapel Hill: University of North Carolina Press, 1990), 221; and Doyle's *Nashville since the 1920s* (Knoxville: University of Tennessee Press, 1985), 3. See also Kelly, "Portrait Painting," 203.

18. Southern States Art League *Bulletin*, 3, No. 8 (1928), Southern States Art League Papers, Southern Historical Collection, Library of the University of North Carolina at Chapel Hill. For a good overview of the League's history, see Amy Kirschke, "The Southern States Art League: A Regionalist Artists' Organization, 1922–1950," *Southern Quarterly* 25 (1987): 1–23.

19. Southern States Art League *Bulletin* (April 1927), Southern States Art League Papers. Permission to quote from the papers, granted by the Southern Historical Collection in the Library of the University of North Carolina at Chapel Hill, is gratefully acknowledged.

20. Southern States Art League Papers; "Biographical Notes on Ethel Hutson," typescript, A-1490, Ethel Hutson Papers, Southern Historical Collection; Kirschke, 2, 19.

21. Kirschke, 5.

22. Michael Grimwood, *Heart in Conflict: Faulkner's Struggles with Vocation* (Athens: University of Georgia Press, 1987), 69. See also Judith L. Sensibar's essay, "Pop Culture Invades Jefferson: Faulkner's Real and Imaginary Photos of Desire," *Faulkner and Popular Culture*, 110–41.

23. Grimwood, 69.

24. See in general, *Thinking of Home: William Faulkner's Letters to His Mother and Father, 1918–1925*, ed. James G. Watson (New York: W. W. Norton, 1992).

25. William Faulkner, *Mosquitoes* (New York: Boni & Liveright, 1927), 51–52. Subsequent references are cited parenthetically in the text.

26. William Faulkner to Mrs. M. C. Falkner [postmarked 10 April 1925], Watson, 198.

27. William Faulkner to Mrs. M. C. Falkner [early Feb. 1925], Watson, 183.

28. William Faulkner to Mrs. M. C. Falkner [late Jan. 1925] Watson, 179.

29. William Faulkner, "Carcassonne," *Collected Stories* (New York: Random House, 1950), 897.

30. See Lois Banner, *American Beauty* (Chicago: University of Chicago Press, 1983), 273, 280; and Carroll Smith-Rosenberg, "The New Woman as Androgyne: Social Disorder and Gender Crisis, 1870–1936," *Disorderly Conduct: Visions of Gender in Victorian America* (New York: Oxford University Press, 1985), 245–96.

31. Quoted in Elaine Showalter, *Sexual Anarchy: Gender and Culture at the Fin de Siècle* (New York: Viking, 1990), 7–8.

32. Quoted in David Minter, *William Faulkner: His Life and Work* (Baltimore: Johns Hopkins University Press, 1980), 55.

33. Minter, 57.

34. William Faulkner to Mrs. M.C. Falkner [postmarked 22 Sept. 1925] *Selected Letters of William Faulkner*, ed. Joseph Blotner (New York: Random House, 1977), 25.

35. William Faulkner, "Elmer," ed. James B. Meriwether and Dianne L. Cox, *Mississippi Quarterly* 36 (1983): 378, 345.

36. Barbara Melosh, "Manly Work: Public Art and Masculinity in Depression America," *Gender and American History since 1890*, ed. Barbara Melosh (New York: Routledge, 1992), 157.

37. Clyde Griffen, "Reconstructing Masculinity from the Evangelical Revival to the Waning of Progressivism: A Speculative Synthesis," *Meanings for Manhood: Construc-*

tions of Masculinity in Victorian America, ed. Mark C. Carnes and Clyde Griffen (Chicago: University of Chicago Press, 1990), 197.

38. Griffen, 198, 185.

39. Michael Grimwood rightly notes the importance of Faulkner's subscription to *American Boy* in *Heart in Conflict*, 22–23.

40. John Starrett Hughes, "The Madness of Separate Spheres: Insanity and Masculinity in Victorian Alabama," in Carnes and Griffen, 66.

41. Griffen, 201, 198, 199.

42. See Judith Sensibar, *The Origins of Faulkner's Art* (Austin: University of Texas Press, 1984), xvii.

43. Ibid., 151.

44. Ibid., 116.

45. See William Faulkner, "After Fifty Years," *William Faulkner: Early Prose and Poetry*, ed. Carvel Collins (Boston: Little, Brown and Company, 1962), 53. See also Sensibar, 73–76.

46. See, for example, William Faulkner to Mrs. M. C. Falkner [postmarked 22 Sept. 1925], *Selected Letters*, 24.

47. Quoted in Sensibar, 118.

48. Griselda Pollack, *Vision and Difference: Femininity, Feminism and Histories of Art* (London: Routledge, 1988), 54.

49. Charles Baudelaire, *The Painter of Modern Life and Other Essays*, trans. and ed. Jonathan Mayne (London: Phaidon, 1964), 30. Pollack discusses this passage in *Vision and Difference*, 71.

50. William Faulkner, "Verse Old and Nascent: A Pilgrimage," *William Faulkner: Early Prose and Poetry*, 117. Michel Gresset argues that Faulkner saw in "Ode to a Grecian Urn" a model for "a masculine literature" (*Fascination: Faulkner's Fiction, 1919–1936*. Adapted from the French by Thomas West [Durham: Duke University Press, 1989], 38, 39).

51. See Minter, 92.

52. Gail L. Mortimer, "The Smooth, Suave Shape of Desire: Paradox in Faulknerian Imagery of Women," *Women's Studies* 13 (1986): 149–61; and Minter, 99–100, 102.

53. Faulkner, "An Introduction to *The Sound and the Fury*, 1933," 10.

54. Minter, 102.

55. Teresa de Lauretis, *Alice Doesn't: Feminism, Semiotics, Cinema* (Bloomington: Indiana University Press, 1984), 109. See, for example, Joseph R. Urgo, *Faulkner's Apocrypha: "A Fable," "Snopes," and the Spirit of Human Rebellion* (Jackson: University Press of Mississippi, 1989), 39; and André Bleikasten, *The Ink of Melancholy: Faulkner's Novels, from "The Sound and the Fury" to "Light in August"* (Bloomington: Indiana University Press, 1990), 19, 46, 61.

56. Introduction, Bleikasten, *William Faulkner's The Sound and the Fury*, 9.

57. William Faulkner, *The Sound and the Fury*, corrected text (New York: Random House, 1984), 203, 206.

58. William Faulkner, *Absalom, Absalom!*, corrected text (New York: Random House, 1986), 148.

59. William Faulkner, "XXXVII," *The Marble Faun* and *A Green Bough* (New York: Random House, 1965), 60.

60. Sigmund Freud, "Medusa's Head," *The Standard Edition of the Complete Psychological Works of Sigmund Freud*, trans. and ed. James Strachey, (London: Hogarth Press, 1959), 18:23.

61. Noel Polk, "The Space between *Sanctuary*," *Intertextuality in Faulkner*, ed. Michel Gresset and Noel Polk (Jackson: University Press of Mississippi, 1985), 20.

62. William Faulkner, *Sanctuary: The Original Text*, ed. Noel Polk (New York: Random House, 1981), 220.

63. Faulkner, *The Marble Faun*, 45.

64. William Faulkner, *Light in August*, corrected text (New York: Vintage, 1987), 533. Subsequent references are cited parenthetically within the text.

65. I would like to thank all the individuals and institutions who granted me permission to use the reproductions accompanying my essay.

The Scene of Writing and the Shape of Language for Faulkner When "Matisse and Picasso Yet Painted"

PANTHEA REID

Before 1925 William Faulkner adopted various poses to cover various insecurities. The most fruitful of these was the wounded aviator pose that enabled Faulkner to pretend to have flown overseas and have been shot down by Germans. Faulkner also adopted literary poses that enabled him to transmute the longing and frustration born of insecurity into art. The most persistent of these poses, as the poetry testifies, were Pierrot and the Marble Faun trapped in "enthrallèd impotence."

In New Orleans on a brief visit in November of 1924, and then between January and July of 1925, William Faulkner resurrected the wounded aviator pose. To his mother and a succession of mother figures, he also adopted a dutiful son pose. In this persona he presented himself as young, naive, inexperienced, and in need of considerable mothering. With Sherwood Anderson on tour, he wrote his mother, "Mrs. Anderson has taken me in to live with them. She is so nice to me—mothers me, and looks after me, and gets things to eat which I like." She even treated the twenty-seven-year-old Faulkner, he claimed, just like her teenage son, sees "that we have enough to eat, and enough cover, and takes care of our money for us."[1]

With his new bohemian friends, the radically different tragic persona of the aviator better masked Faulkner's private self. In this role he explained that, after crashing in battle, he had had a silver plate inserted over his damaged skull. The plate so hurt him he drank prodigious quantities of liquor to anesthetize the pain. These two different personae crossed when Faulkner's mother read Sherwood Anderson's story about a wounded aviator and poet from the South who drank so much he passed out on the brick patio of a New Orleans bordello. The dutiful son Bill tried to deny the wounded aviator Bill by explaining to Maud Falkner that Anderson's tale was not "documentary" or "true" because "[w]hat really happens, you know, never makes a good yarn." He claimed that Anderson had written another story "about me as I really am, not as a fictitious character."[2] Needless to say, such a story never surfaced.

Faulkner played the role of a number of fictitious characters, apparently as a protective carapace. What we who gather in Oxford, Mississippi, to honor Faulkner year after year may too easily forget was just how insecure a young man Faulkner was. Carolyn Smythe said she and her cousin Estelle Oldham looked on him as a sort of "toy."[3] Harold Levy thought him "neurotic," "war-shocked," a "lost ball because of his war wounds."[4] Lillian Friend Marcus thought Faulkner "too unstable to earn a living in any other way" except writing. She sensed a "deep-rooted sense of inferiority in him."[5] Joyce McClure thought of Faulkner as a "nice, pleasant Southern boy who wanted to be a writer & didn't have any money." He carried her groceries, was friendly, civil, and attractive. She fed him out of compassion. She too believed he had been wounded and had cracked up after the war.[6] Harold Dempsey remembered Bill as a gentleman, very introverted and secretive about his work. Dempsey was a flier who argued with Faulkner about flying and writing. Faulkner's RAF uniform carried considerable cachet with Dempsey, with whom Faulkner dropped the wounded aviator pose, no doubt because Dempsey had the expertise to expose it.[7]

Probably all these roles were compensations or excuses for what must have been Faulkner's deepest fear: that he would prove himself a failure as an artist. He already had in one sense, for there is considerable evidence that his mother—and perhaps he himself—had first thought of young Bill as a visual artist. Maud Butler Falkner admitted she had "tried too hard to steer him into being a sketcher and painter." She had her reasons. Once when Faulkner was very young he tried to tell the family of a new watering cart or water wagon which the town of Oxford was using to lay the dust on the unpaved streets. The Falkners couldn't understand what he was talking about, so he drew it. Though Billy was extremely young, the family marveled that he had included significant engineering details of the vehicle and its watering devices.[8] His great aunt Alabama McLean told another version of the same story. When Faulkner was a little boy, a workman was at the house, using a blow torch. Billy told his family he wanted a "blow-tow"; they couldn't understand him, so he drew a picture that "had all its recognizable parts."[9]

That the very young Faulkner had mastered the art of visual representation, rather than oral explanation, was one reason for expecting him to be a painter. Another was that Maud wanted her favorite son to manifest her influence in his career. (After Faulkner won the Nobel Prize, *McCall's* interviewed "Miss Maud." She told their writer she objected to being the Southern Grandma Moses: " 'I'm not a primitive,' she says. 'After all, I had art lessons once.' "[10]) Carolyn Smythe remembered that Maud Falkner told her that the fifteen-year-old Bill had talent to be quite a fine artist and sculptor. Clearly Maud was not thinking of her son as a literary artist. Her evidence was that he had carved a lion out of butter which Maud used as centerpiece on the dining room table.[11] He apparently considered taking art lessons when he went to New York in 1921.[12] Later, Faulkner would perpetuate to his mother the myth of his being a painter. In 1950 he was still buying elaborate sets of oils when he went to New York City, but when he supposedly found he had too little time to paint, he would give them to his mother.[13] Somehow this subterfuge appealed both to her frugality (her son shouldn't buy expensive presents for her) and to her ongoing sense that he really ought to have been a visual artist.

Faulkner's illustrations for his own writing, like his campus publications here at Ole Miss, were highly stylized ink drawings that reduced the subject matter often to simple outlines (figure 1). His drawings often derived from the art nouveau covers of the *Double Dealer* (figure 2). In this early period, he sent Carolyn Smythe a book of poems with a purple velvet cover he sewed together himself. Carolyn remembered that the printing in the now lost volume was elongated and stylized as in *The Marionettes* (figure 3) and that the women in two idealized drawings looked like Estelle Oldham, whom he had then lost to another man. Faulkner accompanied one poem, "Asphodel," with a drawing of a flower pot with a woman, not a flower, growing out of it.[14] The woman-as-flower motif was distinctly art nouveau, dating from the 1890s or so. Faulkner's drawings reduce his subject matter to a minimalist and unthreatening pattern (figure 4). However skillful,[15] they do not engage the artist with his subject. It may be that Faulkner's chief discovery in those hand-printed books lay less in making the stylized drawings, and more in his experience of words as physical

Figure 1. Drawing for *Ole Miss*.

Figure 2. An Aubrey Beardsley cover for the *Double Dealer*.

objects, as shapes to be manipulated in the enclosed space of
the page. His elongated and highly stylized handwriting too was
an experiment in the materiality of language.

Meanwhile in Paris, New York, London, and even New
Orleans, assumptions about the relation between art and the
visible universe were undergoing radical reevaluations. In 1922
Sherwood Anderson, connecting "New Orleans, The Double
Dealer and the Modern Movement in America," defined modernism as liberation from the "speeding up and the standardiza-
tion of life and thought." He saw true culture as the "acceptance
of life, life of the flesh, mind and spirit."[16] That was a lesson that
Faulkner, who had assumed that poetry was inspired by loss
and longing, badly needed. Against that standard, his stylized
early illustrations seemed slight, repetitious, and repressed.

In 1925, when he settled in New Orleans, the Vieux Carré

Figure 3. From William Faulkner's *The Marionettes* (c. 1920). Courtesy of Jill Faulkner Summers and the William Faulkner Collection (Acc. No. 6271aj), University of Virginia Library.

culture permitted, Faulkner claimed, "forty people to spend day after day painting pictures in a single area comprised in six city blocks."[17] Boarding with William Spratling, who painted and taught architecture at Tulane, Faulkner got a graphic taste of art and its pleasures radically different from his own stylized drawings. He regularly mused over a bathroom decorated, as Caroline Durieux insisted, to be "not pornographic but amusing." This bathroom, "a conversation piece" she called it, "had exotic flowers and large nude figures painted in such a way as to incorporate various parts of the bathroom fixtures into anatomical parts of the nude figure" (Carvel Collins did not record whether the nudes were male or female).[18] Such exposure to uninhibited freedom about the body and about how and what one might paint unsettled the aesthetic Faulkner had founded upon what I have termed the economy of desire. Now his

Figure 4. From *The Marionettes*. Courtesy of Jill Faulkner Summers and the William Faulkner Collection (Acc. No. 6271aj), University of Virginia Library.

roommate Spratling thought Faulkner's drawing "lousy."[19] And now Faulkner conceded. Spratling remembered that New Orleans was a "world full of new ideas for most of us."[20] Spratling, who had attended the Beaux Arts in Paris, undertook Faulkner's education in new ideas about art, recommending that he read Faure's *Outline of the History of Art* and Clive Bell's *Art*. In New Orleans Faulkner heard excited discussions of the radical new art that had severed its representational obligations. In this environment, he used the first person for a personal revelation: "I remarked to Spratling how no one since Cezanne had really dipped his brush in light." He described Spratling as a man "whose hand has been shaped to a brush as mine has (alas!) not."[21] The "alas!" testifies to Faulkner's sense of insufficiency as a painter.

John McClure at the *Times-Picayune*, in a generally favorable review of Faulkner's 1924 book of poetry, *The Marble Faun*, faulted the poet for immaturity. Failed as a painter, labeled an immature poet, with his prose sketches not taken especially seriously by his bohemian friends, Faulkner was under enormous pressure to prove himself a novelist.[22] As he progressed with astonishing rapidity on the text of *May Day*, which became *Soldiers' Pay*, he could reflect less subjectively on the nature of art. He often went to the Delgado Museum (now the New Orleans Museum of Art), as he said "looking at the pictures, and [spending] the evenings talking with painters and writers and musicians."[23] These conversations probably fulminated against the generally reactionary tastes of the museum's directors.[24] Among the avant-garde artists in the quarter, however, artistic discussion probably stretched beyond frustration with the museum's acquisition policy and Anderson's simplistic definition of modernism to the exciting au courant notion of the artist's freedom to manipulate shapes and remake reality.

Faulkner had already been exposed to examples of modernist freedom and invention through such little magazines as *The Dial*, that Phil Stone subscribed to in Oxford. *The Dial*, as a recent retrospective explains, appealed to "knowledgeable people who might not have been to Europe and might have been relatively unfamiliar with the work of Pirandello or Proust, Schiele or Vlaminck. They were, like most of us, removed from the most experimental and contemporary arts; yet they were interested in and concerned about them, long before Modernism became an acknowledged movement."[25] Despite such exposure, modernism came alive for Faulkner only after he arrived in New Orleans, began talking with artists, and began writing prose seriously. When John McClure said "we can't all be Shakespeare," a newly confident Faulkner replied "I don't think I'm so bad myself."[26]

From his reading, picture viewing, and conversations with his new artistic friends, Faulkner was revising his aesthetic. He told Dempsey that plot robbed literature of its quality; plot was cheap, absurd, childish, and limited. He theorized that the

modern novel should eliminate plot.[27] His own novel-in-prog-
ress did not eliminate plot, but it fragmented and juxtaposed
bits of plot in a manner that shows, as we shall see, a new
understanding of what Cézanne and the avant-garde painters
were accomplishing. With his novel finished early in the summer, Faulkner and Spratling left New Orleans together on
July 11. Their destination was Italy; Faulkner's was also and
especially Paris.

When Bill Faulkner arrived in Paris in August of 1925, he
first lived in a little hotel on Rue Jacob, from which he moved
at 2 a.m. one morning to take up residence in a hotel on Rue
Servandoni that was so congenial he never locked his door.[28] As
his letters testify, he enjoyed strolling in the nearby Luxembourg Gardens, watching the children sail their boats, and
looking at the pictures in the Luxembourg Museum. The gardens were populated by statues of the men (and at least one
woman) France most honored, chiefly writers and artists, such
as Chopin, Watteau, Delacroix, Sainte Beuve, and George
Sand. Elevated by the company of various mythological and
allegorical statues, these figures testified to France's respect for
the artist.

Inside the museum, however, a major controversy about
France's disrespect for avant-garde painters boiled over after
thirty years of simmering. (This controversy made the Vieux
Carré artists' probable frustration with the Delgado Museum
acquisition policy pale by comparison.) The Luxembourg,
owned by the French government, was a sort of "waiting room"
for works not yet accepted by the Louvre. (At the time there
was no *Musée National d'Art Moderne*.) Leonce Benedite had
been curator of the museum since at least 1894, and he would
continue so until 1931. He was an extremely conservative and
apparently rather incompetent administrator. In 1894 Gustave
Caillebotte had bequeathed his large collection of contemporary
paintings to the state. This collection of sixty-five works included
three Manets, sixteen Monets, nine Sisleys, eighteen Pissarros,
eight Renoirs, two Cézannes, seven Degases, and two Millets.

But a "storm of protest from the die-hards of the old school" erupted. Curator Benedite developed various strategies to avoid hanging these paintings in the Luxembourg. Well-known reactionary painters were interviewed for the *Journal des Artistes*. A typical assessment was: "Only great moral depravity could bring the State to accept such rubbish . . . some paint like this, others like that, in little dots, in triangles—how should I know? I tell you they're all anarchists—and madmen!"[29] (Incidentally, such language would be replicated in 1910 as London's popular press denounced Roger Fry's first Post-Impressionist exhibit.)

Despite two years of negotiation and avoidance, a "depraved" state was forced to accept forty of these examples of "rubbish." It returned twenty-five to the heirs, who continued to try unsuccessfully to follow Gustave Caillebotte's wishes and give, cost-free to the public, all sixty-five paintings to the Luxembourg. The accepted paintings included two Manets, eight Monets, six Renoirs, seven Degases, six Sisleys, seven Pisarros, two Millets, and two Cézannes. Benedite's prejudice against Cézanne is established by his estimates of their value: he priced the Cézannes almost as low as the least valued unimportant sketches by Millet. Forced to accept these early modern paintings, the museum hardly gave them pride of place. In 1907, the year after Cézanne's death, when that artist was already recognized as the major innovator of a new understanding of art, Benedite actually refused a generous gift to the Luxembourg of murals from the artist's home.

Only in 1921 did the Luxembourg reluctantly purchase one Matisse, *Odalisque au pantelon rouge*. Alfred Barr's tone in explaining its purchase conveys how overdue was the acquisition:

[I]n 1921, at long last, the French Government honored Matisse officially by acquiring one of his paintings for the Luxembourg Museum. Perhaps the officials [with Benedite's reluctant acquiescence] had finally been impressed by Matisse's world-wide fame, and perhaps they had been reconciled by the inoffensive and traditional turn his art had recently taken. In any case the museum authorities, still affected by academic pressure, could scarcely have found a milder or more conventional Matisse than the *Odalisque au pantelon rouge*—though it must be said, beautifully painted and quite representative of the period.[30]

In 1921, then, eleven years after Roger Fry's *Manet and the Post-Impressionists* had introduced such painting to London, and nine years after the Armory Show had introduced it to New York, the Luxembourg Museum in Paris was still defensively trying to hold its position against the Post-Impressionist painting that had flowered in Paris and reshaped the history of Western art.

When Faulkner arrived in Paris, then, the embattled Luxembourg contained only one Matisse, two Cézannes, and no Picassos, no Seurats, no Gauguins, no Van Goghs, or any samples of the other painters who had reconceptualized art since the Impressionists. Though it had been forced to accept forty paintings from the Caillebotte bequest, pride of place in the museum seems to have gone to heroic, sentimental, allegorical, and literary painting. (For example, there was an *Homage à Delacroix*, a *Vieux Lithographe*, an *Ishmael*, and a painting of the story of the Prodigal Son.) Other than the bequest, the one Matisse, and the fine collection of Rodin's sculptures Picasso was sometimes seen sketching, I suspect that the only art we would recognize among the museum's holdings would be Whistler's *Arrangement in Grey and Black: Portrait of the Painter's Mother*. A 1922 appreciator of the collection, called this painting "one of [Whistler's] most restful and gentlest deeds."[31] To miss Whistler's experiment with formal design, despite his title, was to be oblivious to the force and intent of the new art.

After thirty-one years as director, when Faulkner arrived in Paris in the summer of 1925, with Cézanne, Matisse, Picasso, and the others established as the important figures in modern French art, Benedite's reactionary position was a matter of public disgrace. Within three years of Faulkner's arrival, the important Caillebotte Bequest that Benedite had almost managed to refuse for the Luxembourg was transferred to a special place of honor in the Louvre. Circumstantial evidence suggests that Faulkner was deeply conscious of his contemporary artists' outrage over the museum's 1925 position. On August 17, 1925, at the Louvre he saw the "Winged Victory, the Venus de Milo, the real ones, and the Mona Lisa etc. It was fine," he said, especially the paintings of the "more-or-less moderns, like Degas, and Manet and Chavannes." (See Degas's *A Ballet Seen from an Opera Box*, Manet's *The Tipsy Woman*, and Chavannes's *The Woodcutters*.) Faulkner wrote as well that he "went to a very very modernist exhibition the other day— futurist and vorticist." (See, e.g., Villon's *Soldiers on the March*.) He told his mother he "was talking to a painter, a real one. He wont go to the exhibitions [presumably the officially sanctioned ones] at all."[32] In his abortive novel "Elmer," Faulkner mentioned Paris as a place where Cézanne (e.g., *The Large Bathers*) "was dragged by his friends like a reluctant cow, where Degas and Monet fought obscure points of color and life and love, cursing Bougereau [sic, figure 5] and his curved pink female flesh." This Bouguereau was at the time probably the most important painting owned by the Delgado Museum in New Orleans. Fraternizing with students of "very very" modernist art, Faulkner now believed the smooth surface and pretty pinkness of Bouguereau deserved a curse. He defined Paris as the place "where Matisse and Picasso yet painted——."[33] (See, e.g., Matisse's *Harmony in Red* and Picasso's *Les Demoiselles d'Avignon*.)

His Parisian friends included a "real painter," a sculptor, a "gang of Chicago art students," and the photographer W. C. Odiorne who had left the New Orleans Vieux Carré for Paris the summer before Faulkner.[34] With his art school friends, Faulkner saw private collections of Matisse and Picasso, "as well as numberless young and struggling moderns." He reused the line from *New Orleans Sketches* about Cézanne's dipping his brush in light and would later describe the Cézannes he saw in Paris.[35] Perhaps because his mother knew little about "very

Figure 5. William Adolphe Bouguereau, *Whisperings of Love* (c.1889). Courtesy of New Orleans Museum of Art: Gift of Mr. and Mrs. Chapman H. Hyams.

very" modern art, he gave no more details, but his distinction between the "more or less" and the "very very" moderns, his contempt for Bouguereau, his viewing private shows of Matisse and Picasso, his excitement about Cézanne, and his friendships with painters and sculptors, art students, and a photographer, establish that he was conscious of the difference between the Impressionists and Post-Impressionists. Also his use of the terms "vorticist" and "cubistic" in his fiction suggests how seriously he took his exposure to this new art.

The paintings he saw and the conversation he must have heard completed the education begun in New Orleans when Faulkner first spoke of Cézanne and disparaged plot. These artists posited a whole new relation between the artist and the world. They proclaimed the autonomy of the work of art, which was manifested in several ways:

1. Art had no more obligation to be representative (e.g., Yves Tanguy's *The Furniture of Time*). One argument was that, since the world cannot be represented on a canvas or anywhere else, the concept of representation itself is a farce. Another was that when we judge a painting by its supposed accuracy, we are thinking more about the world it conveys than about the internal values of the painting itself.

2. Art must be apprehended in terms of its own internal values, rather than in terms of its accuracy of presentation, of the sentiments it stimulates, of the moral values which it inculcates, or of its associations with, say, a narrative, like the story of the Prodigal Son.

3. The internal values of an art work emerge from its form which should express the artist's emotions and achieve harmony from the complex relations of its parts. In this harmony, space may be as important as subject.

4. If the painting is no longer considered a transparent window on the world but a thing-in-itself, the medium itself becomes a focus of attention. Rather than the smooth slick paint of a Bouguereau, Post-Impressionist painters dabbed and smeared and brushed paint on so that its texture was part of the interest of the painting. No longer need the artist pretend that the picture was not a canvas rectangle but a window onto the world. These artists accepted and even celebrated the flat opaqueness of their canvas rectangles (e.g., George Braque's *Vase, Pallette, and Skull*).

5. Autonomy also meant that artists had the freedom to use color as they pleased to express feelings, not to represent appearances. Matisse's 1905 portrait of his wife, often called *Green Stripe*, for example, builds a structure of emotion through color independent of natural appearance.

6. Accepting the flatness of the canvas meant that the relation of planes could be spatially ambiguous. Artists could break and reassemble the planes of nature, bend, facet, and distort them, even show an object from several sides at once. They could reduce basic forms in nature to elemental, even geometric,

shapes. They might even attempt to depict movement on a static canvas (e.g., Marcel Duchamps's *Nude Descending a Staircase*).

7. Being self-sufficient, art could be self-reflexive; artists often used collage to pose fundamental questions such as which is more "real," the painting or the newspaper? Should we view the paper pasted on the canvas practically to read the news or aesthetically to appreciate the design of the painting? Should we look at a ticket pasted on a canvas to see where it would take us or to appreciate its part in the overall design? Clearly collage invites us to respond aesthetically.

I have already explained how this exposure affected Faulkner's aesthetic in the two essays on Cubism and Faulkner I gave at the 1980 Faulkner and Yoknapawtapha Conference and in a recent essay in *The Faulkner Journal* titled "The Economy of Desire: Faulkner's Poetics from Eroticism to Post-Impressionism."[36] Rather than further elaborate what I have already said, I am arguing today that the proof of the effect of exposure to this new art lies in Faulkner's new sense of what occurs at the scene of writing. Rather than translating his emotions into words, as he had largely done with his poetry, Faulkner developed a radical new process of writing fiction that enabled him to overcome his feelings of failure as an artist by appropriating into the art of the pen some of the theoretical understandings and techniques of the art of the brush.

My proof is based on documentary evidence. When Faulkner wrote poetry expressing the economy of desire, his manuscript revisions did not extensively alter the shape of the poems. His method of relating to his models, as Martin Kreiswirth writes, was normally "compression of the prototype's formal structure."[37] No matter how many times he rewrote its lines, no matter how different were the women he remembered in its various redactions, a sonnet necessarily remained a sonnet. And his other poetic forms remained unchanged despite innumerable rewritings.

Faulkner retyped his poems again and again, often making no changes, or only changing incidentals, such as commas. For

example, at the Harry Ransom Humanities Center in Austin
there are four fragments of "And nymphs and satyr follow Pan"
with no visible differences between them, five typings of poem
ten of *A Green Bough*, and seven nearly identical versions of "I
do not weep." Sometimes he rewrote directly after first typing.
Among the fragments in the HRC is one beginning "and an
answering echo within him." There are four lines struck out and
immediately rewritten. Occasionally a typo will be crossed
out and then rewritten. "Leaving Her" (figure 6) shows more
revisions than do the texts of most of his other poems, but they
are all made by substitution, none are structural.

The most common type of alteration Faulkner made was the
substitution of a brief word or phrase. In the "Prologue" to *The
Marble Faun* "graceful slender feet" becomes "slender graceful
feet"; "Roses burn like candles here" becomes "The candled

Figure 6. Burned Manuscript of Faulkner's poem "Leaving Her."
Courtesy of the Manuscript Division, Harry Ransom Humanities
Research Center, University of Texas at Austin.

flames of roses here"; "necklaced cries" becomes "jewelled cries." Poem two of *The Marble Faun* changes "Bent to the unchanging skies" to "Shackled to the curving skies." A fragment of poem six of *Vision in Spring* shows "fainting skies" altered to "faint greenish skies." In "Adolescence" "maiden drowned" becomes "woman drowned" and "find" becomes "look"; in "After the Concert" "wheeling" becomes "reeling"; in "Mississippi Hills" a "blasted" tree becomes a "stricken" one; in "Winter Is Gone" "The shepherd pipes in the dusk, that a maid might follow" becomes "that his love in the dusk may follow"; "following rain" in one version of "Dying Gladiator" becomes "after the rain" in the *Double Dealer* version; in "Estelle" "sup" was altered by hand to "drink," and then a second typed version incorporated the change. A burned fragment of "The World Is Still" shows Faulkner changing "holds the bow" to "Grasps the bow," making "sighing" into "sorrow," and "To the throngs" to "Above the throngs." All these typescript revisions[38] are substitutions of a line, phrase, or word. There are no structural shifts.

Occasionally Faulkner would cannibalize a line or two. An unpublished Prufrock poem includes the line "I should have been a priest in floorless halls" which Faulkner incorporated into the "Love Song" of *Vision in Spring*. He might cancel a quatrain, and sometimes substitute another. Several times in *A Marble Faun* he adds an extra stanza. One of the burned fragments, "Gallows," poem fourteen of *A Green Bough*, shows this cancellation:

> The numbers of your spawning
> You will never name,
> But yours the breast that sucked him
> So take you part the blame.

Four poems among the fragments rescued from Phil Stone's burned office were combined into "The Cave," poem three of *A Green Bough*, but this process made no major structural alteration. Probably the most extensive revision documented in the

Humanities Research Center collection occurs in the poem that follows the prologue in *The Marble Faun* and was titled "Spring." Some of this material was recast; "Nymphs," for example, becomes "spring"; and four lines in the middle and six lines at the end were added. In "Noon" the first stanza becomes the last. Faulkner occasionally shifted the placing of minor units in *The Marble Faun*, and sometimes compressed two lines into one. And there are fragments of *The Marionettes* that integrate lines from *The Marble Faun* into that verse drama.

This alteration in the poetry, however, is basically metonymic; it proceeds by elimination or substitution of one contiguous unit for another. It does not alter the basic shape of the poem. The process Faulkner developed for writing and rewriting his novels, however, bears almost no relation to the process he used for revising his poetry. When Faulkner revised his fiction, as we shall see, his process was sometimes metaphoric, not in a logocentric or hierarchical sense, but rather in an imaginative manner of seeing improbable associations. And sometimes his process was metonymic, making playful and seemingly arbitrary associations. These processes were inspired by a sense of the autonomy of art and hence of the artist's freedom at the scene of creation to experiment, unshackled from traditional forms, unconfined by media prescriptions, uninhibited by bourgeois expectations about art's representational responsibilities.[39]

With fiction, as Margaret Yonce has written, the "writing process for Faulkner was one of elaboration and expansion, never of excision and condensation."[40] This process of "elaboration and expansion" takes units that are logically contingent and separates them. The separation affects readers by making them yearn for connections. Writing *Soldiers' Pay* in New Orleans in the first half of 1925, as Yonce illustrates, Faulkner began the process of fiction writing that he would use from then on. He took two "separate stories or story fragments which were expanded, connected, and grafted onto each other to form the larger unit of the novel." At this point the process was erratic and uncertain, but the manuscript of *Soldiers' Pay* clearly shows Faulkner shifting pieces for maximum effect.[41] Page 76 of the now published "Preliminary Typescript," for example, was not numbered by Faulkner as a page. As the beginning of a section of the book, however, it bears six different numbers. In this typescript, other book, section, and chapter numbers were added and usually (often several times) shifted after the initial typing had been completed.[42] Such a shifting process suggests a spatial sense of arrangement and an affective awareness clearly designed to entice and frustrate readerly involvement.

In Paris, as Faulkner wrote "Elmer" and further distanced himself from the erotic aesthetic, he expanded the method of radical juxtaposition, remaking the shape of "Elmer." In Book One he wrote four chapters, then inserted the fourth after the first two, and hence renumbered the old "THREE" as "FOUR." He followed the same pattern with the major sections of "Elmer." He wrote the first two books about Elmer Hodge, and then he wrote a third book about Myrtle Monson and her mother. Then he took the Monson book and placed it between the two Elmer books.[43] As the renumberings establish, these and similar shifts were impulsive and unplanned, but they suggest an intuitive discovery about the artist's freedom to reshape experience and create affective form.

This process is difficult to trace from surviving evidence about *Mosquitoes*. The Garland manuscript series reprints the complete 462-page ribbon typescript of *Mosquitoes* which was typed in Phil Stone's law office. Faulkner's version, from which this one was typed, apparently does not survive, so we cannot know how much the process of shifting and spreading and filling continued to be Faulkner's method of composing this novel. But since, even in this supposedly fair copy, we see Faulkner's handwritten inserts spreading and filling, we can assume that this practice continues a process by which the whole was assembled. The Garland volume also includes two versions of "Don Giovanni" and a partial typescript of one version of the "Al Jackson letters," materials Faulkner cannibalized in writing his second published novel. When incorporating these disparate materials, Faulkner worked as if making a collage. These inserts do not so much represent a linear process whereby a progression A,B,C might be expanded to become A,A2,B,B2,C; instead, the process is more like M,A,X,C,B.

Of Faulkner's third novel, *Flags in the Dust*, Joseph Blotner writes, "this novel, in both its manuscript and typescript versions, its two published versions [first as *Sartoris*, later as *Flags in the Dust*], and its missing other versions, presents perhaps the most vexed set of problems to be encountered in all of Faulkner's texts." Volume 1 of the Garland series includes a seven-page manuscript story of the death of John (sometimes called Evelyn) Sartoris. Apparently, Faulkner wrote this incomplete story and then abandoned it before he began the 219-page manuscript version also printed in this first volume. There he retold the Sartoris death sequence three times before getting it right. This manuscript shows Faulkner writing, expanding, recasting, and inserting. Apparently, Faulkner typed one version of *Flags in the Dust* (now lost) from that manuscript version; then he typed a third, final version using some of the pages from the second version. Even in this third complete version the process of expanding and shifting continued to an astonishing degree. As Blotner writes, "[I]n the 603 pages of typescript which survive, only the first 6 and the last 92 pages bear only one page number. All the other pages bear at least one other page number and some as many as five other page numbers."[44] At the end of his apprenticeship in fiction, Faulkner's compositional method had set. Consider this manuscript page from *The Sound and the Fury* (figure 7): note that passages of the original text are crossed out and multiple passages are patterned and inserted. We see the same manipulation of prose shapes on this page (figure 8).

With only slight exaggeration I claim that, as Picasso differed from Bouguereau, so Faulkner the prose writer differed from Faulkner the poet. He developed an incremental faceting device of shifting, spreading, and filling, patterned after the artists'

Figure 7. Manuscript page from *The Sound and the Fury.* Courtesy of Jill Faulkner Summers and the William Faulkner Collection (Acc. No. 6074IA), University of Virginia Library.

breaking and bending and reassembling planes on their canvases. We see this process of reassembling again in *Absalom, Absalom!* (figure 9). On this manuscript page from the "Old Man" section of *The Wild Palms* (figure 10) Faulkner literally cut his prose. He cut and pasted the cutoff section (figure 11) of "Old Man" onto another page (figure 12; you can see where the fragment was pasted) with different margins.

From the New Orleans discussions with Spratling and others, from the Paris discussions among Chicago art students, and from the Post-Impressionist paintings he saw in Paris, Faulkner came to understand the autonomy of art. Language in his early poetry had been to some extent transparent, a mere vehicle through which he expressed loss, longing, and desire. As he became an increasingly sophisticated prose writer, he became intensely interested in his medium itself, "thickening" his lan-

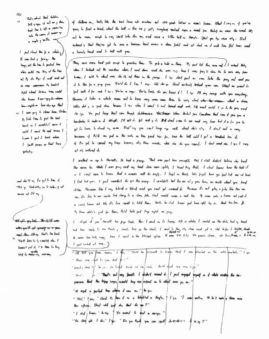

Figure 8. Manuscript page from *The Sound and the Fury*. Courtesy of Jill Faulkner Summers and the William Faulkner Collection (Acc. No. 6074IA), University of Virginia Library.

guage like Van Gogh thickened his paint, and "faceting" its shapes like Picasso and Braque did theirs. A nonmimetic aesthetic empowered him to conceptualize the Benjy section of *The Sound and the Fury.* Not obligated to re-present appearances, he could create spatially and temporally ambiguous surfaces in which various "planes" of time are shifted together in a sequence the artist, not experience, dictated. The harmony of his great works emerged, not from realistic or neatly plotted story lines, but from the complex interrelation of their often "faceted" parts.[45]

Faulkner suspended the basic rules of punctuation and paragraphing to suit his aesthetic purposes. For example, the lack of paragraphing in two parts of the second portion of *The Sound and the Fury* associates, on a visual, typographical level, Quentin's recollections of his conversations with Herbert Head and

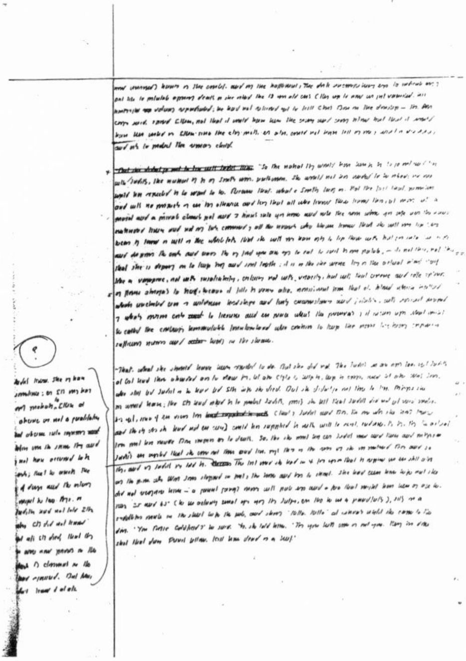

Figure 9. Manuscript page from *Absalom, Absalom!* Courtesy of the Manuscript Division, Harry Ransom Humanities Research Center, University of Texas at Austin.

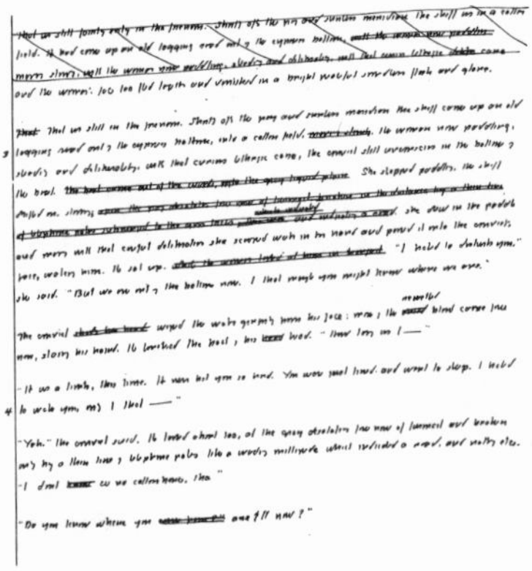

Figure 10. Manuscript page from the "Old Man" section of *The Wild Palms* showing Faulkner's practice of literally cutting up his prose. Courtesy of Jill Faulkner Summers and the William Faulkner Collection (Acc. No. 6074IA), University of Virginia Library.

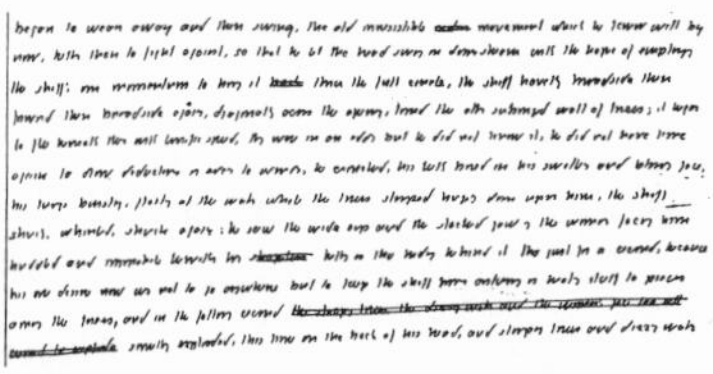

Figure 11. A cut-off fragment of a manuscript page from the "Old Man" section of *The Wild Palms*. Courtesy of Jill Faulkner Summers and the William Faulkner Collection (Acc. No. 6074IA), University of Virginia Library.

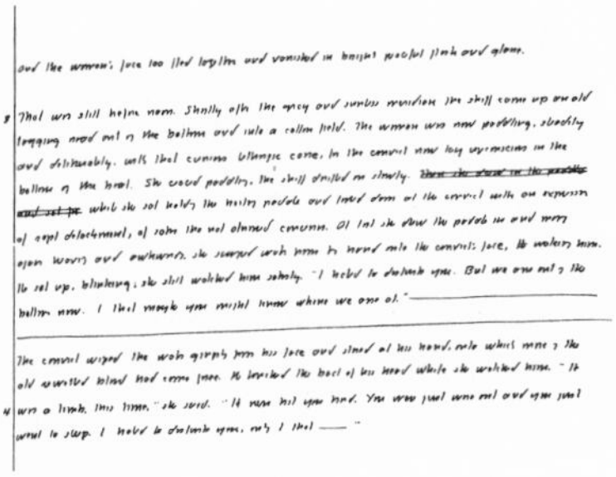

Figure 12. The page onto which the fragment was pasted (before conservationists separated the two). Courtesy of Jill Faulkner Summers and the William Faulkner Collection (Acc. No. 6074IA), University of Virginia Library.

Dalton Ames. Faulkner wanted to use colors to denote time shifts in the Benjy section. He did use italics, section breaks, and interpolated narratives (as in the ledger in "The Bear" or the various letters that appear throughout his fiction). He created collages that call the reader's attention to the interface between word and image by literally drawing figures in the texts of *The Sound and the Fury*, *As I Lay Dying*, and *Go Down, Moses*. He illustrated the limits of language visually by leaving a blank space in the text of *As I Lay Dying*. He paratactically piled clause upon clause, especially in *Absalom, Absalom!* and the fourth part of "The Bear," rather as the Post-Impressionist painter piled paint upon paint. Taking such freedoms with language reminds us, like the green stripe on Mme. Matisse's face, that the work of art is the creation of the artist who is free to use the medium as she or he pleases. This freedom allows the artist to coordinate, arrange, and juxtapose both metaphorically and metonymically.

The relation between poetry and painting, the debate Leonardo termed the "paragone," is as old as Western art. There are various ways in which exchanges between the visual and verbal arts transpire, succinctly summarized by Ulrich Weisstein in an essay entitled "Literature and the Visual Arts." Weisstein mentions several ways in which literature can imitate the visual arts: for example, by *"seeking to reproduce movement styles,"* by borrowing *"certain techniques or modes,"* and by displaying *"features of a common style."*[46] Weisstein, however, does not specifically include a common aesthetic theory or similar compositional process.

The theoretical problem of relating the arts often flounders on the use of terms such as "image," on the concept of "signification," and on the distinction between what is literal in one art and figurative in another. With Faulkner, however, there is no such theoretical impasse. He imported both the abstract theory of autonomy and the actual practice of composition from the visual arts. Always frugal, he put his failed apprenticeship as a visual artist to good use. For him the "visible language of modernism," to use Jerome McGann's term,[47] incorporated an acute sense of the shape of language gleaned first from lettering and illustrating his own early books. And it employed a liberated sense of the artist's freedom to manipulate blocks of language like shapes on a canvas which he imported from his 1925 exposure to Post-Impressionist painting.

Michel Foucault, among others, has said that literature crossed a threshold when it began to be read not as a set of words but as a scene of writing.[48] Empowered by the example of Post-Impressionist painting, William Faulkner crossed that threshold in 1925. For him the issue was not "truth." (All of us who have traveled about Oxford and Lafayette County on the fascinating conference tours have been rereminded how extensive was his mastery of "truth" or "fact.") The issue for Faulkner as he crossed this threshold was how he, the artist, in the scene of writing could manipulate his texts to create his own autonomous works of art. In so doing, he put aside early insecurities and became the master craftsman, the autonomous artist. Rather than feel bested by those whose hands were shaped to the brush as his (minus the "alas!") were not, William Faulkner outmaneuvered modern painters by importing their methods into the scene of his multifarious manipulations of the shapes of language.[49]

NOTES

1. *Thinking of Home: William Faulkner's Letters to his Mother and Father, 1918–1925*, ed. James G. Watson (New York: W. W. Norton, 1992), 173, 174. See the photographs following page 44 of Joseph Blotner's *Faulkner: A Biography*, One-Volume Edition (New York: Random House, 1984) for the juxtapositioning of two 1918 photographs: the boyish Faulkner in his cadet uniform and the manly, heroic Faulkner in his officer's uniform.

2. *Thinking of Home*, 194–95.

3. Bill Faulkner was younger than Carolyn Smythe and her cousin Estelle Oldham and very silent when with them. Collins interview with Smythe, November 23, 1963. The Carvel Collins Archive, housed at the Harry Ransom Humanities Research Center, University of Texas at Austin, is the source for the personal recollections of Faulkner that follow.

4. Carvel Collins interview with Harold Levy, winter, 1962.

5. Collins interview with Lillian Friend Marcus, March 23, 1950.

6. Collins interview with Joyce McClure, March 20, 1950.

7. Collins interview with Harold Dempsey, February 2, 1963.

8. Collins interview with Maud Falkner, April 13, 1950. See Michael Millgate, "William Faulkner, Cadet," *University of Toronto Quarterly* 35 (January 1966), 123, for information on Faulkner's sketching compulsively and giving "no sign" of being a writer during his pilot training in the RAF.

9. Collins interview with Alabama McLean, August 5 or 6, 1951.

10. *"McCall's* Visits 'Miss Maud,' " 84 (October, 1956), 21, 22, 25.

11. Collins interview with Mrs. Will Parks, née Carolyn Smythe, November 23, 1963.

12. Joseph Blotner, *Faulkner: A Biography* (New York: Random House, 1974), 315–16.

13. Collins interview with Maud Falkner, April 2, 1950.

14. Collins interview, November 23, 1963. Carolyn Smythe Parks described the book as quite small, perhaps three and a half inches by five, with twelve to fifteen pages. It included four to eight poems and one short prose vignette, a dramatic conversation. She told Collins the title page bore the inscription "Poems by William Faulkner for Carolyn

Smythe." She said she loaned the volume to a friend whose house burned with this text in it. As Robert Hamblin has kindly pointed out to me, the Brodsky Collection includes a burned fragment of a volume which meets this description, except for a dedication to Phil Stone. Perhaps Faulkner made two distinct volumes with two dedicatées and Phil borrowed Carolyn's to compare them.

15. See Ilse Dusoir Lind's "The Effect of Painting on Faulkner's Poetic Form," *Faulkner, Modernism, and Film: Faulkner and Yoknapatawpha, 1978,* ed. Evans Harrington and Ann J. Abadie (Jackson: University Press of Mississippi, 1979), 127–148.

16. *Double Dealer* 3 (March, 1922), 119, 120.

17. Foreword to *Sherwood Anderson and Other Famous Creoles* (New Orleans: Pelican Bookshop, 1926); rpt. (Austin: University of Texas Press, 1966), unpaginated.

18. Collins interview with Caroline Durieux, March 26, 1963.

19. Collins interview with William Spratling, September 7, 1959.

20. *File on Spratling: An Autobiography* (Boston: Little Brown, 1967), 17.

21. William Faulkner, *New Orleans Sketches,* ed. Carvel Collins (New York: Random House, 1968), 46. From the "Mirror" sketch called "Out of Nazareth," dated April 12, 1925.

22. McClure and Roark Bradford, editor of the Sunday edition, gave Faulkner his first chance to declare himself a mature and presumably self-supporting artist. (Though Joyce McClure's recollection—that Faulkner spent $14 of his $15 fee for each feature on gin and $1 on typing paper—does not suggest a great deal of maturity and responsibility.) John McClure was known for his paternal attitude toward young writers; he encouraged a cub writer whenever he could "by putting his byline in a story at the slightest excuse" (Collins interview with George Tichenor, January 20, 1958). Since everyone in New Orleans knew the patronizing ways of those two kind literary men, writing for the *Times-Picayune* was not as much of a triumph as Faulkner's letters home implied. Furthermore, Lillian Friend Marcus remembered that the *Double Dealer* rejected much of what Faulkner submitted. She personally thought the "New Orleans Sketches" "banal and contrived." Collins interview with Lillian Marcus, February 19, 1958.

23. *Thinking of Home,* 181.

24. My thanks to Judith Bonner of the Historic New Orleans Collection, the Kemper and Leila Williams Foundation, for the information that the Delgado's director, Wellington Boyle, died in 1925 and was replaced by the extremely conservative Ellsworth Woodward. See Prescott Dunbar's *The New Orleans Museum of Art* (Baton Rouge: Louisiana State University Press, 1990).

25. Michael True, "Modernism, *The Dial,* and the Way They Were," in *The Dial: Arts and Letters in the 1920s,* ed. Gaye L. Brown (Worcester: Worcester Art Museum, 1981).

26. Collins interview with John McClure, pre-1950s.

27. Collins interviews with Harold Dempsey, winter, 1963 and August 11, 1963.

28. Collins interview with W. C. Odiorne, February 15, 1963.

29. Gerstle Mack, *Paul Cézanne* (New York: Alfred A. Knopf, 1942), 332. Mack's chapter 36 deals with the bequest and is the source for my information in this and the following paragraph.

30. Alfred H. Barr, Jr. *Matisse: His Art and His Public* (New York: The Museum of Modern Art, 1951), 198. We can be almost positive that Faulkner had seen this painting itself as well as the Bouguereau listed below as figure 5. Other paintings mentioned here serve simply as representative illustrations of the artists' work, not as pictures anyone could claim Faulkner actually saw.

31. E. V. Lucas, *A Wanderer in Paris* (New York: The Macmillan Company, 1922), 176–77.

32. *Selected Letters of William Faulkner,* ed. Joseph Blotner (New York: Random House, 1977), 13.

33. Joseph Blotner, *Faulkner: A Biography* (New York: Random House, 1974), 460.

34. *Selected Letters*, 12, 17, 22. Carvel Collins interview with W. C. Odiorne, February 15, 1963.

35. *Selected Letters*, 22, 24. Richard P. Adams wrote Collins that Faulkner definitely told Kraig Klosson "that he did see Cezanne paintings" in Paris, RPA/CC, September 2, 1962.

36. See *"A Cosmos of My Own": Faulkner and Yoknapatawpha, 1980*, ed. Doreen Fowler and Ann J. Abadie (Jackson: University Press of Mississippi, 1981) and *The Faulkner Journal* 4 (1988–89): 159–77.

37. Martin Kreiswirth, *William Faulkner: The Making of a Novelist* (Athens: University of Georgia Press, 1983), 7.

38. In the Faulkner archive at the Ransom Humanities Research Center.

39. A possible fallacy in this argument, as Robert Hamblin has pointed out to me, is that it rests principally on typescripts of the poems and manuscripts of the prose. Since Faulkner's typescripts of his prose, though not of his poetry, show structural shifts, however, I believe that Faulkner began faceting the structure of his art when he shifted from being a poet to being an increasingly experimental fiction writer.

40. "The Composition of *Soldiers' Pay*," *Mississippi Quarterly* 33 (Summer 1980): 293.

41. Yonce, 293, 315.

42. See *William Faulkner Manuscripts: Soldiers' Pay* (New York: Garland, 1987), 76 and *passim*.

43. See *William Faulkner Manuscripts: Elmer* (New York: Garland, 1987), 34, 49.

44. *William Faulkner Manuscripts: Flags in the Dust* (New York: Garland, 1987), viii.

45. Inter-artistic comparisons can flounder upon the careless use of terms which are precise in one medium, metaphorical in another. I am not contending that words such as "thickening" or "planes" mean the same thing in both media. I suggest instead that the process and effect of, say, "thickening" were similar in Faulkner's and the Post-Impressionist painters' methods.

46. In *Interrelations of Literature*, ed. Jean-Pierre Barricelli and Joseph Gibaldi (New York: Modern Language Association, 1982), 259, 260.

47. See *Black Riders: The Visible Language of Modernism* (Princeton: Princeton University Press, 1993).

48. See McGann, 40.

49. I wish to thank the College of Arts and Sciences at Louisiana State University and the Louisiana State University Research Council under whose auspices research for this work was begun. I am especially grateful to Cathy Henderson, Research Librarian, Harry Ransom Humanities Research Center, University of Texas at Austin; Michael Plunkett, Curator of Manuscripts, Alderman Library, University of Virginia; Denise Klingman, Assistant to the Registrar, New Orleans Museum of Art; Lauren Morgan, Slide Librarian, Louisiana State University, College of Design; and Janice Stern, then a Ph.D. candidate, Louisiana State University, for their kind assistance.

William Faulkner and the
Meaning of Architecture:
The Greek Revival of Yoknapatawpha

Thomas S. Hines

In Faulkner's second novel, *Mosquitoes*, a character "leaned nearer to see the paper. It was a single sheet of a Sunday magazine section: a depressing looking article in small print about Romanesque architecture. . . . 'Are you interested in architecture?' she asked intensely. . . . 'So many people waste their time over things like architecture and such. It's much better to be a part of life, don't you think . . . than to make your life barren through dedicating it to an improbable and ungrateful posterity. Don't you think so?' 'I hadn't thought about it,' Pete said cautiously."[1]

Yet Faulkner clearly *had* thought about it. He believed that the art of architecture—like the art of literature—was indeed a "part of life" and did contribute to the culture and civilization of a not "ungrateful posterity." Architecture was important to Faulkner personally. He had an eye and a feeling for the form, function, and meaning of buildings in his actual surroundings, and he used those elements of his Mississippi environment as the models for the architecture of his invented world: the town of "Jefferson" and the county of "Yoknapatawpha." He gave four of his novels titles with architectural implications: *Pylon*, *The Hamlet*, *The Mansion*, and *The Town*. The first, discarded title of both *Light in August* and *Absalom, Absalom!* was *Dark House*. Several stories have architecturally suggestive titles and themes, and architects appear as characters and symbols throughout the work.

Faulkner's fellow Mississippian, Eudora Welty, once insisted that "place has a more lasting identity than we have . . . fiction depends for its life on place. Location is the cross-roads of circumstance." And of all the masters in the history of literature, Faulkner was one of the greatest in his ability to see, to evoke, to explicate, to use the details and the essence of the physical environment. In his sense of place, of *genius loci*, he was equalled, in the English-speaking world, only by Thomas Hardy, James Joyce, and Henry James. "It sometimes seems to me," observed Malcolm Cowley of Yoknapatawpha in *The Portable Faulkner*, "that every house or hovel has been described in one of Faulkner's novels."[2]

Much has been said and written on the ubiquity of nature in Faulkner's work—the woods, the bear, the natural landscape—but relatively little has been done on Faulkner's equally great interest in the *built* environment—the opposite of nature—as symbol and metaphor of larger issues, attitudes, and moods. There is, in fact, throughout Faulkner criticism a puzzling imbalance between the attention given to nature and that given to architecture. This is unfortunate since "novelistic architecture," according to critic William Ruzicka, "has much to say about the way that characters view the world they inhabit, the effect of the fictive environment upon those who live within it, the image and significance of a fictive place, and the meaning of dwelling there."[3]

Historian Joel Williamson recognized that:

Faulkner early evolved a symbology in which buildings stood for artificial, man-made institutions and the "outdoors" stood for the natural order. In his stories, doors and door frames, windows and window frames became especially important. His characters were forever looking in or looking out, crawling in or crawling out of windows. They passed in and out of doors, faced closed doors and locked doors, and plunged through, paused, rested, or sat in doorways. Very often to go into a house or building was to attempt to enter the modern world and to deal with it on its own terms, to go out was to abandon that effort and seek salvation in nature. Stairs, porches, chimneys, and attics also had easily understood meanings.[4]

Yet, by contrast, it could also be argued that nature in Faulkner did not always represent order, but rather its opposite, and that to escape its wild and scary chaos, one could sometimes find shelter and comfort only in architecture and the built environment, which, in fact, stood for order, sanity, and serenity. On another level, instead of representing the "modern world," architecture, particularly older buildings, could be seen in Faulkner's cosmos as a protective retreat from the stressful demands of modern life.

While cultural and architectural historians have done reasonable justice to the certified "monuments" and the great urban centers, they have had more trouble getting at the essence of the smaller, more rural, more parochial places. Perhaps Faulkner and other writers of what is called "fiction" can, through their particular kind of imaginative probing, help us to locate and explicate the sense and meaning, the smell and ambience of the more elusive, more anonymous architectures of the "Jeffersons" of the world.

Of both the affinities and distinctions between history and fiction, the historian Hayden White has argued that,

> viewed simply as verbal artifacts, histories and novels are indistinguishable from one another . . . unless we approach them with specific preconceptions about the kinds of truths that each is supposed to deal in. But the aim of the writer of a novel must be the same as the writer of history. Both wish to provide a verbal image of "reality." The novelist may present his notion of this reality indirectly, that is to say, by figurative techniques, rather than directly, which is to say, by registering a series of propositions which are supposed to correspond point by point to some extratextural domain of occurrence or happening, as the historian claims to do. But the image of reality which the novelist thus constructs is meant to correspond in its general outline to some domain of human experience which is no less "real" than that referred to by the historian.

"It is not then a matter of conflict between two kinds of truth," White concluded, between the historian's truth of correspondence and the novelist's truth of coherence. "Every history

must meet standards of coherence no less than those of correspondence if it is to pass as a plausible account of 'the way
things *really* were.' " [5]

The same related dualities were likewise suggested in the
title and the text of an article by the historian and psychoanalyst
Erik Erikson: "Psychological Reality and Historical Actuality."
Still, Faulkner's Chick Mallison, in *Knight's Gambit*, may have
been speaking for the author himself in his obvious partiality to
the truth-telling prerogatives of fiction. It was, he asserted,
"only in literature that the paradoxical . . . anecdotes in the
history of a human heart can be juxtaposed and annealed by art
into verisimilitude and credibility." Speaking in the voice of
another alter-ego, Faulkner confirmed this sentiment by insisting that "poets are almost always wrong about facts. That's
because they are not really interested in facts: only in truth:
which is why the truth they speak is so true that even those who
hate poets by simple natural instincts are exalted and terrified
by it."[6]

Whatever the relative significance of nature and architecture
in Faulkner's world, the element that most pervaded his cosmos
and his consciousness, that both linked and differentiated nature
and architecture, was the crucial element of time, or of what
Albert Einstein, in his theory of relativity, would call "the fourth
dimension." Faulkner's obsession with time was in fact the
quality that most linked him with history and that, in turn, has
most attracted historians to his work. While history has been
called the most eclectic of disciplines, substantively and meth-
odologically exploiting whatever seems appropriate to provide
that necessary quotient of coherence and correspondence, the
element, the essence, the sine qua non of historical enquiry,
the element that distinguishes it from all other disciplines, is its
commitment to the primacy of time and of its corollary attributes: sequence, precedence, and consequence.

Philosopher Henri Bergson's concept of time, which Faulkner
acknowledged as applicable to his own, underlay his "fusion of
past and present," critic Elizabeth Kerr observed, and "pre-

vented him from conceiving of different periods as different units. The tendency of the South to live in the past and to be preoccupied with family and tradition may have predisposed Faulkner to feel that 'no man is himself, he is the sum of his past. There is no such thing really as was because the past is.' "[7]

As opposed, however, to the Bergsonian insistence on the undifferentiated flux of time, the philosopher Gaston Bachelard in *The Poetics of Space* linked time *with* space in a manner with which Faulkner should have felt great affinity. As an auxiliary of psychoanalysis, Bachelard coined and defined the term "topo-analysis" as "the systematic psychological study of the sites of our intimate lives. In the theater of the past that is constituted by memory, the stage setting maintains the characters in their dominant roles. At times we think we know ourselves in time, when all we know is a sequence of fixations in the spaces of the being's stability—a being who does not want to melt away and who, even in the past, when he sets out in search of things past, wants time to 'suspend' its flight. In its countless alveoli, space contains compressed time. That is what space is for." And in a related sentiment from *Sartoris*, Faulkner had Narcissa Benbow muse upon the prematurely shortened life of young John Sartoris, killed in a place crash. He had, she thought, "not waited for Time and its furniture to teach him that the end of wisdom is to dream high enough not to lose the dream in the seeking of it." As one of Faulkner's more pregnant phrases, "time and its furniture" possessed prescient implications for the relationship in his world of time *and* architecture.[8]

As opposed to the relative atemporality of nature, architecture, for Faulkner, possessed the qualities of both temporality *and* timelessness. On the one hand, it was drenched with time; on the other, it transcended it. Indeed, for a writer as obsessed with time as Faulkner—the passage of time, the loss of time, the crisscross of time, the presence of the past in the present— architecture offered, if not a stopping of time or prolongation of time, at least a way of carrying through time, of projecting over time, a very tangible part of the past.

Faulkner saw and used architecture *as* the tangible past, the visible past, the tangible document of time suspended and continued. Buildings, he knew, were designed and constructed and observed and used by particular people in particular times and places, but he knew that, if preserved and cared for, they could and would outlast the generations that brought them into being, the generations for whom they stood as monuments and markers of identity. Faulkner, of course, was an architect of books, not of buildings, but he used words in many of the same ways. Yet he appreciated the fact that literature and architecture were very different art forms in their tangible relationship both to "psychological reality" and to "historical actuality."

He was born William Cuthbert Falkner on September 25, 1897, in New Albany, Mississippi, east of Oxford, where his father was working for the family-owned railroad, founded by his great-grandfather, William Clark Falkner, for whom he was named. Soon after his birth, the family moved back to Ripley, the ancestral hometown, northeast of Oxford, where they lived for four years, and then in 1902, when William was five, they moved permanently to Oxford, where he moved through the public schools. After that he attended the University of Mississippi, and there, to his friend and classmate, Ben Wasson, he made his first recorded observations on architecture. "More than once," Wasson recalled, "Faulkner pointed out to me the 'bastard qualities' of the [Ole Miss] campus buildings and said that the Lyceum Building was the best on the campus." With "its good overall Greek quality," Faulkner declared, it possessed "purity and serenity."[9]

Faulkner then left Oxford and ventured out, first to Canada during World War I, then briefly to New Orleans in the early 1920s, and then in 1925 to Europe, where he had a traditional *Wanderjahr* with his friend, the architect William Spratling. Spratling had been commissioned to do sketches of various European buildings for publication in *Architectural Forum*. Faulkner was with him on many of these expeditions, observing the buildings and the drawings in progress. The trip abroad affected him greatly and would show up in his work the rest of his life.[10]

From Milan, for example, he sent his mother a postcard describing the Piazza del Duomo in words that he would later use, almost verbatim in the long story "Elmer." It was an early example of Faulkner's talent for interpreting architectural mood and detail: they "sat drinking beer within the shadow of the cathedral, gazing upward among its mute and musical flanks from which long-bodied doglike gargoyles strained yapping in a soundless gleeful derision, where niched were mitred cardinals like Assyrian kings and lean martyrs pierced dying in eternal ecstasy and young unhelmeted knights staring into space."[11]

Faulkner's memories of Paris would also find their way into several stories and especially into the poignant last pages of *Sanctuary*, where he demonstrated his consciousness of the city's physical and cultural landscape, as his doomed heroine, Temple Drake, sat pondering her stained Mississippi past:

> It had been a gray day, a gray summer, a gray year. On the street old men wore overcoats, and in the Luxembourg Gardens . . . the women sat knitting in shawls and even the men playing croquet played in coats and capes, and in the sad gloom of the chestnut trees, the dry click of balls, the random shouts of children, had that quality of autumn, gallant and evanescent and forlorn. From beyond the circle with its spurious Greek balustrade, clotted with movement, filled with a gray light of the same color and texture as the water which the fountain played into the pool, came a steady crash of music.[12]

Upon returning to America, Faulkner lived a while longer in New Orleans, where he was especially influenced by the older writer, Sherwood Anderson, then living in the French quarter. In his awkward second novel, *Mosquitoes*, a satire on the habitués of his and Anderson's circle, the young writer composed occasionally resonant sentences that predicted the Faulkner that was to come, especially in his keen attention to architecture: "Outside the window New Orleans, the vieux carré, brooded in a faintly tarnished languor like an aging yet still beautiful courtesan in a smokefilled room, avid yet weary too of ardent ways." In a related passage, a character peered across Jackson Square, "across stenciled palms and Andrew Jackson in childish effigy bestriding the terrific arrested plunge of his curly balanced horse, toward the long . . . Pontalba buildings and three spires of the cathedral graduated by perspective, pure and slumbrous beneath the decadent languor of August and evening."[13]

Much later in his career, though earlier in Yoknapatawpha's history, Faulkner trenchantly contrasted the mid-nineteenth-century sophistication of urbane New Orleans with that of neighboring backwoods Mississippi, when in *Absalom, Absalom!* young Henry Sutpen visits the city with his University of Mississippi classmate, Charles Bon, his soul mate, half brother, and probable lover. In densely erotic and seductive prose, which confirmed a decade's progression in his art, Faulkner evoked the way that the exotic Charles took

the innocent and negative plate of Henry's provincial soul and intellect and exposed it by slow degrees to this esoteric milieu, building gradually toward the picture which he desired it to retain, accept. I can see him corrupting Henry gradually into the purlieus of elegance, with no foreword, no warning, the postulation to come after the fact, exposing Henry slowly to the surface aspect—the architecture a little curious, a little femininely flamboyant and therefore to Henry opulent, sensuous, sinful; the inference of great and easy wealth measured by steamboat loads in place of a tedious inching of sweating human figures across cotton fields; the flash and glitter of a myriad carriage wheels, in which women, enthroned and immobile and passing rapidly across the vision, appeared like painted portraits beside men in linen a little finer and diamonds a little brighter and in broadcloth a little trimmer and with hats raked a little more above faces a little more darkly swaggering than any Henry had ever seen before.[14]

Anderson recognized Faulkner's talent, but he was not sure that the city was his metier. "You're a country boy," he told him, "and all you know is that little patch up there in Mississippi where you started from." And long after that, Faulkner indeed realized that "my own little postage stamp of native soil was worth writing about and that I would never live long enough to exhaust it, and by sublimating the actual into the apocryphal I would have complete liberty to use whatever talent I might have to its absolute top."[15]

With his third novel, *Sartoris*, Faulkner half-consciously began his Yoknapatawpha chronicle. One of the most vivid ways in which he sublimated "the actual into [the] apocryphal" in that novel and throughout the saga was in the realm of architecture and the urban and rural landscape. Indeed, in his long *oeuvre* his treatment of architecture encompassed six large categories: Folk Vernacular, Neoclassical, Neo-Gothic, High Victorian, and Modernist, as well as the related art form of Public Sculpture. In those categories, Faulkner used architecture to help him center and focus his narrative, to evoke mood and ambience, to demarcate caste and class, and to delineate character.

To his grandest characters, as to Faulkner himself, the most favored architecture was the neoclassical, especially the local variants of the Greek Revival, the symbol, even in decay, of what Faulkner believed were the better impulses of Southern civilization. The Greek Revival was a romantic, mid-nineteenth-century phenomenon, the latest in a long series of neoclassical movements that had begun with the Italian Renaissance in the fifteenth and sixteenth centuries. The evolution had become more florid in the Mannerist, Baroque, and Rococo styles as they moved northward through France, Austria, and the German states in the seventeenth and eighteenth centuries. Britain, and later America, were less touched by the Baroque and Rococo than by the earlier, less encumbered, Renaissance modes. The most influential architecture on British and American building was, in fact, the world of a single, late Renaissance architect, Andrea Palladio (1508–80), an architect who, though frequently called Mannerist, actually purged Mannerism, especially in his villas, of the excessive affections which that style had acquired. In his penchant for rounded, domed structures, Palladio's models were arcuated Roman variations on trabeated Greek forms, an emphasis that would likewise permeate high style British and American architecture into the early nineteenth century.

Constitutional government, argues historian Leland Roth, "was an experiment in applied Enlightenment philosophy which rejected monarchical absolutism and attempted to recreate the natural society in which it was believed men were meant to live. Thus architects correspondingly rejected Baroque-Rococo complication of form in search of a simpler architecture suggestive of the first civilized state of primal man." Since the founders of the American Republic, moreover, had "borrowed so heavily from the form and terminology of the Roman republican government, it was natural that Roman architectural forms should be among the first used by American architects." Particularly in the work of Thomas Jefferson and Benjamin Latrobe, and especially in the planning of the new national capital at Washington, an abstract version of Roman forms predominated.[16]

The revival in the mid-nineteenth century of simpler, "purer," pre-Roman, Greek architecture was, on the one hand, a logical extension of the Roman Revival and, on the other, a reactive retreat from the Romanist leanings of previous generations. It thus brought into sharper relief the affinities and differences of the Greek and Roman architectures of antiquity. In addition to the formal, geometric differences between Greek trabeation and the Roman amalgamation of trabeated and arcuated forms, there were cultural and contextual differences which further contributed to regional preferences for Greek architecture in the mid-nineteenth-century America, especially in the rural South. While the general image of Roman building suggested urban juxtapositions, annexations, and collisions of forms, as in the Roman Forum, the chief image of Greek architecture was of serenely discrete structures, related to, but interstitially separated from each other, as on the Acropolis in Athens. The Greek temple, avers historian R. Furneau Jordan, was, for the most part, "a shrine, aloof and isolated. The Roman temple . . . was a feature in the street . . . one was a tribute to the deity; the other was an expression of imperial pride, an urban monument."[17]

Further stimulated by the early-nineteenth-century Greek War of Independence from the Turks, the Greek Revival was an international movement which permeated the Western world, including all portions of the United States. Indeed, most Americans, north and south, who built or used neoclassical buildings were unbothered by archaeological distinctions between "Greek" and "Roman." Yet, to philosophically inclined Southerners, the appeal of Greek architecture was more than that of just a new aesthetic fashion. The predominantly rural social structure of the American South helped to contribute to the region's affinity for things Greek. Even in the twentieth century, Faulkner himself would tell a friend that he would "love to go to Greece. All that we learned that's good comes from there."[18]

Aided by James Stuart and Nicholas Revett's seminal eighteenth-century study, *The Antiquities of Athens* (1763), American pattern books, such as Asher Benjamin's illustrated *Practical Home Carpenter* (1830), incorporated proportions and details of Greek orders, and provided what historian Catherine Bishir has called "readily understood instruction to enable local artisans to incorporate the new style into customary building patterns."[19]

The finest Greek Revival building in Faulkner's Lafayette County was the Lyceum Building (1844–48) on the University of Mississippi campus, with its grandly overscaled portico faced with six huge Ionic columns. It was designed by the nationally renowned neoclassicist William Nichols, architect of the Mississippi State Capitol (1833–40) and the Mississippi Governor's Mansion (1836–42), both of which Faulkner would use and analyze in *Requiem for a Nun*. Faulkner admired but never mentioned the Lyceum in his work probably because the University in the work was significantly placed not in the town of Jefferson but in the nearby town of "Oxford," where in reality it resides. This is one of several arguments for the often-stated, though still under-appreciated, contention that the "prototype" for Jefferson is a composite of several places and is at least partially based on Ripley, located some fifty miles northeast of Oxford, the same distance, approximately, between "Jefferson" and "Oxford."

A small, but important, Greek Revival building in Faulkner's personal life was the College Hill Presbyterian Church (1846), four miles northeast of Oxford, an elegantly simple brick structure with a strong Doric-columned portico. After the slave gallery at the rear of the sanctuary was removed, two small, white, outside doors remained as traces high up toward the ceiling of the portico facade, hanging as though suspended in space, the outside stairs accessing them having also been removed. Though Faulkner never used the church directly in his work, it was the scene in 1929 of his marriage to Estelle Oldham Franklin.

Still, the most significant building in all of Faulkner's work was the County Courthouse (figure 1), the symbol not only of law and justice, but spiritually, psychologically, architecturally, the center around which life revolves: "the focus, the hub; sitting looming in the center of county's circumference like a single cloud in its ring of horizon, laying its vast shadow to the uttermost rim of horizon; musing, brooding, symbolic, and ponderable, tall as cloud, solid as rock, dominating all: protector of the weak; judiciate and curb of the passions and lusts, repository and guardian of the aspirations and the hopes; rising course by brick course during that first summer."[20]

Though the name of the actual architect has not survived, the Lafayette County Courthouse was built by the contractors Gordon and Grayson, and was completed on January 12, 1840, at the then sumptuous cost of $25,100. Faulkner later decided that in Yoknapatawpha the designer of the building should be the same "French architect" who designed "Sutpen's Hundred," an analogous "grand design" in the private realm. In a crucial passage in *Requiem for a Nun*, Faulkner emphasized that of all of the county's buildings, the courthouse "came first, and . . .

Figure 1. Lafayette County Courthouse, Oxford, Mississippi, as rebuilt after Civil War. Thomas S. Hines.

with stakes and hanks of fishline, the architect laid out in a grove of oaks opposite the tavern and the store, the square and simple foundations, the irrevocable design not only of the courthouse but of the town too, telling them as much: 'In fifty years you will be trying to change it in the name of what you will call progress. But you will fail . . . you will never be able to get away from it.' " Faulkner then linked the courthouse to the larger town and county, a strong example of his interest in urban design. The building was situated in the center of the Square: "quadrangular around it, the stores, two-storey, the offices of the lawyers and doctors and dentists, the lodge-rooms and auditoriums, above them; school and church and tavern and bank and jail each in its ordered place." Unlike the actual

Oxford Square, which had six roads leading from it—one each from the center of the north and south sides, one each from the corners of the east and west sides—Faulkner devised for the Jefferson Square the more elegant arrangement of four roads leading to and from the exact center of the four sides of the courthouse: "the four broad diverging avenues straight as plumb-lines in the four directions, becoming the network of roads and by-roads until the whole county would be covered with it." It was a reification in the public realm of a frontier Mississippi town of the ancient idea of the "grand design."[21]

In *Requiem*, in the construction of the fictive building,

> eight disjointed marble columns were landed from an Italian ship at New Orleans, into a steamboat up the Mississippi to Vicksburg, and into a smaller steamboat up the Yazoo and Sunflower and Tallahatchie, to Ikkemotubbe's old landing which Sutpen now owned, and thence the twelve miles by oxen into Jefferson: the two identical four-column porticoes, one on the north and one on the south, each with its balcony of wrought-iron New Orleans grillwork, on one of which—the south one—in 1861 Sartoris would stand in the first Confederate uniform the town had ever seen, while in the Square below the Richmond mustering officer enrolled and swore in the regiment which Sartoris as its colonel would take to Virginia [and] when in '63 a United Sates military force burned the Square and the business district, the courthouse survived. It didn't escape: it simply survived: harder than axes, tougher than fire, more fixed than dynamite; encircled by the tumbled and blackened ruins of lesser walls, it still stood, even the topless smoke-stained columns, gutted of course and roofless, but immune, not one hair even out of the Paris architect's almost forgotten plumb, so that all they had to do . . . was put in new floors for the two storeys and a new roof, and this time with a cupola with a four-faced clock and a bell to strike the hours and ring alarms; by this time the Square, the banks and the stores and the lawyers' and doctors' and dentists' offices, had been restored. . . ."

The actual postbellum courthouse was designed and built ca. 1870 by the firm of Willis, Sloan, and Trigg, Builders and Architects, who did virtually identical plans for two other, contemporary courthouses in county seats due north of Oxford: Holly Springs, Mississippi, and Bolivar, Tennessee.[22]

Though Faulkner allowed the Jefferson courthouse to survive the war more completely intact that did its actual Oxford counterpart, and though Jefferson's Square opened to four streets instead of Oxford's six, the similarity of the two environments, both before and after the war, was an exceptional merger of the actual and the apocryphal.

The greatest quantity of neoclassical buildings, and, next to the courthouse, the largest and finest were the Greek Revival houses of the Yoknapatawpha gentry, symbols for Faulkner of a quality of life and a quality of people he admired and emulated despite their personal flaws and despite the flaws of the society that reared them—based upon slavery and a black-white caste system. Just as Jefferson and Yoknapatawpha were amalgamations of several actual Mississippi towns and counties, the homes of Faulkner's characters were composites of actual houses on the North Mississippi landscape.

The most typical regional form of the neoclassical house was a nearly square or rectangular one- or two-story box with a relatively small four-columned porch on one or more sides. Above the front door, and sometimes a side door, there was usually another door in the second story leading onto a small balcony. Window shutters, usually painted dark green, were functional screens against sun and weather as well as decorative counterpoints to the standard white walls. Other ornament in the generally chaste buildings might include a wrought-iron railing for the second floor balconies. On either side of the central hall lay the parlor, library, dining room, and, in one-story houses, bedrooms. The central stairhall in the two-story houses led to upstairs bedrooms. In the middle third of the nineteenth century, this mode was especially popular in Mississippi, Alabama, and Tennessee. Oxford and Lafayette County, during Faulkner's lifetime, contained over a dozen examples of this type of house, as well as several houses of even grander pretention, marked by a six- or eight-columned portico extending across the entire front of the house.

The architect-builder in antebellum Oxford who was most

associated with the four-columned type was William Turner, a talented, though untrained, designer who had come to Oxford as a young man ca. 1840 with his parents, Samuel and Elizabeth Turner, from their home in Iredell County, North Carolina. Turner was the documented designer-builder of several such houses and the possible architect of all or most of the others. If he was not the actual designer for every house of this type, his work could have served as a model for structures by other builders which bore a remarkably close family resemblance. Antebellum houses in this mode in Oxford included the homes of the Craig, Eades, Howry, Shegog, Neilson, Carter, and Thompson families, as well as two successive residences William Turner built for himself. Plantation houses in the four-columned mode were built in the county for various owners, including the Price, Wiley, Shipp, and Jones families.[23]

At least five houses, known to have been designed and built by Turner, were imposing edifices on the Oxford townscape. Two of these, the Carter-Tate and Neilson-Culley homes, were designed in 1859, with two-story, four-column porticoes on the front and one side. The builder of one of these, Dr. Robert Otway Carter, was the great-great-grandson of the legendary Robert "King" Carter, who, in the 1740s, as one of the richest men in Virginia, owned one thousand slaves and three thousand acres of land. Faulkner may have known that "King" Carter allegedly aspired in this grandiose plantation house "Corotoman" to "rival or surpass the Governor's Palace" in Williamsburg, just as Faulkner would later have Thomas Sutpen decree in *Absalom, Absalom!* that "Sutpen's Hundred" should rival or surpass the Yoknapatawpha Courthouse. Like the actual Corotoman, Sutpen's Hundred would ultimately succumb to destruction by fire.[24]

For the merchant, William S. Neilson, the founder of what would become the oldest surviving store in Mississippi (1839), Turner designed a virtual twin of the Carter house. While the latter passed into the family of the Oxford merchant, Henry L. Tate, and fell in the twentieth century into picturesque ruin before it was finally razed, the Neilson house in the twentieth century was acquired by the prominent Oxford physician, John C. Culley, who, with his wife, Nina Somerville Culley, impeccably restored and maintained it. Though Faulkner and Culley had an occasionally strained personal relationship, the two couples were socially amicable, and Faulkner knew the house well, as he did, in fact, other buildings by Turner: the house, later named "Cedar Oaks" (1858) that the architect designed for himself on North [Lamar] Street, two blocks from the Square, and the house between the Carter and Neilson homes that Turner designed for William Thompson, the brother of the eminent Jacob Thompson, Secretary of the Interior in President James Buchanan's cabinet.

For Thompson, Turner designed his usual two-story, four-column mansion with the intention that it should replace two smaller, juxtaposed houses, the earliest of which was built ca. 1837, by John D. Martin, one of the founders of Oxford. With the outbreak of war in 1861, only the front half of the structure had been completed. After the war, Thompson's financial condition rendered him incapable of finishing it as planned, and the older, attached structures at the rear were never demolished. Thompson did, however, after United States troops burned the first county courthouse, acquire and surround his house with the wrought-iron fence that had surrounded the courthouse. Faulkner may have known that, like a tree at the Isom Place, north of the Square, the magnolias on the Thompson lawn were brought as seedlings from South Carolina, a symbolic act that Faulkner would later incorporate into his treatment of the Sartoris house.[25]

One of Thompson's daughters, Lucretia, called Lula, married Dr. Josiah Chandler and moved with him and their growing family back into the family home to care for her aging father. In 1893, the last of the Chandler children, Edwin Dial, was born mentally retarded, a condition known to young William Faulkner. In fact, according to historian Jack Wilson, Faulkner and his brother John "often noticed Edwin behind the massive iron fence when they would walk by the house. Some of the children teased Edwin cruelly, and John Faulkner wrote that William was deeply affected by this inhumanity. The character 'Benjy Compson' in *The Sound and the Fury* is thought to have been partially based on Edwin Chandler." Later, Wilson continues, "one afternoon in January of 1948 Edwin had an accident and was severely burned near the fireplace in the downstairs bedroom that he shared with his brother Wiley. A few days later he died. Once again Faulkner borrowed fact for his fiction and in . . . *The Mansion* he had Benjy Compson burn to death in a fire that destroyed the Compson mansion." Because of these affinities between the actual and the apocryphal, social and architectural, the Thompson-Chandler house, by the mid-twentieth century, was often referred to in Oxford as "the Compson house."[26]

The Turner-designed house that Faulkner knew best was one of the architect's earliest Oxford commissions, the Shegog Place (1848, figure 2) across the Taylor Road from the Greek Revival home of Jacob Thompson, which was destroyed by Federal troops in 1864. After their marriage in 1929, the Faulkners lived for two years in an apartment on University Avenue in the handsome postbellum neoclassical home of Elma Meek, the Oxford dowager who suggested the name "Ole Miss" for the University yearbook, a name subsequently applied to the institution itself. In 1930, with his first substantial royalties, Faulkner purchased the dilapidated Shegog residence and lovingly restored it, getting to know the building and the building process intimately as he worked with the carpenters in its slow resuscitation. Another nearby structure of the four-column type was the Howry-Wright house on University Avenue, begun ca. 1837, probably as a modest structure that evolved, in the prescribed way, into a neoclassical house. Faulkner may have known, since he would later use the idea in his work, that, as at other houses in the region, Union troops dug up the front lawn in search of silver and other valuables purported to be buried there.[27]

Figure 2. Rowan Oak, Oxford, Mississippi. Cofield Collection, Center for the Study of Southern Culture, University of Mississippi.

The grandest house in Oxford that Faulkner knew well was the Avant-Stone mansion, built ca. 1840, on the Old College Hill Road near the northwest edge of town, by Tomlin Avant, the youngest son of a prosperous Virginia family, who had, nonetheless, arrived penniless in Oxford in the late 1830s. The name of his architect has not survived; if it was William Turner, the building was a departure from his usual four-column prototype. By building a great house, on borrowed money, Avant hoped to purchase instant status and ultimately prosperity in his adopted community, and he therefore entertained lavishly in his large, white, two-story residence with its six-columned portico which ran the entire front length of the house. The impressive doorway from the upstairs hall duplicated the scale of the main, first-floor entrance as it opened onto a shallow, wrought-iron balcony. After Avant went bankrupt, the house went through several hands, including University of Mississippi Chancellor Edward Mayes and his famous father-in-law, senator, presidential cabinet member, and Supreme Court Justice,

Lucius Quintus Cincinnatus Lamar. By 1892, the house was vacant and in ill repair when the lawyer, James Stone, purchased and restored it. There, his son Phil, Faulkner's closest hometown friend and mentor, grew up as a child and continued to live as an adult. It was a house that Faulkner knew intimately before it burned to the ground in 1942.[28]

Similar to the four-column Turner-designed homes in town were "Cedar Hill Farm," built ca. 1852 by Yancy Wiley in the northwest quadrant of Lafayette County, and the Shipp plantation house, located south of Oxford near the southern border of the county. Though no such documentation exists, both could easily have been designed by Turner. In 1833, Dr. Felix Grundy Shipp had moved from Hinds County in central Mississippi north into the Chickasaw Cession near the future town of Water Valley. In 1839, he bought his Lafayette County land at the Pontotoc land auction and built his first residence—an inn on the stagecoach road. But Shipp was ambitious, and in the late 1850s began to build his large, imposing mansion.[29]

According to historian Charles B. Cramer, Shipp, with the help of his numerous slaves, built his ten-room house (figure 3) facing the stage road, opposite his first residence: "Bricks used in its construction were made in two brick kilns on the place. The cypress shingles used on the roof of the house were dipped in boiling linseed oil to protect them from the harshness of the weather." The shingles lasted seventy-five years before a tin roof was placed over them. The timber frame was joined with sturdy wooden pegs. Two large rooms lay on either side of the broad central downstairs hall, which ran the depth of the house from the front portico to a porch at the back. An elegantly curved stairway, with carvings by black slave craftsmen, led to the second floor, which contained one huge room above the two first floor parlors, the former of which was specially designed for meetings of the Masonic Lodge and the Methodist Quarterly Conference. Another upstairs space, called the Medicine Room, resembled a drug store with its shelves and cabinets filled with

Figure 3. Old Shipp Place (c. 1850), Lafayette County, Mississippi.
Thomas S. Hines.

jars and bottles of medicine that Dr. Shipp dispensed to his
patients. Plaster walls throughout the house were composed of
sand, molasses, horsehair, and other ingredients. A stunning
plaster medallion in the front parlor was a replica of one in
Andrew Jackson's home, The Hermitage, in Nashville. The
family maintained the property until the death of Dr. Shipp's
daughter, Martha, in the 1920s, after which the house was
boarded up and abandoned.[30]

The family heirlooms left behind fell prey to vandals and
antique hunters and the house slowly decayed. The abandoned
stage road that once ran past it became choked with under-
growth and no longer passable, leaving the house isolated, deep

in the woods. It was a romantic ruin by the time Faulkner would likely have known it in the 1920s, and he possibly found it a suggestive model for the "Old Frenchman Place." Faulkner may or may not have known that the family had originally come from Shipp's Bend, Tennessee. When in 1936 he drew the famous map of his imagined Yoknapatawpha for the flyleaf of *Absalom, Absalom!*, he placed the hamlet of "Frenchman's Bend" and the nearby mansion, "The Old Frenchman Place," in the southeast quadrant of the county, the actual location of the "Old Shipp Place," as it was already coming to be known.

In *Sanctuary*, Faulkner used the Old Frenchman Place to symbolize social, cultural, moral, and spiritual decay:

> The house was a gutted ruin rising gaunt and stark out of a grove of unpruned cedar trees. It was a landmark, known as the Old French-man Place, built before the Civil War; a plantation house set in the middle of a tract of land; of cotton fields and gardens and lawns long since gone back to jungle, which the people of the neighborhood had been pulling down piecemeal for firewood for fifty years or digging with secret and sporadic optimism for the gold which the builder was reputed to have buried somewhere about the place when Grant came through the county on his Vicksburg campaign. . . . The gaunt ruin of the house rose against the sky, above the massed and matted cedars, lightless, desolate, and profound. The road was an eroded scar too deep to be a road and too straight to be a ditch, gutted by winter freshets and choked with fern and rotted leaves and branches.[31]

In *The Hamlet*, near the turn of the century, Faulkner presented the same abandoned house as being no longer owned or occupied by the descendants of Louis Grenier, the "old Frenchman," but by the backwoods entrepreneur, Will Varner, who

> owned most of the good land in the country and held mortgages on most of the rest. He owned the store and the cotton gin and the combined grist mill and blacksmith shop in the village [of Frenchman's Bend] and at least once every month during the spring and summer and early fall . . . he would be seen by someone sitting in a home-made chair on the jungle-choked lawn of the Old

Frenchman's homesite . . . chewing his tobacco or smoking his cob pipe, with a brusque word for passers cheerful enough but inviting no company, against his background of fallen baronial splendor.

He rationalized this habit only to V. K. Ratliff, the itinerant sewing machine salesman: " 'I like to sit here. I'm trying to find out what it must have felt like to be the fool that would need all this . . . just to eat and sleep in. . . . But after all, I reckon I'll just keep what there is left of it, just to remind me of my one mistake. This is the only thing I ever bought in my life I couldn't sell to nobody.' "[32]

Will Varner's attitude toward the Old Frenchman Place, which he owned but did not live in, was one of bemused alienation from the original owners' values and intentions. By contrast, the view of another outsider of another grand house that he not only did not inhabit but had never seen the likes of, was vividly presented in the story "Barn Burning." There, through the mind of the abused and terrorized child, Sarty Snopes, Faulkner suggested the power of architecture to astonish, ameliorate, comfort, and delight:

> Presently he could see the grove of oaks and cedars and the other flowering trees and shrubs where the house would be though not the house yet. They walked beside a fence massed with honeysuckle and Cherokee roses and came to a gate swinging open between two brick pillars, and now, beyond a sweep of drive, he saw the house for the first time and at that instant he forgot his father and the terror and despair both, and even when he remembered his father again . . . the terror and despair did not return. Because, for all the twelve movings, they had sojourned until now in a poor country, a land of small farms and fields and houses, and he had never seen a house like this before. *Hit's big as a courthouse* he thought quietly, with a surge of peace and joy whose reason he could not have thought into words, being too young for that.[33]

Smaller, one-story variants of the same Greek Revival graced Lafayette County in both Oxford and the countryside. Near the hamlet of College Hill, the Buford House (1842) was characterized by crossing central hallways which opened on two sides into identical four-columned porticoes, a partial, modestly rural version of Andrea Palladio's grand Villa Rotonda, Vicenza, Italy (ca. 1550). A smaller, but similar house in town, "The Magnolias," was built the same year by an early settler, William Smither. Such houses, Faulkner wrote in "Knight's Gambit," were "more spartan even than comfortable, even in those days when people wanted needed comfort in their homes for the reason that they spent some of their time there."[34]

The house that so moved Sarty Snopes in "Barn Burning" was in fact the ancestral seat of the de Spain family, but it could as easily have been the nearby country house, "Sartoris," which Faulkner placed in the northwest quadrant of his Yoknapatawpha map, near the actual location of Cedar Hill Farm. It was significant that the Sartoris house had no made-up name like "Longwood" or "Bellevue" but only the name of the family itself, a name Faulkner saw as having both dark and grand connotations: "For there is death in the sound of it and a glamorous fatality, like silver pennons downrushing at sunset, or a dying fall of horns along the road to Rouncevaux."[35]

In the 1920s, Bayard Sartoris returned to and pondered the meaning of his ancestral home, burned by Federal troops during the Civil War and rebuilt over the original cellar and foundations after it. Faulkner used such architectural layering to evoke the even more complex layering of the Sartoris family and indeed of Southern history. Though in most of his later work he would emphasize the exterior of buildings as sculptural monuments on the natural landscape, in *Sartoris* he developed a sense of the layering of interior spaces as well. It was remarkable that here in the first of his Yoknapatawpha novels, he had already developed a sophisticated sense of architectural symbolism: "Then the road approached the railway and crossed it and at last the house John Sartoris had built stood among locusts and oaks and Simon [the driver] swung between iron gates and into a curving drive. . . . Bayard stood for awhile before his house. The white simplicity of it dreamed unbroken among ancient sunshot trees." He then crossed the colonnaded veranda and entered the front hall: "The stairway with its white spindles and red carpet mounted in a tall slender curve into upper gloom. From the center of the ceiling hung a chandelier of crystal prisms and shades, fitted originally for candles but since wired for electricity. To the right of the entrance, beside folding doors rolled back upon a dim room emanating an atmosphere of solemn and seldom violated stateliness and known as the parlor, stood a tall mirror filled with grave obscurity like a still pool of evening water."

Bayard then climbed the stairs and "stopped again in the upper hall. The western windows were closed with lattice blinds, through which sunlight seeped in yellow dissolving bars that but served to increase the gloom. At the opposite end a tall door opened upon a shallow grilled balcony which offered the valley and the cradling semicircle of the eastern hills in panorama. On either side of this door was a narrow window set with leaded panes of vari-colored glass" which John Sartoris's "youngest sister had brought from Carolina in a straw-filled hamper in '69."[36]

The building, the decay, and sometimes the destruction of such houses were crucial to the plots, the ambience, and the delineation of character in Faulkner's work: from the Old Frenchman Place in *Sanctuary* and *The Hamlet*, to similar homes in town of the Compson and de Spain families, to the plantation house, Sutpen's Hundred, in *Absalom, Absalom!* Though such apocryphal grandiosity had no real equivalent on the actual North Mississippi landscape, *Absalom, Absalom!* would have lost much of its power without the prominence and the grandeur Faulkner gave to Sutpen's house, the other Grand Design, the private, monomaniacal counterpart of the public Grand Design of the courthouse, square, and town. It was the symbol for Thomas Sutpen of the security he craved and worked for, a status denied him earlier at another grand house when he had been asked by a haughty servant to go around to the back door. In the middle of what the elder Jason Compson called "a shadowy miasmic region something like the bitter purlieus of Styx," Sutpen decreed his own house into being as a kind of commandment: *"Be Sutpen's Hundred,* like the oldentime *'Be Light.'* " In *Requiem for a Nun,* Faulkner represented the mansion as being: "something like a wing of Versailles glimpsed in a Lilliput's gothic nightmare."[37]

The contrast between the names of the houses on the Sutpen and Sartoris plantations has been noted insightfully by critic William Ruzicka: "Sartoris itself is named, of course, for the family, and the name, in its own way, is an attribute or quality. Sutpen's Hundred is named for the number of square miles it contains—a quantity. The complete name is composed of two words: the possessive form of the owner's name and the quantitative measurement of what is possessed."[38] (figure 4)

The size of the house was, in fact, so colossal that the curious Jefferson gentry, eager to observe the phenomenon, "would make up parties to meet at the Holston House and go out horseback often carrying lunch. . . . Without dismounting

Figure 4. Ruins of Estes Place (c. 1850), Panola County, Mississippi. Thomas S. Hines.

(usually Sutpen did not even greet them with as much as a nod, apparently as unaware of their presence as if they had been idle shades) they would sit in a curious clump as though for mutual protection and watch his mansion rise, carried plank by plank and brick by brick out of the swamp where the clay and timber waited—the bearded white man and the twenty black ones and all stark naked." Sutpen worked in the nude, they surmised, because he was "saving his clothes, since decorum even if not elegance of appearance would be the only weapon (or rather, ladder) with which he could conduct the last assault upon . . . respectability."[39]

Sutpen and his crew of naked slaves

worked from sunup to sundown . . . and the architect in his formal coat and his Paris hat and his expression of grim and embittered amazement lurked about the environs of the scene with his air something between a casual and bitterly disinterested spectator and a condemned and conscientious ghost—amazement, General Compson said, not at the others and what they were doing so much as at himself, at the inexplicable and incredible fact of his own presence. But he was a good architect. . . . And not only an architect, as General Compson said, but an artist since only an artist could have borne those two years in order to build a house which he doubtless not only expected but firmly intended never to see again. Not, General Compson said, the hardship to sense and the outrage to sensibility of the two years' soujourn, but Sutpen: that only an artist could have borne Sutpen's ruthlessness and hurry and still manage to curb the dream of grim and castlelike magnificance at which Sutpen obviously aimed, since the place as Sutpen planned it would have been almost as large as Jefferson itself at the time.[40]

Then, when it became altogether too claustrophobic, too threatening, the "French architect" attempted to escape from it all through the swamp back to the river and south to New Orleans. And in relating this surreal episode, the great Faulkner wit emerged in a novel that is not usually thought to contain much humor, as he turned the word "architect" from a noun into a verb: "It was late afternoon before they caught him . . . and then only because he had hurt his leg trying to architect himself across the river."[41]

Figure 5. Close-up of the entry hall, ruins of Estes Place (c. 1850), Panola County, Mississippi. Thomas S. Hines.

When the work was completed, Sutpen's "presence alone compelled that house to accept and retain human life; as though houses actually possess a sentience, a personality and character acquired, not so much from the people who breathe or have breathed in them inherent in the wood and brick or begotten upon the wood and brick by the man or men who conceived and built them," but rather "in this house an incontrovertible affirmation for emptiness, desertion; an insurmountable resistance to occupancy save when sanctioned and protected by the ruthless and the strong."[42] After surviving the war but not the collisions of Sutpen and his heirs, Sutpen's Hundred, before its ultimate destruction by fire, suffered a decline more ruinous and symbolic even than that of the Old Frenchman Place: *"Rotting portico and scaling walls, it stood, not ravaged, not invaded, marked by no bullet nor soldier's iron heel but rather as though reserved for something more: some desolation more profound than ruin. . . . that barren hall with its naked stair . . . rising into the dim upper hallway where an echo spoke which was not mine but rather that of the lost irrevocable might-have-been which haunts all houses.*"[43] (figure 5)

Indeed, the Greek Revival architecture of Yoknapatawpha was the perfect setting for Faulkner's Greek tragedies.

Thus, in work after work, Faulkner answered resoundingly the question he had posed long before in *Mosquitoes* in asserting and demonstrating that architecture was not only "a part of life," but an art that shaped and reflected its contours. However great the pain and joy in "the tragedy and comedy of being alive"—architecture was an art that was fundamental to life. Indeed, it was—in Jefferson, the town—surely among the things that made up the quest for what Jefferson, the man, Jefferson, the architect, had called "the pursuit of happiness." (figure 6)

Figure 6. South Lamar looking toward square, Oxford, Mississippi. Cofield Collection, Center for the Study of Southern Culture, University of Mississippi.

NOTES

1. William Faulkner, *Mosquitoes* (New York: Boni & Liveright, 1927), 106–7.

2. Eudora Welty, "Place in Fiction," *The Eye of the Story* (New York: Random House, 1978), 118–19; Malcolm Cowley, "Introduction," *The Portable Faulkner* [1946] (New York: The Viking Press, 1951), 5.

3. William T. Ruzicka, *Faulkner's Fictive Architecture: The Meaning of Place in the Yoknapatawpha Novels* (Ann Arbor, Michigan: UMI Press, 1987), 2. This short, insightful analysis by a literary scholar is virtually the only other study that treats the subject at all.

4. Joel Williamson, *William Faulkner and Southern History* (New York: Oxford University Press, 1993), 413.

5. Hayden White, "The Fictions of Factual Representation," *Tropics of Discourse: Essays in Cultural Criticism* (Baltimore: The Johns Hopkins University Press, 1978), 122.

6. Erik H. Erikson, "Psychological Reality and Historical Actuality," *Insight and Responsibility: Lectures on the Ethical Implications of Psychoanalytic Insight* (New York: W. W. Norton & Company, 1964), 159; Faulkner, "Monk," *Knight's Gambit* (New York: Vintage Books, 1978), 39; Faulkner, *The Town* [1957] (New York: Vintage Books, 1960), 88.

7. Elizabeth M. Kerr, *Yoknapatawpha: Faulkner's "Little Postage Stamp of Native Soil"* (New York: Fordham University Press, 1969), 11, quoting Faulkner from *Faulkner in the University: Class Conferences at the University of Virginia, 1957–1958*, ed. Frederick L. Gwynn and Joseph L. Blotner (Charlottesville: University Press of Virginia, 1959), 84.

8. Gaston Bachelard, *The Poetics of Space* (Boston: Beacon Press, 1969), 8; Faulkner, *Sartoris* [1929] (New York: Signet, 1957), 73–74.

9. Ben Wasson, *Count No 'Count: Flashbacks to Faulkner* (Jackson: University Press of Mississippi, 1983), 54–55.

10. Joseph Blotner, *Faulkner: A Biography* (New York: Random House, 1974), 443–83.

11. Ibid., 443.

12. Faulkner, *Sanctuary* [1931] (New York: Vintage Books, 1958), 308.

13. Faulkner, *Mosquitoes*, 10, 14.

14. Faulkner, *Absalom, Absalom!* [1936] (New York: Vintage Books, 1972), 110.

15. Blotner, *Faulkner*, 415; Faulkner, Interview with Jean Stein, first published in *The Paris Review*, Spring 1956; reprinted in *Lion in the Garden: Interviews with William Faulkner, 1926–1962*, ed. James B. Meriwether and Michael Millgate (Lincoln: University of Nebraska Press, 1968), 255.

16. Leland Roth, *A Concise History of American Architecture* (New York: Harper & Row, 1979), 53.

17. R. Furneau Jordan, *A Concise History of Western Architecture* (New York: Harcourt, Brace & World, 1970), 46–47.

18. Wasson, *Count No 'Count*, 55.

19. Catherine Bishir, *North Carolina Architecture* (Chapel Hill: University of North Carolina Press, 1990), 163.

20. Faulkner, *Requiem for a Nun* [1950] (New York: Vintage Books, 1975), 35.

21. Ibid., 34.

22. Ibid., 39–40; Hardeman County [Tennessee] Historical Commission, *Hardeman County Historical Sketches* (Taylor Publishing Company, 1979), 2.

23. Jack Case Wilson, *Faulkners, Fortunes, and Flames* (Nashville: Annandale Press, 1984), 78. This corrects the frequently asserted claim that Turner was "English," an idea apparently accepted by Faulkner himself.

24. Charles B. Cramer, "Ante-Bellum Architecture," Unpublished typescript, Mississippi Collection, University of Mississippi, Oxford, Miss., 25–26.

25. Ibid., 26–28.

26. Wilson, *Faulkners, Fortunes, and Flames*, 66–69.

27. Cramer, "Ante-Bellum Architecture," 9–11; 16–17.

28. Ibid., 14–15; Susan Snell, *Phil Stone of Oxford: A Vicarious Life* (Athens: University of Georgia Press, 1991), 21- 24.

29. Cramer, "Ante-Bellum Architecture," 17–22.

30. Ibid.

31. Faulkner, *Sanctuary*, 7–8, 18–19.

32. Faulkner, *The Hamlet*, 5–6.

33. Faulkner, "Barn Burning," *Collected Stories of William Faulkner* (New York: Random House, 1950), 10.

34. Faulkner, *Knight's Gambit*, 143.

35. Faulkner, *Sartoris*, 303.

36. Ibid., 23–24.

37. Faulkner, *Absalom, Absalom!*, 69, 9; Faulkner, *Requiem for a Nun*, 35.

38. Ruzicka, *Faulkner's Fictive Architecture*, 45.

39. Faulkner, *Absalom, Absalom!*, 36–37.

40. Ibid., 38.

41. Ibid., 256.

42. Ibid., 85.

43. Ibid., 136–37.

Recovering the Teller in the Tale:
An Unfinished Project

WESLEY MORRIS

Although I come here tonight somewhat as an outsider from the world of literary theory, I am genuinely honored to be in the company of so many Faulkner scholars. My reception has been warm, and the opportunity to talk with so many who share my unqualified regard for Faulkner's artistry has been stimulating and challenging. Yet this occasion puts me in a rather compromising posture; for as a student of contemporary literary theory, I must confess that the topic of this conference, "Faulkner and the Artist," is impossible to speak of today.

There are two reasons for this. First, we are now in an age called the postmodern, an era more concerned with cultural critique than literary criticism. In the postmodern age the artist as artist receives only marginal attention from literary theory. I hope, however, to make this obstacle a positive benefit to my reading of Faulkner. The second reason that I cannot speak of the artist is more formidable, for postmodernism has erased the word "artist" from our critical language. The modernist concept of imagination, which suggested genius and was integral to our sense of what constituted artistry, has been thoroughly discredited over the past thirty years. Quite frankly, this is a serious problem for literary critics because the erasure of the artist has left a blank space in many of our critical texts. Faulkner, with the genius of the artist (as I once would have phrased it), knew how to make something significant out of a blank space in the text; you will recall Addie Bundren's description of a particularly poignant blank in *As I Lay Dying* as "a significant shape profoundly without life like an empty door frame."[1] The multiple implications of this particular passage, the empty shape that signifies but has no life, the spot in the text where a murder has happened (or has it?), a space where the body of the text is missing, and the simile of the "threshold" that marks a passage between two unknown realms, has fascinated me as a literary theorist for some time, and I plan to return to it below in order to speculate about how we see through blanks in texts to what is on the other side. Perhaps that is a place where we might recover the artist.

In order to get there I must first confront the missing person of the artist in the postmodern age. I would like to offer, therefore, a particularly suggestive commentary on postmodernism made by Perry Anderson about ten years ago; he observes that one of the great figures of postmodern culture, Jacques Derrida, advocates a rather unsettling "notion of language." Derrida, Anderson correctly states,

> radicalizes [the] pretensions [of language] as a universal suzerain of the modern world, with the truly imperial decree, [that] "there is nothing outside of the text," "nothing before the text, no pretext that is not already a text." The Book of the World that the Renaissance, in its naivete, took to be a metaphor, becomes the last, literal word of a philosophy that would shake all metaphysics.[2]

This ascendency of language over the world, of structure over experience, of the text over history troubles a materialist like Anderson because it fails to account for what he calls the "historical subject," which is both the subject *of* history and the subject *in* history. The historical subject, in this postmortem of the postmodern, is buried in the place where we always find the body, and that is the focus of my effort today: to speak the unspeakable, to rewrite what has been erased, to intrude in the postmodern dust so that I may recover the body of the artist as historical subject prematurely laid to rest by postmodernism.

So Faulkner might ask, "and now what's to do?" I can project where I want to go: *before* the text, but not a straight path for going there *through* my text. I want to entertain the notion that narrative has subjects, that narrative is historical, and that narrative merges art with ethics, even politics, as it represents something outside of the text. But I wish to reach that conclusion by embracing the postmodern dictum that nothing significant lies before the text. Thus, the historical subject that I wish to recover will not take the form of a specific individual. Rather, the historical subject is a story of the forces that produce stories, what Faulkner would call "tales." There is a crucial relationship in this production of stories between the teller and the listener, a historical relationship that is fundamentally ethical and political. The historical subject is itself a relationship, a set of exchanges, a dialogue that forms the structure and the content of the narrative. My argument rests in part on my belief that postmodernism should have done a better job in drawing our attention to the language of narration, particularly that dynamics which is storytelling, to the ways we use words and they use us, to practical problems of community in exchanging knowledge, contracting relationships, and establishing rules; postmodernism should have made us wiser consumers of language, more critical listeners, better informed citizens. But it has not.

Faulkner will be my guide on this journey because of his restless exploration of the social uses of language in storytelling, because of his fascination with words as socially symbolic expressions. Postmodernism also has alerted us to the symbolic character of society, not merely that society uses symbols but that society *is* symbolic, a system of symbols, a pipeline of flows and stops, something like a public water works which provides the citizenry with words to live by delivered to its homes. Consequently, the social symbolic is a mechanism for the circulation of languages and attendant ideas; more accurately it is an ideological pumping system that purifies and distributes stories, stories we learn held in the arms of our mothers and fathers as we listen to the tales they tell. Narrative discriminates for us; it articulates membership and assigns attributes according to an "Us/Them" strategy; it establishes worlds (perhaps we can call them "realities") to live in. The social narratives promote dichotomies, two-party systems within society, not simply in the sense of jingoism or xenophobia but most importantly as an arrangement of groups and individuals within a class system (although "class" must not be read as exclusively "economic"). These dichotomies are structurally stable while they seem to be endlessly mobile.

We may illustrate this by noting how we read character as a series of strategic "moves" or "differences" in the text; what we perceive as subjectivity or identity is what F. Scott Fitzgerald elegantly called "personality," a "series of successful gestures."[3] Faulkner marks these gestures in Chick Mallison of *Intruder in the Dust* by a shift in Mallison's references to Lucas Beauchamp. First Chick repeats what he has heard: " 'They're going to make a nigger out of him once in his life anyway.' "[4] Not long after that, Chick's references designate Lucas as "a man" who is in mortal danger simply "because his skin [is] black" (72). The shift from "nigger" to "a man" who, incidentally, is "black" is a gesture or move in personality or character; we once called it development and it betokened "roundness" or psychological reality in the text. It is also a rather complex reflection of social dialogue ranging from the child's language borrowed from the racist world in which he lives to what we believe is genuine progress, a development of a more liberal racial sensitivity in
· the boy, and maybe it is this in some "personal" sense, in the way that Faulkner or Fitzgerald would have conceived of character. Faulkner, however, insists that we read this personal set of gestures, only part of a long series of such moves that produce the character of Chick Mallison, in a broader perspective. Chick's character emerges only to become more and more isolated from the symbolic structure of the community in which he lives. His identity is linked not only to Lucas but also to other marginalized figures like old maids and young African American boys. The ideological structure of the community remains intact, and Faulkner seemed to have no idea how Chick's personal story might engage the community in a genuine dialogue or how Chick's personality could serve as a critique of

that society which was all too ready to lynch Lucas because his skin was black. What emerges is no real challenge to the structure of the community, merely a personal story, an isolated instance of individual heroism that postpones violence, grants Lucas a stay of execution. The weak ending of the novel, contrary to Faulkner's intentions, I believe, does more to reduce Lucas to caricature than to grant him either justice or dignity.

My goal is not to question the aesthetic or moral dimensions of *Intruder in the Dust* so much as it is to explore the form and function of the narrative which expresses a social symbolic, but it is important to note that ethical and political decisions are not repressed in the examination of the aesthetics of form and style. This is because the social symbolic is not a narrative in the ordinary sense, not simply a "story"; it is multiple stories based on sets of generative elements, potential narratives, contained in what we can call familiar "phrases," recognizable expressions that satisfy collective narrative expectations, that predict endings and thereby establish communities. These generative elements identify the "facts" of the story. In *Intruder in the Dust* Faulkner provides us with a curious and unusually insightful commentary on "facts." Facts are not, we discover, exactly what we have come to think of them in the typical detective novel or court of law. Faulkner argues that facts do not establish truth by anchoring themselves in matter. A fact is not a given "matter of fact," nor is it indisputable. Faulkner urges us to see that a fact is always phrased so that it is recognized in the community and, hence, belongs to the realm of narrative ideology.

I use the term "ideology" to describe what Louis Althusser calls an "imaginary realtionship" to the world.[5] That is to say, an ideology is the sense we have that we relate to a familiar world in a manner that is natural and proper, as a matter of fact. I want to take the term "imaginary" seriously, for it suggests that what we all recognize as our community, as our reality, is, in part, a projection of the capacity we have of extending and completing our "story" of the familiar world that we live in. Society is, in a very significant way, a figment of our imaginations. Narrative (storytelling) is crucial to the production and reproduction of these imaginary realities, to the organizing of facts into patterns of meaning and systems of value. Facts are not fully facts until they have been narrated, "phrased" so as to reaffirm an image of a world and one's ethically proper place in it.

What facts *are*, therefore, is somewhat less important than what facts *do*. A fact satisfies a social, that is, narrative, need. A fact is a double concept, linked, on the one hand, to the realm of human actions, to the material world of things, the register of the body (Vinson's corpse in *Intruder in the Dust* functions as the matter of what is to become a fact) and, on the other hand, linked to the narrative, to the figment of the imagination that designates actions and bodies as reality, that names and describes ideological relationships in the world. A fact is matter phrased or narrated. Narration gives meaning, creates interest, envisions consequences, and judges guilt and innocence; thus the story and not the fact exceeds or falls short of the judicial dictum of "reasonable doubt." A fact, moreover, lends a sense of stability to the story and supports the story in its resistance to change, to revision. It is possible to say, as first Lucas does and then Miss Habersham, that Southern white males are "too busy with facks," with "evidence," to be able to listen to an accounting of events different from the one that they expect to hear (71, 89). The story that reinforces their specific imaginative relation to their world finds Lucas guilty of the murder of Vinson Gowrie because their specific social narrative imagines facts to reflect an ending already written. Or we could say somewhat more dramatically: the ideology of racism speaks through a tyranny of the phrase.

In order to construct the mystery which is at the heart of the plot of his detective story, Faulkner reproduced, in order to dismantle, the dominant narrative of Southern white male society; what he did not or could not construct for us was a genuinely alternative story. In disproving the story that has Lucas killing Vinson Gowrie, Faulkner resolves his plot by telling us that Vinson was killed by his brother, but this substitute story serves more to distract us than to resolve the narrative of Lucas's false arrest and imprisonment. Faulkner shifts the focus to Gavin Stevens, whose long and rambling story of Southern "homogeneity" and theories of mob psychology simply overwhelm any oppositional voices. That is not to say that we are taken in by Stevens's rhetoric or that Faulkner intended for us to be persuaded by Stevens's strained logic. I merely note that Lucas Beauchamp, Miss Habersham, and particularly Chick Mallison, who comprise a trio of possible alternative phrasings, are largely silenced by the scandal of fratricide. It is safer, one might say, for a white male Southerner to forget about the story of class bias (town versus country, middle class Jefferson versus "Beat Four") and racism while pursuing a story of mythological dimensions (the foundations of society in the taboo against fratricide), in a story that Stevens can ultimately declare unspeakable, beyond phrasing. In myth the ethics and politics of race, class, and gender are rendered silent just as Lucas, Chick, and Miss Habersham are spoken for by Stevens's monologue. The story with which the novel began, a powerful story of the movement from repression to liberation, both as Chick Mallison's personal story and Lucas Beauchamp's exemplary story, fades into mere static or noise, into the background of a more powerful story of "original" evil, perhaps a more comfortable story because its familiarity makes us feel at home in it.

Certainly, *Intruder in the Dust* claims our attention because it is more than a detective story resolved by the revelation of the true murderer. Faulkner distances us from the detective story by calling our attention to the social symbolic at play, but that is a risky business. We understand the "real world" issues at stake here, the implications of conflicting stories, of what Jean-Francois Lyotard calls "phrases in dispute."[6] Such dispute defies resolution, even mediation; such dispute generates multiple stories, narrates different facts into an "undecidable." Faulkner, a good modernist, does not seek to submerge his narrative in the undecidable; Lucas *is* innocent, the victim of racist expectations. But this resolution is troubled by the repeated suggestion of an alternative story, of oppositional voices that remain largely muted, another sort of hole in the text. This is the place of the imagination, the domain of storytelling.

We can get closer to this idea of the imaginative relationship to the world that is structured by the tyranny of the phrase by recalling that a significant portion of *Intruder in the Dust* focuses on a phrase that Chick Mallison hears repeated three different times by three different people within a few hours of time: "Lucas ought to thought of that before he picked out Saturday to kill Vinson on" (40). This phrase is a response to the question of whether or not the Gowries will lynch Lucas on a Sunday. It assumes that Lucas shot Vinson Gowrie and that the story will play itself out toward an inevitable conclusion in Lucas's death. The phrase, taken by itself, though meaningful is not wholly intelligible; it is a fragment depending on the untold story that the entire community seems already to have heard. The repetition of this phrase accounts for all the facts necessary for the story's ending and discounts any other possible facts or rephrasings of the facts. Gavin Stevens describes this repetitiveness as the "paucity" or "meagreness" of a language necessary to everyday social interaction (80). That paucity exposes the underlying racist story that ultimately explains the mob which, without any obvious signal, assembles to watch the Gowries lynch Lucas. The mob is the expression of an ideology which can be narrated; it is the representation of communally shared narrative expectations, of a figment of the communal imagination, the sense of an ending.

The phrase that Chick hears repeated in casual talk also functions as a bar to conversation; in each of the three repetitions the phrase signals that nothing more need be said. The same attitude pervades the non-exchanges between Lucas and Gavin, who is to be Lucas's lawyer. Gavin, too, has already written a story of Lucas's guilt; as he interviews his client he interrupts Lucas and often finishes the accused man's sentences. Conversation in Faulkner's world is regulated by a social symbolic, for Gavin does not listen and Lucas must depend upon those *unsocialized*, marginalized figures like the boy, Chick, his young black playmate, Aleck Sander, and the eccentric Miss Habersham to listen and engage in a genuine dialogue with Lucas. Critique, perhaps, can only come from the margins, from the excluded and silent. So it is that Lucas remains almost silent throughout the novel.

Eccentricity is a familiar modernist narrative device, one Faulkner often used to represent resistance, opposition, critique, or revision of the already written stories that tyrranize social action. Yet eccentricity easily lapses into stereotype or caricature. It is interesting that the eccentric anticipates the great postmodern shibboleth of "decentering." Of course, a postmodernist would respond to such a linking of modern and postmodern by noting that eccentricity, as Faulkner cultivates it, is the very focal point of the postmodernist "erasure" of what Derrida called the "before" of the text. A genealogy of the eccentric reveals that it reflects a dying modernist liberalism; it is a version of romantic subjectivism and the avant-garde asocial artist in rebellion against the sterility of bourgeois individualism. All of these notions express the idea of critique, of an oppositional position from within society yet one that is not quite fully regulated or appropriated by society. The force of the idea of postmodern decentering is not unlike eccentricity in this sense when we realize that both undercut the tyranny of the phrase. Eccentricity and decentering are principles of difference, or, I would urge, principles of change. Each locates change in a separate region of social order: the eccentric in that which comes before the text and decentering within the text itself, through the power of symbolic play, through the force of revision that can alter fundamental narrative structure and tell a different story, phrase different facts. The eccentric reaches for the realm of the will, desire, and the body whereas decentering reaches beyond the narration into the depths of symbolic transformation, substitution, and transgression.

The difference between Lucas as caricature and Lucas as

eccentric is the difference between the passivity and quietism of a flabby liberal tolerance and the activism of a militant reformism that liberalism seems to have forgotten along the way to postmodernism. Most importantly, caricature (or stereotype) produces no dialogue; eccentricity, very much in the spirit of postmodern decentering or in the "strange" which subverts the familiar, describes a place for the voice of difference which when narrated, when phrased in a story, becomes the voice of political change: revolution.[7] Eccentricity raises conversation beyond the limits of the tyrany of the phrase. In this context we must recall one of Faulkner's most impressive eccentrics, Rosa Coldfield. Rosa seeks to tell Quentin Compson *her* story in contrast with the tyranny of what has already been phrased in the public domain, what she says *"they will have told you"* concerning her relations with the infamous Thomas Sutpen.[8] She would revise, even displace, what has already been said. She cannot do this, but she can engage the already spoken, reactivating it, bringing it to life in dialogue. It is this level of conversation that I seek here; it is the goal of the narrative artist who must reveal to us the foundation of storytelling in ethics and politics.

There is another Faulknerian device that reveals to us the possibility of opening dialogue within the tyrranizing limits of the phrase. This is a classic psychosocial model, a deeply romantic sense of developmentalism that hinges on the traumatic transition between childhood and maturity, what the postmoderns might call the traumatic accession to language. Becoming an adult and acquiring language focus on rituals of socialization; for Faulkner this was represented predominantly in masculine experiences of growing up. The threshold that the young boy crosses exposes for us the place of the eccentric, somewhere between innocence and experience. This threshold is a dangerous place that constitutes another kind of hole in the text, in the social narrative. It defines for us an opening onto a "before" that defies expression, remains unspoken. This is, of course, a "before" that has no substance; it is the *place* of the

Other or of the unspeakable, that which is excluded, banished from the social norm. It is the symbolic garbage heap of orderly social relations and meaningful interactions.

It is, I suggest, the dwelling place of eccentrics like Lucas Beauchamp, Miss Habersham, and Chick Mallison. The eccentric does not remain silent; the social order must speak and speak endlessly in order to close off the threshold it has itself opened. This is the tension we sense in *Intruder in the Dust* between the story that drives Gavin's familiar world and the eccentric story that Lucas and Chick and Miss Habersham cannot quite phrase. In this novel Faulkner takes the story of a boy's socialization and submerges it in a story of the passage between racial innocence and racist experience. The passing of that threshold takes the form of acquiring a narrative sense of belonging, of the recognition and repetition of the tyrannizing phrase ("Lucas ought to thought of that before he picked out Saturday to kill Vinson on"). The design of this passage to socialization is to interpolate, to assign identity, but it relies on the exposure of the eccentric to reinforce the power of identification with the already narrated. It represses the innocence of the "before," but that innocence becomes thereby a subtext of the already narrated. This repressive entrance into language is perilous and may misfire. Faulkner asks, admittedly in rather sentimental terms, if prior experience does not linger questioningly on the threshold of maturity. Is there not a remnant of the child's "Why?" that foregrounds the interpolative strategies of the socializing language? The answer is beyond the scope of our musings here, but we need not answer this question to grasp the implications of a repressive, socializing process which produces its own fault lines.

Now we can grasp the seeming contradiction that the "before" is not altogether before; it resides within the story as the residue of symbolic expression that can detach itself from the familiar story and link onto another phrase, a different fact, a revised version, a newly imagined world. This alternative symbolic phrasing is neither simply a different point of view nor new evidence; it is a revision based on a realignment of speakers and listeners, on additional conversation, on a reformation of community. Faulkner grasped the revisionary implications of his art: that there is a sense of conspiracy in what can be phrased against what has already been phrased.

Stories consist of phrases which put facts in the service of ideologies, and facts are the realm of desire in storytelling, a reach for truth (if we speak in transcendental terms), an understanding of the consequences of speaking (to phrase it in terms of ethical judgments and political decisions). There is nothing about the matter of facts that is essential, ideal, unchanging; remember how difficult it is for Chick and his conspirators against the social symbolic to dig up Vinson's body, for the grave contains sometimes Vinson and sometimes another body and sometimes no body at all. Vinson's body never is in the same place, sometimes in the grave and sometimes in the quicksand under the bridge. With each alteration of the material world the facts must be rephrased and the story revised. That is to say, the fact that Vinson was not shot with Lucas's gun is in itself meaningless. That *new* fact must be narrated to make sense, and the story it supports is one that Faulkner proposes as fantastic: the murder of brother by brother. Facts do not depend upon the stability of the material body, yet facts incorporate, if I may pun, the body into phrases and narratives. Facts are negotiated. Facts embody (I cannot avoid the pun) decisions and judgments, support arguments, arrange themselves in disputes. They reveal the consequences of narrative production; they expose the *real* world of pain and sorrow, pleasure and joy. There are no stories worth telling that are not about such worlds. At the heart of this consequentiality is conversation, not merely within the fictional plot but also as a manifestation of the relationship of teller and listener, and that conversation is always about being in the (imagined) world together, face to face.

Conversation is essential to the ethics and politics of storytelling. A narrative artist learns narrative as a child through the long and complex process of socialization that culminates in the passage through a threshold into adulthood, into citizenship. In this process we all learn the stories and imagine or reimagine our relationship to the adult world that lies so gloriously before us; we learn the elements of plot, character, and we master the art of conversation which forms links between the individual and the collective. In short, the child learns language by learning the strategies of dialogue with its roles of speaker and listener, its patterns of direct and indirect discourse, and the play of plotting with its hastening and retarding, its deviations and revisions.

In order to fully grasp this process, however, I will have to digress again, this time into the realm of language acquisition. We may describe the developmental process of language mastery as arranged in stages. I will describe a two-stage movement in which the child makes a transition from a simple, context-oriented conversation to a more complex and context-free conversation. M. A. K. Halliday describes the first stage as consisting of an interaction between a speaker (the child) and a listener (a parent or care-giver) and focusing on named objects present in the context of the conversation.[9] For example, the one-word statement "ball" indicates not merely a naming of a thing but a complex relationship that the child wishes to establish with the ball *and* the listener. We must understand that more is communicated than is actually voiced; the single term "ball" may mean, "See the ball," or "I want the ball," or "Give me the ball." All of these involve the listener with the speaker in an action oriented toward the object (the ball). Therefore, the child establishes relationships with the world of objects and persons.

There is a rudimentary narrative involved in this single statement, "ball," a story of expectations and desires within an emerging sense of the established rules of intercourse. The story might go something like this: "Mommy and I saw the ball together. I asked her to give it to me, and she did." The story situates a face-to-face relationship in the context of the facticity of the ball; it negotiates an interaction that defines roles (identities), expresses desires and anticipates satisfactions. The conversation/story places participants in the world, or in an imaginary (ideological) relationship to that world.

This story is not articulated on this preliminary level of conversation, but it will be spoken and elaborated in the second stage of developmental socialization or language acquisition. In this second stage Halliday describes a new element in the child's use of conversation; he calls this element "wording."[10] This is something like playing with words; for Halliday, it involves the sense that words can have more than one meaning, that language is context-free. This stage is crucial in that it signals the advent of symbolic play in the sense of the beginning of the entry into the symbolic realm inhabited by social narratives that are already spoken. There are several ways to express this idea: it allows the child to remember, anticipate, or even imagine situations like the one implicit in the single word statement above. Faulkner experimented with this threshold of entry into the symbolic in *The Sound and the Fury*, for Benjy clearly represents an arrested first-stage development. Benjy's language is trapped in a simple conversation where his crying expresses desire for a lost object, but through the device of stream of consciousness the reader listens to the far more complex, if unspoken, rudimentary narrative that Benjy's simple language implies. Benjy's consciousness exceeds his capacity for conversation, but his imaginary world is rich and meaningful if largely context-oriented. Quentin, on the other hand, has attained the context-free stage of narrative development, but has in the process lost contact with the context-oriented foundation of the developmental process. Quentin endlessly invents imaginary gardens for Caddy and himself, a narrative impulse that carries him too deeply into the merely playful world of "Let's pretend."

In a normal developmental progression the first stage remains embedded within the second as a kind of "reality principle." We use the term "imaginary" to describe the second stage, therefore, in the sense of producing images. In the second stage the capacity for time differentiation develops allowing the narrative game to break free of its dependence on the immediate presence of an object world or context-orientation. The emphasis of this more sophisticated stage of conversation shifts toward relationships and role-playing. The defining of roles is not innocent. Roles ground the child's social identity through dialogue and, ultimately, within the many voices of social polylogue. The "reality" of socially established limits to conversational exchange and interactive behavior can only be entered by means of this dialogue. Narrative and dialogue, Halliday argues, are "prerequisites to the effective functioning of language in the construction of reality."[11] In this function, language and narrative define how the world ought to work, thus providing the users of this language, the citizens, with a stable ground for predicting and judging human behavior. Though the developmental sequence leads away from the purely instrumental function of "Give me the ball," instrumentality, a description of an action in the world, a practical desire, remains vital in the dialogical constitution of reality. Again, according to Halliday, "conversational acts [are] . . . simultaneously both a reflection of and an action on reality."[12]

Literacy develops through gradual elaborations of conversation; in every conversation, moreover, the relationship of speaker and listener, the role-playing, is reimagined with regard to a "reality." No aspect of this is innocent of ideology, power, or ethical and political implications. Stories told by the parent to the child not only create worlds as models of social order (good guys and bad guys), but also define relations of authority and subordination in the structure of relations between teller and listener. As the child learns to tell stories herself, the power of commanding an audience is tried out, and the limits of that power are tested: what stories will the parent listen to and what will be denied, forbidden, repressed? The games of conversation and narration are a delicate structure of ethical and political relationships culminating in the establishing of a balance between ego and communal membership.

My discussion here barely suggests the complexity of the

psychosocial dimensions of language development within the social symbolic. At the base of this narrative situation, however, is an exchange which may best be described by what Emmanuel Levinas calls the "face to face."[13] Levinas suggests here an exchange that establishes the ethical foundations of all human interaction. The exchange between a child and her parent at the stage of language acquisition may range between the extremes of tyranny and anarchy, but within these limits a world of *personal* relationships is formed directed by the social symbolic and oriented toward the region of material existence that we signify by the term "body." To speak and to listen are distinct yet dependent functions; they raise the issues of the ethical right to speak and the ethical obligation to listen. The acquisition of language in conversation is never static, never fixed in a mystical or existential I-thou. The face to face with its ethical dynamics of speaking and listening springs from and returns to the socializing process of storytelling, of imagining relations within and to the real world.

Reality, of course, often seems already constituted, the story already told. That is the central problem for Quentin Compson in *Absalom, Absalom!* when dialogue, with its potential for dominance and represssion, with its uncovering of the "before" or the "ethical" implications of storytelling, explodes into a cacophony of voices. And what a glorious battle is *Absalom, Absalom!*, a thunderous disputation of phrases revising *facts* into myriad imaginative realities: Thomas Sutpen as the "demon," the Greek hero, the innocent, the violator of social taboos, and more beyond the novel as each new generation of readers takes up the fight. The question is not a matter of fact but of ethical relations in the face to face; the question for the reader is not who has the authority to speak or revise but what ethical demand compels one to listen to that which challenges our familiar realities.

Lyotard looks to the level of the phrase in language as the place of disputation because it is there that we hear the struggle for justice. But the play of phrases is much more than a clever use of words; it opens worlds of symbolic exchange, of ideologies embedded in stories told as constructions of reality. Perhaps an imagined relationship with the world (an ideological situation) is best revealed and critiqued by an imaginative representation of that world, particularly if the story is told by one who can listen as well as speak. This is, from my perspective within the postmodern denial of artistic genius, the only place where we can locate the narrative artist. It is the place of the eccentric which whirls out of the vortex of decentering. The peculiar genius of the imaginative storyteller is in hearing the already told and in envisioning how it may be retold in order to foreground the ethical and political. Is this an old romantic misreading of postmodern language games? Or may we see here a correction to a mistaken movement in our conception of language? It is better to ask if our new, postmodern sophistication with language has made us better consumers of stories, better citizens? Has not the retreat from the "before" which began in the seventeenth century and has now rendered the real world inaccessible, resulted in our being less literate as citizens, more subservient to the phrasemongers of our media-driven political society? Postmodernism has given us a diminished language competency, a new "paucity," for the word games of postmodernism satisfy only limited language needs. They cannot address the material needs of life; the endless play of symbols cannot overcome the effects of time on the body nor the consequences of scarcity on human suffering.

After this digression I am ready to return to the blank space in Addie Bundren's narrative. That space is the mark of a total breakdown of conversation, of ethical exchange; it seems to open to the place in the text where we might expect to find Addie's reprobate husband, Anse, whom she has symbolically erased by detaching his bodily presence from his name and then repressing that name. Faulkner reaches for more, however, for the act of erasure of "Anse" is also an act of liberation from being a character in someone else's story; it is a revision of the social symbolic, and an ending that Addie composes for her own life story, a last version of her imaginative relationship to her children, her husband, and her world. Addie's story, we should recall, insists on an accounting of what we have to call her body. The blank space in the text is, therefore, also the place of Addie's body, a body violated by Anse's body, by childbirth, by sin, by labor, and by the social symbolic that genders her and names her "Mrs. Bundren." We read in and through this hole in the text the transaction between symbolic orders and the body.

For Faulkner the modernist the body is the fact of facts, a truth or authenticity, a profound sense of existence that remains a mystery to words, that can be expressed only as an absence of a word. Yet this passage has for us a slightly different significance. It does not express the failure of the word to signify the real, but the fragile relationship between repressive ideology and human dignity, between desire and fulfillment, between marginalization and full participation in the political community, between repression and justice. Addie's story, the one she narrates, the eccentric story, is of hardship, neglect, exploitation, violence, and suffering registered on the body, her dying body that we cannot read as simply inaccessible. Her suffering is projected "before" the text since we read her version only after we read the already written stories of the other characters. These other versions use up her body signified as "Mrs. Bundren" and having used it dispose of it as rapidly as possible. There is, however, a dispute between Addie's story and the others, between two phrases, "I am Addie" and "You are Mrs. Bundren," which cannot be settled out of court. Addie's dying body will not go away and so the identities of Addie and Mrs. Bundren seem irreconcilable. An authorial intervention buries the matter in a symbolic act, and as Anse miraculously remarries on the very day of Addie's burial, the name "Mrs. Bundren" is attached to a different body. Yet Addie's resistance asks the readers to listen more closely to her story from the eccentric margins, to a story that cannot be erased by another Mrs. Bundren.

It is in the nature of societies to count bodies, to account for birth and death; much of language use is in the form of lists and indexes, even genealogies, which are elaborate accountings of bodies as well as relationships. Above all, the stories that express our imaginative relationships within and to our world must account for all bodies, those being born and those that die, and for all that is registered on those bodies in the course of lives, in the passage of time; the social narrative must account for the historical individual. The social narrative that fails to do so represses that which is "before" the text, and it is to this repression that Addie's blank space speaks with silent eloquence. It is a warning, for if we see only the disposable body within the social narrative of endlessly replaceable Mrs. Bundrens, if we do not read through the hole in the text to the place of Addie's body of suffering, we open the door to a play of violence the consequences of which we have yet to imagine.

This is the lesson of the postmodern. Words may well be unattached to things—even Faulkner's Addie argues that this is the case—but narratives phrase words in the production of social realities, imaginative relationships that order and value (or devalue) life. It is, to be sure, the imagination, somewhat in the old and forbidden sense, that passes back and forth through the threshold between words and things, gathering images from the wordless world of sensations and desires and arranging them in stories of triumph and failure, satisfaction and need. It is the imagination that tells of the historical individual and reveals the ethical consequences of narration itself. It is foolish for us to read the commonplace idea that words are not attached to things onto the register of narrative, for narrative is the production of imagined realities, stories that reside in the impossible interface of the symbolic and the experiential, of words and bodies. The symbolic is exactly what Derrida, and other postmoderns, say it is: an infinite structure of revision and substitution, the repository of all phrasing and narration, the production of facts. The symbolic is also the place of the blank spaces that decenter all narratives and disestablish all facts, yet as such it is also the condition of the eccentric's speech, of revision that is also critique. On the other hand, the body, like Addie's dying or Lucas's condemned to die, as the locus of pleasure and pain, is the consequence of the phrasing of facts and narration of ends. Only here can the ethical and political emerge in the demand that we listen to stories as if they mattered.

NOTES

1. William Faulkner, *As I Lay Dying* (New York: Random House, 1957), 165. Additional references to this novel will appear in the text.

2. Perry Anderson, *In the Tracks of Historical Materialism* (Chicago: University of Chicago Press, 1984), 42.

3. F. Scott Fitzgerald, *The Great Gatsby* (New York: Charles Scribner's Sons, 1953), 2.

4. William Faulkner, *Intruder in the Dust* (New York: The Modern Library, 1948), 32. Additional references to this novel will be given in the text.

5. Louis Althusser, "Ideology and Ideological State Apparatuses," *Lenin and Philosophy* (London: New Left Books, 1971), 164–165.

6. Jean-Francois Lyotard, *The "Differend," Phrases in Dispute* (Minneapolis: University of Minnesota Press, 1988).

7. I use the term "strange" here in the same sense as it is used by Judith Butler in *Gender Trouble* to describe the disruptive and deconstructive consequences of certain kinds of parodic performances. That which is strange is that which tests the limits of normalizing social categories, like the gender trouble expressed by drag or cross-dressing within a social context of rigidly binary, heterosexual identities.

8. William Faulkner, *Absalom, Absalom!* (New York: Modern Library, 1951), 134 and after.

9. M. A. K. Halliday, "The Social Construction of Reality," *Modes of Perceiving and Processing Information*, ed. Herbert L. Pick, Jr. and Elliot Saltzman (Hillsdale, N.J.: Lawrence Erlbaum Associates, 1978).

10. Ibid., 86.

11. Ibid., 87.

12. Ibid., 89.

13. Emmanuel Levinas, *Totality and Infinity*, trans. Alfonso Lingus (Pittsburgh: Duquesnes University Press, 1969), 39.

"Paradoxical and Outrageous Discrepancy": Transgression, Auto-Intertextuality, and Faulkner's Yoknapatawpha

MARTIN KREISWIRTH

Undoubtedly one of William Faulkner's great achievements as a literary artist is the creation of Yoknapatawpha, the extensive construct projected discursively from the fourteen or so novels and numerous short stories that deal specifically with his fictional Mississippi county. Constituted by the reader from the perceived interrelations of elements that appear in various texts by Faulkner, the fictional world of Yoknapatawpha is quite simply and clearly a product of intertextuality. Yet, what can we make of this claim? Despite various attempts to isolate or limit its use, *intertextuality* is an almost hopelessly baggy term. It has comfortably accommodated a wide range of practices, from primarily formalist text-centered inquiries, as conceptualized by M. M. Bakhtin, Julia Kristeva, and Roland Barthes, to those directed toward readers, as in the work of Michael Riffaterre. It has also done duty in author-centered inquiries—as in traditional influence or source studies—or those concerned with psychoanalytic agonistics, as in the writings of Harold Bloom.[1] Virtually all these approaches have been used to unravel, pick apart, and reweave Faulknerian textuality. For the last thirty years, from Richard Adams's 1962 study of Faulkner's apprentice borrowings to the 1985 volume on *Intertextuality and Faulkner*, edited by Michel Gresset and Noel Polk, right up to Michael Zeitlin's excellent paper in this volume ("*Pylon*, Joyce, and Faulkner's Imagination"), the intertextual flow into and out of the Faulknerian reservoir has become progressively wider and deeper, as new discursive boundaries are traversed (national, linguistic, historical, but also cultural and ideological), and as the textual features examined move outward from the level of the sign to the trope to the technique, and inward from deliberate borrowing (or what Faulkner called "theft"), to unconscious or perhaps even compulsive reiteration.[2]

In this paper I want to chart what I see as the principal channel of this large and diffuse waterway, the one that, if properly navigated, may lead directly to the heart of Faulkner's fictional county. I want to look at a manifestation of intertextuality that is a special province (and problem) of the Faulknerian canon, that is, the specific movements—transformations, absorptions, and "operative repetitions"—of elements from one Faulkner text to another. And I will attempt to provide a sketch of how this *auto-intertextuality*, as I want to call it, contributes to the particular configuration and reception of Faulkner's intertextually constituted domain, Yoknapatawpha (which is, incidentally, according to Faulkner, a Chickasaw word, meaning "water flowing slow through the flatland"[3]). Moreover, and perhaps more controversially, I want to show that this textual domain achieved its singular genesis and constitution not in *Flags in the Dust* ([1927/73] later called *Sartoris* [1929]), the first extensive projection of these regional materials, or even in the novels and stories that followed it (including *The Sound and the Fury* [1929], *As I Lay Dying* [1930], *Sanctuary* [1931], or *Light in August* [1932]), but rather, somewhat belatedly, in *Absalom, Absalom!* (1936). By both repeating and offering for repetition elements from other Faulkner texts while at the same time configuring a kind of transgressive auto-intertextuality within the various semi-permeable membranes of its own textual boundaries (those that separate the novel proper from the appended Chronology, Genealogy, and map), *Absalom, Absalom!* both engages in and provides a model for dealing with the discrepancies and contradictions that constitute Yoknapatawpha's peculiar textuality. And through its self-reflexive representation of the production and reception of narrative discourse, *Absalom, Absalom!* provides, as well, a model for transgressing or "overpassing" the peculiarly discordant configuration of this fictional world.

It is by now well accepted that Yoknapatawpha has its own intertextual prototypes, most notably in Thomas Hardy's Wessex and in Balzac's *Comédie Humaine*. As Malcolm Cowley, Cleanth Brooks, and Michael Millgate have pointed out, using what he called his "own little postage stamp of native soil" (*LG*, 255), Faulkner created, like Hardy, an isolated rural community, distanced geographically, economically, culturally, and ideologically from his predominantly urban readership; at the same time, he produced a kind of interlocking discursive structure, an "intact world" (*LG*, 217), where, like Balzac's but unlike Hardy's, narratives overlap, characters reappear, and there is significant cross-referencing between texts.[4]

Faulkner himself stated that what appealed to him in Balzac was the way in which the latter's characters traversed textual boundaries: they "don't just move from page one to page 320 of one book," Faulkner said in 1955, but rather contribute to a "continuity" that "flows from page one through to page 20,000 of one book" (*LG*, 217). He also occasionally spoke of his own achievement, the creation of his "cosmos," in similar terms, as the maintenance of a certain stable ground on which he could move his characters from one textual production to another. Here was the fictional assemblage of a common population, occupying a common region, sharing common customs, and participating in a common history.

Studies of Faulkner's auto-intertextuality, especially those dealing with the Yoknapatawpha novels, have tended to stress what we might term these recurrent semic, geographical, and ideological features, the reappearance of *existents* (characters and places) in different textual works. They have thus focused primarily on the level of the represented. But it is worth pointing out that Faulkner's intra-Yoknapatawphan repetitions also have been shown to operate at other semiotic and discursive levels, in reworkings, in different texts, of specific tropes, scenes, and rhetorical techniques, even, as I have shown elsewhere, in reiterations of specific narrative strategies—ways of opening and closing texts—and of structural proclivities, such as the use of an "empty center."[5] Taken together, these centripetal features of auto-intertextuality seem to reinforce the notion that the Yoknapatawpha novels make up a kind of supertext that reduplicates, on a higher plane, some of the various repetitions that form each of the individual works.

Yoknapatawphan intertextuality, in this view, is primarily a discursive mechanism for achieving the overarching design and "referential density"[6] that encompasses, in Faulkner's words, the "whole output or sum" (LG, 255) of his work. And critics who have advanced this position have naturally tended to foreground those intertextual elements that project comprehensiveness, totality, unity, and monologism. They thus valorize Faulkner's imaginative imperialism or hegemony, his insistence, at times, both rhetorically in the fictional texts and discursively in the interviews and letters, that Yoknapatawpha is indeed a consistent and harmonious, if fluid, fictional construct, a "whole world," as Michael Millgate puts it, that "seems to have remained perpetually alive and active in his imagination, as something quite apart from his capacity, as a time-bound human being, to realize that world on paper."[7] From this perspective, auto-intertextuality, intentionality, and integration merge to underwrite the kind of divine founding myth that Faulkner retroactively imposed upon his career in 1955: "Beginning with Sartoris I discovered that my own little postage stamp of native soil was worth writing about . . . and by sublimating the actual into apocryphal I would have complete liberty to use whatever talent I might have to its absolute top . . . so I created a cosmos of my own . . . I like to think of the world I created as being a kind of keystone in the Universe" (LG, 255).

This emphasis on the represented totality, on Yoknapatawphan wholeness and Faulkner's conscious imaginative control is, however, only half the story. It ignores the other side of

Faulknerian auto-intertextuality, the equally emphatic projection of discontinuity, heterogeneity, dialogism, and contingency. And it suppresses those elements that refuse to come together, those semiotic, rhetorical, and narrative maneuvers that leave fissures, gaps, and discrepancies, and point toward instability, indeterminacy, and otherness. It is not hard to show that Yoknapatawpha attempts to achieve a sustained totality at the metatextual level of the represented—in the fictional projection—while at the same exhibiting multiplicity and diversity at the level of representation, the level at which the projection takes place; here, textual production is governed by the juxtaposition of the different rather than the repetition of the same. Distinct or even disparate units or modes of discourse, it can be pointed out, are typically placed in dynamic interaction. Individual texts, for example, set up dialogues (1) between different narrative perspectives (as in the four distinct focalizers in *The Sound and the Fury* or the dizzying merry-go-round of points of view in *As I Lay Dying*); (2) between different styles (compare, for example, Rosa Coldfield's and Mr. Compson's modes of discourse in *Absalom, Absalom!*, or the linguistic registers of Ratliff's narration and that used to narrate the Ike Snopes episode of *The Hamlet* [1940]); (3) between different lines of action (the insular and only tangentially related plot strands that make up *Light in August*, and *Go Down, Moses* [1942], or the essentially incommensurable narratives in *The Wild Palms* [1939]); (4) between different genres (as in the mixing of dramatic and narrative forms in *Requiem for a Nun* [1951]); and, indeed, between different combinations of these various elements. Intratextual recurrence at this level emphasizes repetition with a difference rather than synthetic or homogenizing reiteration.

This equally strenuous and equally Faulknerian move away from coherence, decidability, and toward a constant dialogizing, oppositional or, as I want to argue, transgressive textual activity, is an obsessive copresence, working with and against the concomitant calls for semiotic or hermeneutic closure. There is no reason to rehearse further the manifold devices and strategies—linguistic, rhetorical, narratological, structural—that have become the hallmark of Faulknerian subversions and incongruities, except to recall that they tend to affect virtually every plane of Yoknapatawphan textuality. Faulkner is always breaking what Jacques Derrida has called the "law of genre," flaunting accepted conventions of narrative production and recuperation.[8] Indeed, what appears to be the most repeated intertextual feature in the Yoknapatawpha corpus is Faulkner's inability to play by the rules, to stay within boundaries—whether they be linguistic, syntactical, formal, generic, or textual.[9] In this sense, Yoknapatawphan textuality appears to be compulsively transgressive: no sooner is one element, feature, or structure stabilized or repeated, than another is destabilized and deformed. Each text sets limits whose horizons are traversed and problematized by the addition of other texts.

How are we to concretize the fictional cosmos of Yoknapatawpha from these discursive instabilities? Furthermore, how, are we to deal with the extra-textual "wild card," the profoundly unstable element of the specific texts read and their order of reception? While an individual novel may confront the reader with radically divergent blocks of materials, at least the sequence of these blocks is fixed. There is little to control the way in which we come to the novels and stories that we read in our own particular constructions of Yoknapatawpha—what determines what texts we read and in what sequence? At this level, the individual narrative blocks can assume multiple orders and serial arrangements, sometimes determined by choice, sometimes by chance, but in either case affecting Yoknapatawphan production.

An extension of Michel Foucault's thoughts on transgression may, I think, be helpful here. Foucault sees transgression as a mode of thinking productively unable to stabilize fundamental distinctions between self and other, sexual and sacred, interior and exterior, limit and limitlessness, language and silence. In his essay "A Preface to Transgression," Foucault explores the historical, philosophical, and linguistic implications of such thought in an examination of the relationships between sexuality, speech, and the death of God in the writings of the Marquis de Sade and Georges Bataille, and through this exploration to a contemplation of more general consequences that have relevance for divisions made between texts, genres, and discursive formations.[10]

Transgression, for Foucault, is not a conceptual activity governed by dialectic or even "contradiction" (about which he speculates elsewhere).[11] It "is an action," he writes, "which involves the limit, that narrow zone of a line where it displays the flash of its passage, but perhaps also its entire trajectory, even its origin; it is likely that transgression has its entire space in the line it crosses. The play of limits and transgression seems to be regulated by a simple obstinacy: transgression incessantly crosses and recrosses a line which closes up behind it in a wave of extremely short duration, and thus it is made to return once more right to the horizon of the uncrossable." Transgression implies a writing that is perpetually testing the limits of its own regularity; not for the sake of either stability or instability, but for a positive "contestation" of "values" that "carries them all to their limits."[12]

At the level of Yoknapatawphan textual production, narratively transgressive works themselves characteristically set up boundaries that are then traversed by other texts. For example, the narratively destabilized *Light in August*—where the disparate plot strands (murder and Joe Christmas, birth and Lena Grove) are constantly woven, unravelled, and then rewoven— achieves a certain measure of discursive stability when even more radically discordant forms, such as *The Wild Palms* or *Go Down, Moses*, invade the canon. These later texts engage in the transgressive activity of both broaching and extending the horizon of dialogically non-integrative plots by calling for even less coordinated narrative interplay, as seen in their own discursive strategies and in their workings in the larger auto-intertextual network. *The Wild Palms* is made up of alternating chapters of entirely discrete narratives that never come together (they deal with different characters in different times and places), while *Go Down, Moses* contains seven distinct narrative blocks, only some of which can be seen as connected (the book was originally published with the title *Go Down, Moses and Other Stories*, until Faulkner had it changed). *The Wild Palms, Go Down, Moses,* and indeed *Light in August,* as well, not only play at the textual threshold of generic definition (Are they sustained and coherent narratives? Are they textual wholes? Are they novels at all?) but also operate in the perpetually unstable zone where the borders of that larger discursive construct, Yoknapatawpha, are being simultaneously established and crossed. As Foucault's various speculations on the play of limits can be used to show, this kind of transgressive operation needs *both* the apparent textual boundaries of individual novels *and* the unstable boundarylessness of their represented interaction.

The transgressive process in Yoknapatawpha moves, if you will, in and out, up and down, as well as backwards and forwards, within and between Faulkner's texts: *Requiem for a Nun,* which, in part, "returns" to—and extends—characters, action, and language of *Sanctuary,* obviously alters the earlier text's liminal horizons, just as the two novels taken together force the traversal of *Requiem for a Nun*'s and Yoknapatawpha's textual frontiers. Viewed in this way, and from a great distance, the meta- or super-text of Yoknapatawpha thus appears less like a Balzacian "intact world" than a kind of profuse and multi-dimensional Faulkner novel, where the already unstable, textu-ally interactive blocks—the individual works—become them-selves discursive units in a higher order intertextual dialogue. This description of Yoknapatawpha as a form of transgressive textual activity can be seen, in some sense, as related to Gary Lee Stonum's notion of Faulkner's career as a kind of cybernetic self-regulating system, but without Stonum's insistence on over-riding coherence, comprehensiveness, and control.[13]

More to the point here is Joseph Urgo's recent reevaluation of Yoknapatawpha as an "apocrypha," to the use the term

Faulkner himself repeatedly used (as in the passage on the creation of Yoknapatawpha I cited earlier), rather than as a "saga" or "myth," the terms used by some of his critics. An "apocrypha" is a textual other, an alternative to orthodoxy and the canon; it necessarily exists as dialogic, multiple, inconsistent, and contradictory, and works against monologic authority and hegemony and against, as Urgo points out with particular reference to Yoknapatawpha, attempts to force it into an internally consistent, authoritative, canonical form (as in, say, Malcolm Cowley's attempt to integrate and contain Yoknapatawphan textuality in *The Portable Faulkner* [1946]).[14] Immediately following the passage on transgression quoted earlier, Foucault notes that the operation of incessantly crossing and recrossing a perpetually changing horizon is even more complex than his own description would allow, because "these elements are situated in an uncertain context, in certainties which are immediately upset so that thought is ineffectual as soon as it attempts to seize them."[15] An "apocrypha," unlike a saga, world, or even a cosmos, works precisely at this level of doubt, offering a profanely broken, uncertain discursive context, keeping the boundary between textual inside and outside productively mobile.

Foucault writes that the relationship between transgression and the limit on which it reciprocally depends and crosses is not binary or dialectic. It is "not related to the limit as black to white, the prohibited to the lawful, the outside to the inside." Rather, he continues, "their relationship . . . is like a flash of lightning in the night which . . . gives a dense and black intensity to the night it denies, which lights up the night from the inside, from top to bottom, and yet owes to the dark the stark clarity of its manifestation, its harrowing and poised singularity; the flash loses itself in this space it marks with its sovereignty and becomes silent now that it has given a name to obscurity."[16] There is, I think, something of this self-constituting yet disjunctive mutuality in Faulkner's use of the same figure in a 1957 interview to describe his original and ongoing conception of the Snopes trilogy, which comprises perhaps Yoknapataw-pha's most extended and intertextually resonant project.

The trilogy consists of *The Hamlet* (published in 1940, but conceived of and partly drafted under the title "Father Abraham" in 1926), *The Town* (published a month after the interview, in 1957), and *The Mansion* (published in 1959). Faulkner says that he "thought of the whole story at once like a bolt of lightning lights up a landscape and you see everything but it takes time to write it, and this story I had in my mind for about thirty years, and the one which I will do next—it happened at that same moment."[17] Reading this statement with Foucault's intertextual echoes in mind makes us aware, I think, not only of what critics have tended to stress, the instantaneous comprehensiveness of Faulkner's curiously "anachronic" vision of the "presence" of Yoknapatawpha; it also, and more importantly, opens up a transgressive space for the void upon which its specific energies depend—the blackness of the night, the "harrowing and poised" darkness, the absent other that is co-responsible for the flash of presence that participates in the defining instant by maintaining for the entire temporal duration its unformed "dense and black intensity."

The text or texts of the Snopes trilogy, like the other Yoknapatawphan productions, bear the marks of this destabilizing process not only in some of their larger rhetorical and structural features, of which I've already spoken, but at the most basic plane of linguistic signification—at the level of the sign itself. What I am referring to here are what might be seen, in a sense, as the purest, but decidedly most demanding, auto-intertextual transgressions—the contradictions and discrepancies in semantic details, in, for example, character's names and ages, in dates, places, and specifics of description that appear in different texts throughout the Yoknapatawpha corpus. To give just a few of the many examples that occur: Jack Houston's wife in *The Hamlet* is called Lucy Pate, in *The Town*, she's Letty Bookwright, in *The Mansion*, she goes unnamed; in *Sanctuary* Temple is eighteen when she is raped, in *Requiem for a Nun*, she's seventeen; in

Flags in the Dust, the itinerant sewing machine salesman is named V. K. Suratt, in *The Hamlet*, he's V. K. Ratliff; in *The Sound and the Fury*, the female Quentin climbs down a pear tree, in the appendix to that novel, she climbs down a rainpipe, and so on.[18]

Inconsistencies such as these cause disfunction at the level of the sign itself, the most fundamental and least plural level of semiotic and hermeneutic activity, the level at which we are least likely to admit divergence and undecidability, the level at which it is most difficult to break the rules, and where we tend to ask for editorial law enforcement. These types of incongruities foreground difference and otherness, and function, not as a flash of text-to-text linkage, but as its obscure obverse, transgressing the limits of intertextual repetition itself. Because of this, no doubt, these contradictions have generated a considerable amount of discussion, most crucially, perhaps, among those directly concerned with Yoknapatawpha's material productions, that is, Faulkner himself and his various editors and publishers, who have, not surprisingly, tended to focus on what we might term the multi-textual clusters: the *Snopes* trilogy (*The Hamlet, The Town*, and *The Mansion*), what Michael Millgate has called the "first trilogy" (*Flags in the Dust*—or *Sartoris*—*Sanctuary*, and *Requiem for a Nun*), Malcolm Cowley's *The Portable Faulkner* (a collection of stories and sections from the Yoknapatawpha novels that Cowley, with Faulkner's help, organized chronologically according to the represented fictional action), and those works that have extra-diegetic appendices, *The Sound and the Fury* (with the "Compson Appendix," written originally for *The Portable Faulkner*), and *Absalom, Absalom!* (with its Chronology, Genealogy, and map).

Since I am more interested here in Yoknapatawphan auto-intertextuality than in (admittedly intriguing) questions of intentionality,[19] it doesn't seem relevant to spend time going over the details of, say, Faulkner's exchanges with his editors and the minutia of the textual revisions, balks, reversals, rerevisions, and so on, except to point out that in almost every case, and despite occasionally desperate editorial urgings, Faulkner ended up letting certain textual discrepancies of this kind stand, even going so far, as in the case of the Snopes trilogy, as to provide a kind of public disclaimer or warning for them as a prefatory note to its third volume, *The Mansion*. "This note," Faulkner writes, "is simply to notify the reader that the author has already found more discrepancies and contradictions than he hopes the reader will—contradictions and discrepancies due to the fact that the author has learned, he believes, more about the human heart and its dilemma than he knew thirty-four years ago; and is sure that, having lived with them that long time, he knows the characters in this chronicle better than he did then."[20] Whatever might be said about this preface's valorization of motion and change and romantic faith in the growth of imaginative understanding, I think it is more significant for our purposes to note, first, that it occupies a problematic position as a *paratext*, attached to only one of the trilogy's volumes, and in itself thus immediately opens up the crux of its intertextual relations to its various contexts; second, that from this position at the edge of several textual boundaries it unsettles the issue of the represented fictional "existents," giving, as it were, the characters alluded to the curiously extra-textual ability to have contradictory "authoritative" representations; and, finally, that it, for whatever reasons, foregrounds rather than ignores, effaces or normalizes these auto-intertextual transgressions. In this last respect, as particular defining features of a certain discursive formation, these contradictions tend to resemble some of William Blake's similarly radical and problematic textual destabilizations (in the plates of *Jerusalem*, for example), which, as Jerome McGann effectively argues, create instrumental disfunctions that should not be erased, or gathered together "under an illusory synthesis," but seen, rather, as calling for certain specific responses on the part of the reader.[21]

Quite a number of such first-order discontinuities appear in *Absalom, Absalom!*, undoubtedly one of Faulkner's most transgressive texts, but also, I believe, the one most significant for setting up the particular warp and woof of Yoknapatawphan intertextuality. Within and between its own problematic textual boundaries—the chapters of the novel proper, on the one hand, and the Genealogy, Chronology, and map that appear as appendices, on the other—*Absalom, Absalom!* performs and models Yoknapatawpha's transgressive intertextuality. It also, through its representation of the paradoxes of discursive production and reproduction (in the dialogic interrelationship of the narrators and their transferential interpretive activities), performs and models the transgressive pragmatics of Yoknapatawphan reception.

Absalom, Absalom! was written during a period in Faulkner's career when the issue of auto-intertextual connection was becoming an increasingly important factor in the development of his *oeuvre*. In the months preceding his start on *Absalom, Absalom!* and during the long period of the writing itself, he began or revised a number of Yoknapatawphan projects, including early forms of *The Hamlet* and *Requiem for a Nun*, and some of the stories that would be included in *The Unvanquished* and *Go Down, Moses*. He had also recently gone over *The Sound and the Fury* in detail, marking the text, and writing several draft introductions for a projected three-color limited edition, which most likely contributed, in some way, to Quentin Compson's retextualization in the later work. He also spent a great deal of time looking over the various Yoknapatawpha short stories for a possible collection, and began to draft "A Golden Book of Jefferson and Yoknapatawpha," which, like the Genealogy of *Absalom, Absalom!* or the Compson Appendix, contained biographies of the region's inhabitants. During an imposed break from the difficulties of writing *Absalom, Absalom!*, moreover, he completed *Pylon*, a decidedly non-Yoknapatawphan novel, set in New Orleans, which, by its very absence of auto-intertextual connectives, may have, as well, brought these issues to the surface.[22] Finally, *Absalom, Absalom!*'s thematics of dynastic creation, of world-building ("Let there be Yoknapatawpha") is certainly also not irrelevant. Yet, I think it is the text's three addenda or appendices—the Chronology, Genealogy, and the map of Yoknapatawpha—and the formal relationship that is established between them and the narrative proper that is most crucial here. These addenda directly introduce intertextual materials from other Yoknapatawpha novels, from *The Sound and the Fury* in the Genealogy, for example, and from virtually every previous Yoknapatawpha text on the map; more importantly, they are placed both within and without the boundaries of the text, at the limits of the discursive unit, thus opening up a transgressive zone that provides Faulkner with an experimental space for the modelling of Yoknapatawpha's peculiar brand of stabilizing/destabilizing auto-intertextuality.[23]

The discrepancies between the narrative chapters and the appendices of *Absalom, Absalom!* have frequently been pointed out: in the body of the text we read, for example, that Judith and Charles Etienne de St. Velery Bon die of "yellow fever," the Chronology says they succumb to "smallpox"; the gravestone depicted in the narrative proper gives Ellen Coldfield Sutpen's dates as 1817–1863, the Chronology and Genealogy give them as 1818–1862; the main text indicates that Charles Bon was born in New Orleans, the Chronology says he was born in Haiti; and the earlier chapters indicate that Quentin Compson's and Rosa Coldfield's visit to Sutpen's Hundred occurred in September 1909, while the Chronology dates the visit as September 1910, which, of course, also profoundly contradicts *The Sound and the Fury*, which insists that Quentin died June 2 1910.[24] Like what might now be termed "classical" Derridian *aporias*, these base level auto-intertextual incongruities appear in the textual margins—in the Chronology and Genealogy; they function, however, as I've been arguing, not just to point up semantic and rhetorical indeterminacies that unravel attempts at homogenizing closure for this text, but to produce and indeed model precisely the transgressive activity that underwrites the whole of Yoknapatawphan intertextuality itself. In this way, the particular sign or trace that points up the hermeneutic disfunction and semiotic noise is not as important as the fact that it produces such disfunction; the destabilizing contradiction itself thus operates positively as a sign and accomplishes its work. Specific meaning is thus subordinated to its performative transgression.

While revising *The Mansion*, Faulkner told his editor, in what had by then become a characteristic response, that if consistency was to be striven for in this, the Snopes trilogy's final text, the earlier two (*The Hamlet* and *The Town*) should be the ones made to conform. He then added: "Unless of course the discrepancy is paradoxical and outrageous."[25] It is the interpretive violence of the transgressive contradiction that is important, not the particular channel that it disrupts. Yoknapatawpha requires the paradoxical and outrageous discrepancy that challenges representation as well as the potentially connecting recurrence of the represented to activate both the seesawing repetition/contradiction of the auto-intertextuality and the transgression that keeps it mobile.

At moments such as these the logic of the sign is poised at the limit of signification, tracing the line of foam (to borrow Foucault's metaphor) at the shifting horizon of textual boundaries. The subversive energies of these constantly changing forces do not deconstruct Yoknapatawphan textuality, do not open it up to a limitless, arepresentational realm, but rather only slightly displace it, reconfiguring it and the conventions by which it is received. By maintaining a transgressive context of intertextual connection *and* its disruption, Yoknapatawpha, it seems to me, moves slightly away from the world-creating of fiction and toward the curiously less stabilized domain of historical discourse, whose constitutive representations of past actualities— whose "facts," that is—are constrained by referential rather than purely textual or aesthetic conventions.

What I mean here is that the language of doubt and discrepancy that Yoknapatawpha tactically exhibits is a discursive effect of factual statements—such as those that make up historiography—not of those that are constituted solely by authorial fiat in fictional constructs. It is the discourse of history that must deal with the possibility of contradictory signification at the level of the sign. Without the fictional authority to set a limit, the represented fact can only be stabilized by lining it up with other corroborating representations. Yet, to place such nonfictive contradictions within an extensive and overarching context of fictional discourse, as Yoknapatawpha strategically does, pushes at the limit of fictional and nonfictional discursive formations, transgressively partaking, to some degree, in the interpretative conventions of both forms.[26] If, as Faulkner states, the artist who creates this world becomes "like a god," it is not so much because he can "move these people around in space and time" within a comprehensive and coherent construct; rather it is because his texts project a self-contradictory plenitude that denies ultimate coherence, performatively inviting responses that perpetually cross the borders between fiction and history.[27] An imaginative "cosmos"[28] that actively calls for interpretative discrepancy is, one might argue, more like "*the* world" than "*a* world," and, to continue the underlying generative metaphor, its creator, paradoxically, more godlike because of his discrepancies, insufficiencies, and "failures."

In discussing the possibility of Egyptian influence and corruptions of the Bible in *Moses and Monotheism*, Sigmund Freud points out the "noticeable gaps, disturbing repetitions and obvious contradictions" which he sees as having come about during the process of textual transmission. "In its implications," he goes on, "the distortion of a text resembles a murder: the difficulty is not in perpetrating the deed, but in getting rid of its traces." This distortion [*Entstellung*], he notes, has a "double meaning": it signifies "not only 'to change the appearance of something' but also 'to put something in another place, to displace.' " "Accordingly," Freud continues, "in many instances of textual distortion, we may nevertheless count upon finding what has been suppressed and disavowed hidden away somewhere else, though changed and torn from its context."[29] In Yoknapatawphan intertextuality, distortion—particularly as intertextual displacement—is suppressed, disavowed and hidden between or at the edges of texts, at the same time as it actively participates in its discursive construction and pragmatics of reception. As in *Absalom, Absalom!*, the novel that contains Faulkner's most significant meditation on textual production, interpretation, and reception, the reader (somewhat like the novel's interactive narrators) must ultimately confront hermeneutic incoherence: small pox or yellow fever? or, to extend the issue, pear tree or rainpipe? These irresolvable base-level contradictions are not ambiguities, not interpretive irregularities, but textual instabilities, and signify, like Freud's distortions, that something always will be suppressed, disavowed, and hidden away. The murder, either of Freud's text or indeed of Charles Bon, may not be able to be solved; the traces or clues can only be placed within that larger "marriage of speaking and hearing . . . where," as is stated in *Absalom, Absalom!*, "there might be paradox and inconsistency but nothing fault nor false."[30] For Yoknapatawphan intertextuality, the false and the fault are not errors or discrepancies but performatives. And what they perform is transgression—textual, semiotic, and generic—which calls on the reader to engage in a certain kind of transgressive interpretative activity, a transferential "overpassing," itself poised in a zone between intertextual limits. What might be false and fault would be a kind of reading (which, I guess, would include a kind of editing) that ignored or stabilized contradiction, paradox, and transgression, that "overpassed" difference, otherness, and the "apocryphal," that searched for a field of unified "fictional" illumination rather than for uncanny and contingent flashes of "actual" lightning.

NOTES

1. An introduction to this vast subject (in English) might include: Mikhail M. Bakhtin, "Discourse in the Novel," *The Dialogic Imagination*, ed. Michael Holquist, trans. Caryl Emerson and Michael Holquist (Austin: University of Texas Press, 1981), 259–422, "The Problem of the Text in Linguistics, Philology, and the Human Sciences," *Speech Genres and Other Late Essays*, ed. Caryl Emerson and Michael Holquist, trans. Vern W. McGee (Austin: University of Texas Press, 1986), 103–21; Roland Barthes, "The Death of the Author," trans. Stephen Heath, *Image, Music, Text* (New York: Hill and Wang, 1977), 142–48, "From Work to Text," *Image, Music, Text*, 155–64, S/Z, trans. Richard Miller (New York: Hill and Wang, 1974), *The Pleasure of the Text*, trans.

Richard Miller (New York: Hill and Wang, 1975); Harold Bloom, *The Anxiety of Influence: A Theory of Poetry* (New York: Oxford University Press, 1973), *A Map of Misreading* (New York: Oxford University Press, 1975); Linda Hutcheon, "Literary Borrowing . . . And Stealing: Plagiarism, Sources, Influences, and Intertexts," *English Studies in Canada* 12 (1986): 229–39; Julia Kristeva, *Desire in Language: A Semiotic Approach to Literature and Art*, trans. Thomas Gora, Alice Jardine, and Leon Roudiez (New York: Columbia University Press, 1980), *Revolution in Poetic Language*, trans. Margaret Waller (New York: Columbia University Press, 1984); Owen Miller, "Intertextual Identity," *Identity of the Literary Text*, ed. Mario J. Valdés and Owen Miller (Toronto: University of Toronto Press, 1985), 19–40; Thäis E. Morgan, "Is There an Intertext in This Text?: Literary and Interdisciplinary Approaches to Intertextuality," *American Journal of Semiotics* 3 (1985): 1–40; Michael Riffaterre, "Interpretation and Undecidability," *New Literary History* 12 (1981): 227–42, "The Making of the Text," *Identity of the Literary Text*, ed. Mario J. Valdés and Owen Miller (Toronto: University of Toronto Press, 1985), 54–70, *Semiotics of Poetry* (Bloomington: University of Indiana Press, 1978), "Syllepsis," *Critical Inquiry* 6 (1980): 625–38, "Intertextual Representation: On Mimesis as Interpretive Discourse," *Critical Inquiry* 11 (1984): 141–62, *Text Production*, trans. Terese Lyons (New York: Columbia University Press, 1983). Also see Michael Worton and Judith Sill, *Intertextuality: Theories and Practices* (Manchester: Manchester University Press, 1990); Heinrich F. Plett, *Intertextuality* (Berlin: Walter de Gruyter, 1991); Jay Clayton and Eric Rothstein, "Figures in the Corpus: Theories of Influence and Intertextuality," *Influence and Intertextuality in Literary History* (Madison: University of Wisconsin Press, 1991), 3–36; Jonathan Culler, "Presupposition and Intertextuality," *The Pursuit of Signs: Semiotics, Literature, Deconstruction* (Ithaca: Cornell University Press, 1981), 100–118; and John Frow, "Intertextuality," *Marxism and Literary History* (Cambridge: Harvard University Press, 1986), 125–69.

2. Richard P. Adams, "The Apprenticeship of William Faulkner," *Tulane Studies in English* 12 (1962): 113–56; *Intertextuality in Faulkner*, ed. Michel Gresset and Noel Polk (Jackson: University Press of Mississippi, 1985); Michael Zeitlin, "*Pylon*, Joyce, and Faulkner's Imagination," in this volume. The studies dealing with intertextuality and Faulkner, in all its forms, are simply too numerous to mention.

3. William Faulkner, *Lion in the Garden: Interviews with William Faulkner, 1926–1962*, ed. James B. Meriwether and Michael Millgate (New York: Random House, 1968), 134; subsequently abbreviated *LG*.

4. See, e.g., Malcolm Cowley, "Introduction," *The Portable Faulkner* (New York: Viking, 1946), 1–24, and Cleanth Brooks, *The Yoknapatawpha Country* (New Haven: Yale University Press, 1963), *passim*, for the earliest discussions of the "world" of Yoknapatawpha. These extremely important critics argued that the Yoknapatawpha novels created a comprehensive "myth" or "saga"; their studies influenced an entire generation of Faulkner critics. Also see, e.g., Michael Millgate, *Thomas Hardy: His Career as a Novelist* (New York: Random House, 1971), 345–50, for the specific relationships between Yoknapatawpha and Wessex, and Roxandra V. Antoniadis, "Faulkner and Balzac: The Poetic Web," *Comparative Literature Studies* 9 (1972): 303–25, for those between Yoknapatawpha and the *Comédie Humaine*.

5. Martin Kreiswirth, "Centers, Openings, and Endings: Some Faulknerian Constants," *American Literature* 56 (1984): 38–50, rpt. in *On William Faulkner: The Best from American Literature*, ed. Louis J. Budd and Edwin H. Cady (Durham: Duke University Press, 1990), 201–14.

6. "Referential density" is a crucial component for postulating fictional worlds; see Thomas Pavel, *Fictional Worlds* (Cambridge: Harvard University Press, 1986), 101.

7. Michael Millgate, " 'A Cosmos of My Own': The Evolution of Yoknapatawpha," *Fifty Years of Yoknapatawpha*, ed. Doreen Fowler and Ann J. Abadie (Jackson: University Press of Mississippi, 1980), 38–39.

8. Jacques Derrida, "The Law of Genre," *Critical Inquiry* 7 (1980): 55–81.

9. This "formal inventiveness" and "ruthlessness toward his own prior inventions," Richard H. Brodhead notes, connect Faulkner to his great predecessors in American

fiction: Melville, James, and even Whitman and Emerson ("Introduction: Faulkner and the Logic of Remaking," *Faulkner: New Perspectives*, ed. Richard H. Brodhead [Englewood Cliffs, N.J.: Prentice-Hall, 1983], 6–7).

10. Michel Foucault, "A Preface to Transgression," *Language, Counter-Memory, Practice: Selected Essays and Interviews*, ed. Donald F. Bouchard, trans. Donald F. Bouchard and Sherry Simon (Ithaca: Cornell University Press, 1977), 29–52. Foucault appropriated the term *transgression* from Georges Bataille (primarily from *Eroticism*) and put it to his own uses; it has now, in turn, become appropriated, elaborated, and placed in new contexts. In the following discussion I use transgression less as a description of metaphysical (or indeed physical) than of linguistic relationships; on Foucault and transgression, see Simon During, *Foucault and Literature: Towards a Genealogy of Writing* (New York: Routledge, 1992), 7–8, 80–84. During notes that Foucault's use of *transgression* "commits some violence on Bataille's thought" (83); in the same spirit, I commit some violence on Foucault's thought. Also see Charles C. Lemert and Garth Gillan, *Michel Foucault: Social Theory and Transgression* (New York: Columbia University Press, 1982); and John Rajchman, *Michel Foucault: The Freedom of Philosophy* (New York: Columbia University Press, 1985), chapter 1.

11. See Foucault, "A Preface to Transgression," 37, n. 18.

12. Foucault, "A Preface to Transgression," 33–34, 36.

13. Gary Lee Stonum, *Faulkner's Career: An Internal Literary History* (Ithaca: Cornell University Press, 1979). Probably the most interesting and useful speculations on the development of Yoknapatawpha and Faulkner's career can be found in Michael Millgate's various essays on the creation of Faulkner's fictional world; see, e.g., " 'A Cosmos of My Own': The Evolution of Yoknapatawpha," *Fifty Years of Yoknapatawpha*, 23–43, "Faulkner's First Trilogy: *Sartoris, Sanctuary*, and *Requiem for a Nun*," *Fifty Years of Yoknapatawpha*, 90–109, and "William Faulkner: The Shape of a Career," *New Directions in Faulkner Studies*, ed. Doreen Fowler and Ann J. Abadie (Jackson: University Press of Mississippi, 1984), 18–36.

14. Joseph Urgo, *Faulkner's Apocrypha: "A Fable," "Snopes," and the Spirit of Human Rebellion* (Jackson: University Press of Mississippi, 1989), chapter 1.

15. Foucault, "A Preface to Transgression," 34.

16. Ibid., 35.

17. William Faulkner, *Faulkner in the University: Class Conferences at the University of Virginia, 1957–1958*, ed. Frederick L. Gwynn and Joseph L. Blotner (Charlottesville: University of Virginia Press, 1959), 90.

18. On the relationship of these contradictions to a developing concept of the hero in the Yoknapatawphan fiction, see James B. Carothers, "The Myriad Heart: The Evolution of the Faulkner Hero," *"A Cosmos of My Own": Faulkner and Yoknapatawpha*, ed. Doreen Fowler and Ann J. Abadie (Jackson: University Press of Mississippi, 1981), 252–83.

19. For an interesting discussion of Faulkner's relationship to the auto-intertextual world created by his fictional discourse, see Philip M. Weinstein, *Faulkner's Subject: A Cosmos No One Owns* (Cambridge: Cambridge University Press, 1993).

20. Faulkner, *The Mansion* (New York: Random House, 1959), [xi].

21. Jerome J. McGann, "William Blake Illuminates the Truth," *Towards a Literature of Knowledge* (Oxford: Clarendon Press, 1989), 9–37.

22. See, e.g., Joseph Blotner, *Faulkner: A Biography*, 2 vols. (New York: Random House, 1974), chapters 39–43; Elizabeth Muhlenfeld, "Introduction," *William Faulkner's "Absalom, Absalom!": A Critical Casebook* (New York: Garland, 1984), xi–xxxix; and David Paul Ragan, "Introduction," *William Faulkner's "Absalom, Absalom!": A Critical Study* (Ann Arbor: UMI Research Press, 1987), 1–18.

23. From a rather different perspective, Weinstein has also recently argued that *Absalom, Absalom!* is the pivotal text in Faulkner's career, one contributing specifically to the kind of textuality that produces "a cosmos no one owns" (*Faulkner's Subject*).

24. Much has been written on the intriguing and problematic relationship between the appendices (the Chronology, Genealogy, and map) and the preceding text of

Absalom, Absalom!. See, e.g., Duncan Aswell, "The Puzzling Design of *Absalom, Absalom!*," *Kenyon Review* 30 (1968): 67–84; Pamela Dalziel, *"Absalom, Absalom!*: The Extension of Dialogic Form," *Mississippi Quarterly* 65 (1992): 277–94; Daniel Ferrer, "Editorial Changes in the Chronology of *Absalom, Absalom!*: A Matter of Life and Death?" *The Faulkner Journal* 5 (1989): 45–49; Michael Millgate, "The Unending of *Absalom, Absalom!*," unpub. paper, Modern Language Association Conference (1986); Susan Resneck Parr, "The Fourteenth Image of the Blackbird: Another Look at Truth in *Absalom, Absalom!*," *Arizona Quarterly* 35 (1979): 153–64; Robert Dale Parker, "The Chronology and Genealogy of *Absalom, Absalom!*": The Authority of Fiction and the Fiction of Authority," *Studies in American Fiction* 14 (1986): 191–98; and David Paul Ragan, *William Faulkner's "Absalom, Absalom!": A Critical Study*, 13, 164–65. Also see, Cleanth Brooks, *William Faulkner: The Yoknapatawpha Country*, 424–26; Gerald Langford, *Faulkner's Revision of "Absalom, Absalom!": A Collation of the Manuscript and the Published Book* (Austin: University of Texas Press, 1971), 11, 32–33, 38; Michael Millgate, *The Achievement of William Faulkner* (New York: Random House, 1966), 323–24; Elizabeth Muhlenfeld, "Introduction," *William Faulkner's "Absalom, Absalom!": A Critical Casebook*, xxxii–xxxiii; and Noel Polk, "Introduction," *William Faulkner Manuscripts 13: "Absalom, Absalom!" Typescript Setting Copy and Miscellaneous Material* (New York: Garland, 1987), x–xii.

25. William Faulkner, letter to Albert Erskine (received March 12, 1959), *Selected Letters of William Faulkner*, ed. Joseph Blotner (New York: Random House, 1977), 426.

26. For a rather different, Marxist-oriented discussion of the relationship between textual contradiction and the discourse of history, specifically in *Absalom, Absalom!*, see Leon S. Roudiez, *"Absalom, Absalom!*: The Significance of Contradictions," *The Minnesota Review* 17 (1981): 58–78.

27. Faulkner also crosses this line by indicating, in the Genealogy, that Shreve, a fictional character, a product solely of linguistic and discursive projection, "is now a practising surgeon, Edmonton, Alta." On this point, see Dalziel, *"Absalom, Absalom!*: The Extension of Dialogic Form," 291–92.

28. In "Faulkner's Cosmos and the Incarnation of History in *Light in August*" (*Rewriting the South: History and Fiction*, ed. Lothar Hönninghausen and Valeria Gennardo Lerda [Tübingen and Basil: Franke Verlag, 1993], 324–34) Thomas L. McHaney shows that Faulkner's conception of Yoknapatawpha as a "cosmos" is based on an understanding of the past, of history; McHaney, however, emphasizes the underlying, lawlike order of history, not the inevitable contradictions of historical representation. There are numerous discussions of *Absalom, Absalom!* and the problematics of history; see, e.g., Colleen E. Donnelly, "Compelled to Believe: Historiography and Truth in *Absalom, Absalom!*," *Style* 25 (1991): 104–22; and Carl Rollyson, "The Re-Creation of the Past in *Absalom, Absalom!*," *Mississippi Quarterly* 29 (1976): 361–74.

29. Sigmund Freud, *The Standard Edition of the Complete Psychological Works of Sigmund Freud*, ed. and trans. James Strachey et al. (London: Hogarth Press, 1964), 23:43.

30. William Faulkner, *Absalom, Absalom!: The Corrected Text* (New York: Vintage, International Edition, 1990), 253.

Pylon, Joyce, and Faulkner's Imagination

MICHAEL ZEITLIN

*Yet this sphinx has its secret and keeps it closely, a secret
whose answer even it does not know . . .*
            —REYNOLDS PRICE, Introduction to *Pylon*

And yet Pylon *may well provide us with the key to
Faulkner's imagination.*
            —MICHEL GRESSET, *Fascination*

Pylon is the most elusive of Faulkner's novels, the one most
likely to disorient even experienced Faulknerians. Perhaps in
compensation we have attempted to establish its place in the
oeuvre: the novel has generally been considered an anomalous
minor work, abrupting with bizarre effect upon the scene of
Faulkner's suspended narrative, *A Dark House*, the one to
which Faulkner would return after *Pylon* and bring to comple-
tion under the new title, *Absalom, Absalom!* But why *Pylon* (of
all things), there, then, at *that* moment in Faulkner's career?
Faulkner's well-known explanation is not as illuminating as one
might wish: "I wrote that book," Faulkner said at the University
of Virginia in 1957, "because I'd got in trouble with *Absalom,
Absalom!* and I had to get away from it for a while so I thought
a good way to get away from it was to write another book, so I
wrote *Pylon*. . . . It seemed to me interesting enough to make a
story about, but that was just to get away from a book that
wasn't going too well, till I could get back at it."[1] As we have
come to expect of all such public accounts of his own creativity,
Faulkner's anecdote promises its usual quota of truth even as it
offers an obviously reductive and incomplete solution to one of
the most complex and unaccountable scenes of his writing.

To be sure, there is no reason to deny that, in one important sense, *Pylon* may actually be the book Faulkner said it was, the one he wrote, in Cleanth Brooks's paraphrase, as an "escap[e] . . . from the special problems of writing *Absalom, Absalom!*"[2] But the prevailing assumption inherent in the act of framing the novels in this way is that *Pylon* is less a "major" work of imagination in its own right than a peculiar warm-up exercise to another book—the book, in fact—against which *Pylon* must always be defined as radically inferior. As Judith Wittenberg once put it (in a valuable discussion of the novel, I should add), "[*Pylon*'s] major importance is as a precursor of Faulkner's masterpiece, *Absalom, Absalom!* . . . . the disparity between the effectiveness of these novels is [therefore] mysterious, for they were written during the same period of time in virtual counterpoint." A similar sense of disparity impels John Duvall to categorize the novel before he can go on to grant it serious (and illuminating) attention: *Pylon*, writes Duvall, is "Non-Yoknapatawpha, atypical, secondary, and supplemental," terms which, long affixed to the novel in one form or another, have tended to constrain and prefigure what might be said or discovered about its potent forms of narrative imagination.[3]

In the interest of helping to shake *Pylon* free of the stigma of the minor and the secondary, I raise, then, these questions: How clearly can *Pylon* itself be seen if we leave it tucked in under the shadow of *Absalom, Absalom!*? How fully can *Pylon* be appreciated if our attention remains divided and perhaps intimidated by the imposing moral presence of that great work? Or, putting it still another way, how, as critics of *Pylon*, can we hope to hit the ball if we come up to the plate with one eye on Babe Ruth? In attempting to grasp more of what *Pylon* actually accomplishes, I'll proceed from the premise that, for the most part, we have been too rapid and too confident in understanding the meaning of *Pylon* within Faulkner's overall thinking as an artist in the year 1934; that if we wish to keep pace with *Pylon*'s rapid and peculiar logic, we need to read the novel more slowly (one cannot read it too slowly); and that there is still much to be discovered about the book, especially when we set it within the various literary and cultural contexts of what Faulkner called his "contemporary scene." An early and important essay on the book, Donald Torchiana's "*Pylon* and the Structure of Modernity," attempted to do this.[4] More recently, Karl Zender and John Matthews have found rich meanings in the book by treating *Pylon* and its author as fully "embedded . . . in the economic and social conflicts of [their] times."[5] Here I want to suggest that *Pylon*'s engagement with its contemporary history is both mediated and enabled by its implication in a network of literary (as well as cultural and social) texts, especially, in this case, James Joyce's *Ulysses*. As Joseph Blotner has pointed out in his catalogue of Faulkner's library, Faulkner owned a copy of the book (Paris: Shakespeare & Co., 1924) which he inscribed, "William Faulkner/ Rowan Oak. 1924."[6] I stress the specific text of literary and biographical history at the outset, for it gives basic support to my initial act of interpretation: the setting of *Pylon* and *Ulysses* for purposes of contrast and comparison within the same analytical frame.

Immediately that act invokes the contesting assumptions of two formally opposed (but perhaps not finally incompatible) theoretical paradigms, with respect to which I should attempt briefly to locate my own comparative approach.[7] On the one hand, there is the notion of influence, and its fundamental concern with the artist's creative process. On the other hand, there is the notion of intertextuality, a term advanced by Julia Kristeva to characterize what she has called the "anonymous" and "impersonal" intersection of linguistic surfaces constituting textuality itself. With its stress on impersonality, the critical discourse of intertextuality would tend to efface or neutralize the terminology and assumptions of any "influence study," for which author, agency, source, origin, biography, reference, meaning, intention, etc., must be fundamental concepts and categories of literary analysis. In the purest poststructuralist notion of intertextuality, the author of a literary text must remain ambiguous if not irrelevant in his or her basic ontological terms, a figure dispersed into his or her own discourse and so fundamentally inaccessible except as a series of "traces," traces promising at best only the mirage or perhaps the hallucination of authorial presence.

In Kristeva's model, that is, neither authors nor originating subjects but language itself is the principal agency of intertextual process: "the notion of intertextuality replaces that of intersubjectivity."[8] In the intertextual theory of Roland Barthes and Jacques Lacan, equally it is language, not the author or ego, "which speaks," and so (in their view) it would be vain or simply misguided to seek in literary texts the contours of a "person-to-person" relationship of influence. Writes Barthes, "The intertextuality in which any text is apprehended, since it is itself the intertext of another text, cannot be identified with some *origin* of the text: to seek out the 'sources,' the 'influences' of a work is to satisfy *the myth of filiation* [my emphasis]; the quotations a text is made of are anonymous, irrecoverable, and yet *already read*; they are quotations without quotation marks."[9]

The myth of filiation: Naturally, such a conception of anonymous, sourceless, unaffiliated intertextuality would more or less rule out the comparative analysis I am interested in pursuing here, which proceeds from the unremarkable assumption that Faulkner read, rewrote, and "cathected" other texts, and that the signatures of such (intersubjective) intertextual contact can be identified and interpreted by analysis. Hence I need the notion of influence in order to make intelligible what is not simply a literary but also in important respects a historical and psychological inquiry into the relative "positionalities" of culturally situated texts and subjects, and hence into what might be called the element of historicity inherent in the meanings generated by *Pylon's* "absorption and transformation" of parts of *Ulysses*. But I also need to retain Kristeva's sense of intertextuality in order to follow through on the acknowledgment that literary relationships imply not only "lines" of dyadic transmission, spanning subjects and linking aspects of a literary tradition, but also wider "nets" of interconnecting cultural discourses generally (Faulkner's term for this was "the pollen of ideas"). The point, then, would be not to "reduce" *Pylon* to certain underlying patterns of signification implicit in a postulated scene of reading and rewriting (Faulkner at his desk with a copy of *Ulysses* and the unfolding manuscript of *Pylon*). Rather, it would be to stress that such unmistakable patterns are incorporated within that "something wider" which is signalled by the term intertextuality in its broadest sense: any given pair of communicating texts is also entangled with "myriad" other historical and contemporary texts and contexts, hence its fundamentally "overdetermined" and problematically "mixed" nature.

In what follows I shall focus on intertextuality's dynamic principle: as Kristeva has put it, "any text is the absorption and transformation of another,"[10] a formulation indispensable to my own conception of what the text of *Pylon* actually is—to how, as a text, it may be said to "act" or "perform" in relation to the text *Ulysses*. If, however, I compare the texts of Faulkner and Joyce, it is not primarily in this case to examine the multiple interconnections of language *per se*. Rather, it is to signal *Faulkner's* imaginative work of affiliation, imitation, and revision; *his* reading, rewriting, and transformation of Joyce's text in an intense, playful, and sometimes polemical process of "dialogue, parody, and contestation;"[11] borrowing, imitation, and "theft" (perhaps Faulkner's favorite word in this context)— and all the other as yet uncatalogued let alone exhausted ways in which an author can engage any other author's work.

In other words, I invite "the return of the . . . historically specific [authorial] subject into the discourse of intertextuality."[12] The return of the author: or perhaps, as André Bleikasten has noted, the author has been there all along: " 'the death of the author,' periodically reannounced since Mallarmé, has not laid his ghost to rest."[13] I would suspect that among Faulkner's readers in this room, for example, a more or less insistently felt presence, a more or less biographically informed idea, a more or less emotionally charged image of William Faulkner helps inform one's grasp of the rich and complex and shifting meanings of his texts. One deploys an idea of the author in order to orient and give shape to what would otherwise be the radical and one suspects relatively empty interpretive freedom posited by the insistent literal claims of the poststructuralist ethos: "boundless" or "borderless" texts; "endless" trace, dissemination, *différance*; "infinitely expanding" contexts of intertextuality.[14] As Fredric Jameson has polemically written,

> I suspect, indeed, that there are only a finite number of interpretive possibilities in any given textual situation, and that the program to which the various contemporary ideologies of pluralism are most passionately attached is a largely negative one: namely to forestall th[e . . .] articulation [of . . .] interpretive results which can only lead to embarrassing questions about [. . .] the place of history and the ultimate ground of narrative and textual production.[15]

"The place of history and the ultimate ground of narrative and textual production": in one important and unmistakable sense, this metaphor of the "ultimate ground" must also imply the active, creative, and *laboring* human subject in history, William Faulkner, who must be given a place in our minds as the artist and prime mover of his text, as a "discharge of mental energy," and as what Eliot called "a particular [discursive] medium . . . in which impressions and experiences combine in peculiar and unexpected ways."[16]

PYLON, PYLON!

Having cleared, perhaps, a little theoretical space for myself, I am ready to proceed with my proper argument, which begins with what many critics have identified as the central irritating feature of *Pylon*, a feature which in this case the critics do not hesitate in linking directly with the figure of an author, his choices and intentions. This would be Faulkner's apparently imitative, stylized, and unaccountable return to the twin pylons of modernism, Eliot and Joyce, as he composed his weird novel about New Valois, Franciana, and airplane racing. Reynolds

Price has given one of the most extravagant and entertaining of all such complaints:

> Any tenth-grader can see, at first glance, what its weaknesses are—the willful havoc with grammar and spelling, the homemade artiness (the resort to Eliot and Shakespeare in chapter titles, the tired stream of unilluminating compounds and obstructive neologisms, which even in 1935 must have been old hat); the flirtation with objects and events which appear to be gathering emblematic functions but which finally are abandoned, unemblematic debris. . . .[17]

That is why, as we have already noted, for Price *Pylon* is a sphinx. Indeed, from the first sentence onward, the language—in its very look and sound—calls attention to itself as a riddle to be solved: "For a full minute Jiggs stood before the window in a light spatter of last night's confetti lying against the windowbase like spent dirty foam, lightpoised on the balls of his greasestained tennis shoes, looking at the boots."[18] In a recent essay John Matthews situates the general play of Faulkner's language in *Pylon* within the context of the novel's "carnival material," which threatens to "unsettle," if only temporarily, prevailing economic and social structures:

> The carnival's truly ambivalent, universal laughter decays into the reduced versions of literary parody or irony. *Pylon*'s peculiar resurrection of Joyce and Eliot at this point in Faulkner's career I attribute to the carnival material, which inevitably drives a modernist like Faulkner to the storehouse of literary parody. Faulkner draws on the most potent forms of parody in his literary heritage, on Joyce's efforts to resuscitate the common imagination through a polylogic music, and on Eliot's early shoring of the fragments against ruin. (266)

I shall return to the carnival in a moment; but first I would like to ponder Matthews's formulation, "*Pylon*'s peculiar resurrection of Joyce," which implies that Joycean high modernism was, by 1934, already "dead" in the literary culture at large—"old hat," as Reynolds Price has put it (vi)—and so was available

to an artist like Faulkner only for parodic purposes (whether
Eliot and Joyce themselves are the main targets of parody or
whether they are primarily being used to generate the idiom of
an outwardly directed cultural critique). Leaving aside the
question of the disposition of Faulkner's own rather complex
and intimate relationship with Joyce in the novels he had
written before *Pylon*, here I want to suggest that in *Pylon* Joyce
takes up residence in Faulkner's text as what Foucault has
called a "founder of discursivity," as one who produces "the
possibilities and rules for" further textual invention and elaboration.[19] In my reading, accordingly, Faulkner absorbs and trans-
figures Joyce not only for parodic purposes but also to solve a
range of narrative problems uniquely relevant to Faulkner's
predicament as both an artist and a historical subject in the
year 1934. For Faulkner writing *Pylon*, Joyce was a means of
structuring an apocryphal geography, of "contemplating sheer
language calmly,"[20] of widening the scope of his representational
possibilities, and, accordingly, of probing into some of the
dominant structures of contemporary history itself.

ULYSSES LANDS!

James Joyce was on the cover of the January 29, 1934, issue of
Time magazine and the subject of its lead story, "*Ulysses*
Lands"—a commemoration of the lifting of the ban that had
made the importation and possession of the book a crime. About
two weeks later, on February 15, Faulkner arrived in New
Orleans to attend the opening of the Shushan Airport, where he
observed the events that would emerge, transfigured, in *Pylon*.
The *Time* article is a crucial piece of the *Pylon* puzzle; in it
Faulkner would have read the following:

> Trusting readers who plunge in hopefully to a smooth beginning
> [of *Ulysses*] soon find themselves floundering in troubled waters.
> Arrogant Author Joyce gives them no help, lets them sink or swim.
> But thanks to the exploratory works of critics, and notably such an
> exegetical commentary as Stuard [sic] Gilbert's *James Joyce's Ulys-*

ses (TIME, Jan. 5, 1931) . . . the plain reader can now literally find out what *Ulysses* is all about. Without a key to its plan this stream-of-consciousness Bible, with its elliptical shorthand, its apparently confused and formless method, may well seem an esoteric work of art. Confusing *Ulysses* sometimes is, but rather from too much plan than too little. The key to the plan is the title. . . . Other obvious parallels: Hades, the graveyard; the Cave of Aeolus, the newspaper office; the Isle of Circe, the brothel.[21]

My preliminary claim, then, is this: for Faulkner, the process of "getting away" from *Absalom* (in order to return to it with renewed energy) involved revisiting a book that had been in his workshop ever since he began writing novels in 1925, that is, *Ulysses*, and now specifically its "Aeolus" chapter. Moreover, we need to find in Faulkner's *Pylon* workshop not only the text of "Aeolus" but also Stuart Gilbert's exegesis of that episode in his own celebrated book. (Faulkner, as always, took what he needed wherever he could find it.) Faulkner would have read sections of Gilbert's book simply out of curiosity: to test the "accuracy" of his grasp of Joyce's mythical method as he read and rewrote major aspects of *Ulysses* in the course of composing his first novels in the mid twenties. But there are more compelling reasons for a close reading of Gilbert in 1934: Gilbert would have given Faulkner a detailed account of the multiple interconnections linking the "Aeolus" episode of *Ulysses* with Book X of *The Odyssey*. I believe there is strong evidence to suggest that Faulkner combined his own narrative with this elaborate "intertext," weaving Joyce's city narrative into the innermost structure of his own apocryphal, mid-Depression New Valois.

Indeed, the "signatures" of "Aeolus" pervade Faulkner's narrative: the city room of a mass circulation newspaper (one of the novel's principal settings); the squalls of screaming newsboys; the invasive power of overcharged rhetoric; the bizarre presence in the discourse of quasi-Homeric neologisms, bold-type "headlines," and other, strikingly experimental effects of style, language, and typography; the phallic monuments, Pylon and

Nelson's Pillar, and their associated images of circulatory paralysis, fetishism, and fascination (the airplanes revolving in dizzying, pointless, and ultimately fatal elliptical orbits; the encircling
tramlines "becalmed in short circuit"; the diminutive human
figures gazing upward); and the deployment of these images as
signatures of "foreign" domination (the prototype, the Hebrews
in Egypt, controlling successive analogies: the Irish in the
British Empire, the South in the Union).[22] Equally important
are the multiple and overlapping interconnections linking the
reporter, Leopold Bloom, and Odysseus; Hagood, Myles Crawford, and Aeolus; Feinman, the Amplyfier (Faulkner's spelling),
and the Searchlight—as one extended reification—and the fused
gods, Aeolus and Cyclops.

The inference is unavoidable: rereading "Aeolus" in the light
of Gilbert, Faulkner renewed his excitement in the multiple
possibilities inherent in the Joycean "mythical method," and, at
a critical moment in his career, transfused into the narrative he
wrote in one "forced draft" that dose of iconoclastic verbal
"jouissance" he felt he needed.[23] But he was also interested in
channeling into his own discourse the power of "Aeolus"'s
(suddenly no longer latent) indictment of modernity. For it is
worth recalling that *Pylon* is singular in Faulkner's work in being
set entirely within or at the margins of a modern metropolis,
the great collecting-place of modernity's hostile, alien, and
oppressive forces. If Faulkner then uses the "Aeolus" chapter of
Ulysses as a screen on which to project his ideas, and as a
principal energy source to drive his own project of cultural
criticism, that is because "Aeolus" is the city chapter par excellence of literary high modernism, the episode plunging the
reader, at the turn of a page, deep **"IN THE HEART OF
THE HIBERNIAN METROPOLIS."** Here Faulkner found the
material he needed to help him shape an apocryphal geography
and so carry out his fictional analysis of the contemporary
scene.[24]

CONFETTISPATTER

There are myriad gateways at which the texts of Faulkner, Joyce, Homer, and Gilbert open into one another; but perhaps the best place to enter is through what John Matthews has designated the novel's "carnival material," which I shall here take in its literal sense: the "confettidrift" and "confettispatter," the "broken serpentine" and "the purple-and-gold bunting" (*P* 782). Immediately we encounter a promising difficulty, to which Susie Paul Johnson alerts us: "As he discards the traditional green, Faulkner adds a detail *not* a tradition of Mardi Gras in New Orleans. *Confetti and serpentine have never been part of this celebration, as Faulkner would have known.* Yet they are a repeated image of accumulating significance in *Pylon*" (emphasis added).[25]

Where, then, do the confetti and serpentine *come from*? In attempting to answer this question, we need to reject outright Reynolds Price's unfortunate (though understandable) suggestion that we ought to read the narrative "with eyes . . . trained for avoiding debris" (ix). As in Freud's notion, after Nietzsche, of "the transvaluation of all psychical values"—a principal mechanism not only of the dreamwork but of the literary "work" of imagination itself—the small, seemingly insignificant details are often the most "highly cathected" with psychical energy or meaning. The reader's, like the psychoanalyst's, challenge, therefore, is to attempt to determine, as Lacan has put it, "which 'part' of this discourse carries the significative term."[26] A "significative term" would be one highly "invested" by numerous ideas, and so "predestined," in Freud's formulation, to ambiguity and complexity, "condensation and disguise."[27] Our fascinating trouble in *Pylon* is that there seem to be no *insignificant* terms in it. And so it is the debris—the scattered, obsessively reiterated, apparently trivial elements which both overwrite and underwrite an apocryphal reality—that yields the first insight into the nature of Faulkner's intertextual imagination.

VOLCANIC

At this point, deus ex machina, Stuart Gilbert hands us the key to reading the hieroglyphs and so to finding out "where we are": "A buoyant debris, vomited by the printing machines, *like pumice from a volcano* [my emphasis], litters the offices— 'strewn packing paper,' 'limp galleypages,' light 'tissues' which, 'rustling up' in every draught, 'floated softly in the air blue scrawls and under the table came to earth.' . . . Among the volcanic products found on this island [Stromboli] is a metallic ore which adheres in flakes to the surface of the rocks" (emphasis added).[28] Flowing into New Valois from Gilbert's Homerized reading of the Joycean episode are the transformed pumiceflakes of a volcanic eruption, the proliferated signatures of the invisible (though no less proscriptive) gods themselves. As we read near the novel's opening:

> There was confetti here too, and broken serpentine, in neat narrow swept windrows against wallangles and *lightly vulcanised* [my emphasis] along the gutterrims by the flushing fireplugs of the past dawn, while, upcaught and pinned by the cryptic significant shields to doorfront and lamppost, the purple-and-gold bunting looped unbroken as a trolley wire above his head as he walked, turning at last at right angles to cross the street itself and meet that one on the opposite side making its angle too, to join over the center of the street as though to form an aerial and bottomless regalcolored cattlechute suspended at first floor level above the earth, and suspending beneath itself in turn, the outwardfacing cheeseclothlettered interdiction which Jiggs, passing, slowed looking back to read: **Grandlieu Street CLOSED To Traffic 8:00 P.M.—Midnight**. (P 782)

In its uncanny, oneiric, and overdetermined way, New Valois is not only the conical volcanic island, Stromboli, mythological home of Aeolus, but also the labyrinth of the Minotaur (half man, half bull, Jiggs is the Minotaur in the maze) and Pompeii after the eruption, a city of the dead. Michel Gresset has implied as much: "The air show takes place against the backdrop of a ground show: the Mardi Gras parade, Grandlieu Street, the whole tawdry pageant of the (dreary) city festival, with streets littered with rubbish and confetti, without mirth, *without even a crowd*. The earthly, horizontal show is not part of a festival but part of *the bitter aftermath of a festival*" (emphasis added).[29]

A reiterated figure, Faulkner's crowd is anonymous, intimidated, mesmerized, "static"; the effect is grotesque and often poignant: a "static curbmass of amazed confettifaces" (*P* 810); a "static human mass" (*P* 813); "a small violent backwater of motionless backturned faces" (*P* 812); "the gaped and upturned faces which choked the gangway" (*P* 933); "the throng huddled in the narrow underpass beneath the reserved seats" (*P* 799); the "tide which still set toward the apron and talking to itself with one another in voices forlorn, baffled, and amazed: 'What is it now? What are they doing out there now?' " (*P* 799). In my reading of Faulkner's crowd, possibilities for popular subversion and rebellion, for "universal laughter," in Matthews's Bakhtinian sense, are significantly absent.

If the urban core of New Valois is awash in volcanic effluent—"a building 'floats,' a car 'drifts,' a train station 'flows up,' the city 'dissolves,' " (Johnson, *Annotations*, 4)—the airport and the upstairs newspaper offices are Faulknerian versions of Aeolus's windy floating island. Again it is Gilbert who brings things into focus by citing the Homeric source: "The Aeolian island rose sheer from a wide belt of buoyant pumice-stone on which it seemed to float" (*G* 179): "Then we came to the isle Aeolian, where dwelt Aeolus . . . in a floating island, and all about it is a wall of bronze unbroken and the cliff runs up sheer from the sea. . . . And the steaming house echoes all around its outer court by day" (*G* 183).[30] Thus aroused, our Homeric expectations are certainly fulfilled as we catch a first glimpse of *Pylon's* airport:

there was only the soft pale sharp chimaerashape above which pennons floated against a further drowsy immensity which the mind knew must be water, *apparently separated from the flat earth by a mirageline so that, taking shape now as a doublewinged building, it seemed to float lightly* like the apocryphal turreted and battlemented cities in the colored Sunday sections [. . . .] (*P* 786, emphasis added)[31]

Like a city in the colored Sunday sections: the airport is indeed a "paperspace"[32] (Joyce's word) within a larger space of print and language, what Faulkner calls "the garblement which was the city" (*P* 918). That garblement repeats itself, *mis-en-abime*, in the Homeric idiom Faulkner, with his genius for language, fluently picked up and made his own:

> Now the cityroom (he scratched this match on the door itself) the barncavern, looming: the copydesk like a cluttered island, the other single desks beneath the single greenshaded bulbs had that quality of profound and lonely isolation of buoymarked shoals in an untravelled and forgotten sea, his own among them. (*P* 914)

Nor would Faulkner fail to have noticed the signal feature of the Aeolian island in its modern incarnation as newspaper office, namely its protean forms of wind. Writes Gilbert,

> A gale of wind is blowing through this episode, literally and metaphorically. Doors are flung open violently, Myles Crawford blows violent puffs from his cigarette, the barefoot newsboys, scampering in, create a hurricane which lifts the rustling tissues into the air; swing-doors draughtily flicker to and fro. (*G* 192)

> —Throw him out and shut the door, the editor said. There's a hurricane blowing. (*U* 128)

> The door opened and clashed behind him [. . . .] "Get out of the door," the elevator man said. "There's a draft in here." It clashed behind the reporter again [. . . .] (*P* 809–10)

Along with the Joycean geography which Faulkner extends into his own narrative come the major "subject positions" of a prior dramatic scene. Here we are at the point of solving another perennial *Pylon* "problem": just who *is* the reporter? There has been much speculation. He has been identified as Lazarus, Death incarnate, Ichabod Crane, J. Alfred Prufrock, St. Christopher, Don Quixote; as Vampire, Scarecrow, Frankenstein's monster, Satan; as the real-life reporter, Herman Deutsch, and William Faulkner himself.[33] In Faulkner's symbolic discourse, that is, "a complication of motives, an accumulation and conjunction of mental activities—in a word, overdetermination—is the rule."[34] Our hermeneutic task is therefore to trace the intertextual figure "home" to a complex of sources.

NOMAN THEY CALL ME

Susie Paul Johnson brings us to the verge of uncovering an additional identity when she notes that the reporter is blown about by the wind:

> However, the lightness of the reporter's "ballooning suit," which allows him to be blown about so, like "a scarecrow . . . now poised for the first light vagrant air to blow it into utter dissolution" . . . or like a "scarecrow in a gale" . . . parallels the biblical description of those who are evil: "Let them be as chaff before the wind: and let the angel of the Lord chase them" (*Psalms* 35:5). Or, "the ungodly . . . are like the chaff which the wind driveth away" (*Psalms* 1:4).[35]

So complex, clever, and devious are the man's disguises that he seems to have eluded identification in even this keen hermeneutical instance. But who can he be, this figure who is blown about by the winds, who descends across the underworld river into nighttown (offering absinthe instead of blood to the shades that they may speak) but the man with no name, the wandering arch-dissembler and many-sided trickster, NoMan himself, whose return Aeolus reads as proof he has been forsaken by the gods?[36]

Specifically, the reporter can be read as an essentially modernist variation on the figure of Odysseus-as-Leopold Bloom: certainly it is Bloom who establishes the pattern the reporter is destined to repeat. Wandering the city, Bloom is attacked without warning by a newsboy who screams in his face an ominous news:

> A newsboy cried in Mr Bloom's face:
> —Terrible tragedy in Rathmines! A child bit by a bellows! (*U* 146)

This is clearly an omen of the "violent" event to come: Bloom, the child, will be bit by the bellows, Myles Crawford, and in this inflated atmosphere, the event is certainly a **TRAGEDY**. *Pylon* takes this prototypical encounter further in the direction of hyperbole, violence, and assault:

> But even before [the reporter] reached the corner he was assailed by a gust of screaming newsboys apparently as oblivious to the moment's significance as birds are aware yet oblivious to the human doings which their wings brush and their droppings fall upon. They swirled about him, screaming: in the reflected light of the passing torches the familiar black thick type and the raucous cries seemed to glare and merge faster than the mind could distinguish the sense through which each had been received: "Boinum boins!" **FIRST FATALITY OF AIR** "Read about it! Foist Moidigror foitality!" **LIEUT. BURNHAM KILLED IN AIR CRASH** "Boinum boins!" (*P* 811)

Reading "Aeolus" Faulkner clearly noticed the insistent figure of the swarming newsboys who, in the metaphorical texture of the narrative, render the sudden siroccos, squalls, and breezes of Aeolus's island; in their darting motions and sudden cries, the newsboys are also screeching seagulls careening on the winds:

> A telegram boy stepped in nimbly, threw an envelope on the counter and stepped off posthaste with a word.
> —*Freeman!* (*U* 118)

> Screams of newsboys barefoot in the hall rushed near and the door was flung open. (*U* 128)

> The first newsboy came pattering down the stairs at their heels and rushed out into the street, yelling:—*Racing special!* (*U* 144)

> A bevy of scampering newsboys rushed down the steps, scampering in all directions, yelling, their white papers fluttering. (*U* 146)[37]

Moreover, Faulkner grasped the manner in which the newsboys, metonymically representing the newspaper industry itself, reify the voice of the city's own fascination with the grotesque new forms of violence it has invented. It is accordingly appropriate that Burnham's violent death, his crashing and burning in his rocket plane—the prototypical traumatic event of this narrative of modernity—should be reiterated not only at the level of plot and event (Roger Shumann's crash and death), but also within the literal substance, texture, and rhythm of narrative discourse itself. The hysterical boldface of the newspaper headlines which, as Gresset has noted, "strike out aggressively at the reader" (239), insist on the message of a shattering violence even as they become the principal form of the narrative's "compulsion to repeat."[38] Echoing Freud's theory of repetition and mastery in *Beyond the Pleasure Principle*, Walter Benjamin's formulation seems pertinent to the fundamental narrative logic and therapeutic function of *Pylon* in Faulkner's unfolding narrative project: "The more readily consciousness registers these shocks, the less likely are they to have a traumatic effect":[39] "as they entered a newsboy screamed at them, flapping the paper, the headline: **PILOT KILLED. Shumann Crashes Into Lake. SECOND FATALITY OF AIRMEET.** as it too flicked away" (*P* 939–40).

Nowhere is the figure of the assaulting media more intense than in Faulkner's description of newsprint itself, whose type generates a kind of hysteria of signification whose final effect is a form of paralysis (another of "Aeolus'"s characteristic figures):

> a thick heavy typesplattered front page filled with ejaculations and pictures [. . . .] heavy, blacksplotched, staccato [. . . .] the fragile web of ink and paper, assertive, proclamative; profound and irrevocable if only in the sense of being profoundly and irrevocably unimportant—the dead instant's fruit of forty tons of machinery and an entire nation's antic delusion. (*P* 783, 850)

The assault is so penetrating that it is as if it brings about a transmogrification of the organs of perception themselves:

> The eye, the organ without thought speculation or amaze, ran off the last word [. . . .] that vision without contact [. . .] like two dead electric bulbs set into his skull [. . . .] his eyes hot blank and dead as if they had been reversed in his skull and only the blank backsides showed [. . . .] the hot impenetrable eyes, the membrane and fiber netting and webbing the unrecking and the undismayed. (*P* 850, 858, 859, 875)

The figure of the aggressive media of signification is intimately associated with the newspaper editor-gods themselves, Hagood and Crawford. Once again, as in the psychoanalytic notion of "acting out," a prior script (one, for which, as always, there are ones prior still) blocks out the major positions available in the contemporary enactment of the scene (in this way "Aeolus" might be thought of as *Pylon's* intertextual unconscious). We might adumbrate the scene's multilayered structure by noting, with Gilbert, the parallels between Bloom-Odysseus and Myles Crawford-Aeolus. Odysseus, bestowed with favorable winds by Aeolus, is in sight of Ithaca when the wind is let out of the bag and he is blown back to a rude reception on Aeolus's island (as Michael Seidel points out, the episode is "the least heroic of all the *Wanderings*") (167):

> "So I spake, beseeching them in soft words, but they held their peace. And the father answered, saying: 'Get thee forth from the island straightway, thou that art the most reprobate of living men. Far be it from me to help or to further that man whom the blessed gods abhor! Get thee forth, for lo, thy coming marks thee hated by the deathless gods.'
>
> Therewith he sent me forth from the house making heavy moan." (*Odyssey* 146)

Bloom, in turn, after receiving Crawford's blessing, "Begone! [. . . .] The world is before you" (*U* 129), is given a hostile and tempestuous reception upon successive requests for an audience. In the modern version of the Homeric event, the editor-gods—Hagood and Crawford—use telephones to transmit their hostility and aggression:

> —Bloom is at the telephone, he said.
> —Tell him go to hell, the editor said promptly. (*U* 137)

The Faulknerian version of the scene is characteristically more brutal and direct:

> "Fired! Fired! Fired! Fired!" the editor screamed. He leaned halfway across the desk beneath the greenshaded light, telephone and receiver clutched to him like a tackled halfback lying half across the goalline [. . . .] "Do you hear me?" he screamed. (*P* 825)

As this passage might suggest, much of *Pylon* is carried out under the sign of "Aeolian" hyperbole, exaggeration, expansion, augmentation; the novel represents the logical continuation of Joyce's Aeolean modes of inflation and intimidation into a more explicitly mechanized world. The brazen voice of the amplifyer, the menacing sweep of the search beam, the "downwardglaring" attitude of lights and stares and gazes throughout—all represent a brilliant and unpredictable fusion and development of Joycean and Homeric modes of proscription and hyperbole. Like the god Aeolus, who "from a seagirt palace, controls the air of the multitudinous seas" (*G* 191), the amplifyer narrates—indeed appears to generate and control—the novel's central repeating event, the turning of the airplanes around the pylons during an airshow at the opening of the city's new airport.

CLANGING RINGING!

Continuing to follow the pathways of the signifier, one arrives at another of Joyce's dominant figures, the traffic and transportation systems of a busy metropolis, systems located and controlled by reference to Nelson's Pillar. As Marilyn French has put it, "This is a mechanistic world, its heart is a pillar erected to a conqueror, and its lifeblood is machines, tramcars."[40] As we read at the opening of Joyce's chapter,

> BEFORE NELSON'S PILLAR TRAMS SLOWED, SHUNTED, CHANGED trolley [. . . .] Right and left parallel clanging ringing a doubledecker and a singledeck moved from their railheads, swerved to the down line, glided parallel [. . . .] At various points along the eight lines tramcars with motionless trolleys stood in their tracks [. . .] all still, becalmed in short circuit. (*U* 116, 149)

Faulkner takes up this text in two principal ways. The first might be termed conceptual and structural: the Joycean source is translated into Faulkner's stunningly overdetermined figure for modernity—the pylon around which the flyers revolve in a demonic parody of humanity's most recent attempt toward Transcendence: "the furious, still, and legendary tale of what man has come to call his conquering of the infinite and impervious air" (*P* 800).[41] The second way in which Faulkner takes up the Joycean material is aural, rhythmic, mimetic, citational:

> Now they could cross Grandlieu Street; there was traffic in it now; to clash and clang of light and bell trolley and automobile crashed and glared across the intersection, rushing in a light curbchanneled spindrift of tortured and draggled serpentine [. . .] ordered and marked by light and bell [. . . .] (*P* 827)

If here Faulkner appears to be announcing his playful affiliation with the Joycean source, he is also rewriting a prior text that "failed to go far enough."[42] Darker, more cynical than anything found in the daytime "Aeolus" chapter, Faulkner's version places isolated and forlorn human figures *right in the middle of the traffic* (which nearly slices them apart):

> As the woman and the parachute jumper stepped onto the curb light and bell clanged again and merged into the rising gearwhine as the traffic moved; Shumann sprang forward and onto the curb with a stiff light movement of unbelievable and rigid celerity, without a hair's abatement of expression or hatangle; again, behind them now, the light harried spindrift of tortured confetti and serpentine rose from the gutter in sucking gusts. The reporter glared at them all now with his dazed, strained and urgent face. "The bastards!" he cried. "The son of a bitches!" (*P* 828).

Leaving his offices at night the reporter reenters a viciously fragmented system, "threading [his] way between the blatting and honking, the whining and clashing of gears, the glare of backbouncing and crossing headlight beams" (*P* 972).

One comes to appreciate Faulkner's problem, and so his motivation for turning to Joyce in a time of representational "need": so alien, so fast-paced, so beyond the range of conventional literary language did he find the contemporary scene, that he needed to find a new idiom—an appropriately "alienated" narrative voice—one now determined by the imperatives of a mechanized culture. And so in *Pylon* the characteristic form of that language is the composite, the portmanteau word, the neologism, an invention allowing for multiple investments from inner and outer, intertextual and extratextual realities: "corpse-glare," "wirehum," "gasolinespanned," "pavementthrong," "trafficdammed," "machinevoice," "gearwhine," "slantshim-mered," "typesplattered"— weird, defamiliarizing "machine-language" appearing with Joycean strangeness upon the page. As Walter Benjamin (in an analogous context) has observed, the crisis of language "which manifests itself in this way can be seen as an integral part of a crisis in perception itself."[43] And hence, to meet that "crisis," "*Pylon*'s peculiar resurrection of Joyce" (in Matthews's formulation). If Faulkner's words, images, and structures are never quite Joyce's, it is by that difference that we can measure the rhythm of his imagination, the way he finds a vocabulary (and the conceptual modes inherent in it) and transforms it to solve representational problems unique and historically contingent.[44]

Faulkner's sustained reading and augmentation of the Joycean text literally transform, by "deferred action" as it were, the meaning of that text. After Faulkner's reading of it, "Aeolus" can never be the same. It is in this sense that *Pylon* and "Aeolus" constitute one seamless "intertext," one continuous network of discourse. The proofs of this are easy to find: the reporter leaves his mark at the newspaper office by striking matches on the surfaces around him: "Now the cityroom (he scratched this match on the door itself)" (*P* 914). "[R]aking the match across the frame as he disappeared. But the first match broke; the second one he struck on the bellplate while the elevator was rising" (*P* 809). "Just above the button on the bellplate the faintly oxidised streak of last night's match still showed; the match now, without calculation, without sight to guide it, almost followed the mark" (*P* 913–14). Descending the staircase which leads to the *Evening Telegraph* office, Leopold Bloom responds, "Who the deuce scrawled all over these walls with matches?" (*U* 123).

At another point, Faulkner grabs a sheet of paper out of "Aeolus" and stuffs it into the pocket of the reporter:

Stephen handed over the typed sheets, pointing to the title and signature. (*U* 130)

Myles Crawford crammed the sheets into a sidepocket. (*U* 132)

He flung the pages down. (*U* 136)

He fumbled in his pocket, pulling out the crushed typesheets. (*U* 142)

He thrust the sheets back and went into the inner office. (*U* 142)

Then he folded it and tried to thrust it into the pocket with the other folded one just like it. (*P* 810)

the suit that looked as if someone else had just finished sleeping in it and with one coat pocket sagging with yellow copy paper and from the other protruding, folded, the cold violent stilldamp black

ALITY OF
BURNED (*P* 802)

Whether Faulkner has taken the sheet in play or in transgression, he has also done so in order to serve his own fictional investigation of reality. One notes his peculiar, cubistic way of placing the sheet and then of focusing on it; he is giving us a new angle of vision, of things heretofore unnoticed in precisely *that* way. The illuminating analogies would appear to be those of cinema and psychoanalysis, as Walter Benjamin, in another context, suggests:

> By close-ups of the things around us, by focusing on hidden details of familiar objects, by exploring commonplace milieus under the ingenious guidance of the camera, the film, on the one hand, extends our comprehension of the necessities which rule our lives. . . . With the close-up, space expands; with slow motion, movement is extended. The enlargement of a snapshot does not simply render more precise what in any case was visible, though unclear: it reveals entirely new structural formations of the subject. . . . Evidently a different nature opens itself to the camera than opens to the naked eye—if only because an unconsciously penetrated space is substituted for a space consciously explored by man. . . . The camera introduces us to unconscious optics as does psychoanalysis to unconscious impulses.[45]

Faulkner's manner of taking Joyce up into his own narrative implies not only the reading of a literary but also the reading of a historical "text." "Aeolus," for Faulkner, was an instrument of vision, focalization, and analysis:

> A typesetter brought him a limp galleypage. (*U* 121)

> Into the round target of light a hand slid the first tomorrow's galley: the stilldamp neat row of boxes which in the paper's natural order had no scarehead, containing, since there was nothing new in them since time began, likewise no alarm:—that crossection out of timespace as though of a lightray caught by a speed lens for a second's fraction between infinity and furious and trivial dust:
>
> ### FARMERS REFUSE   BANKERS DENY
> ### STRIKERS DEMAND   PRESIDENT'S YACHT
> ### ACREAGE REDUCTION   QUINTUPLETS GAIN
> ### EX-SENATOR RENAUD CELEBRATES TENTH
> ### ANNIVERSARY AS RESTAURATEUR (*P* 825–26)

THE LAST PYLON AND THE BEGINNING
OF LITERATURE

It has been observed that "Aeolus" stages a competition between human and inhuman voices; hence the role of bombast, inflated rhetoric, dramatic set speeches. The celebrated orators, Dawson, Bushe, and Taylor, were men who could raise their voices above the din of the presses. *Pylon* appears to stage the battle as one already lost: the dominant voices, those of the newspaper and amplifyer, seem to invade and transform the novel's very language and vision. The compelling magic of the book has much to do with the fact that Faulkner's rendering of this alienated language and vision is a rebelliously human achievement. Indeed, the metafictional logic of *Pylon* tends toward that moment, on the penultimate page, when we are brought into the presence of "the beginning of literature" (*P* 991). This is the reporter's discovery (and Faulkner's rediscovery) of his own creative narrative voice, a voice promising to take him beyond "news" if he can ever extricate himself from Amboise Street. In "Aeolus" Stephen Dedalus will escape the pressgang and emerge (as James Joyce) to write *Ulysses* ("On now. Dare it. Let there be life") (*U* 145). Somehow "Aeolus" is involved in the "beginning of literature" too, the literature that was *Pylon* and the literature that will be *Absalom, Absalom!*

NOTES

1. *Faulkner in the University: Class Conferences at the University of Virginia, 1957–1958*, ed. Frederick L. Gwynn and Joseph L. Blotner (New York: Vintage, 1965), 36.

2. Cleanth Brooks, *William Faulkner: Toward Yoknapatawpha and Beyond* (New Haven: Yale University Press, 1978), 178.

3. Judith Wittenberg, *Faulkner: The Transfiguration of Biography* (Lincoln: University of Nebraska Press, 1979), 140, 130; John N. Duvall, *Faulkner's Marginal Couple: Invisible, Outlaw, and Unspeakable Communities* (Austin: University of Texas Press, 1990), 82.

4. *Modern Fiction Studies* 3 (Winter 1957–58): 291–308.

5. John T. Matthews, "The Autograph of Violence in Faulkner's *Pylon*," in *Southern Literature and Literary Theory*, ed. Jefferson Humphries (Athens: University of Georgia Press, 1990), 247–69; Karl F. Zender, *The Crossing of the Ways: William Faulkner, the South, and the Modern World* (New Brunswick: Rutgers University Press, 1989).

6. *William Faulkner's Library—A Catalogue*, ed. Joseph L. Blotner (Charlottesville: University Press of Virginia, 1964), 77. Blotner notes the strange conjunction of "1924" with "Rowan Oak": "There is only one reliable sign of esteem for books in his library. Those he cared about he inscribed, usually with his name, the date, and place in ink. . . . Only eleven of them are dated in the 1920's. . . . One is in Eric Dawson's *Henry Becque: Sa vie et son theatre*. The other is James Joyce's *Ulysses*. This is a notable entry for two reasons. One somehow welcomes this evidence of the young writer's admiration for his great predecessor. But, curiously, the book is inscribed 'Rowan Oak' six years before the Faulkners moved there. (Three other such anomalies appear. Perhaps Faulkner sat down one day in the study of the new home and added to the inscription as a part of the process of settling in . . .)" (7).

7. My discussion of these issues has been informed by *Influence and Intertextuality in Literary History*, ed. Jay Clayton and Eric Rothstein (Madison: University of Wisconsin Press, 1991), especially the editors' introductory chapter, "Figures in the Corpus: Theories of Influence and Intertextuality" (3–36).

8. Julia Kristeva, *Desire in Language: A Semiotic Approach to Literature and Art*, ed. Leon Roudiez, trans. Thomas Gora et al. (New York: Columbia University Press, 1980), 65.

9. Roland Barthes, *The Rustle of Language*, trans. Richard Howard (New York: Hill and Wang, 1986), 60.

10. Kristeva, *Desire in Language*, 66.

11. Roland Barthes, "The Death of the Author," in *Image- Music-Text*, trans. Stephen Heath (New York: Hill and Wang, 1977), 148.

12. Susan Stanford Friedman, "Weavings: Intertextuality and the (Re)Birth of the Author," in Clayton and Rothstein, 146–80, 173.

13. André Bleikasten, *The Ink of Melancholy: Faulkner's Novels from "The Sound*

and the Fury" to "Light in August" (Bloomington: Indiana University Press, 1990), vii–viii.

14. Foucault has noted that an idea of the "author allows a limitation of the cancerous and dangerous proliferation of significations within a world where one is thrifty not only with one's resources and riches, but also with one's discourses and their significations. The author is the principle of thrift in the proliferation of meaning" ("What Is an Author," in *The Foucault Reader*, ed. Paul Rabinow [New York: Pantheon, 1984], 119). In this view, a sense of Faulkner and his location as both a "subject in history" and as an artist working within a "structured area of problems" (Ernst Kris, *Psychoanalytic Explorations in Art* [New York: International Universities Press, Inc., 1952], 21) would be the "necessary or constraining figure" (Foucault, 119) through which any reading of his text ought (at some point or other) to pass.

15. Fredric Jameson, *The Political Unconscious: Narrative as a Socially Symbolic Act* (Ithaca: Cornell University Press, 1981), 32.

16. T. S. Eliot, "Tradition and the Individual Talent," in *Selected Prose of T. S. Eliot*, ed. Frank Kermode (London: Faber, 1975), 42. The phrase "discharge of mental energy" is from Bleikasten's *Ink of Melancholy*, xiii.

17. Introduction to *Pylon* (New York: Signet, 1968), vi.

18. William Faulkner, *Pylon* (New York: Library of America, 1985), 775–992, 779, hereafter abbreviated as *P* and cited parenthetically in the text. My ellipses will appear in brackets to distinguish them from Faulkner's.

19. "What Is an Author," 114.

20. See Faulkner's review of *Test Pilot* by Jimmy Collins (*American Mercury*, November 1935), in *Essays, Speeches, and Public Letters by William Faulkner*, ed. James B. Meriwether (New York: Random House, 1965), 189.

21. "Ulysses Lands," *Time* 23 (January 29, 1934): 49–51. See also "Joyce Translated," *Time* 17 (January 5, 1931), 48: "JAMES JOYCE'S ULYSSES—Stuart Gilbert—Knopf ($5). . . . *Ulysses* readers may now cease head-scratching; [Gilbert's] 379-page commentary should make all plain. More, Translator Gilbert's interpretation (unlike earlier ones) is guaranteed correct, for it was written under the supervision of Maestro Joyce himself. . . . With his running comment, frequent quotations, scholarly footnotes, Translator Gilbert gives you almost a substitute for the book itself" (48).

22. "But the South, as Chicago is the Middlewest and New York the East, is dead, killed by the Civil War. There is a thing known whimsically as the New South to be sure, but it is not the south. It is a land of Immigrants who are rebuilding the towns and cities into replicas of towns and cities in Kansas and Iowa and Illinois, with skyscrapers and striped canvas awnings instead of wooden balconies, and teaching the young men who sell the gasoline and the waitresses in the restaurants to say O yeah? and to speak with hard r's . . ." ("An Introduction to *The Sound and the Fury*," ed. James B. Meriwether, *Mississippi Quarterly* 26 [1973]: 410–15, 411).

23. In October 1934 Faulkner wrote to his agent Morton Goldman, asking him to send the story "This Kind of Courage": "I am writing a novel out of it, so please return it." Then, in a letter of early or mid-December, 1934, Faulkner wrote: "Dear Morty: Excuse not writing. I have worked forced draft on the novel and finished it yesterday" (*Selected Letters of William Faulkner*, ed. Joseph Blotner [New York: Random House, 1977], 85).

24. James Joyce, *Ulysses* (New York: Random House, 1961), 116, hereafter abbreviated as *U* and cited parenthetically in the text. My ellipses appear in brackets to distinguish them from Joyce's. Several critics mention John Dos Passos, especially in *Manhattan Transfer* (1925), as a likely source of the neologisms in *Pylon*. This may be true, but it should also be remembered that Joyce was Dos Passos's source. The same can be said for the "headlines." In her extremely useful book, *Annotations to William Faulkner's "Pylon"* (New York: Garland, 1989), Susie Paul Johnson cites as a possible source for these the "Aeolus" chapter as first published in the *Little Review* in October 1918. However, the headlines were not yet a feature of that version of the episode. Joyce added the headlines in proof, and they appeared only in the book as published in

1922. See Michael Groden, *"Ulysses" in Progress* (Princeton: Princeton University Press, 1977): "For a reader who had followed *Ulysses* as it appeared serially in the *Little Review* from 1918 to 1920, the least recognizable episode in the published book would certainly have been 'Aeolus' " (64).

25. Susie Paul Johnson, *"Pylon*: Faulkner's Waste Land," *Mississippi Quarterly* 38 (Summer 1985): 287–94, 290–91.

26. Sigmund Freud, *The Interpretation of Dreams*, in *Standard Edition of the Complete Psychological Works of Sigmund Freud*, ed. and trans. James Strachey, 24 vols. (London: The Hogarth Press, 1986), 4:330; Jacques Lacan, "The function and field of speech and language in psychoanalysis," in *Écrits: A Selection*, trans. Alan Sheridan (New York: W. W. Norton & Co., 1977), 30–113, 44.

27. Freud, *The Interpretation of Dreams*, 408n.

28. Stuart Gilbert, *James Joyce's "Ulysses"* (London: Faber & Faber, 1930), 186, 184; this text will be abbreviated hereafter as G and cited parenthetically in the text. My ellipses will appear in brackets to distinguish them from Gilbert's.

29. Michel Gresset, *Fascination: Faulkner's Fiction, 1919–1936*, adapted from the French by Thomas West (Durham: Duke University Press, 1989), 243.

30. *The Complete Works of Homer: "The Iliad" and "The Odyssey,"* trans. Andrew Lang, Walter Leaf, Ernest Myers, S. H. Butcher (New York: Modern Library, n.d.). Gilbert quotes from this edition, a copy of which Faulkner owned (see Blotner, *Faulkner's Library*, 80).

31. In *Epic Geography: James Joyce's "Ulysses"* (Princeton: Princeton University Press, 1976), Michael Seidel writes: "Berard explains that the volcanic activity on Stromboli casts huge rocks afloat in the sea, giving approaching navigators the illusion of floating islands. Moreover, the volcanic ash, blown by the south wind, poses its own threat to seamen in the navigational lanes down from Cumae" (165).

32. Patrick McGee, *Paperspace: Style as Ideology in Joyce's "Ulysses"* (Lincoln: University of Nebraska Press, 1988).

33. In *The Achievement of William Faulkner*, Michael Millgate notes that "it is tempting to see [the reporter] as the figure of Death stalking Roger Shumann" (144). In *Faulkner's Fables of Creativity: The Non-Yoknapatawpha Novels* (London: Macmillan, 1990), Gary Harrington identifies the reporter as an ironical St. Christopher, "the patron saint of motorists and aviators" (52). In "The Killer in *Pylon*," *Mississippi Quarterly* 40 (Fall 1987), Susie Paul Johnson identifies the reporter as a scarecrow: "The image of the scarecrow, given the novel's other allusions to the poetry of T. S. Eliot, links the reporter to the spiritual emptiness of Eliot's 'Hollow Men,' and it reinforces what the frequent comparisons of the reporter to a corpse or cadaver suggest, that he is essentially dead" (404). Naturally, the epigraph of the poem is from Conrad, and as I have pointed out elsewhere, the reporter also resembles Kurtz in important respects (Michael Zeitlin, "Faulkner's *Pylon*: The City in the Age of Mechanical Reproduction," *Canadian Review of American Studies* 22 [Fall 1991]: 238n). We should also add Hawthorne's Myles Coverdale, from *The Blithedale Romance*, to the list.

34. Sigmund Freud, "Fragment of an Analysis of a Case of Hysteria" ["Dora"],in *Standard Edition* 7:1–122, 60.

35. Susie Paul Johnson, "The Killer in *Pylon*," 404.

36. The oneiric scene (*P* 830ff) is written through and through by the opening pages of the "Circe" episode of *Ulysses*. In Book IX of *The Odyssey*, Odysseus assumes the name of Noman in his encounter with the Cyclops, whose signatures are multiple in *Pylon*: Consider the "fierce white downwardglaring beam" of the searchlight (*P* 945); "the long sicklebar of the beacon [which] swept inward from the lake, to vanish at the instant when the yellow eye came broadside on" (*P* 948); and Jiggs's "blue and swollen eye" (*P* 947): "He stared at Jiggs, who stared back at him with blinking and oneeyed attention" (*P* 958). As the reporter looks at Jiggs, moreover, one encounters another unmistakable inscription of the Cyclops narrative: "When he spoke again [. . .] the reporter thought of a man trying to herd a half dozen blind sheep through a passage a little wider than he could span with his extended arms" (*P* 947). Cf. "But the Cyclops,

groaning and travailing in pain, groped with his hands, and lifted away the stone from the door of the cave, and himself sat in the entry, with arms outstretched to catch, if he might, any one that was going forth with his sheep, so witless, methinks did he hope to find me" (*The Odyssey* 138). One also notices the following correspondence between the "tinseldung" scattered in piles in the streets of New Valois and the "dung which was scattered in great heaps in the depths of the cave" of the Cyclops (*The Odyssey* 135). Finally, Gilbert again seems a likely support for Faulkner's game: "A curious feature of the last seven pages of the episode is that any reference to Mr Bloom by name is carefully evaded" (*G* 267), etc.

37. Cf. *The Sound and the Fury*, Corrected Edition (New York: Random House, 1984): "At the corner two bootblacks caught me, one on either side, shrill and raucous, like blackbirds" (83).

38. In the game of matching Faulkner's signs with those of Joyce's, let Burnham and Shumann be linked with Paddy Dignam, the dead man whose absence presides over so much of *Ulysses*'s action. In "Aeolus," Dignam's death is appropriately associated with dismemberment and mutilation as Bloom listens to the "Thumping thump" of the machines: "Hynes here too: account of the funeral probably. Thumping thump. This morning the remains of the late Mr Patrick Dignam. Machines. Smash a man to atoms if they got him caught" (*U* 118).

39. Walter Benjamin, "On Some Motifs in Baudelaire," in *Illuminations*, ed. Hannah Arendt, trans. Harry Zohn (New York: Schocken Books, 1968), 189.

40. Marilyn French, *The Book as World: James Joyce's "Ulysses"* (Cambridge: Harvard University Press, 1976), 99. See also Groden: "The 1920 schema that Joyce wrote for his friend Carlo Linati described the meaning of "Wandering Rocks" as 'the hostile environment' (Linati Schema), and Joyce begins to present this aspect of the city in the newspaper office" (*"Ulysses" in Progress*, 73).

41. According to the Linati schema, the theme of "Aeolus" was "The Mockery of Victory." Faulkner could not have known this, and yet, uncannily, Momus, the god of mockery, presides over New Valois' apocryphal Mardi Gras. In *The Achievement of William Faulkner* Millgate makes clear the target of that mockery: "An even more direct and specific source of irony, in February 1934, was the fact that the theme of that year's Mardi Gras parade was 'The Conquest of the Air' " (45).

42. Harold Bloom, *The Anxiety of Influence: A Theory of Poetry* (London: Oxford University Press, 1973), 14.

43. Benjamin, "On Some Motifs in Baudelaire," 189.

44. For a highly pertinent discussion of Joyce's "hellenization" of style, his invention of "post-Homeric epithets" like "snotgreen" and "scrotumtightening sea," and his exercises in "Homer's formulaic composition" ("Grossbooted draymen rolled barrels dullthudding out of Prince's stores," etc.), see Richard Ellmann, *The Consciousness of Joyce* (New York: Oxford University Press, 1977), 25–26.

45. Benjamin, "The Work of Art in the Age of Mechanical Reproduction," *Illuminations*, 235–37.

The Signifying Eye: Faulkner's Artists and the Engendering of Art

CANDACE WAID

In his fiction Faulkner reveals a complex and often obsessive association between art and gender, especially when he enters into the realm of the visual arts: depicting the relation of the artist and the work of art, representing acts of artistic reproduction, and even incorporating graphic representation into his texts. With the exception of his first novel, *Soldiers' Pay*, Faulkner's earliest works are preoccupied with works of art and contain his most specific portrayals of artists: the painter in "Elmer," the sculptor and writers of *Mosquitoes*, and the glass blower of *Sartoris*. All of these artists (as well as Eva Wiseman, the allegorically named lesbian poet) are troubled by female sexuality and fecundity and the meaning of women as they attempt to incorporate these elements into their work. In both "Elmer" and *Mosquitoes*, Faulkner's artists seem to be under the spell of Swinburne as they allude to the mysterious erotic drive embodied in the concept of *Hermaphroditus*.[1] Faulkner seems obsessed with gendering the materials of art and the work of art itself as artists in these works describe the conception, genesis, and origins of a work of art in strongly sexualized accounts of creation. In these eroticized descriptions, Faulkner's artists seem aware of the profound if familiar connection between creation and procreation; yet as they are driven in their efforts to make a work of art, they seem both haunted and lured by the troubling presence of the female body.

Faulkner's interest in these themes appears as early as 1925 in one of his first longer works of fiction, "Elmer," which tells the story of a troubled young man with strong visual and tactile obsessions with smokestacks, cigars, jars filled with brightly colored liquids, and slender pipelike structures. Critics have speculated (and Faulkner himself intimated) that "Elmer" remained unfinished because Faulkner's account of the aspirations and inspirations of the artist as a young man became too intimate and, if not precisely autobiographical, cloyingly confessional in tone. Elmer is a painter who as a child enjoyed crayons (cylindrical shapes that leave their mark) and even as an adult he approaches a "new unstained box of paints" with an almost painful awareness of the erotic valences of the materials of art:

> To finger lasciviously smooth dull silver tubes virgin yet at the same time pregnant, comfortably heavy to the palm—such an immaculate mating of bulk and weight that it were a shame to violate them, innocent clean brushes slender and bristled to all sizes and interesting chubby bottles of oil . . . Elmer hovered over them with a brooding maternity, taking up one at a time those fat portentous tubes in which was yet wombed his heart's desire, the world itself—thick-bodied and female and at the same time phallic: hermaphroditic. He closed his eyes the better to savour its feel. . . .[2]

Elmer savors the moment before creation, the moment before possibility is violated by the artist's effort to conceive; the materials themselves are "portentous," the paint tubes not just containers but generative, the place in which "his heart's desire, the world itself" seems "wombed."

Elmer dwells on the idea of a self-contained object which seems complete in itself, "an immaculate mating of bulk and weight." "Thick bodied and female and at the same time phallic," the tubes are provocatively hermaphroditic from the outset; "virgin yet at the same time pregnant," they seem to embody "an immaculate mating." In the hermaphroditic materials of his art, these strangely phallicized wombs of desire, Elmer sees both the masculine and feminine forces of conception and creation. In a transfer of fertility, this immaculate mating of virginity and pregnancy seems to inspire the "brooding maternity" of the artist. Paradoxically, however, the "innocent clean brushes" and the "immaculate mating" seem to describe a virgin birth that would remove art from a sexuality which threatens to taint both creation and procreation. As "Elmer" focuses on the moment before conception, the artist seems to have a closer link to God's creation than woman's procreation: the desire that lies "wombed" is nothing less than the "world itself." The very images that charge the male artist's act of creation with gender and sexuality seem to distance this process from the sexual defilement that is part of the traditional story of female procreation.

In *Mosquitoes,* Faulkner's novel about Bohemian life in 1920s New Orleans, there are repeated conversations about the tensions between life and art that recall the concerns of "Elmer." Neither Mr. Talliaferro (an admirer of art and the female form and a sales clerk in the sensitive area of women's clothing) nor Mrs. Maurier (a self-styled patroness of the arts) is an artist. However, when the two meet on the street carrying packages, each turns out to bear an icon which, like everything else in this novel, becomes the occasion for a meditation on art and artists. Mrs. Maurier's object is "a dull lead plaque from which in dim bas relief of faded red and blue simpered a Madonna with an expression of infantile astonishment identical with that of Mrs. Maurier." After she reveals the object she is carrying, the curious woman insists on finding out what is in Mr. Talliaferro's parcel, which contains a bottle of milk. With her own "breast heav[ing] with repression," she asks, " 'A bottle of milk? Have you turned artist, too?' " Laughing with "abortive heartiness," Talliaferro responds: " 'An artist? You flatter me, dear lady. I'm afraid my soul does not aspire so high.' " As he tries to represent himself as a "Maecenas" (the classical figure who is credited with bringing the arts to the Emperor Augustus), Mrs. Maurier's androgynous niece interrupts his assertion, " 'I am content to be merely a—' " and completes his sentence with the devastating word " 'Milkman.' "

Earlier, near the opening of *Mosquitoes,* the sculptor Gordon has sent Mr. Talliaferro out on a mundane errand to return an empty bottle and get a new bottle of milk. As he sets out, Mr. Talliaferro is embarrassed by the bottle itself. Walking past "two people indistinguishably kissing" in a "darkling corridor," the "unwashed milk bottle" he clutches in his hand feels "clammy" and "unbearably dirty." Hoping to conceal the increasingly suggestive object in a newspaper, in desperation he wraps it in "his immaculate linen handkerchief . . . thrusting the bottle beneath his coat" where "it bulged distressingly under his exploring hand." Embarrassingly phallic in this uncomfortably masturbatory imagery, the empty bottle bulging beneath his coat becomes an appendage which (like the embarrassing appellation "Milkman") seems disturbingly hermaphroditic. In Mr. Talliaferro's hands, it is a dirty vessel that is as suggestively seminal as it has been innocently bovine. Talliaferro is described as "nursing his bottle" when it is both empty and full; the grocer identifies the full milk bottle as feminine, agreeing to " 'make her in a parcel.' "[3] Mrs. Maurier's odd joke about the milk bottle identifying Talliaferro as an artist is consistent with the associations in "Elmer" that gender the materials of art in images that picture them as simultaneously phallic and maternal.[4]

The icons associated with art in *Mosquitoes*—the simpering face of the virgin mother on Mrs. Maurier's plaque and the milk bottle—are juxtaposed with the work of art that has been carved by Gordon. This work is described as "motionless and passionately eternal—the virginal breastless torso of a girl, headless, armless, legless, in marble temporarily caught and hushed yet passionate still for escape" (*M* 11). According to Gordon, his statue represents his "feminine ideal: a virgin with no legs to leave me, no arms to hold me, no head to talk to me" (*M* 26). (Gordon's virgin is inviolable, he argues later, only because man has not found a way to defile marble.) Gordon's ideal woman is female yet unmaternal, virginal yet not entirely sexless. This virginal torso is similar to the vases that Horace Benbow blows from glass in Faulkner's third novel, *Sartoris*, vases which also are described as idealized feminine figures.

Emphasizing the purity of his work, Benbow describes one of
his early creations as "a small chaste shape in clear glass . . .
fragile as a silver lily and incomplete."[5] Like Gordon, Benbow
seems driven by the need to make a virginal woman; his other
work of art is described as an "almost perfect vase of clear
amber, larger, more richly and chastely serene, which he kept
always on his night table and called by his sister's name." This
vase, honored in the place of Benbow's sister, would be called
"Narcissa"; and this name for the work of art suggests that this
"chastely serene" object is not just an echo but it is also a
reflection of the artist in a feminine form. Quoting a line from
Keats's "Ode on a Grecian Urn," Benbow addresses both his
sister and the vase without distinction as " 'Thou still unravished
bride of quietness' " (S 154).

To Horace Benbow, the works of the glass blowers whom he
watches in Europe are " 'Sheerly and tragically beautiful, like
preserved flowers. . . . Macabre and inviolate' " (S 147).[6] Unlike
the defiled urns which haunt Joe Christmas's imagination in
Light in August, the cracked vessels exuding "something liquid,
deathcolored and foul"—what Faulkner in an earlier scene calls
"periodic filth"[7]—and unlike Caddy Compson, who is called a
"frail doomed vessel,"[8] these works of art are presented as
"unravished," virginal, and "chaste." Like Faulkner himself,
who would later recall bending over the blank sheet, "unmarred" and "inviolate,"[9] as he began to write *The Sound and
the Fury*, Faulkner's artists seem obsessed with the virginity
and chastity of their works of art. Like Faulkner himself, who
would compare his own effort in *The Sound and the Fury* "to
make myself a beautiful and tragic little girl"[10] to the making of
a vase, Faulkner's artists seem driven to create art which is
modeled on the female form. These emblematic images—the
pregnant virginity of paint tubes, painted icons of the Virgin
Mary, dirty and peculiarly embarrassing milk bottles, sculpted
female torsos without breasts, chastely feminine vases, and
virginal blank pages—form the suggestive background for works

which speculate on the troubling place of the female body in male artists' drives toward creation.

In the misogynist world of *Mosquitoes*, real artists are men (or women such as the lesbian, Eva Wiseman) who are driven in their art at least in part by the desire for women. For some of them, the addiction to words is "like morphine" and as one says " 'the Thing is merely the symbol for the Word' " (*M* 130), but repeatedly these words and other forms of art focus on women. Fairchild argues that " 'every word a writing man writes is put down' " to impress " 'some woman. . . . [M]aybe she ain't always a flesh and blood creature. She may be only the symbol of a desire' " (*M* 250). As in the story Gordon tells about Cyrano, who has trapped the woman he loves in the pages of a book (a story which, as Mrs. Maurier's epicene niece recognizes, explains Gordon's own relation to his sculpture of the virginal torso arrested in the moment of flight), art seems to be a way of "making" women in both senses of the verb. Not only is art seen as a way to seduce women (in the words of one of the aesthetes from *Mosquitoes*, " 'the illusion that art is just a valid camouflage for rutting' " (*M* 71); it also becomes a way of replacing women as both love objects and as creators. As if to compensate for their inability to create life from flesh, to procreate from their loins, these artists seem obsessed with the desire to embody the female. However, the female form embodied seems to be in virginal suspension: unmarried and unmarred, without child, breasts, or maternal milk. These objects are unchanging and inviolable. Just as Gordon insists on the purity of his materials and insists that marble cannot be defiled, Elmer feels happiest when he approaches "a new unstained box of paints" and Horace Benbow can only make his art because the "crucible and retorts" (elsewhere called "tubes") arrive "intact." Intact, untouched, and unstained, the materials of art are described in terms which suggest a kind of presexual innocence that represents simultaneously an erotic, generative, and procreative potential in the hands of the artist.

In one of the revealingly gendered arguments about why men

need to create, a writer in *Mosquitoes* argues that creating art is
" 'getting into life, getting into it and wrapping it around you,
becoming a part of it.' " He explains: " 'Women can do it
without art—old biology takes care of that. But men, men . . .
[Faulkner's ellipses] A woman conceives: does she care afterward whose seed it was? . . . And bears, and all the rest of her
life—her young troubling years, that is—is filled. Of course the
father can look at it occasionally. But in art, a man can create
without any assistance at all.' " The writer calls this a
" 'perversion,' " but, he argues, " 'a perversion that builds
Chartres and invents Lear is a pretty good thing.' " Raising the
idea of "[c]reation, reproduction from within," he asks: " 'Is the
dominating impulse in the world feminine . . . as aboriginal
peoples believe?' " Here, in a surprising turn, the writer recalls
the female spider who devours her mate " 'during the act of
conception' " (*M* 320), but this is not seen as an example of
female dominance, but rather as a description of the voracious-
ness of the artist who paradoxically devours life as he stands
apart from it with notebook in hand. In these overdetermined
images, artists are linked to the female force in nature; but this
particular spider recalls the women represented in *Mosquitoes*
who seem to threaten to devour man, artist, and the possibility
of art in their acts of conception. Women in Faulkner's work in
general are seen as sexual creatures whose erotic pull (like the
spider's) is a harbinger of death. Women in *Mosquitoes* are
feared as all-consuming, threatening to consume man and his
seed; it is " '[a]s though the earth the world, man and his very
desires and impulses themselves, had been invented for the
sole purpose of hushing their little hungry souls by filling their
time through serving their biological ends. . . .' " [Faulkner's
ellipses] (*M* 305). The artist's drive to create not only imitates
and rivals the female act of reproduction; it seems locked in a
death struggle, trying to devour the world before the artist
himself is devoured by the seemingly omnivorous force of
female reproduction.

In *Sartoris* (and in the slightly different version in *Flags in the Dust*), Faulkner presents one of his most powerful scenes linking the creation of art with human procreation. The site of artistic creation is figured as a scene of procreation witnessed by Horace Benbow as he takes a journey which seems to lead him into the belly of the beast—or more specifically, into the womb of a woman. Visiting a glass blowing foundry in Europe, Horace Benbow discovers the primal scene of his art as he descends into the fired furnace among the grotesque shadows of a benignly presented Inferno. He tells his sister, Narcissa:

> They work in caves . . . down flights of stairs underground. You feel water seeping under your foot while you're reaching for the next step; and when you put your hand out to steady yourself against the wall, it's wet when you take it away. It feels just like blood. . . . And 'way ahead you see the glow. All of a sudden the tunnel comes glimmering out of nothing; then you see the furnace, with things rising and falling before it, shutting off the light, and the walls go glimmering again. At first they're just shapeless things hunching about. Antic, with shadows on the bloody walls, red shadows. A glare, and black shapes like paper dolls weaving and rising and falling in front of it, like a magic-lantern shutter. And then a face comes out, blowing, and other faces sort of swell out of the red dark with faces like painted balloons. (S 146–47)[11]

This descent into a cave with "bloody walls" or wet walls that feel "like blood" (in both novels) also seems to be a descent into the human body. The "tunnel" which appears "all of a sudden" coming "out of nothing" marks a moment of origin. Like the newly born coming into light and life, the "face [which] comes out blowing" and the "other faces [which] swell out of the red dark like painted balloons" emerge from the "red dark" head first. However, in this scene, in which the source of the light is also the crucible of art, the faces which appear "blowing" are those of the artists who breathe and blow shape into their malleable materials. These pristine shapes, formed by the breath of the body, balloonlike, are articulated by the artist's breath and made in his image. Descending into a womblike site of creation, Horace Benbow finds a scene of creation in which artists seem to be born and to give birth to their works of art.

The "chaste" vases that Benbow creates, like the one that he "called by his sister's name" and addressed as a "still unravished bride," are feminine figures; even as they (like Gordon's statue) represent only part of a woman, they figure the female body as a potential container or vessel. For Faulkner, who called the "beautiful and tragic little girl" he was trying to make in *The Sound and the Fury* "a frail doomed vessel," and who referred to a woman he fancied at the time as "a lovely vase,"[12] virginal women seem to be empty vases while other women are vessels that are already filled—perhaps with the bloody signs of procreative potential, like the filth which seems to pour from the cracked urns in Joe Christmas's fantasy about menstruation in *Light in August*. Although Benbow sees the balloonlike heads of artists emerge as the vases are made, neither his vases nor the fleeing marble virgin created by Gordon have heads. In *Light in August*, before the castration and murder of Joe Christmas, Faulkner returns to what might be seen as a scene of female castration. In a scene which in some way recalls Gordon's abbreviated statue and looks forward to the decapitation of does in "Delta Autumn," Joanna Burden's head is found nearly severed from her body in an enactment of the traditional Western insistence on the mind/body split. (While the figure of the headless woman emphasizes the idea of a female body untroubled by the mediating and potentially masculine part located in the head, the does in "Delta Autumn" have their heads removed because they tell a story of signifying absence: an absence of antlers which announces that the animals were female creatures. By cutting off the does' heads, the hunters conceal the fact that they have not respected the laws against slaughtering females, the sources of generation.) Despite the liplike rim which Faulkner elsewhere imagines being kissed, the virginal vases are headless figures which like Gordon's statue represent women only as an "incomplete" or dismembered and truncated body.

It is Gordon, Faulkner's most serious artist, who realizes that there is something missing—but he locates this lack not in his breastless, armless, legless, and headless sculpture of a girl who seems defined by absence and dismemberment, but rather in an actual woman. Returning from the boat trip he has taken to look at Mrs. Maurier's niece (the girl who resembles his statue so much that she might have been the model for it), Gordon molds a female head in clay. The head, however, does not have the masculine jaw of the young woman whose body resembles his marble girl; it represents the face of the aged virgin who has not escaped time by being frozen in stone.

> It was clay, yet damp, and from out its dull, dead grayness Mrs. Maurier looked at them. . . . Her eyes were caverns thumbed with two motions into the dead familiar astonishment of her face; and . . . behind them, somewhere within those empty sockets . . . there was something else—something that exposed her face for the mask it was, and still more, a mask unaware. (M 322)

Speculating on her emptiness, one of the aesthetes (recalling the story of Mrs. Maurier's youth being traded in a marriage to a much older man) sees " 'something thwarted back of it all, something stifled, yet which won't quite die.' " In a story reminiscent of Sherwood Anderson, Fairchild, the writer Faulkner based on Anderson, declares: " 'A virgin. . . . She missed something: her body told her so, insisted, forced her to try to remedy it and fill the vacuum. But now her body is old; it no longer remembers that it missed anything, and all she has left is a habit, the ghost of a need to rectify something the lack of which her body has long since forgotten about' " (M 326). Once a muse in her own right who inspired painters with her cold "Dresden china" beauty, Mrs. Maurier is now a hollow woman who no longer tries " 'to fill the vacuum' " or " 'to rectify . . . the lack.' " Gordon dismembers Mrs. Maurier at the neck, allowing her cavernous "thumbed" eyes and "empty sockets" to tell her story. Earlier, preoccupied with the body of the virginal niece who is identified with his sculpture of the truncated female torso, Gordon takes Mrs. Maurier's face in his hands and exclaims: " 'Why aren't you her mother, so you could tell me how conceiving her must have been, how carrying her in your loins must have been?' " (*M* 154). This is perhaps the clearest expression of womb envy in all of Faulkner's work. The hollow and empty Mrs. Maurier cannot tell him what he longs to know because she has missed exactly what he has missed. Although he can make women out of marble, he cannot make them out of flesh, as she might have; he cannot be a vessel for the origination of life.

In *Sartoris*, as Benbow witnesses the primal scene of his art, within the seemingly bloody dungeon " 'all of a sudden, the tunnel' " is said to come " 'glimmering out of nothing.' " This description of the furnace seems to stand for what is not described: the way in which the vases emerge from the breath of the blowing men as tunnels coming out of nothing. Both the scene and the activity witnessed in it evoke a frightening channel of birth. In *Mosquitoes*, the fog-shrouded shore is associated, in Faulkner's words, with a primal "first prehistoric morning of time; it might have been the very substance in which the seed of the beginning of things fecundated." The trees which "might have been the first of living things" are described as "too recently born to know either fear or astonishment, dragging their sluggish umbilical cords from out the old miasmic womb of a nothingness latent and dreadful" (*M* 169). In this fantasy, as with Elmer's experience of his tubes of the paint, the "whole world" lies "wombed"—or rather the whole world seems to emerge from "the old miasmic womb of a nothingness." Both of these scenes locate moments of birth and creation in an originary nothing.

In a related passage, Mrs. Maurier's niece, the androgynous muse with the treelike body, masculine jaw, and "buttocks that . . . might well belong to a boy of fifteen,' " also has a vision of a nothing at the center of the female body. She speculates on the difference between her body and that of Jenny, the other desired female in the novel, whose breath is said to be "a little regular wind come recently from off fresh milk" and whose body seems to have what Fairchild calls "the soft bulging rabbitlike things women used to have inside their clothes" (*M* 240). Fascinated with the shape of the uncovered body of this most feminine of forms, as "Jenny's angelic nakedness went beyond her vision" and disappeared past a window, the boyish muse is struck by an almost philosophical vision about the significance of woman. After looking at the naked female body, "suddenly she stared at nothing with a vague orifice vaguely in the center of it, and beyond the orifice a pale moonfilled sky" (*M* 140).

Much earlier, near the opening of *Mosquitoes*, when the niece sees Gordon's statue for the first time and recognizes it as being like herself, she has another precocious insight into the female form and art. Looking at the female torso, Mrs. Maurier asks, " 'What does it signify' "; and the niece, an unlikely reader of Shakespeare, answers: " 'Nothing.' " Long before he had begun to fashion his "tale/ Told by an idiot, full of sound and fury/ Signifying nothing," and the novel which stands as an explication of Macbeth's famous soliloquy, Faulkner—like Macbeth—was concerned with what it meant to be "of woman born." In his early work *Mosquitoes*, he includes at least two visions of the naked female form "signifying nothing." Both of these muses in *Mosquitoes*, the woman associated with milk and fecundity who becomes an image of nothing with a hole in it and the dismembered torso that is said to signify nothing, seem to represent the dreadful womb of nothingness from which men are born.

I have been suggesting that we find in Faulkner's early works a relentless series of images and figures which almost obsessively associate the artist and the work of art with the troubling presence of the female body. In this complex and often contradictory series of associations, the conventional notion of the artist as creator is translated into highly charged sexual terms in which not only the act of creation but even the materials of art are eroticized—yet at the same time, the notion that the artistic process is either hermaphroditic or an immaculate conception (or both) seems to deny the necessity of a sexual union. Male or

masculine artists, defined by their desire for women, make
works of art which are the figures and objects of their desire;
yet these female figures seem inviolable. Made from hard
materials like marble and glass, these sculptural forms seem
frozen in a state of virginal reluctance. Gordon's sculpture and
Benbow's fragile forms represent the female body and the
ostensible site of the womb, but these figures are cut off
from the threatening maturity of the maternal breast and the
possibility of a nurturance which is depicted as consuming man.
Indeed, while women are defined in *Mosquitoes* as "merely
articulated genital organs" (*M* 241), men are depicted as part
of the materials consumed in the unwavering female drive
toward procreation.

As he incorporates the language of procreation and birth,
Faulkner seems to display a kind of womb envy; yet he also
suggests a fear of feminizing the artist by putting him in the
woman's place. The emphasis on art as a way of bypassing
women, the singular creation which is called "a perversion,"
suggests the artist's fear as he seems to take the place of a
woman. These images, which seem to proliferate as if out of
control, reveal the artist's desires to control, usurp, and deny
female sexuality: to create, become, and somehow nullify the
woman through the creation of art. Faulkner's artists seem to
be at the center of an anxiety about origins. Like the world
which is created out of the "miasmic womb of a nothingness
latent and dreadful," the act of birth, even the moment of
conception, seems to be a terrifying creation from a female
abyss. The womb which creates is also the site of absence. The
work of art may seem idealized in the form of the female body:
virgin, chaste, undefiled, potentially but not yet fertile; but its
dismembered state recalls the frightening fact that the female
form is the site of a crucial absence—a terrifying and signifying
nothing.

"Wild Palms" contains Faulkner's most intimate and tender
portrayal of the female body; and the graphically flesh-driven

woman at the heart of the story is a woman artist. Published in 1939 along with "Old Man" in the volume entitled *The Wild Palms*, which is comprised of two ostensibly unrelated stories presented in the novel in alternating chapters and separated by a decade in historical time, both story lines ("Old Man" and "Wild Palms") focus on, among other things, the haplessness of men as they confront forces of nature, the bodies of women, and the inevitability of pregnancy. "Old Man" tells the story of various people, including a pregnant woman, who are caught in the flow of the flooded Mississippi in 1927. "Wild Palms" in Faulkner's description is "the part of it about the doctor who performed the abortion on his own sweetheart."[13] "Wild Palms," like Faulkner's early fiction and *The Sound and the Fury*, is about art and sexuality, about the problem of writing and reproduction and the crisis of creation and procreation. Written a decade after the publication of *The Sound and the Fury*, "Wild Palms" in many ways marks Faulkner's return to the explicit dramatization of the concerns about art, artists, and the effort to embody the female that form the fertile matrix for so much of his early fiction.

In "Wild Palms," a doctor with the evocative name of Wilbourne becomes a writer; with this twist, "Wild Palms" develops into a shockingly explicit allegory about the relation between sexuality and art. Returning like a bad dream to the scenes and themes of Faulkner's early fiction, this work emerges as a disturbing culmination of Faulkner's past obsessions. "Wild Palms" not only dramatizes but also literalizes the relationship between creation and procreation as they come into violent conflict. One might flesh out Faulkner's summary of the plot by saying that "Wild Palms" tells the story of a male writer who performs an abortion on a female sculptor and woman artist. As we shall see, Faulkner's story also depicts an artist who kills a living woman in his effort to rob the mother.

Mosquitoes centers on questions about art and creation and finally on speculations about art and sexual desire. In "Wild Palms," sexual desire is consummated and the making of art appears to be almost as physical. In a tawdry hotel where the lovers meet to consummate their relationship, Charlotte Rittenmeyer refuses to have sex because she does not want their erotic union to begin in "back alleys." As Wilbourne stands over her, "holding her wrists," Charlotte abruptly justifies her refusal by evoking her art: " 'I told you how I wanted to make things, take the fine hard clean brass or stone and cut it, no matter how hard, how long it took, cut it into something fine, that you could be proud to show, that you could touch, hold, see the behind side of it and feel the fine solid weight.' "[14] In what otherwise might seem to be a peculiar interruption, Charlotte's suggestion that the hardness of her materials brings purity to her work recalls the sexual aesthetics advanced by Faulkner's other serious artist, Gordon, the sculptor from *Mosquitoes*, who praises the hardness and inviolability of his marble. Making love in "Wild Palms" is closely related to the making of art. Repeatedly in "Wild Palms," Charlotte insists that she likes "bitching"—her raw word for sex—"and making things with [her] hands" (*WP* 88).

The narrative of "Wild Palms" opens near the end of the lovers' story, circling back to relate the events of the year in which the young intern Wilbourne leaves New Orleans with the married Charlotte Rittenmeyer. The abortion already has taken place at the beginning of the book and it casts an ominous light over the chapters which tell the story of the couple's lives before the narrative brings them back to the Gulf Coast and the scene of Charlotte's death. In the opening section of the book, the landlord (who is also a physician) tries to understand which "organ" is causing Charlotte's apparent illness, and like the reader he looks for the truth of a living woman that he can glimpse only through a screen of leaves: "It seemed to him that he saw the truth already, the shadowy indefinite shape of truth, as though he were separated from the truth only by a veil just as he was separated from the living woman by the screen of oleander leaves. . . . *I will have plenty of time in which to learn just which organ it is she is listening to* (*WP* 6). The landlord asks Wilbourne what he does and Wilbourne inexplicably tells him that he is " 'trying to be a painter.' " Explaining that he is not a house painter, he adds, " 'I paint pictures. . . . At least, I think I do' " (*WP* 18).[15] This claim is never explained but the landlord's assertion that follows declaring that the woman is "probably still bleeding" turns out to provide an ominous commentary on Wilbourne's art.

In the second section of "Wild Palms," which recalls the initial scenes of *Mosquitoes*, Charlotte Rittenmeyer and Harry Wilbourne meet for the first time in "French town" in an artist's studio filled with unframed paintings. Charlotte's assertion to the young intern that she is a painter reveals an echo in Wilbourne's surprising assertion (at the beginning of the text but later in the sequence of the narrative) to the landlord/physician. Before the evening is over she tells him, " 'Listen. I lied to you. I don't paint. I work with clay, and some in brass, and once with a piece of stone, with a chisel and maul. Feel.' " Instead of handing him a piece of her art, she asks him to feel her hand. She takes "his hand and drew his finger-tips along the base of her other palm—the broad, blunt, strong, supple-fingered hand . . . the skin at the base and lower joints of the fingers not calloused exactly but smoothly hardened and toughened like the heel of a foot" (*WP* 40–41). Linked with passion, works of art, "transformed steadily and endlessly beneath [Charlotte's] deft untiring hands" (*WP* 89), emerge from and are equated with the palms of the living woman. Having given him her palm, the part of her body which stands in for the sculpture and which has itself been sculpted by the act of shaping art, Charlotte explains the difference between sculpture and painting: " 'I make . . . something you can touch, pick up, something with weight in your hand that you can look at the behind side of, that displaces air and displaces water.' " Introducing a hierarchy of the arts, she insists this is not like painting, " '[n]ot poking at a piece of cloth with a knife or a brush like you were trying to put together a jig-saw puzzle with a rotten switch' " (*WP* 41). When Wilbourne comes to call

himself "a painter" as well, the questionable claim has become
filled with horror since Charlotte herself has been put in the
place of the work of art. The living woman has become a "jig-
saw puzzle" to be "put together" by her lover "with a knife."
Wilbourne's gratuitous lie that he is a painter becomes increasingly bizarre and disturbing as the novel progresses, especially
when he advances from brushes to knives.

As we will see, Wilbourne does make a single significant
painting but he is figured most graphically as a writer. Fired
from his low level position at a hospital, Wilbourne writes
stories for "confession magazines" that begin with sentences
such as, " 'I had the body and desires of a woman yet in
knowledge and experience of the world I was but a child' " and
" 'If I had only had a mother's love to guard me on that fatal
day' " (WP 121). He appears to fear the "respectability" that
makes men into "chiropractors and clerks and bill posters and
motormen and pulp writers"—the respectability that makes
even sinning and writing pulp fiction seem routine; yet, like the
author of sensationalist works such as Sanctuary and The Wild
Palms, Wilbourne is confident that he can write to " 'make all
the money [he and Charlotte] will need' " because " 'there
seems to be no limit to what I can invent on the theme of female
sex troubles' " (WP 135-36). As the winter descends, he sits
"before an unfinished page in the typewriter, believing he was
thinking of nothing, believing he was thinking only of the
money" (WP 126). Yet it is not only the money; there is an
intensity that surrounds Wilbourne's frenzy of writing which
suggests that he has become entangled in the process itself: " 'I
had tied myself hand and foot in a little strip of inked ribbon,
daily I watched myself getting more and more tangled in it like
a roach in a spider web' " (WP 134). While the artist in Mosquitoes is likened to the female spider who devours her mate,
Wilbourne seems to have become entrapped in the web. Characters travel light in "The Wild Palms," but as Wilbourne
admits near the close of section three, he would not have
dared to desert his typewriter any more " 'than I would my

eyelashes' " (*WP* 134). Wilbourne writes the stories "from the first capital to the last period in one sustained frenzied agonising rush" (*WP* 121), neglecting to eat while he is writing.

The obsessiveness of the bland Wilbourne's writing of pulp fiction seems out of proportion, as if invested with the intensity of Faulkner's own obsessive writing.[16] Wilbourne's most significant act of creation in the story is not his fiction but rather a strange painting. In the same section of the novel, before he becomes a writer, we see Wilbourne's effort to be a painter. Day after day he sits in a clearing near their cabin in the woods with "his half of the sketch pad and his converted sardine can color-box intact and pristine beside him." Then, bizarrely, he begins to paint a calendar. As he unravels "one by one out of the wine-sharp and honey-still warp of tideless solitude the lost Tuesdays and Fridays and Sundays," he realizes "that he could prove his figures, establish mathematical truth out of the sunny and timeless void into which the individual days had vanished by the dates and intervals between Charlotte's menstrual periods" (*WP* 113–14). Recalling Elmer with his "new unstained box of paints" and Horace Benbow with the "intact" tubes, crucible, and retorts which are the tools of his art, in a phrase which echoes Elmer's idea of "immaculate mating," Wilbourne claims that his decision to paint time in the form of a calendar measured in relation to Charlotte's bodily cycles came from a notion which was "innocently conceived." Indeed, his painting is shaped by the tidal flow which marks the absence of conception and paradoxically establishes "truth" from the midst of a "tideless solitude" and a "timeless void." In this painting of days, Wilbourne initially constructs a six-week month as he tries to deny the coming of winter; this long month in terms of the narrative as a whole is a troubling detail, quietly introducing the specter of pregnancy long before the actual moment of conception.

Charlotte, who returns from her own painting expedition to find that Wilbourne is uncharacteristically happy, asks: " 'Have you painted a picture or have you discovered at last that the

human race really doesn't have to even try to produce art—' "
(*WP* 115). Her query and its air of significance remain unex-
plained. Wilbourne indeed has made a painting, and this painting may also be read as posing a question about the "human
race" and the drive "to produce art." Wilbourne's painting, like
the torso sculpted by Gordon in Mosquitoes, is measured
against the truth embodied by a living woman.[17] This painting
of the absence of conception, even without its anomalous six-
week month, suggests a procreative potential. Wilbourne's art,
articulated and measured through Charlotte's blood flow, calls
attention to the other possibility, an absence of blood, the
absence of a period which might demonstrate how completely
Wilbourne's art and his painted calibration of days can be
supplanted by procreation, by creation in flesh and blood.

Charlotte Rittenmeyer already has created in flesh and blood;
she is the mother of two children, daughters who are left behind
with her husband when she leaves New Orleans to run away
with Wilbourne. From the opening of the novel, the landlord
and physician realizes: "His wife would have noticed the faint
mark of the absent wedding ring, but he, the doctor, saw more
than that: *She has borne children. . . . One, anyway; I would
stake my degree on that*" (*WP* 11). As a mother as well as a
sculptor, Charlotte Rittenmeyer bears the marks of her experience on her body. Wilbourne, too, despite their passionate
affair, also sees Charlotte as a mother. At the close of the third
and most extensive section of "Wild Palms," the portion of the
book which is devoted to the description of artists and art, he
confesses to McCord, the journalist friend who first loaned him
his typewriter, that " 'there is something in me [Charlotte] is
not mistress to but mother' "; and, with surprising intensity, he
adds: " 'there is something in me you and she parented between
you, that you are father of' " (*WP* 141).[18] What has been born of
Wilbourne remains mysterious, but his reference to Charlotte
and McCord as parents suggests that he sees himself as the
child of an artist and a writer. The intensity which surrounds
Wilbourne's creation of what he calls "moron's pap," suggests

that there is something primal in the frenzied acts of writing in which he imagines " 'the body and desires of a woman' " and " 'a mother's love.' "

After leaving her family, Charlotte begins to make figures, some of which are said to be the size of "small children." Working with paper soaking in water, wire, paint, shellac, and wood-fiber, Charlotte makes her first "collection of little figures—deer and wolfhounds and horses and men and women, lean epicene sophisticated and bizarre, with a quality fantastic and perverse" (*WP* 87); and even after she tells Wilbourne that she is " 'not an artist' " anymore, she seems unable to stop. Faulkner, the author of a play called "The Marionettes" which he illustrated with drawings, pictures his woman artist making "puppets, marionettes" to be used in photographs "for magazine covers and advertisements" and possibly even for use in "charades, tableaux [in a] hired hall." Modeled out of shaped paper among other things, Charlotte's art shifts focus from animals, people, and humorous historical figures to great figures from literature: "a Quixote with a gaunt mad dreamy uncoordinated face, a Falstaff with the worn face of a syphilitic barber and gross with meat . . . Roxane with spit curls and a wad of gum . . . Cyrano with the face of a low comedy Jew in vaudeville" (*WP* 91). Whereas Wilbourne in his writing assumes the confessional voice of the fallen woman, following a tradition in the novel which extends from Moll Flanders to the unrepentant though severely punished sexually transgressive heroine of *The Wild Palms* itself, Charlotte Rittenmeyer's rendition of great figures of literature "almost as large as small children" recalls her creative and procreative potential, her status as a mother and a creator of works of art. A creator of bodies as both mother and artist, Charlotte here creates literary characters in figures that seem to both parody and give life to the characters in books.

Charlotte's "fragile perverse and disturbing" figures, at first "lean" and "epicene," become caricatures of literary characters. Falstaff, "gross with meat," is described as "a single figure, yet when [Wilbourne] looked at it he seemed to see two: the man and the gross flesh like a huge bear and its fragile consumptive keeper; it seemed to him that he could actually watch the man struggling with the mountain of entrails as the keeper might wrestle with the bear, not to overcome it but to pass it, escape it, as you do with the atavistic beasts in nightmare" (*WP* 91). Wilbourne seems to see in the fat of Falstaff the female form of body within a body. The entrails and the fate of man and woman as bearers of flesh is the nightmare of "Wild Palms" in which Charlotte goes beyond the pure essences represented in the "epicine" or androgynous figures of her earlier art to embody the fate of woman as the keeper of flesh.

Wilbourne has another glimpse of the strange physicality of art and its representations of bodies when he visits Charlotte at her night job as a window dresser in a department store in Chicago. Waiting amidst the manikins, "surrounded by jointless figures with suave organless bodies and serene almost incredible faces," Wilbourne watches as the women who clean the store on their knees move about like "another species just crawled molelike from some tunnel or orifice leading from the foundation of the earth itself" (*WP* 120). In contrast to this graphic image of the animal-like women who seem to emerge from the earth's "orifice," the "organless bodies" (who, like Charlotte's puppets, are designed to perform in tableaux devoted to advertising art) have an unbelievable serenity, a more pristine form that is reminiscent of Gordon's sculptures.

Early in "Wild Palms," in a bizarre and strangely self-reflective reverie, Wilbourne muses over what is wrong with the role of characters in books in relation to people like himself. "*Maybe I can read*, he thought. Then he cursed, thinking, *That's it. It's all exactly backward. It should be the books, the people in the books inventing and reading about us—the Does and the Roes and the Wilbournes and Smiths—males and females but without the pricks or cunts*" (*WP* 52). While it is not entirely clear here whether the readers or characters are organless, Wilbourne himself is, of course, also a character in a book. In Jonson's *Bartholomew Fair*, the Puppet Dionysus wins a debate with a

Puritan by pointing out that "your old stale argument against the players" about wearing the clothes of the opposite sex will not hold because puppets "have neither male nor female amongst us."[19] Unlike the organless bodies of the manikins, the literary creations of "Wild Palms" seem to have genders and bodies, bodies that become too real. Wilbourne is a character in a book who becomes a writer of stories about "Wilbournes" and tales of women whose fate is not unlike that of the "Does" (if not Roes) who are the sacrificial figures of "Delta Autumn" in Faulkner's *Go Down, Moses*. By the end of Charlotte's story, it is clear to the doctor *"just which organ it is she is listening to."* Like one of Wilbourne's characters with an unwanted pregnancy ("At sixteen I was an unwed mother" [*WP* 123]), the object of the writer's fantasies and speculations about the maternal body, Charlotte dies after becoming "two" in her "gross flesh." Although a literary character, a puppetlike figure, as artist and as mother she pays the price of making bodies and having a body.

We can read in "Wild Palms" a horrible culmination of Faulkner's earlier concerns with the source of art and the struggle between creation and procreation. The writer who composes melodramatic and confessional stories in the name of passion, if not art, performs an abortion on the woman who is the sexually vital artist and the embodiment of the mother. As Charlotte dies in a hospital room, a policeman, who calls Wilbourne by the name of "Webster," as if he somehow recognizes his charge's professional association with words, tells him: " 'You played hell, didn't you? Using a knife. I'm old-fashioned; the old way still suits me. I don't want variety' " (*WP* 299). Earlier, as Wilbourne prepares to perform the abortion, Charlotte herself makes the same bitter joke. In a remark which recalls the sexualized scene with the knife in *The Sound and the Fury*, she quips: " 'All right. We'll wait a minute. It's simple. It's funny. New, I mean. We've done this lots of ways but not with knives, have we? There. Now your hand has stopped' " (*WP* 221). In Charlotte's words, which recall the mad desires of Quentin Compson, this extreme version of a negative primal scene will mean it " 'will be us again forever and ever' " (*WP* 220). Much later, after they have returned to Mississippi, Wilbourne looks at Charlotte's dying body, sensing "a black wind" which fills "the room but coming from nothing . . . no croaching shadow of ineradicable blackness, no shape of death cuckolding him; nothing to see, yet it was there, he not permitted to watch his own cuckolding but only to look down upon the invisible pregnancy of his horning" (*WP* 285). The abortion, repeatedly imaged as a knifing, or in this instance as a horning, is presented as a novel and horrible revision of the sexual act: the knife which replaces the phallus in this construction has been already implicated in "Wild Palms" as one of the tools of a lesser art.

In a grotesque literalization of the early themes of his work, Faulkner has invented a writer who sees no end to the market for stories about the sex troubles of women; and this writer, who claims to be a painter, takes his knife to life, "poking" at the body of the woman he loves, the figure of fecundity who is both mother and artist. With horrible appropriateness, the woman who is in pain from Wilbourne's earlier horning with "the knife" seems to ask him to go beyond painting, to go beyond "poking" at her as if she were "a piece of cloth." Asking him to become a sculptor, she begs him to carve her out: " 'take the knife and cut it out of me. All of it. Deep. So there wont be anything left but just a shell to hold the cold air' " (*WP* 286). Here, the woman suffering from the abortive attempts of a writer as he assumes the role of a painter asks to be freed from life by being made into a shell. Although she cannot by any means become the virginal vase, this woman artist desires to be emptied of her procreative organs and pleads for the death which will come from being an emptied container, a version of the idealized work of art which takes the female form in Faulkner's early works.

In *Mosquitoes*, the sufficiency of Gordon's ideal woman, the truncated and inviolable statue, "passionately eternal," is called into question by the appearance of the young woman who in her flesh seems to mirror yet miraculously transform art. Preferring hard substances like marble, perhaps because it will not melt like wax to the shape of his touch, Gordon has no hope of becoming a Pygmalion whose work, infused with the heat of his desire, will turn into flesh. He is, however, haunted and temporarily lured away from his art by a breathing Galatea whose bodily presence as she stands in his studio seems to suggest the limits of his "feminine ideal." Gordon does not mate with the muse to produce art; instead he seems troubled by his susceptibility to the siren call of woman. Seen in this light, Gordon's art seems to be an effort both to bypass sexuality and to replace the need for reproduction—to create female figures (on one occasion, a body, and on the other, a head) without reproductive organs. Although procreation seems to provide both the model and the impetus for the human need "to produce art," Faulkner reveals through Gordon another driving force in art, the desire to create objects which erase the means of reproduction.

In *As I Lay Dying*, the absence of a period after Darl's sentence, "*Addie Bundren is dead,*"[20] suggests a lack of closure. This is not in the otherworldly sense of Dickinson's claim that "This world is not conclusion" but rather in the sense that death, in itself inconclusive, is part of a collective social process. Addie Bundren's only daughter, Dewey Dell, explains in her next monologue, "God gave women a sign when something has happened bad" (*AILD*, 58). The female sign of "something . . . bad" is a sign of absence. This sign, a missing period, does not mean death;[21] instead like the earlier missing period it marks the initiation of a process—the beginning of a life which will lead to death. If Wilbourne's first painting with a brush is calibrated on the absence rather than just the alleged innocence of conception, his second and more horrible "painting" with a knife is also based on the fact of a bleeding woman; in his effort to thwart procreation with art, he tries to bring the blood which will signal the absence of conception. Wilbourne's art, like art born of William and indeed all art when read against the natural world, can only be (as Welty's painter, Audubon, realizes) "a dead thing."[22]

In the "Wild Palms," the woman is killed by the writer. As she lies dying and unconscious, Charlotte Rittenmeyer returns briefly to herself and becomes, as her name suggests, a curiously written figure. Standing with his hand on the doorframe, Wilbourne sees "the eyes open full upon him though still profoundly empty of sentience. Then he saw it begin: the *I*. It was like watching a fish rise in water—a dot, a minnow, and still increasing; in a second there would be no more pool but all sentience." As he tells her repeatedly to " 'Go back,' " she hears him "from somewhere because at once the fish became the minnow again and then the dot; in another second the eyes would be empty again and blank." Finally, her eyes in a rapid transformation become "a vortex of cognizant pupil" and while he watches, "the black shadow" which has been linked with death is "not on the belly but in the eyes" (*WP* 284–85). The *I*, of course, stands for her identity, but there is also a play between the eyes and the *I* in which Charlotte's sentience becomes strangely alphabetic. In an image which describes the fishlike body and jump of the capital letter "I" in cursive writing, this passage also acknowledges Charlotte's closeness to death as she (like Quentin Compson in his final moments of narration and life) is reduced from the signifying "I"—the fish—to the minnow and the dot, the fragile and diminished identity of the lower case "i." The dot here, while pointing to the shape of a letter, also marks a site of origin, the beginning of what will be transformed from minnow to fish and back again before emerging in what is described as a "vortex of cognizant pupil."

Pleading to be cleaned out, to be released from her abortive life, the body of Charlotte Rittenmeyer, whose identity and sentience is embodied through the eyes in the shape of letters, becomes increasingly flat. In death, Wilbourne sees "the shape of Charlotte's body just indicated and curiously flattened beneath the sheet" (*WP* 305). He witnesses what appears to be the

"collapsing of the entire body as undammed water collapses . . .
lower than the prone one of the little death called sleep, lower
even than the paper-thin spurning sole." Her body in death is
likened to "the flat earth itself and even this not low enough."
The most tenderly embodied of all of Faulkner's female characters, Charlotte Rittenmeyer is herself paper-thin and destined
to vanish with "no trace left above the insatiable dust." She has
become the opposite of her sculptures. We read: "There was no
especial shape beneath the sheet now at all and it came onto the
stretcher as if it had no weight either" (*WP* 306). The flattened
figure concealed by sheets that cover the fact that her eyes have
been drained of their alphabetic intensity erases the troubling
space of the female body and seems to suggest a desire to go
back to a point of origins before this woman was conceived and
given shape, blood, breath, and finally murdered through
writing.

In 1946, when Random House approached Faulkner about
reprinting *The Sound and the Fury* and *As I Lay Dying* in a
single volume, Faulkner expressed his disapproval, insisting
that he "had never thought about [*The Sound and the Fury*] and
As I Lay Dying in the same breath."[23] The two novels were
finally published together in a Modern Library edition, but
Faulkner believed that *The Sound and the Fury* should have
been paired with "Wild Palms." The fact that he had thought
about these two works in the same breath and that he continued
to read one novel through the other is recorded in the language
of "Wild Palms," which echoes both the words and concerns of
Faulkner's earlier novel; and the significance of this connection
is confirmed by the 1946 Appendix to *The Sound and the Fury*,
an addition which Faulkner saw as the fifth section of this work.
This genealogy, among other things, focuses attention on the
female maidenhead; to describe this place of origins, Faulkner
borrowed both words and images from a related passage in
"Wild Palms."

In what might be imagined as a transmigration of literary

souls, Harry Wilbourne of "Wild Palms" is born in the year of
Quentin's death.[24] It is Harry Wilbourne, not Quentin Compson
who seems fated to follow Miss Rosa's suggestion in *Absalom,
Absalom!* about writing to obtain material goods. Unlike his
literary predecessor, Harry Wilbourne has become a writer and
he (again running counter to Quentin) consciously refuses to
commit suicide. Assuming the voice of fallen female characters,
Wilbourne generates fictions about sexual experiences and also
goes into great detail about his own. In many ways, as he leads
the life which Quentin refuses to pursue, he is also able to
continue Quentin's philosophical obsessions with origins, with
being and time, with the meaning of virginity and finally with
the drama of the moment of conception. Wilbourne, in his most
Quentin-like reverie, speculates about " 'the current of time
that runs through remembering, that exists only in relation to
what little of reality . . . we know, else there is no such thing as
time. You know: *I was not*. Then *I am*, and then time begins,
retroactive, is was and will be. Then *I was* and so I am not and
so time never existed. It was like the instant of virginity . . .
that condition, fact, that does not actually exist except during
the instant you know you are losing it ' " (*WP* 137). Both
Harry Wilbourne and his predecessor, Quentin Compson, seem
obsessed with the idea of meaning which is generated through
loss and absence, in particular the significance of female absence
as a place of beginnings. However, as we have seen, as a writer
Wilbourne can create characters; unlike Quentin, he is able to
intervene in the competing story of female procreation even
after the point of conception.

As I suggested earlier, it is significant that when Faulkner
wrote the Appendix to *The Sound and the Fury*, he borrowed
an image from "Wild Palms" to describe the bodily signifier (the
sign of presence and absence) that is the crucial site of origins
in *The Sound and the Fury*. In the Appendix, Quentin is said to
have "loved not his sister's body but some concept of Compson
honor precariously and (he knew well) only temporarily supported by the minute fragile membrane of her maidenhead as a

miniature replica of the whole vast globy earth may be poised on the nose of a trained seal" (*SF* 411). "Wild Palms" contains closely related lines which represent not virginity but rather the equally "fragile" and suggestively "intact" moment of physical union—the "joint life" of a man and a woman. Pictured in bed with Charlotte, as Wilbourne lies "still and relaxed in the darkness while she held him, not even bothering to be aware whether his eyes were open or not, he seemed to see their joint life as a fragile globe, a bubble, which she kept balanced and intact above disaster like a trained seal does its ball" (*WP* 92). Both Charlotte and Caddy, two women whose prowess is associated with masculine nerve, are described with the same suggestive image indicating their sexual potency and erotic potential. Just as, earlier, for Faulkner's Elmer Hodge, the "world itself" lies "wombed" in the untouched—intact—materials of his art, the "fragile globe" and "whole vast globy earth," the balls associated with these sexually active female figures (however precariously poised), suggest their worldly potential. These balls are meant to be broken.

Long before he wrote "Wild Palms" and long before he wrote the 1946 Appendix, Faulkner had begun to speculate on the origins of *The Sound and the Fury*. There is no recognizable artist figure in *The Sound and the Fury*, but one might argue that at least in retrospect Faulkner cast himself in the role of the artist. Indeed, in his accounts of the novel's origins, Faulkner seems to echo the gendered terms he had used to frame the idea of art and the making of art in his earlier fiction. Whereas the cuckolded husband of *Mosquitoes* takes *The Decameron* to bed with him every night, Faulkner in the introduction he drafted for the proposed 1933 edition of *The Sound and the Fury* reveals his own fantasies about the comforts of art. Describing sitting down to write this novel, Faulkner recalled thinking: "Now I can write. Now I can make myself a vase like that which the old Roman kept at his bedside and wore the rim slowly away with kissing it." As he compares the writing of his novel to the making of a vase and tells of his desire to "make a beautiful and tragic girl,"[25] Faulkner clearly casts *The Sound and the Fury* in the role of the sexualized and idealized work of art described in the early works.

Like Gordon, Faulkner conceives of his art as a making of girls and like Benbow, whose art is also articulated though breath, Faulkner sees himself as a maker of vases. However, if Faulkner links himself to Horace Benbow and his creation of sisterly vases, the repeatedly crossed female thresholds of *The Sound and the Fury* represent a dramatic change from the earlier focus on the inviolable feminine form as providing the structure for the idealized work of art. Caddy Compson, the female figure whom Faulkner equates with the novel itself, is not finally just a virginal vase or a "tragic girl"; from the outset, she is (as the Appendix suggests) "a frail, doomed vessel." In *The Sound and the Fury*, Faulkner seems to realize that the work of art will never be chaste; he seems to know, to borrow a line from David Lodge, that words are "never virgin: words come to the writer already violated by other men."[26]

Endowing Quentin with his earlier artists' obsessions with chastity, Quentin returns again and again in this novel to the moment of conception. *The Sound and the Fury* repeatedly recalls and re-enacts the juncture of male and female as a site of origins which is crucial to art; in this sexualized conjunction, words seem to be coded as masculine and linked with impotence, and pictures (or more precisely, the pictorial) seem to be coded not just as feminine, but as gestures toward embodiment, efforts to picture the female body as an originary space. Relatively rare in Faulkner's work, these pictorial forms—the coffin [▱] of *As I Lay Dying*, the upside down delta [▽] of "Delta Autumn," and the eye 👁 of *The Sound and the Fury*—call attention to their author's interest in the visual arts; and, at the same time, each of these pictures serves as a graphic portrayal of a female container, a vessel associated with fecundity and generation. Even more suggestively, perhaps, these pictorial forms are linked by the fictions themselves to the shapes of instruments used to tell time.

The least obvious yet the most obsessively represented of these images is the eye of *The Sound and the Fury*; in this novel, the eye is not merely the window to the soul but also the displaced gateway of the female body: the site of lost virginity and the site of human origin. *The Sound and the Fury*, a book which returns again and again to the signifying eye, is obsessed with the moment of origin, the sexualized conjunction which is implicated in both the reproduction of offspring and the production of art. In this novel, Faulkner is obviously concerned with the virginity or chastity of his characters but like the artists of his earlier works, he is also concerned with questions about the chastity of art. In *The Sound and the Fury*, Faulkner seems to focus on the concept of purity as a lost ideal. Obsessed with the idea of loss, *The Sound and the Fury* turns repeatedly to the moment of conception, the site of a fertile breaking which marks a scene of origins. While these fertile conjunctions produce art and discover a potency in words, the male Compsons (the first three narrators of *The Sound and the Fury*) are faced with the threat of impotence as they find themselves caught in and taunted by the futility and sterility of words. Again and again, the Compson brothers tell stories in which they find themselves feminized by their experience of dangerous female thresholds. Benjy goes through the gate which he associates with his missing sister and he is literally dismembered as a result of his pursuit of a schoolgirl, castrated for his only effort at speech in the novel as he describes himself as "trying to say." Associated with money robbed from women and pawing at his mother's empty pockets, Jason Compson seems to feed on telling and retelling his story of "outrage" and "impotence." In contrast, Quentin repeatedly insists on his own sexual experience; however, this experience exists only in the form of words. As Donald Kartiganer argues, Quentin is driven by his desire "to see words as the originator rather than the imitator of deeds . . . [insisting] that words have a substance more real than bodies."[27] Entrapped in their own narratives, the Compson brothers find themselves defined by the impotence of words, particularly in relation to the potency of sexually active women (Caddy Compson, Miss Quentin, and Lorraine) who threaten to embody life and death.

In *The Sound and the Fury,* Faulkner is not merely concerned with the virginity or chastity of his characters, as the artists of his earlier works are concerned with the chastity of art. The novel itself is generated to fill the vacuum left by a missing woman, the lost sister. André Bleikasten describes *The Sound and the Fury* and *As I Lay Dying* as "novels *about* lack and loss" that themselves "have sprung *out* of a deep sense of lack and loss—texts spun around a primal gap."[28] Caddy Compson, the figure who combines the sexual and maternal, is the absence around which Faulkner structures his entire novel. Speaking to students at the University of Virginia, Faulkner explained the novel's genesis: "To me she was the beautiful one, she was my heart's darling. That's what I wrote the book about . . . to try to tell, try to draw the picture of Caddy."[29] Gary Lee Stonum, commenting on Faulkner's return to the terms of "his earlier, image-based art" to explain the "gestation of the novel," notes that in this description "Faulkner abandons a narrative term, 'tell,' for a pictorial one."[30] This pictorial image of Faulkner's artistic enterprise in *The Sound and Fury* is significant because Caddy Compson embodies the source of vision in the novel; and this image of her as a picture helps to locate Faulkner's inscription of himself as an artist in the text. If *The Sound and the Fury* does not explicitly portray an artist, it recapitulates Faulkner's representation of the conceiving of art and it stages Faulkner's own surprising and overdetermined entry into the graphic representation of the visual.

Indeed, Faulkner locates Caddy in what may be considered the primal scene of the novel. In this scene, she climbs the tree, exposing her muddy drawers, to look in through a window onto death. As she tries to understand what is going on, she sees a forbidden scene that reveals the death of Damuddy—a name that seems to join "Daddy" and "mother," as well as call attention to Caddy's suggestively stained underclothes. This association of soiled sexuality, death, and the witnessing of a forbidden sight might be enough to evoke a scene of origins in Faulkner's psychic landscape; but this is also recalled as a primal scene of literary conception, a glimpse into the origins of the novel itself. Faulkner claimed that this scene of Caddy looking in on death with muddied drawers was the originary germ of the novel—just as, with equal appropriateness, he would locate the origins of *Light in August* in what we can now recognize as a related vision of a pregnant woman "walking along a strange country road."[31] (Whether one questions Faulkner's historical accuracy as he associates the origins of his books with the presence of sexually marked and fecund females, the use of the word "Damuddy" alone would mark this suggestive passage as a primal scene of language for Faulkner, because he, as the oldest grandchild, would have been the originator of the resonant term which became the Falkner children's name for their maternal grandmother.)[32] We can see in this scene of Caddy looking through a window at a scene not only an image of the novel's conception but also a frame through which we understand both the novel's concern with the visual and the significance of its focus on the eye.[33]

At a crucial moment in the career of the fainting and bleeding Compson brothers, having been threatened with a hatchet, and fearing that his head is bleeding where he has hit it, Jason sees a sign. Nearly blind, he is led to an "empty platform" where "grass grew rigidly in a plot bordered with rigid flowers" and he sees "a sign in electric lights: Keep your 👁 on Mottson, the gap filled by a human eye with an electric pupil" (*SF* 388). As he represents a slogan of the New South (and alludes to the dollar bill), Faulkner actually reproduces the sign, breaking into the words of his text in what is for him an unprecedented way and filling "the gap" with a pictorial eye. This sign of the visual is given a visual form which changes the way we read the words encoded in the sign. Like everything else in Faulkner, this overdetermined sign signifies too much. This sign instructs the viewer to "Keep your 👁 on Mottson," replacing a word with

a picture. On one level we might see Faulkner indulging in the
Joycean bilingual wordplay that appears elsewhere in the novel:
as the word is eschewed for a picture, one might see French
words and read the sign as warning: "Keep your 👁 on *Mot*
son"—as if to say, "Keep your eye on the word, son" (speaking
the unspoken word that is the troubling absence at the core of
Absalom, Absalom!). Or, still keeping our eye on French, we
might read: "Keep your 👁 on Mot son"—"Keep your eye on
the word-sound," on the sound of the word that does not
appear, "I." Whether one wants to hear this wordplay or not,
this passage is crucial because it pictures the sound of a word (a
word sound) and replaces a verbal sign with a pictorial symbol.
It opens up a gap in the text and dramatizes a graphic illustration
that stands in the place of a word.

To understand what it means for Faulkner to fill this gap with
a picture rather than a word, we need to speculate on the
meaning of the eye in *The Sound and the Fury*: the signifying
eye which must also be understood as "signifying nothing."
Obsessed with incest and driven by Oedipal tensions, the novel
is particularly concerned with eyes. The placement of the sign
of the eye "in a plot bordered with rigid flowers" takes us back
to the beginning of the book, to one of the novel's many bizarre
scenes of sexual displacement and the first definition of Caddy's
name (based on the sound of the word). Here, Benjy watches
"through the curling flower spaces" to see men hitting balls with
sticks and calling their "caddies." The wordplay is obvious as
Benjy and Luster look for lost balls. When Luster asks the
young woman at the branch, " 'You all found any balls yet,' " he
is told " 'Aint you talking biggity. I bet you better not let your
grandmammy hear you talking like that' " (*SF* 17). Later the
word itself has become unnecessary as Benjy looks down at
himself and Luster tells him simply, "Looking for them aint
going to do no good. They're gone" (*SF* 90). The inventory of
castration symbols in Faulkner's novels is well known and I will
not catalogue the one-handed men, one-armed straight jackets,
one-handed clocks, or the biblical association of the Ethiopian

queen Candace with eunuchs; but in this scene, which brings together the "curling flower spaces" and men with sticks, we might well ask: does a Caddy look for balls because she has them or because she lacks them?

Preoccupied with castration, *The Sound and the Fury* also repeatedly returns to potential moments of generation and conception. Throughout the novel, the eye is linked to the mystery of women's sexuality and the question of what sort of ball Caddy might have. In the Appendix to *The Sound and the Fury*, Faulkner insists on this image as he describes "the minute fragile membrane of [Caddy's] maidenhead" balanced like "a miniature replica of all the whole vast globy earth . . . poised on the nose of a trained seal." The language in this passage, which as we have seen echoes a passage in "Wild Palms," is also closely related to an even earlier image in *Sanctuary* in which eyes are specifically associated with lost virginity. Horace Benbow, inspired by Temple Drake's story of her rape and the bloody breaking of her maidenhead, has a wild reverie which, with macabre appropriateness, concludes as he recalls the eyes of a dead child, seeing them as "two empty globes in which the motionless world lurked profoundly in miniature."[34] In his description of these eyes, Benbow anticipates both the imagery and the words used in the description of Caddy's maidenhead in the Appendix as "a miniature replica of all the whole vast globy earth."

These images and associations underline the symbolic association between eyes and the female genitals which is already present throughout *The Sound and the Fury*. Both Mrs. Compson and Benjy sense irrevocable change as they look into Caddy Compson's eyes. Insisting that there is "no halfway ground . . . a woman is either a lady or not," Caddie's mother concludes, "I can look at her eyes and tell" (*SF* 127); and what might just be a cliché as it comes from her mouth is supported by her more insightful idiot son. Earlier when Benjy sees Caddy on the swing with Charlie (probably kissing because it is the sight of kissing which precipitates this memory), he takes her into the

kitchen, where she washes her mouth out with soap. In a later
related scene, the problem becomes more severe as it focuses
on the eyes rather than just the mouth. As Benjy describes the
scene, "Caddy came to the door and stood there, looking at
Father and Mother. Her eyes flew at me. . . . Her eyes ran,"
and finally, "Her hand was against her mouth and I saw her
eyes and I cried" (*SF* 84–85). Benjy drags her through the house
again but according to Faulkner's morphology of houses the
kitchen is no longer appropriate; Caddy tries to enter her
bedroom but Benjy pulls her toward the bathroom. In this
displacement upward, Faulkner seems to have chosen to focus
on the eyes as the site of the female genitals. Perhaps familiar
with the vulgar nineteenth-century euphemism for sexual intercourse, "to be poked in the blind eye," Faulkner builds as much
on the fact that Caddy's formal name "Candace" means "the
one eyed warrior queen" as he does on its allusion to the
incandescence of "white fire." The broken eyes and balls of *The
Sound and the Fury* (such as Quentin's bloody eye) are signs of
feminization.

The eyes are of crucial importance in the scenes that Quentin
recalls from the past in which he symbolically loses possession
of the phallus in the form of a knife and a gun. In the scene of
attempted suicide in which Quentin ultimately drops his knife,
the narrative reads as an almost embarrassing lesson in sexual
intercourse or masturbation: "will you close your eyes/ no like
this youll have to push it harder/ touch your hand to it/ but she
didnt move her eyes were wide open." Almost immediately
Quentin recalls the primal scene of Caddy seeing; but faced
with her eyes, he instead remembers her muddy panties:
"Caddy do you remember how Dilsey fussed at you because
your drawers were muddy" (*SF* 189). A few lines earlier, he has
asked out of nowhere: "do you remember the day damuddy
died when you sat down in the water in your drawers." This
query has followed another fertile conjunction of symbols put
together in Quentin's mind as he announces "I could see a rim
of white under her irises I opened my knife." Here, Quentin

announces that he has dropped his knife after we learn that Caddy's "muscles gathered." In his related confrontation with Dalton Ames, Quentin refuses a gun that is presented to him "butt first" (*SF* 200) in what is understood to be the feminine position. In this seminal scene, in which smoke streams from the barrel of Ames's gun while cigarette smoke streams from his nose, Quentin refuses the gun and instead (in his words) "passe[s] out like a girl." Having given himself a bloody or broken eye, Quentin recalls "looking at [Dalton Ames] through a piece of coloured glass" (*SF* 200); in the relentless symbolism of *The Sound and the Fury*, this wound seems to confirm Quentin's feminization. Broken glass and bloody eyes appear in a dense conjunction of images which bring Quentin back to the present and memories of a more recent past. The pain from his punch in the eye brings him back to the feeling of his face "cold and sort of dead, and my eye, and the cut place on my finger was smarting again" (*SF* 203).

The word "rim" is used twice by Quentin to describe the edges of Caddy's eyes. It first appears in Quentin's narrative in another representation of the sexual act which emphasizes the novel's obsession with dismemberment; he smashes the glass face of his watch, twists off its hands, and carefully removes the glass from the rim. (The symbolic associations between watching and eyes and eyes and watches are of course underlined repeatedly in the opening scenes of Quentin's narration.) Wrenching off the hands, he cuts his own hand and the cut finger leaves a bloody smear on what is later in this section called the "eye of the clock" (*SF* 149). The blood on the watch is suggestive here. Quentin is confused about blood in acts which involve males and females ("*Oh her blood or my blood Oh*" [*SF* 167]) and he is particularly confused about castration and sexual difference. In an important juxtaposition of thoughts, as he tells Versh's story of a man who castrates himself, Quentin immediately thinks of the female body and is stumped: "It's not not having them. It's never to have had them then I could say O That That's Chinese I don't know Chinese" (*SF* 143). One of the rare occasions in the novel when the "O" is rendered without an "h," as in "Oh," we might read the "O" in this discussion of the female absence as a turn to the pictorial. (Faulkner already had used this form of the pictorial in *Mosquitoes* where he describes a woman's mouth as "a small red O" [*M* 197]). Whether one accepts this "O" as a picture of absence—the zero, aught, or naught, what was referred to in common slang as "the divine monosyllable"—when faced with the female and the source of generation, Quentin seems to find words to be inadequate, as if somehow from the wrong language. For Quentin, female difference is like Chinese: an unknown, exotic foreign language—perhaps not coincidentally made up of pictographs.

Caddy's ball, what is described in the Appendix as "the minute fragile membrane of her maidenhead" and "a miniature replica of all the whole vast globy earth . . . poised on the nose of a trained seal," is there to be broken; and although the loss or breaking of balls signals impotence in men, in Caddy Compson and other women like her it paradoxically marks the initiation of potency. When broken, Caddy's ball-like hymen establishes her potency as a sexual figure. If we accept that "purity is a negative state," the loss of virginity is arguably a positive state, marking the possibility of generation, a beginning of being and of time. The awareness that time begins at conception causes Quentin repeatedly to wish to return to the moment before conception. Near the opening of his narrative, Quentin has fantasies of thwarting beginnings as he imagines himself as Dalton Ames's mother refusing to lie with her husband and preventing the birth of Caddy's seducer: "If I could have been his mother lying with open body lifted laughing, holding his father with my hand refraining, seeing, watching him die before he lived" (*SF* 98). Quentin has equally desperate fantasies in which he tries to use language to become his own father so that he can act to preclude both his and Caddy's existence as individuals as well as characters in a book.[35]

Despite these imagined states, there is a fatalism in Quentin's understanding of generation. One meditation about this negative primal scene significantly focuses on a picture in a book. Quentin recalls a picture in one of his childhood books which shows two people trapped in a dungeon, a "dark place into which a single weak ray of light came slanting upon two faces lifted out of the shadow." To him, this seems to be a picture of his parents and the horror of generation. Caught in an obsessive cycle of rereading, Quentin recalls: "I'd have to turn back to it until the dungeon was Mother herself she and Father upward into weak light holding hands and us lost somewhere below even them without even a ray of light." Imagining himself and his siblings in the darkness below their parents, Quentin understands that his mother is the "dungeon," the bodily room which will trap them into life. In an act which shows her potency, Caddy, who "never was a queen or a fairy [but] always a king or a giant or a general," is said to declare that if she were a king she would *break that place open*; and then we read: "[i]t was torn out, jagged out" (*SF* 215). Paradoxically, this power to tear out the page which seems to picture generation and the inevitability of conception involves an act of "breaking" and tearing which signals woman's potency and the crossed threshold of female sexuality.

Quentin's memory of a picture that has been torn out, this absent image of the "dark place" of the mother, is another indication of Faulkner's deep associations between the work of art, the visual image, procreation and reproduction, and the female body. As the overdetermined image of the "eye of the clock" suggests, these associations are also related to Faulkner's obsession with time. I do not have time to do more than gesture toward Faulkner's other uses of pictorial images and their associations with the gendering of art and the problem of the creative and procreative. We might briefly recall, however, the picture of the coffin in *As I Lay Dying*, which critics have seen as a womb with the corpse upside down in the position for birth.[36] Like a caddy, a small box for holding things, this structure, ⬡ (*AILD* 88), which is repeatedly called a "box," functions as a container for the body of the mother, herself a vessel for so many children, as she returns to the earth. The coffin is said to be "clock-shaped" but the picture tells us that this clock is not like an eye but rather like a grandfather clock, again framing the process of generation in patrilineal terms. Buried in the ground, the coffin is like the fecund, triangular wedge pictured in "Delta Autumn" in *Go Down, Moses* to represent a "∇-shaped section of earth."[37] Yet this funnel-like figure (described as "brooding" and "impenetrable"), pointing downward in the shape of the mound of Venus, the triangle of fertility, is also the Greek letter delta turned on its head—a rather abstract but still evocatively pictorial depiction of the fertile flanks of the Mississippi Yazoo delta. Like the top of an hour glass built up through the alluvial sands of time, this triangle of wilderness is becoming smaller as its tangled growth and earthen banks are being eroded by an encroaching civilization.

In *As I Lay Dying*, Faulkner also pictures a blank space, an actual gap between words. Addie Bundren speaks of Anse's "name"—"I could see the word as a shape, a vessel"—and "a significant shape profoundly without life like an empty door frame," and she describes herself thinking: "The shape of my body where I used to be a virgin is in the shape of a   " (*AILD* 172). Faulkner leaves a blank space on the page to represent the look of the place where Addie Bundren's virginity used to be. This absence is anticipated in *Flags in the Dust* in Horace Benbow's fantasy about the pinkness of unnamed female parts which leads to the single word "unchaste" followed by a word-sized blank space and a question mark: "Unchaste   ?"[38] For the writers in Faulkner's *Mosquitoes* and for Addie Bundren in *As I Lay Dying*, words are instruments of masculine desire, but Addie Bundren has learned to despise the words that from her husband's mouth are "just a shape to fill a lack" (*AILD* 172). Addie, who has experienced unmediated life as a "dark voicelessness in which the words are deeds," insists that "the other words that are not deeds . . . are just the gaps in people's lacks" (*AILD* 174). Each of these pictorial images might be said to signify nothing; not only the actual gaps or blank spaces on the page but also the images that stand for an eye, a coffin, and the landscape. Like the eye that stands as a symbol of the sexual presence and absence at the center of the woman, these figures evoke female sexuality: both its terrifying embodiment of nothing and the transformative force of the female form. They represent the "nothing" which in the slang of Shakespeare referred to the female genital and what comes from nothing. Faulkner seems to try obsessively to fill the gaps in these lacks with words; but sometimes, as if declaring himself an artist, he resorts to pictures that signify the absence of language and the tensions inherent in the artist's acts of creation.

NOTES

1. Hermaphroditus is the title of a poem attributed to the character Eva Wiseman in *Mosquitoes*. Faulkner himself published virtually the same poem under the same title in *A Green Bough*, a collection of his early poems.

2. William Faulkner, "Elmer" and "A Portrait of Elmer" in *William Faulkner Manuscripts I*, introduced and arranged by Thomas L. McHaney (New York: Garland Publishing, Inc., 1987), 3–4. Further citations from this text will refer to this edition.

3. William Faulkner, *Mosquitoes* (New York: Boni and Liveright, 1927), 13–18. Further citations from this text will refer to this edition.

4. For an interesting reading of this scene which discusses the milk bottle as a fetishized object, see Michael Zeitlin, in *Faulkner and Psychology*, ed. Donald M. Kartiganer and Ann J. Abadie (Jackson: University Press of Mississippi, 1994), 219–41.

5. William Faulkner, *Sartoris* (New York: New American Library Signet Classics, 1964 [1929]), 146. Further citations from this text will refer to this edition. See David Minter, *William Faulkner: His Life and Work* (Baltimore: The Johns Hopkins University Press, 1980), 99–103. Minter distinguishes among Faulkner's early artist figures: "Elmer and Horace work in their art toward a female figure that is actual; they make art a substitute for love of a real woman. Gordon . . . makes art a way of approaching an ideal whose identity remains vague." See Minter's important discussions of Faulkner's obsession with the feminine vase and the way this figure informs Faulkner's understanding of the relationship between sexuality and art in "Faulkner, Childhood, and the Making of the Novel," *The Sound and the Fury*, ed. David Minter (New York: W.W. Norton & Co., 1994), 343–58.

6. William Faulkner, *Flags in the Dust* (New York: Random House, 1974), 153. *Flags in the Dust* was the original manuscript which in a cut and edited form appeared as *Sartoris*.

7. William Faulkner, *Light in August* (New York: Vintage, 1985 [1932]), 189, 185.

8. William Faulkner, *The Sound and the Fury* (New York: Vintage, 1954 [1929]), 412. Further citations from this text will refer to this edition, unless otherwise noted.

9. William Faulkner, "An Introduction to *The Sound and the Fury*," in *The Sound and the Fury*, ed. David Minter, 226). Written by Faulkner for a 1933 edition of the novel, the two versions of this introduction were not published in Faulkner's lifetime.

10. Ibid., 227–28.

11. In *Flags in the Dust*, the "shapeless things" are said to be "Antic, with shadows on the wet walls, red shadows; a dull red gleam, and black shapes like cardboard cut-

outs rising and falling like a magic-lantern shutter" (153). The spectacle of a magic-lantern show suggested by Faulkner's original representation of "the card board cutouts" casting black shadows and the "red shadows" of the furnace is revised in *Sartoris* to focus on "paper dolls," which suggest the creations of the literary artist.

12. Minter, "Faulkner, Childhood, and the Making of the Novel," 344.

13. William Faulkner, *Selected Letters of William Faulkner*, ed. Joseph Blotner (New York: Random House, 1978), 228.

14. William Faulkner, *The Wild Palms* (New York: Random House, 1966 [1939]), 47. Further references to this text refer to this edition.

15. Wilbourne's reference to himself as a painter has baffled readers. Referring to Wilbourne's claim to be a painter in the opening chapter, Michael Millgate concludes: "There is much about *The Wild Palms* which does not seem wholly explicable in terms of the thematic patterns of the book or the psychology of the characters. It is, indeed, in many ways a strange and uncomfortable book" (*The Achievement of William Faulkner* [New York: Random House, 1966], 178–79).

16. Millgate speculates that there seems to be "some kind of autobiographical or peculiarly personal significance" for *The Wild Palms*. He bases this view on the "curious personal quality of many of its incidents and allusions" and "the almost masochistic intensity of Wilbourne's agony" (179).

17. There are few critical comments about this painting. Thomas L. McHaney suggests that "Charlotte's sexuality in its most basic terms brings Harry back to an awareness of time" (*William Faulkner's "The Wild Palms": A Study* [Jackson: University Press of Mississippi, 1975] 91–92).

18. McHaney calls this "one of the most cryptic passages in the novel." Speculating that the source is autobiographical, he reads this passage as a "blending of references to a romantic disappointment with references to [Sherwood] Anderson's art" (*William Faulkner's "The Wild Palms": A Study*, 22).

19. Ben Jonson, *Bartholomew Fair*, ed. Edward B. Partridge (Lincoln: University of Nebraska Press, 1969), V, v, 90–97.

20. William Faulkner, *As I Lay Dying: The Corrected Text* (New York: Vintage, 1990 [1930]), 52. Further citations from this text will refer to this edition.

21. I am grateful to my student Jarret Sonta for pointing out this connnection.

22. Eudora Welty, "A Still Moment" in *The Collected Stories of Eudora Welty* (New York: Harcourt Brace Jovanovich, 1980), 198.

23. Quoted by Donald Kartiganer in *The Fragile Thread: The Meaning of Form in Faulkner's Novels* (Amherst: University of Massachusetts Press, 1979), 3.

24. For a related discussion, see Gary Harrington, *Faulkner's Fables of Creativity: The Non-Yoknapatawpha Novels* (London: The MacMillan Press, 1990), 88–93.

25. "Introduction," *The Sound and the Fury*, ed. Minter, 227–28.

26. Cited by Susan Gubar in "The Blank Page," *Writing and Sexual Difference*, ed. Elizabeth Abel (Chicago: University of Chicago Press, 1982), 77.

27. Kartiganer, *The Fragile Thread*, 13.

28. André Bleikasten, *The Most Splendid Failure: Faulkner's "The Sound and the Fury"* (Bloomington: Indiana University Press, 1976), 53. For an important discussion of the significance of Caddy and the role of loss in the novel, see John T. Matthews, *The Play of Faulkner's Language* (Ithaca: Cornell University Press, 1982), 17–23, 91–114.

29. *Faulkner in the University: Class Conferences at the University of Virginia, 1957–1958*, ed. Frederick L. Gwynn and Joseph L. Blotner (Charlottesville: University of Virginia Press, 1959), 6.

30. Gary Lee Stonum, *Faulkner's Career: An Internal History* (Ithaca: Cornell University Press, 1979), 76.

31. "Introduction," *The Sound and the Fury*, ed. Minter, 226.

32. In an interesting discussion, Eric J. Sundquist insists that Faulkner's comments on *The Sound and the Fury* are part of his retrospective mythologizing of this novel. In particular, he speculates that the scene of looking up at Caddy drawers is not actually the founding image of the novel. Putting aside the vexed question about whether

anyone can truthfully describe the origins of a work of art, for my purposes here it is important that Faulkner persisted in telling what was for him already an old story about works of art and women and vases, and that he focuses even in retrospect on the image of Caddy looking into the window onto death. See *Faulkner: The House Divided* (Baltimore: The Johns Hopkins University Press, 1983), 3–27.

33. André Bleikasten links this scene to the " 'primal fantasies' postulated by psychoanalysis." Noting the emphasis on looking, he associates the scene with Freud's description of the male fear of castration upon discovering the difference of the female genitals. He reads this image as "the emblem of a dual revelation: the simultaneous discovery of the difference between the sexes and of death" (*The Most Splendid Failure*, 54–55). Michel Gresset comments on "the exorbitant privilege the eye and the act of looking enjoy in Faulkner's novels" and the significance of "the impotent Popeye's exophthalmia." He argues that "Freud went as far as to say that an organ, the eye for instance, could assume 'as the consequence of an exaggerated erogenous zone, the conduct peculiar to the genital organ.' " In his understanding of the erotic potential of the eye, Gresset focuses on the idea of the penetrating gaze and writes about what he calls "The Optical Rape" in *Sanctuary* (*Fascination: Faulkner's Fiction, 1919–1936* [Durham: Duke University Press, 1989], 177; 157–211). See also Sigmund Freud, *Three Contributions to the Theory of Sex*, trans. A. A. Brill (New York: The Nervous and Mental Disease Publishing Co., 1925), 23–24.

34. William Faulkner, *Sanctuary* (New York: Random House, 1958 [1931]), 214.

35. John Irwin describes this process in terms of Quentin's desire to gain control of the narrative. He also discusses the idea of taking revenge by supplanting the father as the narrative authority and through the telling of the tale. (*Doubling and Incest/ Repetition and Revenge* [Baltimore: The Johns Hopkins University Press, 1975], 82–135).

36. See André Bleikasten, *Faulkner's "As I Lay Dying"* (Bloomington: Indiana University Press, 1973), 120. Doreen Fowler writes: "It is motherhood—symbolized by Addie's reversed, head-to-foot position in the coffin like a fetus in the mother's womb, a position imposed by 'them durn women' (80)—that disturbs the balance" ("Matricide and the Mother's Revenge: *As I Lay Dying*," *The Faulkner Journal: Special Issue on Faulkner and Feminisms* 4 [Fall, 1988/Spring, 1989], ed. John T. Matthews and Judith Bryant Wittenberg: 118).

37. William Faulkner, *Go Down, Moses* (New York: Vintage International, 1990 [1942], 326.

38. William Faulkner, *Flags in the Dust*, 173.

The Complex Art of Justice: Lawyers and Lawmakers as Faulkner's Dubious Artist-Figures

MICHAEL LAHEY

> " '—but you're a lawyer; you don't think I got into this
> without reading a little law first myself, do you?' "
> —WILLIAM FAULKNER, *The Town* (1957)

Faulkner's fiction is laced with law, lawyers, and legal matters, as several critics have noted. Richard Weisberg points out that with the recurrent Gavin Stevens Faulkner engages legal matters "ranging from racial politics to real estate conveyancing, and criminal litigation to college admissions counselling."[1] Weisberg examines the personal qualities of Gavin and of lawyers in literature generally, asserting that Gavin Stevens "becomes the first major literary lawyer to develop positively as a human being in the direction of, and not in rebellion against, his professional strengths" (197). In "William Faulkner: Author-At-Law," Joseph Blotner observes that law permeates Faulkner's fiction from "beginning to end over a broad range of subjects" and that Faulkner's "sympathies most often lie with the defendants."[2] In "Faulkner's Knowledge of the Law," Morris Wolff, analyzing the court judgment in "Spotted Horses," states that "as often happens in Faulkner's 'legal situations,' our expectations of justice and financial award are jarred by the intervention of the law which produces an unfair result."[3] Wolff states further that "for those who are victimized by the irrational application of the law, the reaction is outrage and a sense of defeat" (251). The issues these critics raise thus address the personal development of the professional as individual, the plight of individuals, particularly defendants, caught in the mechanisms of law and the court, and the intrusion and violence of bureaucratic law wrongly argued, applied, and judged in the lives of those before the court or living with the results of its proceedings.

Central to these concerns is the sense that law is delicate and always shifting, sometimes dangerously, as interpretation, but that legal proceedings are conducted indelicately by apparatus: that once the machine starts only lawyers and other legal officials can work within its churnings as the literate technicians, inscribing on, with, and against its mechanisms. Yet if law can be shaped and rechannelled while it is proceeding, it also seems a strangely organic as well as merely procedural creation, encompassing always a collaborative of creators, all legally inventing, applying, reinterpreting to the benefit or detriment of those directly represented and of those outside the court—society at large—who are affected by the creation. The lawyer may be seen as a deeply invested personal and political creator and not only the hired spokesperson of facts, evidence, statements, narrative, impressions, and carefully contrived arguments that eventually exist as artifacts on the record. This always complex, often insidious, organic-mechanistic art of law—not only the artistry of words, logic, debate, and interpretations but the completed and often compromised production of the judgment itself—seems, in fact, to haunt Faulkner through his writing career. Accordingly, law as art form and lawyer as artist figure can be closely examined in his fiction to understand better some of the central tensions in Faulkner's content, structures, style, and concerns. The recurrent notions of law and their surrounding issues—such as who can ever justifiably weigh the credibility of multiple and conflicting voices, what new accounts can successfully challenge entrenched evaluative hierarchies, and what unacknowledged elements determine the conditions and contexts that determine formal conditions and contexts—all of these may be productively interrogated to examine Faulkner's own methods of creation, as well as his presentation of the creation of social reality.

The qualities of the artist common to the lawyer are several, but their reflection from one identity to the other is distorted. Certainly twisted and refracted in the movement from the world of art to the arena of law, the qualities of creativeness, presentation, engagement, and response serve to destroy as much as construct, hurt as much as heal, when at the disposal of a determined lawyer. And if legal arguments and techniques can be considered strange and curious works of art and artfulness, their creative aim concerns itself primarily, usually exclusively, with a narrow persuasion, seldom recognizing moral, ethical, philosophical or other outside claims upon the works themselves. What a defense lawyer might call a "beautiful argument" which serves well the interests of his client may clearly be, even to the lawyer, morally and socially reprehensible in its implications. The lawyer, then, is the artist-figure with a difference, the willing creator of art forms that may be false in every manner but legally, the paid shaper of a craft whose artistic success can destroy as well as body forth.

In many ways, Faulkner's art is a social, creative, healing practice that explores the productions, extensions, and applications of law as a social, narrowly creative, never healing practice. In *Sanctuary*, for example, the law destroys a sense of community or the hope for convincing pursuits of justice. The trial exposes its own fraud as judicial enterprise and reveals that the substance of what is being so vigorously tried exists wholesale and is endorsed throughout the society supposedly so outraged. In "Law in Faulkner's *Sanctuary*," Noel Polk observes that law in the novel is represented as a corrupt parent, that the legal system is "a capricious set of lawyers, judges, legislators, policemen, jurors, preachers, and even Jefferson society, all of whom, like fathers, make laws and break them with impunity."[4] As with the generative powers of parents and artists, the legal power to create, in this case "make laws," is both self-affirming and dangerous, reckless in sheer creative range and resource, particularly when dealing, as law usually does, without a critical audience of any balancing power. Like a father, law creates in its own image, and the communal audience it creates for has little voice to comment further. But while Faulkner's depiction of law throughout this work is certainly that of an unresponsive, unreachable authority, the nature of this authority's ambiguity and suppleness precludes thinking of it as monolithic construct. The fact that Goodwin and Popeye are both convicted for crimes not committed by them in the novel, though other crimes are theirs, instead suggests the dangerous indeterminacy—the decentered quality of both origin and destination—of the social, legal narratives the instruments of law write every time they function.

Sanctuary further explores the figurings of law and of justice as corrupted art forms in Yoknapatawpha, ones relying on the qualities of spectacle and not essence. In Horace Benbow's case, his attempt to conduct a defense, to create through his own legal narrative the possibility for acquittal of the wrongly accused Lee Goodwin, fails to meet and counterargue the claims of the District Attorney, Eustace Graham, a most artful attorney, an evoker of impressions hurtful and false to the defendant and flattering and fictional to the jury and observers. Graham stage-manages his case rather than trying it outright, depending on the production of effects more than the pursuit of evidence toward the establishment of facts. He creates his particular sense of theater with the dramatic corn cob, a stunning visual prop and legal exhibit that Horace is not previously aware of because of Lee's unwillingness to speak of the facts of that night at the Old Frenchman's Place. The bloodied cob is coordinated, in all its increasing sense of threatfulness and illicit physical intrusion, with Graham's additional construction of "woman" as sacred object in the eyes of the court; as expert witnesses, the chemist and gynecologist are called to testify on "the most sacred affairs of that most sacred thing in life: womanhood. . . ."[5]

The District Attorney's prosecution thus calibrates professional and emotional rhetoric with visual display in order to play to and upon audience. When examining Temple, "he caught her gaze and held it and lifted the stained corn-cob before her

eyes. The room sighed, a long hissing breath" (345). As the
District Attorney plays to his house, he conjures himself as
juridical avenger and also conjures his audience as outraged
participants in justice as sexual morality play. Since law as ritual
and ceremony, as Foucault has noted, historically relies on "the
anger of the threatened people,"[6] the DA constructs dubious
categories of morality, criminality, sexuality, and gender so that
he can be enabled to act, exaggerates threat to a community of
his own construction so he can legislate against it.[7] Jefferson's
willingness to be scripted as mobilized legal avenger is belied,
however, by the male population's vicarious sexual self-imagin-
ing, their wish for substitution as Temple's violater: " 'I saw
her. She was some baby. Jeez. I wouldn't have used no cob' "
(352). So law as the art of convincing social construction in
Sanctuary, let alone as the art of a possible justice, fails everywhere but in the courtroom, where the legal enterprise's own
interests at this moment are subtly peddled as the community's.

In Forensic Fictions: The Lawyer Figure in Faulkner, Jay
Watson suggests that for the Southern community, many of
whom were "shackled to the soil and starved for any kind of
diversion, courtroom trials served as an important form of
entertainment, a poor man's playhouse."[8] The lawyer as performance artist, as public thespian on a stage alternately playing
to expectation and platitude and then shocking, testing limits of
outrage and community standard, proceeds in Sanctuary with
the dual aims of juridical audience engagement and promised
catharsis, but only if the outcome of the trial appears to sweep
from the life of the community the contentious issues. That
social, moral restoration in this particular novel and this particular trial is thorough illusion is made clear by Lee's own presumed copycat sodomizing with a broom handle, as well as his
subsequent burning and murder by the mob (354–55). The
District Attorney's performance paradoxically succeeds both at
painting a picture of communal solidarity, protectiveness, and
masculine moral excellence that does not exist in Jefferson and
at inciting a murderous mob that rampages on cue, enacting

itself contrary to the belief in its own discretion, conscience, and lawfulness believed only moments ago. Ironically, one of the important social functions and responsibilities of law is the disruption of the revenge cycle, law's public duty to stop, often with its own threats and force, the cycle of ongoing action and reaction that accompanies individual grievances and transgressions. Law must act so that society as a whole will not be pulled into the vortex of retaliation and revenge of the particular wrongs in its midst. Against this chief responsibility of law, *Sanctuary* explores how the dynamics of insidious legal creation and false communal creation contrive to produce injustice and vigilantism as response. The successful lawyer in this novel is merely, and also powerfully, giving the audience what it wants, but only after manipulating its demand.[9]

Faulknerian lawyer as artist figure also takes on dangerous implications in *The Town*. The law and its workings in this novel become a mechanism equipped to invent itself for its own ends, as Gavin, the County Attorney, contributes false evidence against Montgomery Ward Snopes. Stevens collaborates with the sheriff, Hub Hampton, and Flem Snopes, the embarrassed relative and rising businessman, to plant bootleg corn whiskey in Snopes's studio,[10] out of which pornography is being viewed and sold to customers "two counties wide in either direction" (163). Their effort suggests how Faulkner can conceptualize law as becoming always ever more an ambiguously creative and self-inventing endeavor. Gavin's false production of alternative evidence in the planting of the whiskey so that Jefferson will not be embarrassed by a criminal charge of illicit sexual material here marks the State's lawyer as moral fabricator as well as legal conjuror. Since Gavin's willingness to proceed legally against alcohol rather than pornography is an attempt to protect Snopes's almost endless list of male clients (some of them probably as influential as Gavin) and the collective reputation of Jefferson, law strives in this account to construct a legal, moral, communal standard that is ungrounded in communal reality. There results, then, an argument, a version calling for a reckoning, that is floating along authorizing itself for its own ends. The law's collaboration in this novel with Flem, the amoral, unscrupulous business venturist, against his hapless relative is also disturbing and strongly suggests that law too is merely a naked vested interest on the part of its practitioners. The business of law in this Faulknerian moment is the business of images—domestic, orderly, predictable—which best allow business to operate. Since even such easily manipulated desire as that generated by the pornographic photos threatens the predictable order, and so the pathways of business, this material becomes urgently criminal at Flem's intervention. Backed up by law, Flem's efforts against criminality are exclusively to safeguard his own continued progression as entrepreneur. The pathways of private business and supposedly generalized law are now completely entangled in Jefferson, their interests each other's. And again, an authorized impression of community and its standards is legally produced that does not reflect its constituents but exists in its own account, replacing one proliferation of images with its own.

In "The Violence of Masquerade: Law Dressed Up as Justice," Drucilla Cornell explores the possibility of legal justice and "the deconstruction of the identification of law as justice."[11] Drawing on other Critical Legal Studies scholars, she argues that the law is a machine: "[t]he law just keeps coming. . . . Once it is wound up there is no stopping the law, and what winds it up [are] its own functions as elaborated in the myths of legal culture" (1051). Cornell thus sees law as efficiently and dangerously automatic, autocritical, automotive, autoinscriptive. In Faulkner's *The Town*, the prospect of the self-winding machine which can operate on a logic of perpetual ejaculation ("just keeps coming") offers increased complications to a consideration of the law and its resources of creative capacity, of an autonomous and even autoerotic authority and its art of legitimacy and effects. Gavin's production of illegality, after all, will have the fullest embodiment of the law itself—a judge—as audience. Since Gavin and Hampton as State Attorney and Sheriff are themselves the office-holders and intermediary embodiments of the law, their last-minute invention of a more acceptable illegality for a judge presents the unsettling proposition of law inventing entirely from the inside-out, expanding itself for the sole purpose of interaction between its own levels. Legal enterprise is now not only insidiously self-winding but chillingly self-contained, sealed: it is its own scriptwriter, patron, player, audience, critic; its art produces itself for itself precisely along the lines of Cornell's notion of a perpetual legal motion machine. The threat that Snopes's print pornography poses to the community may or may not exist; as a contentious issue, it is certainly never evaluated in *The Town*. The danger that law poses, however, and not only to the opportunistic Montgomery Snopes but to a community ignorant, complacent or powerless to comment on, dissent against, or partake of its law's happenings, seems almost completely unaddressable as threat, beyond evaluation as presented in the novel. Invented and inventing, law as creator of social narrative here, and in the whole of the Snopes trilogy, possesses what Cornell sees as "the power of law to enforce its own premises as the truth of the system," thereby "eras[ing] the significance of its philosophical interlocutors, rendering their protest impotent" (1055). For Faulkner, too, there seems little prospect of writing back against the law's inscriptions in Jefferson.

Law as represented in *The Town*, then, is indifferent to the community it still appears to serve. The creative legal enterprise to end Snopes's creative commercial enterprise—the photos—will invent what it has to in order to invent again that fictional sense of order and place that law justifies itself as existing to serve and protect anyway. Gavin as Faulkner's favorite lawyer is indeed partial artist and "forger" of his craft, for as the sheriff observes, suggesting both the law's suppleness and fixity through the medium of individual personality, power, and desire, " 'You're the County Attorney. . . . You're the one to say what the law is before I can be it' " (161).

The depiction of law as a fascinating fiction writing itself in order to write the world exists elsewhere in Faulkner. In

The Wild Palms the Tall Convict's additional penalty after his voluntary return to prison is an institutional fiction—that of the prison officials—to account not for the Convict's unexpected, unhelpable absence during the Mississippi River's flooding, but for his surprise return after being prematurely recorded as dead.[12] The Convict's rescue of the pregnant woman and their heroic, poetic survival on the Mississippi are now violently recast by law, represented falsely with the approval of all, including the Convict. Faulkner again shows how systematic institutional rendering of theoretically acceptable possibilities takes primacy over lived realities, ones that are both factual and certainly more emotionally true than official accounts. In fact, the reason for this particular legal imagining is to preserve the consistency of prison paperwork, the consistency and power of its initial misreading, rather than amend it to register shifts in the reality it purports and has the responsibility to record:

> 'This man is dead.'
> 'Hell fire, he aint dead,' the deputy said. 'He's up yonder in that bunkhouse right now. . . .'
> 'But he has received an official discharge as being dead. Not a pardon nor a parole either: a discharge. He's either dead, or free. In either case he doesn't belong here.' (326–27)

With the addition of ten years for imaginary escape, a provision that the Warden calls "bad luck," then "hard luck" (331), law in this Faulknerian moment becomes only a paper reality, a recording of its own will to create itself always more strongly so that it can create routinely what it touches, perceives, rules upon. Clearly, this hasty creation of law by its managers and interpreters functions as authoritarian justification only, not as justice nor as any genuine struggle with the burden of attempted representation. In fact, the deputy's rejected suggestion that they hold a mock trial to reconvict the Tall Convict, who because he is not dead must now be free, makes plain Faulkner's sceptical suggestion of the law's capacity to stage itself as false production able to back up its large claims with mystifying ritual, dubious hoops, and confident reference to its own range of processes: " 'Just call twelve men in here and tell him it's a jury—he never seen but one before and he wont know no better—and try him over for robbing that train. Hamp can be the judge' " (328). And the tentatively amusing fact that a procedure of law must be created and wrongly applied to the returned Convict in order to get around another procedure of law presents the law upon further consideration as unamusingly irreversible and barely containable authority, one uncannily applying itself independently of even its own attendants, spokespeople, practitioners. Law here thus swings free as a powerful block of language that its handlers are powerless to work with, where the only countermeasure is to create another powerful block of language to outmaneuver this one. Blind and autonomous to all but its own concerns in unsettling and not the supposedly ideal or reassuring ways, the law speaks, regenerates itself, operates as screen for its churnings, intentions, misfirings. Ironically, it is able to commit transgressions against itself, intentionally undercut itself, in order to conserve itself as law.[13]

Legal episode and dangerous fictiveness also intertwine in *The Sound and the Fury*, where law again creates itself, by allowing unsubstantiated allegation to hang in the air. Quentin's outdoor ad hoc trial in the Justice of the Peace's makeshift court for mistakenly alleged sexual misconduct with a minor suggests an added layer of dubious creation in law's imaginings of itself and the world. Faulkner suggests that law can travel at will beyond the boundary of the individual self and appropriate that self's interiority as a stage of operations. There having been no incident whatsoever to substantiate an allegation, the law sees fit to assign guilty intent to Quentin: " 'He [the sheriff] aims to charge you with meditated criminal assault.' "[14] In what can perhaps be seen as an initially comic episode, law here nonetheless supposes for itself a pervasive, even transcendent, quality of everywhereness that can appropriate Quentin's inner life and recast it as a set of motives thoroughly alien to him. Quentin's restitution payment to Julio, the girl's brother, and the sheriff (180)—really an extortion payment to resolve the increasingly misrepresented matter—further presents the necessity of individuals before the workings of the law to collaborate for their own benefit in any initial fictiveness so as to avoid more greatly damaging subsequent fictions and expanding contexts.

Law as artful creation that is always in a state of its own becoming emerges as insidious and increasingly problematic; if law has the self-legitimating authority not only to invent itself independently of any addressed reality but also to become coercive, duplicitous art form, sheer implicating artifice, then its self-creation and -reflexity can threaten possible, though unestablishable, hurtful readings upon the lives of its subjects and viewers at will. While much meaningful art is ideologically, socially unsettling, law as invented, inventing form can go farther than the conceptual challenges of other art forms, can reach from its canvas, off its stage, beyond the scene of its writing to damage immediately its audience. Displacing whatever set of social relations it chooses or is set in motion against, law works briefly but with a universally determining quality in *The Sound and the Fury*, as in *The Wild Palms*, "Spotted Horses," and *The Town*, to force individuals and situations into legal channels and contexts already prearranged, to make through its own brand of violence the presumed matter fit. Faulkner consistently shows how law in his Yoknapatawpha omits, edits, decontextualizes, and recontextualizes; the real force of the law presented in his work may be read as its ability to transform entirely all that is available to it.[15] Quentin's restitution payment is both his admission to the preliminary of a startling and dangerous show and deposit for the privilege of early exit.

Although they are legally equipped creators of suspect realities, Faulkner's lawyers are sometimes pulled into the community events from which they strive to be distant.[16] As detached intellectual, Gavin, for instance, occasionally trades the extravagant arrogance of the lawyerly voyeur for an imperfect, personal involvement.[17] In *Go Down, Moses*, in particular, Gavin's arrangement in the title story of a town collection for the funeral of Samuel "Butch" Beauchamp suggests the pull of community events which involve the County Attorney individually. While not a central character in this work in the sense that his life is not a pressing concern, Gavin certainly orchestrates and stage manages the action. He also controls the presentation of the official and unofficial language within the community by effortlessly blocking newspaper stories about the alleged murderer in deference to the grandmother: " 'I have already talked with Mr Wilmoth at the paper. He has agreed not to print anything.' "[18] But Gavin's charitable production of the public funeral ceremony in "Go Down, Moses" becomes merely another Faulknerian construct of the empty image of community, a charade whose enactment destroys further rather than props up any fleeting hope for the possibility of the meaningful interaction of a collective:

> [T]hey followed the hearse . . . circling the Confederate monument and the courthouse while the merchants and clerks and barbers and professional men who had given Stevens the dollars and half-dollars and quarters and the ones who had not, watched quietly from doors and upstairs windows, swinging then into the street which at the edge of town would become the country road.

> "Come on." he [Stevens] said. "Let's get back to town. I haven't seen my desk in two days." (382–83)

In the staged hometown funeral, the County Attorney and City Editor provide a social narrative that nobody, not even perhaps Mollie Worsham Beauchamp, believes representative of anything. As the stage master of "Go Down, Moses," Gavin— whom the narrator refers to in the midst of the charade of ceremony and community as "the designated paladin of justice and truth and right, the Heidelberg PhD" (382)—becomes a fiction maker on the grandest scale, one capable of securing audience complicity by writing the entire town into a plot for which no one suspends disbelief. If the funeral represents anything significant in the life of Jefferson it is merely that Gavin's procession, with its own accompanying newspaper stories (383), substitutes for an absence which is the genuine response of the community: indifference to this former black member's death and therefore, life. The false representation of a communal concern standing in for the genuine absence thereby calls attention to the increasing ambiguity about the distance and distinctions separating the real and the represented and the potential for manipulation of this space by those, such as County Attorneys and City Editors, who are professionally invested in the reproduction and continuation of such images. Although custodians of public representations in language and actions—representations of the public to itself—in the name of both order and place, County Attorneys and City Editors are also dependent for livelihood on the proliferation of images of the communal, whether true or false.

In "Crying in the Wilderness: Legal, Racial, and Moral Codes in *Go Down, Moses*," Thadious M. Davis observes that the spiritual, "Go Down, Moses," from which Faulkner takes his title, has "three levels of authority and sources of law affecting the lives of human beings": God (transcendental), Moses (moral representative), and Pharaoh.[19] At the lowest level of law, Pharaoh is merely legal "ruler of the land and representative of the state" (313). Davis thus identifies Faulkner's linking of the law in his title piece to a deep history of moral wrongdoing, to oppression and a slavery into which the unfortunate and voiceless are sold. Several times Mollie Beauchamp makes this parallel within the story when she says that Roth Edmonds sold " 'my boy. . . . Sold him in Egypt. Pharaoh got him' " (371). Her efforts to have Samuel "Butch" Beauchamp returned from Chicago rely on Gavin because " 'you the Law' " (371). Mollie may or may not realize that she thereby casts Gavin with the forces of Pharaoh, the ruler of the laws of land, property, individuals as commodity, and racial and social codes. Rather than gracefully paper over the possibly damaging issues surrounding the dead criminal's social, racial, psychological, and legal circumstances, the orchestrated funeral achieves exactly the opposite: it displays the community's and by implication Gavin's commitment to surfaces only, though the town continues to cling to its own social and racial formalizations. As Davis observes, "the townspeople are mainly quite content to believe that somehow Butch is merely the bad son of a bad father, but not that the duality of legal, racial, and moral codes followed by their society and which persistently dehumanize blacks or undermine the ability of blacks to be or to do may be equally responsible for what Butch becomes" (315).

The community has a sense of determinism, then, but one genetic rather than social. They will not acknowledge that in their social structures is the power to shape and enforce identities, despite the charade enacted before their eyes which is the half-hearted attempt at social construction. Gavin's implication as "the Law" (371) in the plight of Beauchamp, of the black in white society, also implicates him, though after the fact, in all the various uses and abuses of property, race, gender, written and unwritten codes, laws, games and other puzzles haunting *Go Down, Moses*. As an artist figure, Gavin the lawyer contributes most in this novel to the creation of white myths about white justice, to the inability to account compassionately for rather than continue to construct the black presence in its midst.

As artist-figures, lawyers also often attempt to revise and rework the law and justice already produced and existing. *Requiem for a Nun*, Faulkner's sequel to his trial novel *Sanctuary*, attempts to revise some of the issues of that first novel as the characters of *Requiem* attempt to revise the processes and judgments of law in which they are embroiled. *Requiem* raises several interesting issues central to reading law as dubious art form. The novel-play attempts to set in motion against the administrative judgment of law the notion of love and forgiveness, the humane naked against the process. Faulkner suggests, however, that the art of law in this work seems itself illegitimate as a self-declared totalizing system that purports to address all conceivable matters of human conflict, error, and grievance. In *Requiem*, the art of law (the process) and art of justice (the ideal but also humane) instead seem inaccessible to each other, despite Gavin's last-minute attempt at intercession and petition:

Temple: Wait. He said, No.
Stevens: Yes.
Temple: Did he say why?
Stevens: Yes. He can't.
Temple: Cant? The Governor of a state, with all the legal power
            to pardon or at least reprieve, cant?
Stevens: That's just law. If it was only law, I could have plead [*sic*]
            insanity for her at any time.[20]

So the workings of formal law in this instance mask the
informal workings of community behind them: "[i]f it was only
law. . . ." Gavin's suggestion that the letter of law is backed up
by social judgments and presumptions about Nancy as woman,
black, and prostitute, as well as killer, underscores the unwritten community laws that cannot be successfully appealed. Custom, the supposed expression of "Volkgeist," or the spirit of the
people, fuels here the impulse of law, and law in this text is
temporarily reconnected to the community, but only insofar as
prevailing cultural conditions add to the momentum of the
authoritarian vector. Since law cannot be turned back by emotional claims and the Governor will proceed with death, law's
fatal inscription will write on its socially and legally constructed
subject, Nancy Mannigoe, despite Temple's plea for clemency
as mother of the murdered infant. Faulkner seems to suggest
that the infanticide is a desperate act of mercy—to save the
baby from the world in which Nancy and Temple have had to
live. This proposition, even if ultimately nihilistic, cannot be
credibly pursued philosophically in the courts, however, because of their prior investment in upholding the social, political,
gender, and racial claims and power imbalances of such a world
as it already exists, never formally acknowledging that for some
individuals such a world traffics in personal and social despair as
the inevitability of its structure. Like Morrison's careful and
caring portrayal of the infanticidal Sethe in *Beloved*, *Requiem*
thus figures a double punishment of Nancy, first in her socially
and racially constructed identity and secondly in the legal
judgment on both her conformity to that construction (as perpet-

ual victim) and her rebellion against it (as murderess prepared to kill and die for the statement of her pain). Like Butch Beauchamp in "Go Down, Moses" and Morrison's Sethe, Nancy may be seen as first victim, then criminal, despite the law's own reordering identifications.

The attempt to revise law's judgment in *Requiem* further suggests the hope of some of the characters that law is an organic and amorphous work itself, unfixed, responsive and changeable, subject always to experienced or concerned viewers' ongoing considerations. The perception of law's passing from works-in-progress responsive to alternative claims and concerns into hardened, permanent fixtures is perhaps similar to a perception of the evolving creations of the artist that register a range of possibility until the work enters the record permanently. It seems that any such perception of possibility for enlightening recognitions and beneficial revealings within the workings of law in the Faulknerian world, however, is a misplaced hope, as Gavin, Temple, and Nancy discover here, as did Horace, Ruby, and Lee in *Sanctuary*, Mrs. Tull and Mrs. Armstid in the "Spotted Horses" section of *The Hamlet*, and, perhaps tellingly, Gavin himself early in his career in the short story "Tomorrow."

Contrary to the possibilities of a responsive art form, Faulkner's vision of law does not seem to include possibility, even after early points of beginning: no possibility for further comment, interpretation, readings. In particular, Faulkner's various legal depictions seem to develop from an increasingly complex perception that law does not guarantee responsiveness and equality as a condition of its own existence, nor is there any point outside law—a precious if paradoxical site of extralegal, impossibly transhistorical and apolitical jurisprudence—that can ensure that inner workings are functioning as vital instruments of attempted representation rather than are always already edging toward the casting of themselves as autonomous systems, as in Cornell's disturbing view. Indeed, the anxieties and politics that constantly swirl around the notion of the individual as legal subject, as abstract bearer of rights and duties, are always poised between the inability to fulfill the dream of a responsive jurisprudence and the fear of entering into the nightmare of its system. The risk of law as our society's most dangerous art is its continuing power to shape a reality in which we live entrapped after legal argument's authorization as admissible version before the courts. In "Terror and the Law," David A. J. Richards remarks that, at the Nuremburg war crimes trial known as "The Justice Case," the indictment of Nazi S.S. lawyers baffled one particular legal observer who saw these defendants as " 'highly educated, professional men' " who had " 'attained full mental maturity long before Hitler's rise to power' " and who had " 'had special training and successful careers in the service of the law. They, of all Germans, should have understood and valued justice.' "[21] Richards goes on in his essay to remark that "[i]ndeed, there is no aspect of the Nazi terror more incomprehensible, nor more offensive to an American lawyer . . . than the complicity of lawyers in the terror" (171). Yet legal complicity in terrifying social constructions is present all through American literature, not the least of which includes Faulkner. Indeed, Faulkner seems to suggest that legal realities in his fictional universe—from *The Hamlet* and *Intruder in the Dust* to *The Sound and the Fury* and *Go Down, Moses*, from *The Wild Palms* to "Barn Burning," from *Sanctuary* and "Smoke" to "Tomorrow" and *The Town*—are all highly suspect, contrived, and often dangerous, a series of legal fictions only: fables of both legality and of the greater reality outside juridical space.

NOTES

1. Richard Weisberg, "Faulkner's Knowledge of the Law," *Mississippi College Law Review* 4 (Spring 1984): 193.

2. Joseph Blotner, "William Faulkner: Author-At-Law," *Mississippi College Law Review* 4 (Spring 1984): 275, 180.

3. Morris Wolff, "Faulkner's Knowledge of the Law," *Mississippi College Law Review* 4 (Spring 1984): 249.

4. Noel Polk, "Law in Faulkner's *Sanctuary*," *Mississippi College Law Review* 4 (Spring 1984): 237.

5. William Faulkner, *Sanctuary* (New York: The Modern Library, 1932), 340. Two contradictions inform Graham's strategy here, though they bolster instead of weaken his case. First, the expert witnesses are specialists in the scientific particulars of the body,

yet are called to loan whatever support they can to the idea of woman as special space of mystified processes. The second contradiction is more subtle and follows from the success of the first: if the testimonies can "elevate" Temple to the status of a sacred object, they unwittingly erase in logic (though reinforce emotionally) the possibility that a crime has been committed, insofar as profane object of cob has violated sacred object of woman. As the DA would probably be aware, there are no provisions under law for objects committing crimes against other objects.

6. Michel Foucault, *Discipline and Punish: The Birth of the Prison* (New York: Vintage, 1979), 73.

7. Foucault's ideas may be profitably explored further in such a reading of authority in *Sanctuary* (as well as elsewhere in Faulkner of the constantly recurring presentation of the spurious construction of community). The visual display orchestrated by the DA features as centerpiece Temple as violated, sexually punished female body. The relationship between the spectacle of the punished body and the rituals and power of law as shapers of a communal identity is explored in detail in Foucault's *Discipline and Punish: The Birth of the Prison*. In Temple's case, law itself does not punish her body but, by staging her, attempts to reap the authoritarian benefits of violation as spectacle.

8. Jay Watson, *Forensic Fictions: The Lawyer Figure in Faulkner* (Athens: The University of Georgia Press, 1993), 34–35.

9. The complex question immediately arises, however, of what the extra-legal audience presumably wants, of, once again, whether a public desire for justice pre-exists the juridical drama or whether that drama produces the public desire it would seem only to address and satisfy. While provoking it, *Sanctuary* leaves open this pressing question at the heart of its action and of legal culture generally. A related issue here is the role of media in modern legal conflicts, where news reports stage a type of institutionalized trial before the trial, unavoidably conditioning community expectation of and response to the formal workings of justice, blurring the lines, in fact, of where formal justice begins and what it takes into account.

10. William Faulkner, *The Town* (New York: Vintage, 1961), 173.

11. Drucilla Cornell, "The Violence of the Masquerade: Law Dressed Up As Justice," *Cardozo Studies in Law and Literature* 11 (1990): 1049.

12. William Faulkner, *The Wild Palms* (New York: Vintage, 1966), 327.

13. For another Faulknerian instance of law collapsing in on itself to achieve its ends, see "Smoke" in *Knight's Gambit*. In this story Gavin falsifies enough to call the Grand Jury inquest as legal enterprise into question, at least in the eyes of the narrator, also a juror.

14. William Faulkner, *The Sound and the Fury* (New York: Vintage, 1956), 174.

15. And all is available to it, as Peter Fitzpatrick points out in *The Mythology of Modern Law* (London: Routledge, 1992). Discussing the deific (and circular) aspects law arrogates onto itself, he notes that "law's omnipotence attributes to law not the ability to do everything but the ability to do anything. Law remains pervasive, able to intervene at any point but not intervening at every point . . . . [L]aw maintains its imperial and universal character against the particular" (57).

16. The professional legal identity of certain characters and the events of a plot already or not yet in progress are sometimes linked in Faulkner. Bayard (II) Sartoris in *The Unvanquished*, for example, is a law student who will not accept pistols from his law professor to avenge his father, a lawyer among other things, shot down by the lawyer Ben Redmond. In refusing to resort to personal violence, Bayard disrupts the blood feud, the revenge cycle, that law masks but promotes in this novel. For more on law as both a type of communal mask and blood feud, see John Duvall's "Silencing Women in 'The Fire and the Hearth' and 'Tomorrow,' " *College Literature* 16 (1989): 75–82.

17. Consider Gavin's roles, characterized by abstracted speech and disengaged observation, but not action, in *Light in August* and *Intruder in the Dust*, and even as complacent listener to a second- or third-hand story about a beautiful and troubled romance in "Hair." The lawyerly voyeur par excellence remains, of course, Dickens's

Jaggers in *Great Expectations*, who certainly orchestrates situations and events but seems to enjoy most stepping back to watch them unfold along one of their possible trajectories. Other curiously distanced legal observers, often remote from their own lives and communities, include the unnamed narrator in Melville's "Bartleby the Scrivener," David Wilson in Twain's *Pudd'nhead Wilson*, Clamence in Camus's *The Fall*, and Todd Andrews in John Barth's *The Floating Opera*.

18. William Faulkner, *Go Down, Moses* (New York: Vintage, 1973), 375.

19. Thadious M. Davis, "Crying in the Wilderness: Legal, Racial, and Moral Codes in *Go Down, Moses*," *Mississippi College Law Review* 4 (Spring 1984): 313.

20. William Faulkner, *Requiem for a Nun* (New York: Vintage, 1975), 177–78.

21. David A. J. Richards, "Terror and the Law," *Human Rights Quarterly* 5 (1983): 171.

"Longer than Anything": Faulkner's "Grand Design" in *Absalom, Absalom!*

ROBERT W. HAMBLIN

> *"[Man] can't live forever. He knows that. But when he's gone somebody will know he was here for his short time. He can build a bridge and will be remembered for a day or two, a monument, for a day or two, but somehow the picture, the poem—that lasts a long time, a very long time, longer than anything."*
> —FAULKNER AT NAGANO, JAPAN, 1955[1]

1

Many critics have written extensive commentaries on Thomas Sutpen's "Grand Design" in *Absalom, Absalom!*[2] Indeed, one of the most thorough treatments of the topic, Dirk Kuyk, Jr.'s book-length study, carries the title *Sutpen's Design.*[3] Less has been written, however, about another "design" in the book that counters Sutpen's, providing an upward, transcendent movement that contrasts sharply with Sutpen's tragic fall. This second pattern is Faulkner's, the creator's; and to understand that design is to understand a great deal about Faulkner's views of art and the artist.

I begin with a rarely cited passage that characterizes not only the type of novel that *Absalom, Absalom!* is but also the kind of writer that William Faulkner is. The passage, which appears early in chapter 8, is, significantly, one of the few in the novel narrated by the omniscient author. The passage describes Quentin's and Shreve's reconstruction of the conversation between Thomas and Henry Sutpen in the library of the Sutpen mansion a half-century earlier. As Quentin and Shreve imagine the scene, Henry, while he listens to his father speak, looks through the window and sees Judith and Charles Bon walking together in the garden, "the sister's head bent with listening, the lover's head leaned above it while they paced slowly on in that rhythm which not the eyes but the heart marks and calls the beat and measure for, to disappear slowly beyond some bush or shrub starred with white bloom—jasmine, spiraea, honeysuckle, perhaps myriad scentless unpickable Cherokee roses" (236).[4]

Then, abruptly, without even a sentence break, the omniscient narrator retracts what has just been said by pointing out that it would have been impossible for Henry to see what Quentin and Shreve want to believe he saw because it was both wintertime (specifically Christmas Eve) and nighttime: "and hence no bloom nor leaf even if there had been someone to walk there and be seen there." Then, just as abruptly, three times in rapid succession, the narrator offers a judgment on the apparent contradiction by observing that Quentin's and Shreve's misconceptions "did not matter," since what really matters for Quentin and Shreve (and for Faulkner as well) is the power of the creative imagination to bridge the gap between present and past and thus to enable "the immortal brief recent intransient blood" (237) of the dead to "course" once again.

No passage better illustrates the degree to which the narrative strategy of *Absalom, Absalom!* turns upon the mythologizing tendency of the human imagination. For Quentin and Shreve the scene between Henry and his father is characterized by sunlight, blooming flowers, youth, idealism, and love—symbols of life and regeneration. For the narrator, whose role as realist is to demythologize, or deconstruct, the myth, the actual scene is one of winter and darkness—universal symbols of death. Thus are presented the polarities of Faulkner's greatest novel—death versus life, history versus myth, actuality versus art, the lost, irretrievable past versus the past as resurrected and revivified in poetic fabulation.

2

Throughout his career Faulkner was interested in—even, one might justifiably argue, obsessed with—the paradoxical relationship between art and life. "The aim of every artist," he once said, "is to arrest motion, which is life, by artificial means and hold it fixed so that 100 years later when a stranger looks at it, it moves again since it is life" (*LIG* 253). At Charlottesville he spoke of the writer's goal in similar terms: "You catch this fluidity which is human life and you focus a light on it and you stop it long enough for people to be able to see it" (*FIU* 239). Such statements acknowledge that art is a created object, an artifact, a stoppage of life and motion and hence antithetical to the flux and mutability that characterize the human condition. In this sense, of course, all art is ultimately a divorcement from actuality; as Gail Hightower observes in *Light in August*, "How false the most profound book turns out to be when applied to life" (455). At the same time, however, Faulkner's statements also assert that whatever success is possible for the artist is directly proportionate to the degree that his art is interrelated with actual experience.[5]

Faulkner's fictional *oeuvre* may be viewed as an ongoing dialectic on the relationship between art and life. At times Faulkner seemed to favor the realists' theory of art as *mimesis*, a view which asserts the dependence of art on life and thereby implies a superiority of life over art; at other times, drawing upon the practice of the neo-Romantics, the Symbolists, he stressed art as *poiesis*, a position that emphasizes the artist's originality and creativity and thus argues for the supremacy of art over life. While a tension between these two positions is evidenced throughout his career, in general Faulkner may be identified with the life-over-art school of thought during his apprenticeship and with the art-over-life school after he reached his literary majority.

In one of his earliest essays, published in 1922, Faulkner characterizes Joseph Hergesheimer as an author who seeks to divorce his art from life. Faulkner claims that Hergesheimer is "afraid of living, of man in his sorry clay," and adds that *Linda Condon* is "not a novel" but "a lovely Byzantine frieze: a few unforgettable figures in silent arrested motion, forever beyond the reach of time and troubling the heart like music." Faulkner further observes: "One can imagine Hergesheimer submerging himself in *Linda Condon* as in a still harbor where the age cannot hurt him and where rumor of the world reaches him only as a far faint sound of rain" (*EPP* 101–2). Clearly, Faulkner views Hergesheimer's art as escapist, and therefore incompatible with the truth of actual experience.

Recognition of the paradoxical tension that exists between art and life seems to account in part for the characterization of the faun in Faulkner's first published book, *The Marble Faun*. In this pastoral cycle of poems a marble faun, reminiscent of both Praxiteles' statue in Rome and Hawthorne's novel based on the statue, is exposed to the changes wrought in nature by the advancing seasons of the year. The mutability observable in nature contrasts sharply with the "marble-bound" existence of the faun. One might expect such a contrast to be employed, as it often is in the poetry of the Romantics, to assert the superiority of art over nature, but just the opposite seems to be the case.

> Why am I sad? I?
> Why am I not content? The sky
> Warms me and yet I cannot break
> My marble bonds. That quick keen snake
> Is free to come and go, while I
> Am prisoner to dream and sigh
> For things I know, yet cannot know,
> 'Twixt sky above and earth below.
> The spreading earth calls to my feet
> Of orchards bright with fruits to eat,
> Of hills and streams on either hand;
> Of sleep at night on moon-blanched sand:
> The whole world breathes and calls to me
> Who marble-bound must ever be.
> (12)

Although the faun exists in an immutable, deathless world, this realization, in a manner that recalls Calypso in Homer's *Odyssey*, occasions no joy.

> And we, the marbles in the glade,
> Dreaming in the leafy shade
> Are saddened, for we know that all
> Things save us must fade and fall.
>
> (31)

In the Epilogue the faun continues to lament the fact that he is forever excluded from both the ecstasies and sorrows of real life:

> Ah, how all this calls to me
> Who marble-bound must ever be
> While turn unchangingly the years.
> My heart is full, yet sheds no tears
> To cool my burning carven eyes
> Bent to the unchanging skies:
> I would be sad with changing year,
> Instead, a sad, bound prisoner.
> For though about me seasons go
> My heart knows only winter snow.
>
> (50–51)

Unlike Hawthorne's Donatello, Faulkner's faun is never allowed to become humanized, to exchange his innocence for experience in the actual world. He remains, at the end as in the beginning, trapped in his artificial, marble-bound existence.

Faulkner's most explicit treatment of the paradoxical relationship between art and life is found in his second novel, *Mosquitoes*. In fact, this book, in which Faulkner portrays a group of New Orleans artists, would-be artists, intellectuals, and socialites on a four-day outing aboard a yacht, may be viewed primarily as a colloquium which allows the author to examine various theories of art and the artist. As Michael Millgate pointed out in his seminal study a quarter-century ago, the novel contains "statements of artistic principle and belief which seem most fully to embody Faulkner's own position—almost as if the book, with its exploration and exposition of many different viewpoints, had been the means by which he had argued out his own uncertainties and arrived eventually at a clearer conception of his role as an artist."[6] Although many different topics (not all of them literary) are discussed, the principal concern, as in *The Marble Faun*, appears to be the relationship between life and art; and the characters may be grouped according to their views regarding this central concern.

At one extreme are such young people as Patricia, David West, Jenny, and Pete, who are intensely involved in living but utterly indifferent to art. As Julius, the Semitic man, observes, "Look at our books, our stage, the movies. Who supports 'em? Not the young folks. They'd rather walk around or just sit and hold each other's hands" (229). At the other extreme are the dilettantes like Ernest Talliaferro and Mrs. Maurier and such artist-pretenders as Mark Frost, Eva Wiseman, and Miss Jameson. Like J. Alfred Prufrock, with whom Talliaferro is specifically paralleled, these characters are all fearful of life (as with Prufrock, the revealing metaphor is sex) and prefer conversation to action. Their discussions, lengthy and often tiresome, are appropriately described as "talk, talk, talk: the utter and heartbreaking stupidity of words" (186). Ironically, Mrs. Maurier mistakes the detachment from life symbolized by such verbalization as a prerequisite to artistic endeavor: "To live within yourself, to be sufficient unto yourself. . . . To go through life, keeping yourself from becoming involved in it, to gather inspiration for your Work—ah, Mr. Gordon, how lucky you who create are" (152–53).

Standing alone as the one character who is capable of at least partially reconciling these extremes, of bridging the gap between life and art, is the sculptor Gordon. Not only is he the most perceptive and creative among the artist group (he manages to capture in the clay bust of Mrs. Maurier the very essence of her character, whereas Dawson Fairchild, who has been acquainted with the lady much longer, discovers that he hardly knows her at all), but he is also the least talkative. Moreover, his involvement with Patricia, while not altogether satisfying, nonetheless suggests an openness to life denied the aesthetes and pseudoartists. Gordon's refusal to withdraw from life in the manner of the other artists is symbolized by his encounter with the prostitute toward the end of the novel. "Gordon entered and before the door closed again they saw him in a narrow passageway lift a woman from the shadow and raise her against the mad stars, smothering her squeal against his tall kiss" (338–39). This act of engagement with life is immediately juxtaposed with the image of Gordon's statue of the young virgin: *"Then voices and sounds, shadows and echoes change form swirling, becoming the headless, armless, legless torso of a girl, motionless and virginal and passionately eternal before the shadows and echoes whirl away"* (339). The point seems clear: only the artist with the courage and passion to engage life honestly and directly can hope to transform that experience into authentic art.

3

Faulkner wrote his review of *Linda Condon, The Marble Faun,* and *Mosquitoes* during a period of his life when art seemed rather poor compensation for missed adventures in living. Like the frustrated poet in "Carcassonne," that early story which reveals so much about its creator, Faulkner wanted *"to perform something bold and tragical and austere"* (CS 899). His recent disillusionments in military service and love doubtless contributed to a sense of unfulfillment, but he had not yet lost his youthful idealism. Despite his disappointments, he was still inclined to identify with Dawson Fairchild's tendency in *Mosquitoes* to "prefer a live poet to the writings of any man" (246). Indeed, as he had confessed in his 1924 essay, "Verse Old and Nascent: A Pilgrimage," poetry was primarily a way of "furthering various philanderings in which [he] was engaged"; only, he continues, after he found his "concupiscence waning" did he turn to "verse for verse's sake" (*EPP* 115). As such statements evidence, to the young Faulkner life, not art, was the magical realm where happiness could best be found.

By the time he wrote *Absalom*, however, Faulkner's view of life had become much more jaded and cynical—and, conversely, as I shall subsequently demonstrate, his view of art much more positive. The former attitude derived partly, one suspects, from the time period in which the novel was written. In the mid-1930s the nation was in the midst of the Great Depression; and Faulkner, unlike his contemporary Margaret Mitchell, could find little encouragement in the situation. Whereas Mitchell's novel, *Gone with the Wind* (coincidentally published the same year as *Absalom, Absalom!*), stresses the popular theme of the resiliency of the human spirit to bounce back from defeat and hardship, Faulkner's politically incorrect novel offered no such hopeful vision. On the contrary, Faulkner's message was more akin to that of his Hollywood hunting companion Nathanael West, whose *Miss Lonelyhearts* (1933) depicted an America being overwhelmed by chaos, violence, alienation, and despair.

In addition to the Great Depression context of the novel, there was also, as Faulkner's biographers have helped us to realize, a personal element in the bitterly pessimistic view of life expressed in Faulkner's rendition of Sutpen's fate.[7] The approach of middle age, the failure to achieve the literary and financial success that he desired and felt he deserved, the growing conviction that he was trapped in an unhappy marriage, the chronic drinking—such factors contributed to Faulkner's discontent and malaise. Then, too, there was the cruel, untimely death of his brother Dean in the crash of the plane that Faulkner had provided. Given such developments, it is not at all surprising that the Faulkner of this period was coming to perceive human history in the terms he would employ at the end of *Absalom, Absalom!* to describe the collapse of Sutpen's dream: "it was all finished now, there was nothing left now, nothing out there now but that idiot boy to lurk around those ashes and those four gutted chimneys and howl" (301). The echoes of the famous quotation from *Macbeth*, from which

Faulkner had taken his title for *The Sound and the Fury*, are ummistakable—and very likely intentional.

Even Faulkner's mail brought him suggestions that life and history are futile. As Joseph Blotner has documented, about the time Faulkner was beginning the work that would become *Absalom, Absalom!* he received from Hal Smith a copy of André Malraux's *Man's Fate*.[8] This novel, which traces the betrayal and defeat of a group of Chinese revolutionaries, depicts the ongoing but pathetic struggle of man's idealism in an indifferent and absurd cosmos. Faulkner's novel would develop much the same theme—but without Malraux's redeeming "beginning again" conclusion.

4

Viewed as history, Thomas Sutpen's story is exceedingly tragic, deterministically so. As we know from a number of other Faulkner works, particularly *The Sound and the Fury*, "The Bear," and (as Noel Polk so persuasively argued in his presentation at last year's conference) *A Fable*, Faulkner's ultimate view of history was decidedly pessimistic. In fact, it could be called Spenglerian.[9] Individuals age and die, cultures rise and inevitably fall, dreams and ideals are constantly frustrated and thwarted, remaining alive only as hope and memory. As Harry Wilbourne, a character not altogether unlike Thomas Sutpen, comes to understand, the common lot of humanity is "grief," the only alternative, as Quentin Compson has already discovered, being "nothing" (*WP* 324).

It is, I think, to stress the inevitability of grief and loss that Faulkner accounts for Sutpen's failure to realize his design in deterministic terms. As every reader comes to recognize, Sutpen's defeat is inextricably tied to the question of race. Sutpen is undeniably and unapologetically "racist," but it becomes instructive to examine carefully the influences that make him so.

Faulkner treats Sutpen's first encounter with a black almost casually—in fact, parenthetically—but the experience has profound ramifications, foreshadowing as it does Sutpen's subsequent career. The encounter occurs when Sutpen is a ten-year-old boy, accompanying his family as it migrates from the mountains of western Virginia to the Tidewater region to the east. As Sutpen recalls for General Compson, a good portion of that journey was spent sitting in the family's cart outside taverns waiting for the alcoholic father to complete his drinking binges. Frequently the father would become so drunk that he had to be physically carried from the tavern and loaded onto the cart. On one occasion that chore had been accomplished "by a huge bull of a nigger, the first black man, slave, they had ever seen, who emerged with the old man over his shoulder like a sack of meal and his—the nigger's—mouth loud with laughing and full of teeth like tombstones" (182).

Sutpen's Negrophobia has its origin in this scene. Readers should not underestimate the shocking and lasting effect of a young boy's watching his father's being manhandled and ridiculed by a large, powerful black stranger. Significantly, the description of the scene conveys two images that symbolize forces that Sutpen will later contend against in his quest to build a family dynasty: the twin fears of dehumanization (the father is handled "like a sack of meal") and death (the black's teeth look "like tombstones").

This negative experience, which made such a startling impression upon the young Sutpen that the adult would still recall and repeat it more than a quarter century later, is followed by others just as traumatic and influential. Once, as he and his sister walk along a dirt road, the young girl is nearly run down by a carriage driven by a "nigger coachman in a plug hat" (187). On another occasion he listens as his father, in a voice of "fierce exultation, vindication" (187), recounts the beating of a black slave by a group of night riders. Then, when he is about thirteen or fourteen years of age, Thomas is sent by his father with a message to the "big house," whereupon he is turned away from the front door and told to go to the back by a "monkey-dressed nigger butler" (187).

All readers agree, following Sutpen's own assessment of the incident, that the rejection at the door is the central experience of Sutpen's childhood. But most readers, I think, have been too quick to follow Sutpen's lead in affixing blame for the humiliation. Although Sutpen consciously insists that his anger and desire for revenge are directed toward the owner of the plantation and not the black butler, it is hard to believe that his subconscious has completely exonerated the black butler of guilt. [10] In fact, Sutpen's redundant reiteration that it was "not the nigger" who was at fault seems excessive, the futile effort perhaps of an uncertain man to persuade himself of a truth of which he is not altogether convinced. No reader takes Quentin's protestation, *"I dont hate it! I dont hate it!"* (303), at face value; neither should we necessarily believe everything that Sutpen says. As psychologists recognize, it is not at all unusual for individuals to find it extremely difficult, at least subconsciously, to separate a message from its deliverer. His use of the demeaning phrase "monkey nigger" certainly seems to suggest that Sutpen has been unable to do so.

The terrifying, near-death experience in Haiti further exaggerates the Negrophobia that Sutpen's early conditioning has already established. In fact, the Haiti episode merely repeats on a wider, adult scale the tragic initiation pattern of the young boy's Tidewater experience. As General Compson notes, Haiti is "a theatre for violence and injustice and bloodshed and all the satanic lusts of human greed and cruelty," located at "the halfway point between what we call the jungle and what we call civilization" (202). Compson associates Sutpen's journey to the island as a journey to "the heart of the earth" (202), a phrase that recalls the experience of another character from one of Faulkner's favorite books—Kurtz in Joseph Conrad's *Heart of Darkness*. Although Faulkner chooses to present Sutpen's Haitian terror indirectly, through suggestion and implication (as he does the terror element in such stories as "A Rose for Emily" and "Dry September"), his references to voodooistic ritual, the eight-day siege, the paralyzing fear of those under attack, and

Sutpen's life-threatening wounds persuade most readers that Sutpen is not exaggerating when he characterizes the episode as "more than flesh should be asked to stand" (205).

Unlike Kurtz, Sutpen survives his Descent into Hell; but he does not escape unscathed: the horrors he saw and experienced there have a catastrophic effect upon his subsequent life and career. In fact, so intense is his association of those terrible days with his memory of the smell of burning sugar cane that "he had never been able to bear sugar since" (201). Undoubtedly, like Kurtz (and like Captain Delano in another horror story that Faulkner may have known, Melville's "Benito Cereno"), Sutpen also comes to associate such atrocities with black skin.

Sutpen's subsequent effort to create Sutpen's Hundred and establish a family dynasty in Yoknapatawpha County represents a heroic, though eventually maniacal, attempt to control the forces of dehumanization, disintegration, and death that he has come to associate, albeit perhaps subconsciously, with the condition of blackness. To prove his superiority to and control over this condition, he coerces a subhuman "band of wild niggers like beasts half tamed to walk upright like men" (4) to build his mansion. For the same reason he engages in hand-to-hand combat with some of these beastlike creatures. Rosa Coldfield is right at least on this point, viewing Sutpen's motivation for the no-holds-barred fights "as a matter of sheer deadly forethought toward the retention of supremacy, domination" (21). The picture of Sutpen standing triumphantly over the body of a vanquished black is an obverse image of his watching his father's being manhandled by a huge slave, or his being turned away from the Tidewater plantation house by a "monkey nigger," or his being pinned down for days and nearly killed during the slave insurrection in Haiti. The desperate need for a plantation house and a family dynasty is merely a further extension of his desire to prove to himself and to the world that he is forevermore impervious to such threats.[11]

Ironically, in seeking to prove his invincibility, to escape his fear of powerlessness and dehumanization, he oppresses and abuses the very group in the novel with which he originally has so much in common, that is, the blacks, three of whom are his wife, his son, and his daughter. While Sutpen's treatment of Eulalia Bon, Charles Bon, and even Clytie is sad and disgraceful, it is, given his past experience, altogether logical and predictable. The shrewd manipulation of Henry to prevent Bon's marriage to Judith is not merely consistent with Sutpen's character, it is inescapable. Given his personal history, the last thing that Sutpen could allow would be to have his "design" tainted by any trace of black blood. The logic of the racist may appear to others to be confused and irrational, but to the racist it has the precision and inevitability of a mathematical equation.

I am aware that the explanation I have presented for Sutpen's behavior is not consistent with Sutpen's own understanding of his motives. He believes—and he is partly right—that it is the owner of the big house, not the black butler, who is to blame for his youthful humiliation and thus responsible for the genesis of his "design." He also genuinely believes that on two crucial occasions in the pursuit of that design he has exercised free will in the making of choices: the first time, in Haiti, when he elects to set aside his first wife and child as incompatible with his life's purpose, and again, years later in Mississippi, when he rejects his mulatto son a second time.

I believe, however, that Sutpen is at least partly mistaken on both counts. In the final analysis, Sutpen's adult behavior seems as rigidly predetermined as that, say, of Quentin Compson, Joe Christmas, or Popeye Vitelli. When the defining moment of his destiny presents itself in the person of Charles Bon at his door, Sutpen thinks that he makes a choice; but that choice has already been been made for him long ago. Were he more self-aware, he might say with Joe Christmas, "I have never got outside that circle. I have never broken out of the ring of what I have already done and cannot ever undo" (*LIA* 321).

I have stressed the deterministic aspects of Faulkner's handling of the fate of Thomas Sutpen to suggest how thoroughly bleak and pessimistic is the view of history expressed in *Absa-*

lom, Absalom! That pessimism is evidenced not only in the death of Sutpen, the destruction of his mansion, and the ironic survival of Sutpen's blood lineage only in the "idiot negro" (301) Jim Bond, but also in the degree to which Sutpen's fall is linked to circumstance, geography, and the ineradicable imperfections of human nature. Sutpen's "innocence," therefore, is in part his belief, his illusion, that history can be anything other than what it already, inexorably is.

5

But history is only one aspect, the negative one, of this great novel; art is the other, the redeeming feature. Whereas Sutpen's historical "design" plunges downward to defeat and death, Faulkner's artistic "design"—far grander than Sutpen's—moves upward and outward, defeating both time and geography through the immortality of art and the universality of myth. His faith in life diminishing, and not having the solace of a belief in an afterlife, Faulkner, like many of the Symbolists before him, elevated art into a religion and the artist into a high priest. Years later he would speak of art as "the salvation of mankind" and "a proof of man's immortality" (*LIG* 71, 103). One of his earliest and most forceful dramatizations of this exalted view of art is *Absalom, Absalom!*

The point that *Absalom, Absalom!* is as much about art as it is about history is encoded in Faulkner's text in several significant ways. For example, there is the letter that Judith Sutpen passes on to Mrs. Compson. Like the statue of John Sartoris at the end of *Sartoris* or the McCaslin family ledgers in "The Bear" or the signature that Cecilia Farmer scratches into glass in *Requiem for a Nun*, Bon's letter to Judith serves as an art-surrogate that symbolizes the capability of works of art to withstand the ravaging effects of time. The artist's driving impulse, Faulkner repeatedly said, is "to say No to death," and he frequently cited his favorite poem, Keats's "Ode on a Grecian Urn," as both an expression and realization of that desire.[12]

It is hardly coincidental that Judith's explanation of why she wants to pass Bon's letter into another person's hands—someone who will live after her—almost exactly parallels Faulkner's statements on the artist's attempt to defeat time.

> "Because you make so little impression [Judith says] . . . and then all of a sudden it's all over and all you have left is a block of stone with scratches on it. . . . And so maybe if you could go to someone, the stranger the better, and give them something—a scrap of paper—something, anything . . . at least it would be something just because it would have happened, be remembered even if only from passing from one hand to another, one mind to another, and it would be at least a scratch, something, something that might make a mark on something that *was* once for the reason that it can die someday, while the block of stone cant be *is* because it never can become *was* because it cant ever die or perish." (100–1).

Judith may be uncertain as to her motive for giving the letter to Mrs. Compson, but Faulkner is not. He knows that her attempt "to make that scratch, that undying mark on the blank face of the oblivion to which we are all doomed" (102) is akin to the artist's denial of death. "Since man is mortal," Faulkner told one interviewer, "the only immortality possible for him is to leave something behind him that is immortal since it will always move. This is the artist's way of scribbling 'Kilroy was here' on the wall of the final and irrevocable oblivion through which he must someday pass" (*LIG* 253).

Faulkner similarly links Thomas Sutpen's "design" to the artist's quest for immortality.[13] Carving Sutpen's Hundred out of a frontier wilderness becomes an analogue to what Wallace Stevens has called the artist's "Blessed rage for order."[14] Significantly, in this connection Sutpen is identified with the divine, *ex-nihilo* creator of the Genesis myth: "Then in the long unamaze Quentin seemed to watch them overrun suddenly the hundred square miles of tranquil and astonished earth and drag house and formal gardens violently out of the soundless Nothing and clap them down like cards upon a table beneath the up-palm immobile and pontific, creating the Sutpen's Hundred, the *Be Sutpen's Hundred* like the oldentime *Be Light*" (4).[15] Even more revealingly, Sutpen is linked to the artist's resistance to time and death and to Carcassonne, Faulkner's personal symbol for artistic creation.[16] Conscious of "a need for haste, of time fleeing beneath him" (25), Sutpen is described in a key passage as "a madman who creates within his very coffin walls his fabulous immeasurable Camelots and Carcassonnes" (129). One need not, of course, be negatively influenced by the use in this passage of the word "madman." Like Shakespeare in his creation of King Lear or Melville in his characterization of Captain Ahab (characters with whom Sutpen has a great deal in common), Faulkner occasionally associates madness with special knowledge or insight.[17]

Even in his ruthlessness to realize his dream Sutpen may be compared to Faulkner's notion of the artist. "They did not think of love in connection with Sutpen," the reader is told. "They thought of ruthlessness rather than justice and of fear rather than respect, but not of pity or love" (32). Faulkner, one recalls, made similar statements about artists. "The writer's only responsibility," he once said, "is to his art. He will be completely ruthless if he is a good one. . . . If a writer has to rob his mother, he will not hesitate; the 'Ode on a Grecian Urn' is worth any number of old ladies" (*LIG* 239). So too, Sutpen believed, was a dynasty. The comparison is underscored by the fact that Sutpen is continually identified as a "demon"—the same word Faulkner occasionally used to describe the artistic impulse within an individual (*FIU* 19, 159).

As noted at the very outset, however, the most significant statement on art in *Absalom, Absalom!* is to be found in the imaginative reconstruction of the Sutpen story by Quentin and Shreve in their Harvard dormitory room. Whereas the first five chapters of the novel present the characters' search for historical facts, the remaining four chapters abandon (necessarily, in Faulkner's view) a concern for fact in favor of intuition and imaginative invention. In these concluding chapters history is usurped by fiction; actuality is superseded by art. In repeating the ancient ritual of storytelling, in the shared act of narrating and hearing, in the dead of winter, a story about events that happened a half-century previously, Quentin and Shreve dramatize the capability of art to defeat time and death. Faulkner would repeat the symbolism in his next novel, *The Unvanquished*. Like Drusilla's story to Bayard and Ringo of the Confederates who defy their conquerers by racing a locomotive along tracks supposedly controlled by the Yankees, the Sutpen story will never be "gone or vanished either, so long as there should be defeated or the descendants of defeated to tell it or listen to the telling" (*U* 112). Rosa Coldfield is linked to the same faith in the resurrectional power of storytelling when she tells Quentin, "So maybe you will enter the literary profession as so many Southern gentlemen and gentlewomen too are doing now and maybe some day you will remember this and write about it" (5). *"It's because she wants it told,"* Quentin thinks, *"so that people whom she will never see and whose names she will never hear and who have never heard her name nor seen her face will read it . . ."* (6).

6

Reading *Absalom, Absalom!* as a celebration of the superiority of art over life contributes to an understanding of the significance of the map of Yoknapatawpha County which Faulkner drew and allowed to be tipped into the back of his novel. Though the point has been generally ignored by readers and critics, the end of *Absalom, Absalom!* is not Quentin's tortured and passionate assertion that he doesn't hate the South. Nor is it the appendix listing the Sutpen "Chronology" and "Genealogy." The end of *Absalom, Absalom!* is Faulkner's map.[18] As I hope to demonstrate, that map functions in much the same way as the title does, that is, by extending the province of the novel beyond the regional to the universal, by converting the "facts" of history into the "truth" of myth. In fact, the title and the map serve as matching bookends, or, better, a symbolic parenthesis enclosing the tragic history of Thomas Sutpen. Taken together, they are the Alpha and Omega, the first word and the last, of the novel, and both express Faulkner's faith in the triumph of art over the inevitable, downward spiral of history.

Most critics have interpreted Faulkner's title as an ironic commentary on the Sutpen family history. As John Hagopian has pointed out, the Sutpen narrative parallels the biblical story of David and Absalom in its emphasis on "revolt, incest, and fratricide," but it differs in that Faulkner's David, unlike the biblical one, is unable to feel love and compassion for his rebellious son. Hagopian views this key difference as "the main point of the Sutpen story."[19]

While he is undoubtedly right in his point-by-point comparison of the two stories, Hagopian ignores the broader implications of Faulkner's biblical allusion. Faulkner's interest in the David-Absalom story, as in the Greek and medieval legends with which it is clustered, is rooted in its mythic dimension—the manner in which it captures and reiterates, in its retelling, important aspects of the universal human condition. Faulkner's view of the Bible is pertinent here. As he made quite clear, his reading of the Bible was always literary, mythic, never religious. Like Ike McCaslin, Faulkner viewed the authors of biblical myths as "human men" who "were trying to write down the heart's truth out of the heart's driving complexity, for all the complex and troubled hearts which would beat after them" (*GDM* 260). What impressed Faulkner primarily about the David and Absalom material was that it was a story that had been written and preserved through the centuries for generations of readers. That preservation had little to do with the religious significance or the historical accuracy of the story—in point of fact King David was a petty tyrant in a petty kingdom whose story would have been quickly forgotten had it not been recorded in "The Book." The real hero of the narrative is neither David nor Absalom but the anonymous bard/scribe who told/ wrote a story that has outgrown and outlasted the author, the subject, and the historical era that produced it—that, in short, like Quentin and Shreve's retelling of the Sutpen myth, has conquered time and death to live on as art.

Just as the biblical allusion of the title extends Sutpen's regional, temporal story into the realms of the universal, the mythic, and the timeless, so too does the map that ends the novel. Like the title, the map functions at three different levels: the realistic, the ironic, and the symbolic.

As Jules Zanger has explained, one of the most obvious purposes of a literary map is to provide clarification and verisimilitude for the story it accompanies.[20] Faulkner, of course, would have been familiar with numerous maps employed in this manner: for example, biblical maps tracing the migration of the Hebrew people or the missionary journeys of Paul, Bulfinch's maps depicting the settings of the Greek and Roman myths and the wanderings of Ulysses, Sir Thomas More's map of Utopia, Jonathan Swift's maps of the travels of Lemuel Gulliver, Thomas Hardy's maps of Wessex, Sherwood Anderson's map of Winesburg. Like other authorial devices such as Hawthorne's "discovery" of the scarlet A and the papers of Jonathan Pue in the Salem custom house, or the "missing" parts of Henry Mackenzie's *The Man of Feeling*, the literary map enables the reader to suspend disbelief and momentarily accept a fictionalized world as authentic and actual. To visualize Sutpen's Hundred on a map makes it easier to view Thomas Sutpen as a historical character inhabiting a real world.

On this level Faulkner's map reiterates and extends the tragic view of life and history that the Sutpen narrative has already conveyed. Through the handwritten entries that Faulkner made, the landscape of Yoknapatawpha is presented primarily as a setting for grief, villainy, and death. At the top is the "fishing camp where Wash Jones killed Sutpen"; at the bottom is the place "where Popeye killed Tommy." In between are references to the deaths of other characters—old Bayard Sartoris, John Sartoris, Addie Bundren, Joe Christmas, Joanna Burden, Lee Goodwin. The cemetery and the jail are highlighted, as also are the unscrupulous actions of Flem Snopes and Jason Compson. Even the courthouse, which sits at the center, as Faulkner says in another place, "laying its vast shadow to the uttermost rim of horizon" (RFN 35), and which ideally should be identified with order and stability and justice, is instead associated with Temple Drake's perjury and the pathetic fate of Benjy Compson. Like the story of Thomas Sutpen, Faulkner's map of Yoknapatawpha depicts history literally as a dead-end, or, to use the phrases that Faulkner later directed to Malcolm Cowley, a "pointless chronicle," "the same frantic steeplechase toward nothing everywhere" (FCF 7, 15).

But a map is not merely a representation of place; it is also a guide, a means of assisting a traveler in getting from one point to another. "You are here," we read in the subway or museum and chart our intended destination, trusting the map to show us the way, to keep us from getting lost. In this regard a map serves as an ideal corollary to a novel of quest and initiation. *Absalom, Absalom!*, of course, is just such a novel, being filled with travel references and journeys of one kind or another: Thomas Sutpen's journey from the mountains to the Tidewater and thence on to Haiti and Mississippi; Charles Bon's migration from Haiti to New Orleans to Oxford to Sutpen's Hundred; Henry Sutpen's travels to Oxford, New Orleans, the war, Texas, and back to Mississippi; the various characters' trips back and forth between Sutpen's Hundred and Jefferson; Quentin Compson's trip to Harvard. All such journeys represent psychological quests as well: Sutpen's attempt to escape his threatening past by creating a "design" of safety and security, Bon's search for a father, Henry's search for personal and cultural identity, Quentin's desperate hope to understand both himself and the South.

In this connection, however, Faulkner's map, like his title, functions ironically. All of the personal quests in *Absalom, Absalom!* end in futility and failure. Bon dies, unackowledged by his father; Sutpen dies, frustrated in his design; Henry dies, outcast and condemned; Quentin will soon die, still troubled and confused about the meaning of existence. Faulkner's map, like the plot of the novel it underscores and supports, is, so far as it is a map of history and the human condition, a map charting failed ambitions and pointing the way to death. Had Faulkner chosen an epigraph for his drawing, it might well have been the quotation from Shakespeare alluded to earlier, the one he used for the title of his second-greatest novel:

> Tomorrow, and tomorrow, and tomorrow,
> Creeps in this petty pace from day to day
> To the last syllable of recorded time,
> And all our yesterdays have lighted fools
> The way to dusty death. Out, out brief candle!
> Life's but a walking shadow, a poor player
> That struts and frets his hour upon the stage
> And then is heard no more: it is a tale
> Told by an idiot, full of sound and fury,
> Signifying nothing.

Any map, however, as Faulkner surely understood and appreciated, is more than a graphic representation of an actual place and a practical guide for travelers; it is simultaneously a metaphor. Despite its seeming verisimilitude, every map remains, like the familiar Mercator projection, a distortion of the actual, a substitution for the real, an evocation of an order and harmony that exists, finally, only in the mapmaker's mind and imagination. Cartography, therefore, is not only a science but also an art.

Moreover, even to the degree that a map may be considered metaphorically "true," as opposed to "factual," that truth is always temporary and partial. Thus maps must be periodically redrawn, as medieval maps were rendered obsolete by the discovery of the New World and as celestial charts were altered by the invention of the telescope. Thus, too, maps must always be understood in relation to a larger whole. Maps end at their edges, but reality and meaning do not. Counties merge into states, states into nations, nations into continents, continents into hemispheres and worlds, and so on outward through the cosmos.

All such observations suggest why Faulkner's map of Yoknapatawpha County provides an appropriate ending for *Absalom,
Absalom!* Just as the map blends both "factual" information and
metaphor, the novel fuses actuality and art. Just as the map—
with its roads, rivers, and railroad leading off the edge and its
arrows pointing to Memphis and Mottstown and ultimately, as
Faulkner claimed in *The Town*, "from Jefferson to the world"
(*T* 315)—suggests a geography beyond Yoknapatawpha, the
novel links local, time-bound history with universal, timeless
myth. Just as Faulkner's map, like every map, must eventually
be revised and redrawn,[21] the novel presents truth as partial
and relative, changing with the addition of new information and
constant shifts in perspective.

Faulkner's map of Yoknapatawpha is the artistic equivalent of
the historical Sutpen's Hundred. Each is the result of its creator's great "design" to impose order and meaning on chaos.
But whereas Sutpen's, as a part of what Faulkner considered to
be a fatally flawed human history, is inevitably doomed to fail,
Faulkner's, by being elevated to the level of great art, is
timeless. On Faulkner's fictional "historical" map Sutpen's Hundred is a tiny, finite circle, ending where it began. On Faulkner's real map, however—the one that depicts the mythical
"Jefferson, Yoknapatawpha Co, Mississippi"—Sutpen's Hundred survives and endures, a lasting symbol of the redeeming
power of art. Like the novel of which it is such an integral
part, and the title which it complements, Faulkner's map both
evidences and celebrates the artist's capacity to defeat time and
death by crafting a work of art that will last "a long time, a very
long time, longer than anything" (*LIG* 103).

NOTES

1. *Lion in the Garden: Interviews with William Faulkner, 1926–1962*, ed. James B.
Meriwether and Michael Millgate (New York: Random House, 1968), 103.

2. I have borrowed this term from Elizabeth M. Kerr, *Yoknapatawpha: Faulkner's
"Little Postage Stamp of Native Soil"* (New York: Fordham University Press, 1969), 87;
but numerous other critics, including Malcolm Cowley, Melvin Backman, Ilse Dusoir
Lind, Eric Sundquist, and Frederick Karl have similarly referred to Sutpen's dream as

a "grand" or a "great" design. The adjectives, of course, are supplied by the critics: in Faulkner's text the term employed is merely "design." My intent, as I hope my title conveys, is to contrast Sutpen's "design" with Faulkner's "grand design."

3. Dirk Kuyk, Jr., *Sutpen's Design: Interpreting Faulkner's "Absalom, Absalom!"* (Charlottesville: University Press of Virginia, 1990).

4. Quotations from Faulkner's works, all cited internally, are taken from the following editions: *Absalom, Absalom!* (New York: Vintage International Edition [Corrected Text], 1990); *Collected Stories of William Faulkner* [*CS*] (New York: Vintage Books, 1977); *Go Down, Moses* [*GDM*] (New York: Vintage Books, 1973); *Light in August* [*LIA*] (New York: Vintage Books, 1972); *The Marble Faun* (Boston: Four Seas Company, 1924); *Mosquitoes* (New York: Boni and Liveright, 1927); *Requiem for a Nun* [*RFN*] (New York: Vintage Books, 1975); *The Town* [*T*] (New York: Vintage Books, 1961); *The Unvanquished* [*U*] (New York: Vintage Books, 1966); *The Wild Palms* [*WP*] (New York: Vintage Books, 1966).

The following works are also cited parenthetically within the text: *William Faulkner: Early Prose and Poetry*, ed. Carvel Collins (Boston: Little, Brown and Company, 1962), cited as *EPP*; *The Faulkner-Cowley File*, ed. Malcolm Cowley (New York: Viking Press, 1966), cited as *FCF*; *Faulkner in the University*, ed. Frederick L. Gwynn and Joseph L. Blotner (Charlottesville: University of Virginia Press, 1959), cited as *FIU*; *Lion in the Garden: Interviews with William Faulkner*, ed. James B. Meriwether and Michael Millgate (New York: Random House, 1968), cited as *LIG*.

5. By the time he wrote the prefatory note to *The Mansion* (1959) Faulkner had discovered a happy oxymoron to express his notion of the ideal interrelationship between life and art. There he describes his entire life's work as an attempt to create "a living literature." He goes on to explain that "since 'living' is motion, and 'motion' is change and alteration and therefore the only alternative to motion is un-motion, stasis, death, there will be found discrepancies and contradictions in the thirty-four-year progress of this particular chronicle." This statement should be viewed not merely as an attempt to excuse the chronological errors in the successive volumes of the Snopes trilogy (Abner Snopes's age, for example), but rather as another expression of Faulkner's conviction that great literature is both superior to and allied with the actual life process. The inconsistencies in the Snopes narrative, Faulkner says, are "due to the fact that the author has learned, he believes, more about the human heart and its dilemma than he knew thirty-four years ago; and is sure that, having lived with them that long time, he knows the characters in this chronicle better than he did then." In other words, the complexities and contradictions in the Snopes saga result from Faulkner's attempt to be faithful to his evolving definition of the human condition. Still, as Faulkner readily acknowledged, regardless of its degree of verisimilitude, ultimately art is art, not life. "Living literature," therefore, is a paradoxical literature that seeks to be faithful to both art-as-life and art-as-art.

6. Michael Millgate, *The Achievement of William Faulkner* (New York: Random House, 1966), 74.

7. Elisabeth Muhlenfeld, in "Introduction," *William Faulkner's "Absalom, Absalom!": A Critical Casebook* (New York: Garland Publishing, Inc., 1984), has also discussed the novel in the context of Faulkner's personal situation. She concludes: "A brief look at this period suggests, perhaps, that the intricacy, force and sustained intensity of *Absalom*, with its relative lack of humor and its overriding tragic vision, may be due in part to the very elements in Faulkner's life during the writing of the novel which he had to confront, to endure, and ultimately to control, at least to the extent that he was not shackled or defeated in his role as artist" (xii–xiii). See also Frederick Karl, *William Faulkner: American Writer* (New York: Weidenfeld and Nicolson, 1989), 549, 573n.

8. Joseph Blotner, *Faulkner: A Biography* (New York: Random House, 1974), 827.

9. Oswald Spengler's monumental work on the philosophy of history, *Der Untergang des Abendlandes* (English title, *The Decline of the West*), one of the most influential books of the twentieth century, appeared in German from 1918 to 1923 and

in English from 1926 to 1928. Spengler's ideas had a profound effect upon a number of American writers, including Eliot, Hemingway, Fitzgerald, and Faulkner.

10. In this regard it seems significant that in Faulkner's prototype of the scene of the boy at the door of the big house—appearing in an earlier, unpublished story entitled "The Big Shot"—the hostility is clearly directed at the servant as well as the owner. Faulkner's description there makes explicit the cultural antipathy between white and black that is only implied in the corresponding passage in *Absalom, Absalom!*: "There was a negro servant come to the door behind the boss, his eyeballs white in the gloom, and Martin's people and kind, although they looked upon Republicans and Catholics, having never seen either one, probably, with something of that mystical horror which European peasants of the fifteenth century were taught to regard Democrats and Protestants, the antipathy between them and negroes was an immediate and definite affair, being at once biblical, political, and economic: the three compulsions—the harsh unflagging land broken into sparse intervals by spells of demagoguery and religio-neurotic hysteria—which shaped and coerced their gaunt lives. A mystical justification of the need to feel superior to someone somewhere, you see." *Uncollected Stories of William Faulkner*, ed. Joseph Blotner (New York: Random House, 1979), 508.

11. For broader applications of Sutpen's desire for power and control, see James Guetti, *The Limits of Metaphor: A Study of Melville, Conrad, and Faulkner* (Ithaca, New York: Cornell University Press, 1967), 88–91, and Panthea Reid Broughton, *William Faulkner: The Abstract and the Actual* (Baton Rouge: Louisiana State University Press, 1974), 85–86, 105.

12. For an extended discussion of the centrality of this concept to Faulkner's view of art, see Robert W. Hamblin, " 'Saying No to Death': Toward William Faulkner's Theory of Fiction," in *"A Cosmos of My Own": Faulkner and Yoknapatawpha, 1980*, ed. Doreen Fowler and Ann J. Abadie (Jackson: University Press of Mississippi, 1981), 3–35.

13. For a helpful discussion of this point see Ruth M. Vande Kieft, "Faulkner's Defeat of Time in *Absalom, Absalom!*," *Southern Review* 6 (1970): 1100–1109. Vande Kieft argues that the novel stands as "a comprehensive symbol of [Faulkner's] relationship to time as an artist," mirroring "not only his obsession with time, but his battle against the oblivion which threatens all human achievement" (1100).

14. Wallace Stevens, "The Idea of Order at Key West," *The Collected Poems of Wallace Stevens* (New York: Alfred A. Knopf, 1955), 130.

15. For an extended analysis of this analogy see William D. Lindsey, "Order as Disorder: *Absalom, Absalom!*'s Inversion of the Judaeo-Christian Creation Myth," in *Faulkner and Religion: Faulkner and Yoknapatawpha, 1989*, ed. Doreen Fowler and Ann J. Abadie (Jackson: University Press of Mississippi, 1991), 85–102.

16. I have previously discussed the influence of Carcassonne upon Faulkner's thought in " 'Carcassonne': Faulkner's Allegory of Art and the Artist," *Southern Review* 15 (Spring 1979): 355–65, and "Carcassonne in Mississippi: Faulkner's Geography of the Imagination," in *Faulkner and the Craft of Fiction: Faulkner and Yoknapatawpha, 1987*, ed. Doreen Fowler and Ann J. Abadie (Jackson: University Press of Mississippi, 1989), 148–71.

17. The best example, of course, is Darl Bundren of *As I Lay Dying*.

18. The most detailed treatment of Faulkner's map of Yoknapatawpha is Elizabeth Duvert, "Faulkner's Map of Time," *Faulkner Journal* 2 (Fall 1986): 14–28. Duvert's essay is an an excellent discussion of the map in relation to the entire corpus of Faulkner's Yoknapatawpha fiction but says nothing of its function in *Absalom, Absalom!*
To my knowledge, Pamela Dalziel, in "*Absalom, Absalom!*: The Extension of Dialogic Form," *Mississippi Quarterly* 45 (Summer 1992): 277–94, is the only previous critic to link the map to the text of *Absalom, Absalom!* She views Faulkner's drawing as "the final narrative" (292) of the novel and argues that it contributes to the pattern of inconsistency and ambiguity that characterizes the novel as a whole.

19. John V. Hagopian, "The Biblical Background of Faulkner's *Absalom, Absalom!*," *CEA Critic* 36 (January 1974): 22–24; reprinted in *William Faulkner's "Absalom, Absalom!": A Critical Casebook*, ed. Muhlenfeld, 131–34. See also Ralph Behrens,

"Collapse of Dynasty: The Thematic Center of *Absalom, Absalom!*," *PMLA* 89 (1974): 24–33.

20. Jules Zanger, " 'Harbours Like Sonnets': Literary Maps and Cartographic Symbols," *Georgia Review* 36 (1982): 773–90.

21. Faulkner redrew his map in 1945 for Cowley's edition of *The Portable Faulkner*, published in 1946. A variant of that map is reproduced as the endpapers for volume 1 of *Faulkner: A Comprehensive Guide to the Brodsky Collection*, ed. Louis Daniel Brodsky and Robert W. Hamblin (Jackson: University Press of Mississippi, 1982).

The Ephemeral Instant: William Faulkner and the Photographic Image

Thomas Rankin

In 1947, the French photographer Henri Cartier-Bresson went to Rowan Oak to photograph William Faulkner. Cartier-Bresson's visit to Oxford was just one of many such trips throughout America to photograph various writers and artists. His photograph of Faulkner, published widely over the years and available to a mass audience on a FotoFolio postcard, is a compelling portrait of the writer with two of his dogs [figure 1].[1] Without question, the presence of the dogs and their own unique postures are just as important to the success of the image as the striking pose of Faulkner. Cartier-Bresson's photographic influence is powerful, his images a compelling witness to his idea of the success of a photograph resting on "the decisive moment." In his 1952 book *The Decisive Moment*, Cartier-Bresson set forth his point of view: "He [the photographer] composes a picture in very nearly the same amount of time it takes to click the shutter, at the speed of a reflex action. . . . Composition must be one of our constant preoccupations, but at the moment of shooting it can stem only from our intuition, for we are out to capture the fugitive moment, and all the interrelationships are on the move."[2]

Cartier-Bresson's notion of arresting motion decisively is similar to William Faulkner's idea of motion that he explained in an interview in *The Paris Review*: "The aim of every artist is to arrest motion, which is life, by artificial means and hold it fixed so that 100 years later when a stranger looks at it, it moves again since it is life."[3] This "arresting of motion" is at the foundation

Figure 1. William Faulkner at Rowan Oak, 1947. Photograph by Henri Cartier-Bresson. Courtesy of Magnum, Inc.

of the famous portrait of William Faulkner taken by Cartier-Bresson as well as other photographs made of Faulkner and the land in which he lived and wrote.

Cartier-Bresson made a number of photographs during his trip to Rowan Oak in 1947. Despite the clarity, grace, and resonance of several of his other portraits of Faulkner, it is the portrait with the two dogs that is most often seen, the image that has taken on a life of its own.

A story circulates in the oral tradition in and around Oxford based on the famous Cartier-Bresson portrait of Faulkner.[4] Local legend has it that an admirer came up to Faulkner's house, as happened frequently towards the end of his life, and knocked on the door. Mr. Faulkner came to the door, visibly irritated by this stranger's disruptive knock.

The stranger introduced himself: "Mr. Faulkner, I've been such an admirer of yours for so long I just want to talk to you for a minute." Faulkner reluctantly consented, came out on the porch, and began walking toward his horse lot.

The visitor said, "This is such a beautiful home you have here. I've never seen a house so impressive. What style of architecture it?"

"Oh, its a neo-Greek revival, classical something," replied Faulkner, inventing some hybrid architectural type on the spot.

"So graceful, such an elegant house, so wonderful," the man exclaimed.

As they approached the pasture the visitor eyed Mr. Faulkner's horse.

"That horse is such a beautiful horse. I've never seen a horse like that. So stately and fine. What breed of horse is that?"

"A Murfreesboro Tennessee walking horse," replied Mr. Faulkner, perhaps accurately.

"So beautiful, so impressive," replied the young man.

As they continued to walk slowly, a number of small dogs followed near their feet.

"And these dogs," the stranger said. "I've never seen anything quite like these dogs. What a beautiful breed, what a special kind of dog this is. Just what kind of dog is this, Mr. Faulkner?"

"Oh, those are Cartier-Bresson dogs, a very special breed."

This story, certainly related to the Southerner-takes-advantage-of-the-stranger motif type, suggests the resonance that photographs may have locally as well as the permanent mark made by the photographer. Photographs that arrest moments in time can leave their mark on the wall of oblivion as well as other places. As small dogs can chase their own tails incessantly, so can photographs circulate with multiple meanings, this one having grown to iconographic proportion.

Recognizing the power of the photographic image not only to arrest a fleeting moment but also to reinforce existing truths and create new realities, I will discuss a select group of images of William Faulkner and his world. From the first photograph made of him in his mother's arms some three months after his birth in 1897 to the many photographs made of his funeral, William Faulkner was enshrined and at times plagued by the lense and shutter of the many photographers that confronted him. As photographers pursued the visage of Faulkner as their photographic subject, a number also attempted (and still attempt) to evoke "the world of William Faulkner" and his literature through photography. This paper investigates the photographs of Faulkner and the context of their making, attempting to suggest Faulkner's feelings toward photographers and photography. Connected to my discussion of Faulkner and photography is also the attempt by visual artists to render the cultural environment of his place. Three major groups of photographs are the focus here: the Cofield portraits and related photographs made by Colonel J. R. and Jack Cofield; Martin J. Dain's photographs taken during 1961–62 in Lafayette County, some of which were published in *Yoknapatawpha: Faulkner's County*; and Alain Desvergnes's images made from 1963 to 1965 and published in 1990 in *Yoknapatawpha: The Land of William Faulkner*.

As historical and cultural context, it is instructive to think for a moment about the role of photographs in William Faulkner's early life. Like most children of his standing and time, Faulkner was photographed a number of times as a child, with the first picture made in Oxford in 1897 in the Sanders and Sweezy Studio. Other childhood images were made, many of those now very familiar to scholars and Faulkner enthusiasts as a result of the numerous times they've been published. How did William Faulkner feel about the medium of photography? How did he understand photography? Other scholars—David Madden and Judith Sensibar among them—have posed these questions and looked to the literature for clues. Faulkner's writings are laced with photographic descriptions, and photographs show up throughout his fiction. It is a photograph that's at the root of the remembrance in the short story "All the Dead Pilots." Faulkner uses photographs throughout *Absalom, Absalom!*; David Madden has discussed the role of photography in *Sanctuary*.[5] And there are other examples. To be sure, however, a close reading of the literature for the role of the photographic image is a topic for another time and, most certainly, for a different writer.

Judith Sensibar, in her article "Faulkner's Real and Imaginary Photos of Desire," acknowledges that Faulkner's early experiments with visual images—mostly drawings—extended to photography.[6] Martha Cofield remembered that William Faulkner made some drawings of a horse once in order to explain fully to Jack Cofield how to photograph him on his horse. Martha recalls that her husband Jack had previously made some photographs of Faulkner on his horse that both agreed were dreadful. Faulkner's knowledge of horses and photography provoked him to give Jack Cofield a little primer on photographing a horse. J. R. "Colonel" Cofield, Jack's father, recalled Faulkner's experience with photography. Colonel Cofield developed rolls of William Faulkner's film early in his career. In "Many Faces, Many Moods," Colonel Cofield offered his recollections of Faulkner the photographer:

> In the mid-thirties Bill was a devout camera fiend. In his rambles in Europe he had picked up a genuine old Zeiss camera with one of the finest German mechanisms ever made. The only drawback was that you practically had to hold a Georgia Tech degree in order to operate the thing. He'd rush out wildly and shoot up a film and bring it in to me to develop. It usually turned out to be a hodge-podge of double exposures, overtimed or undertimed, general mediocre craftsmanship that most any dunderhead with $1.50 Hawkeye box Kodak could beat a mile.
>
> He finally gave it up in disgust, even though cameras always did fascinate him.[7]

How much photography Faulkner did himself is difficult to gauge. Presumably, he made pictures of his own family, though few have been published. In his 1940, 1951, and 1954 Last Will and Testament, he included a Leica camera which he left to his daughter Jill. Curiously, he lists the Leica in item 13 of his will along with his binoculars and an assortment of six guns.[8] Perhaps he shot with a camera just as he shot with guns. Martin J. Dain remembers seeing several cameras on the mantel in Rowan Oak in the early 1960s.[9] And photographs taken in Rowan Oak at this time support Dain's recollection. So Faulkner himself may have made pictures, and it would be very interesting to see what he found worthy of a photograph.

An early indication of his understanding of the power of photography can be seen in his use of a 1918 portrait of himself as an RAF lieutenant [figure 2]. As he created his mythological war hero identity, the photograph served as very supportive

Figure 2. William Faulkner as RAF lieutenant, 1918. Photograph from Cofield Collection, copyright Center for the Study of Southern Culture, University of Mississippi.

evidence. His posing as a wounded war hero illustrates an early understanding of the manipulation of the photo-eye to serve his personal narrative. J. R. Cofield's first encounter with Faulkner was when he came in with a copy of the RAF photo, wanting Cofield to make a copy negative and enlarge it: Faulkner instructed him "to hurry up and copy it so I can put it back in Mother's bureau before she misses it."[10] Presumably, he needed more copies to reinforce the war hero mythology or simply to establish his military background. In any event, he recognized the power of the photograph both to convince and to distort; this understanding may have contributed to his reticence toward photographers later in life.

Colonel J. R. Cofield, a photograper from Georgia, moved to Oxford in 1928 and purchased the local photography studio from Tom Majure. A third generation photographer, Colonel Cofield's grandfather John B. Cofield opened a studio in Hawkinsville, Georgia, soon after the Civil War. In addition to being an accomplished photographer, he was also a painter and specialized in retouching black and white photographs. His son, John Isaac Cofield, learned the photographic trade and opened his own studio around 1900 in the new town of Cordele, Georgia. He operated this studio until his retirement. With one studio in Hawkinsville and another in Cordele, the Cofields were expanding. In 1928, Colonel Cofield, who was born in 1900, left Cordele for Oxford and bought Mr. Majure's studio. His son Jack also was raised within the family photography tradition. Martha Cofield, Jack's widow, remembers an advertisement by Kodak in the mid-1920s that featured four generations of Cofields, with a very young Jack being the fourth, obviously too young to have chosen his own career, but labeled a photographer nevertheless.[11]

Colonel J. R. Cofield (the title of "colonel" given to him as an informal Southern honor), who always referred to Faulkner as his "friend," grew to be an avid collector of local history and the history of William Faulkner's family and community. Along with his son Jack, Colonel Cofield made copy negatives of any and all photographs he could find or that people would loan him, assembling a personal archive of images documenting the Faulkner family and their life in Mississippi. In his 1964 " 'Memoirs' of his friend William Faulkner" prepared for Dr. James Webb of Ole Miss, Cofield traced his first "incidents" involving Faulkner. Colonel Cofield wrote:

> William came upstairs to my studio and brought me my "first" of many assignments for him, it was a tiny little Kodak photo his mother had saved him made back in the WWI days, in his R.A.F. uniform, lookin very casual as usual (I always said Bill should have been in Hollywood as an ACTOR, not a writer), as I have yet to ever see him phazed by a mere camera—he was just a *natural*, I never had to pose Bill Faulkner for any photograph in his life— everything just "fell into place" without any sweating over getting the proper angles of the lens eh?[12]

Unique to the Cofield Studio portraits is the fact that at times William Faulkner looks directly into the lense [figures 3, 4]. In many of the portraits taken by other photographers, Faulkner tends to look off, away from the lense, and seldom shows a smile. The Cofield Studio portraits show a different Faulkner, partly a result of the friendship and genuine dialogue that existed between the Cofields and William Faulkner.

All photographic portraits are part dialogue, with the subject presenting him or herself to the camera and the photographer attempting to capture what he or she desires. Unlike photojournalists or documentary photographers, the studio photographer makes a portrait when asked and hired. When an individual engages the service of a studio photographer he or she may have as much influence on the resulting portrait as the photographer. People make choices of how they want to be seen in pictures and in turn how they do not want to be seen. In the Cofield sessions William Faulkner was in control. He made the appointments, arrived dressed as he wished to be seen, and presented his "look" to the camera on his own terms. The Cofield portraits are in sharp contrast to others taken of Faulkner by photographers who had to pursue him in order to make a picture. In the case of both Colonel Cofield and his son Jack, they photographed Mr. Faulkner only when asked.

Figure 3. Publicity portrait made by Col. J. R. Cofield in 1929–1930 with the publication of *Sanctuary*. Cofield Collection, copyright Center for the Study of Southern Culture, University of Mississippi.

On Valentine's Day, 1986, the Cofield Studio, then located in the old warehouse building in Oxford, caught fire. The negatives of Faulkner and all others in the Cofield Studio were subjected to the two greatest catastrophes a photo collection can suffer— fire and water. The story of the fire that destroyed the Cofield Studio in Oxford lives on as a tragic reminder of the fragility of photographic negatives when exposed to heat and moisture.

Martha Cofield remembers the event:

> Happened in the middle of the night. We got a phone call about four o'clock in the morning. And this voice from the police station, it was a woman, said, "Mrs. Cofield, there is smoke coming out of the warehouse. What do you want us to do?"
> And I said, "For God sake call the fire department."
> And she said, "We already did that."

Figure 4. Portrait from Faulkner's second session at Cofield Studio, 1942. Cofield Collection, copyright Center for the Study of Southern Culture, University of Mississippi.

Before they had completely put the thing out there was a volunteer fireman from the Lafayette County fire department. He had been in the studio for four or five weeks before the fire and he was interested in Faulkner. I think he was in school out here. And he was real interested in the pictures and we talked a lot and he came two or three times I think. So he went in there and he got some of the stuff off the walls. Particularly the oil and the picture Jack has taken that's autographed. He brought those two out. The table underneath that oil was on fire when he got that.

I said, "Can't you all go back in? If we could just get the Faulkner stuff out." One of them got me a pair of boots. They said, "Let's take her in." So I got on firemen's boots that were too big. And there was still fire. It wasn't blazing, but still burning. Took me down there and, of course, the ceiling had caved in. I was able to show them, and they just came out with this drawer full of stuff. And they started getting other stuff out. They just got what they could get.

We put it in the back of one of the boy's pick-up trucks to take it home, and on the way home the whole thing caught on fire again in the back of the truck. The wind ignited a small spark, I guess. We had to stop and put it out.[13]

The fire itself appears to have been intimidated, burning carefully and delicately around the edges of the 4″ × 5″ and 5″ × 7″ negatives, thus unable to violate the space of the negative that contains Faulkner's face [figure 5]. If the fire spared some of the most important elements in the negatives, however, it also left its permanent mark of destruction, burning many of the studio prints and most of the negatives of everyday life in Oxford and Lafayette County. While the negatives of Faulkner were salvaged, the majority of the studio collection burned, including many images the Cofields had made of ordinary life in Oxford since the family acquired the studio in 1928, as well as glass negatives made by the studio under Tom Majure's ownership.

Cofield's portraits of Faulkner may well be the most powerful of all those taken. Perhaps it was the directness of the process and the power and dignity inherent in the simplicity of the studio portrait. In many ways, the Cofield approach—large studio view camera, large negative—represented the unspoiled landscape of the photography of the time. The camera, stationary and mounted on tripod using available light, was pointed at someone only when a person asked and arranged to be photographed.

Another photographer of Faulkner and his Oxford-Lafayette County surroundings, Martin J. Dain, was born in Boston, Massachusetts. The son of a pharmacist in Cambridge, he attended Boston Latin School and the University of Miami. His work as a photographer centered primarily on magazine work and advertising; at times he worked on corporate annual reports [figure 6]. From an early age he was an avid Faulkner reader. "I can't remember a time," recalls Dain, "when I didn't read Faulkner."[14]

In 1964, his book of photographs, *Yoknapatawpha: Faulkner's County*, was published by Random House. It was a work he began in August 1961 and one that always was aimed at "evoking" William Faulkner. "All my life I had been reading Faulkner, and you mature along with your reading and you discover

Figure 5. Example of negative damage from Cofield Studio fire. Negative is from March 20, 1962, portrait session. Cofield Collection, copyright Center for the Study of Southern Culture, University of Mississippi.

Figure 6. Left to right, Martin J. Dain with Mr. and Mrs. E. W. Wells at their home. Photographer unknown. Martin J. Dain Collection, copyright Center for the Study of Southern Culture, University of Mississippi.

this man has said and known everything that's worth knowing and saying in your entire life," asserts Dain. "And I asked various people, 'If I go to Mississippi, am I going to be able to show this country? Will I be able to find things that will evoke a great author?' Evoke is the key word. Don't take the pictures literally. Evoke." At the end of his book Dain wrote a brief statement, "Explanatory Notes," in which he attempted to emphasize his perspective:

> The personality of William Faulkner will remain an enigma, but the country around him, our world, is as clear as one is willing to see. . . . On the preceding pages I have tried to evoke some of this world. It is by no means all. There is much of contemporary life that is not shown; such as the housing developments and the modern glass store fronts.[15]

Dain's images emphasize the older, more traditional look of the community. When Dain came to Oxford and the surrounding area he brought with him his own vision of Yoknapatawpha, a vision derived from his own readings and understanding of Faulkner [figure 7]. He wanted to "evoke" in images the feelings that the literature had instilled in him. Reading Faulkner over and over, Dain said, prepared him uniquely for the task: "I read everything. Multiple times. Four or five times. With the exception of *A Fable* which I just couldn't get through because I'm ignorant about Biblical things. I don't like too much reference to God because it makes me feel guilty."

In 1961, Dain went to Mississippi on the defensive. He was self-conscious and sensitive about being from the North, concerned about how hill country Mississippians would view his Jewish background, and worried about his mostly liberal political opinions. He believed that his general appearance, which he felt included his Northern style and dress, combined with the cameras he carried around his neck, would attract negative, if

Figure 7. Lafayette County, Mississippi, in the early 1960s, identified by Martin Dain simply as a "rural scene." Photography by Martin J. Dain. Copyright Center for the Study of Southern Culture, University of Mississippi.

not aggressive, attention. He feared being taken for a civil rights worker. Ed Meek, then a student at Ole Miss, accompanied Dain around Lafayette County. Meek remembers Dain saying that he needed help being accepted. After first meeting Martin Dain, Meek agreed that there was a need for a guide, a liaison. Meek ushered Dain throughout the community, providing introductions to select local residents. [16]

Dain's main contact in Oxford was historian Jim Silver. Dain wrote to Silver and asked him for assistance while he was in Oxford, and Silver consented to help. Dain's enthusiasm for Faulkner was so contagious that Silver, who had been William Faulkner's friend, became more interested in reading his books. Silver wrote to Linton Massey in January of 1962 that "Dain has a real scholarly interest in a man he considers a great writer. He got me so interested that I have just completed my fourth Faulkner book since his arrival."[17]

At the outset of his project Dain had no idea where, or even if, he might publish his photographs. His idea was to complete a book, but he had no publisher. And the key to the project, he believed, was his ability to "get to Faulkner." In late 1961 or early 1962, Jim Silver took Dain to Rowan Oak. The Faulkners were out of town and Silver encouraged Dain to photograph the house and the grounds. Soon after that trip, in a letter to Silver, Dain expressed his reticence to photograph in William Faulkner's absence: "Until I can learn something more of Faulkner's attitude toward photos I don't wish to antagonize him."[18]

In March of 1962, several photographers requested sessions with William Faulkner. As Joseph Blotner reports in his biography, Faulkner declined *Vogue* magazine's request to send Henri Cartier-Bresson back for another photo session. Perhaps no longer in need of the rare Cartier-Bresson dog, his response was succinct: "I don't want to be photographed by anybody anywhere."[19] But Dain somehow made it through, with the help of Silver and Victoria Fielden. He photographed the horses, the barn, and in and around the paddock area. While many of the images portray the writer in a natural context, Faulkner eventually tired of the visit and, according to Blotner, of Dain's request that he pose for the camera. Dain remembers Faulkner being very accommodating, even to the point of holding his camera bag [figure 8]. While perhaps only an obligatory act of gentlemanly hospitality, Dain points to his photograph of Faulkner with his equipment bag as evidence of the writer's ultimate cooperation. But something changed suddenly, and Faulkner ended the session abruptly.[20] The photographs Dain made were of Faulkner in the well-worn attire of his home at Rowan Oak, providing what appears to be a very intimate look at the man. However, Faulkner must have reconsidered his cooperative hospitality after the visit, for he wrote Jim Silver on April 4 a specific message for Dain:

> We are leaving this afternoon, so I probably wont see you or Mr Dane (Dain?) either before that. So will you please get word to him to please dont make any more photographs on my property while we are gone, and also that I will not authorise the reprinting or publishing or disseminating of the ones he has made here (I mean

Figure 8. William Faulkner with horse and holding Martin Dain's camera bag. Photograph by Martin J. Dain, 1962. Copyright Center for the Study of Southern Culture, University of Mississippi.

on my property, of me and my animals and servants) in any form. Please impress upon him that I dont want photographs of myself and home and animals etc. in newspapers or magazines or books or in the possession of strangers.[21]

For all his good intentions and his sincere respect for Faulkner, Dain had obviously violated William Faulkner's privacy, enough to have him play with the spelling of his name. With the lifetime ambition of being the last private individual on earth, Faulkner had good reason to be concerned. And while Dain's pictures of Faulkner show a heartfelt commitment to an honest and natural portrayal of the writer and his place, Faulkner could never have known that. He certainly understood the possibility of distortion, of misrepresentation. William Faulkner simply wanted his privacy, something that was increasingly hard to secure. And he understood how much photographers and editors coveted pictures of him and his environment.

Dain, on the other hand, had made some compelling images, and he knew it. After he returned to New York, he wrote Silver that potential publishers "had been waiting to see if I could get to the old man." His letter continued, "Let me assure you that I think I have enough of Faulkner around the fields with horses and dogs and Vickie to take me over the hump."[22] William Faulkner's photograph was clearly seen as a commodity, one that seemed to beckon the symbolic power of the man's literature [figure 9].

Dain was nowhere near finished, however. When William Faulkner died in July of 1962, the interest in Dain's project grew. Dain himself has suggested that it was Faulkner's death in 1962 that really spurred on the project and resulted in the book. But at the time of Faulkner's death Dain had much more he needed to photograph in order to truly make a statement about "Faulkner's world," about Yoknapatawpha. He felt he needed photographs of a hog killing, sorghum molasses making, of a deer hunt, to mention a few, all symbols to Dain of the traditional culture of hill country Mississippi that he had read about in Faulkner and wanted to declare as part of the world of

Figure 9. Faulkner at his horse barn in 1962. Photograph by Martin
J. Dain. Copyright Center for the Study of Southern Culture, University of Mississippi.

the writer. Contrary to the way Dain normally worked, he "set up" several scenes that he felt pivotal to his work, including sorghum making, which had to be "re-enacted" by locals out of season to accommodate Dain's shooting and publishing schedule. In a letter to Jim Silver in October of 1962, Dain explained his needs:

> The time is becoming so critical so I would like to ask the following question. Apparently hog killing is dependent on the weather and the proximity of holidays, so about when would you expect that someone kill some hogs? Would you be able to find someone in a picturesque atmosphere who is going to do that? Would it be in October?
>
> The man with the sorghum mill is Mr. J. H. Moody whose phone number used to [be] 480-R-4. He said that he would grind stuff and that he would have to first fix his mill and that might cost money. I am prepared to assist with that.[23]

Any reticence about contriving images or recreating events out of season simply in order to photograph was overwhelmed by Dain's desire to make his evocation of William Faulkner comprehensive and thorough [figure 10].

Alain Desvergnes, a French photographer who came to Oxford in 1963 to live and work in Oxford, begins his introduction to *Yoknapatawpha: The Land of William Faulkner*, clearly articulating his photographic approach, his pictorial point of view: "You want to go into all the streets of all the cities men live in. To look into all the darkened rooms in the world. Not with curiosity, not with dread nor doubt nor disapproval. But humbly, gently, as you would steal in to look at a sleeping child, not to disturb it."[24]

His photographs are humble and gentle and quiet and have the appearance of being taken by an outsider quietly moving through the landscape, trying not to disturb but only to observe [figure 11]. Everything in the landscape, in the towns, seems to be of interest to Desvergnes. Unlike Dain, who shied away from more modern facades in an attempt to capture reflections of earlier times, Desvergnes makes little delineation between the

Figure 10. "Making sorghum molasses in the early fall—a craft becoming rare," wrote Martin Dain in the explanatory notes to his book. Photograph by Martin J. Dain. Copyright Center for the Study of Southern Culture, University of Mississippi.

old and the new. His sensibilities are heightened by his distant origin. He sees what others may not see, and while he was very aware of the Southern and Mississippi culture, he seems to arrive with fewer preconceptions of how "Faulkner's world" should look. Desvergnes's book, which he dedicated to his daughter, "a southern belle from Ole Miss," includes a broad range of images from Oxford and the surrounding cultural

Figure 11. Oxford Square in 1963–64. Photograph by Alain Desvergnes. Reprinted by permission.

landscape of Mississippi and the South. Not confining himself to
any particular subject matter, Desvergnes photographed cotton
pickers, beauty queens, football players, rich and poor townspeople, blues musicians, and an abundance of roadside attrac-
tions [figures 12 and 13]. He attempted, like Dain, to find visual
equivalents to Faulkner's prose. "I photographed as would a
novelist, who writes as he sees," said Desvergnes, "without
interruption, without order or apparent coherence, without
reassuring logic or enticing benefits."[25] He is not literal in his
quest for visual equivalents, but rather photographs constantly
over several years anything in the landscape that his eye sees as
an analogy to his understanding of Faulkner. To Desvergnes,
the greater Southern cultural landscape is all Faulkner's world.

Noel Polk, in his article " 'Polysyllabic and Verbless Patriotic
Nonsense': Faulkner at Midcentury—His and Ours," recounts
an exchange between William Faulkner and Phillip "Moon"
Mullen on the 1952 Omnibus television program.[26] On the

Figure 12. Beauty contest, probably in Oxford. Photograph by Alain Desvergnes. Reprinted by permission.

program, Mullen is greeted by Faulkner at Rowan Oak and invited inside. Mullen tries to convince Faulkner that since someone will do a "story" on him, that someone should be Mullen himself. Faulkner eventually concurs and adds, "Do your story. But no pictures." All of this discussion occurs on film, in "picture." However, Faulkner's statement of "no pictures" does reflect his yearning for privacy, his disdain for the constantly peering cameras, and the persistent journalists. Regardless of his reluctance to be pictured on film and his various attempts to limit the photographic record or control his own portrayal, it is the photographs of him that profoundly shape our image of the man. We think we know him better because we can see him look into the lens or walk about his yard in front of his house. We believe we understand his literature better because we can see photographic images from his world.

The photographs of Faulkner—all of those discussed above as

Figure 13. Mississippi Fred McDowell at his home. Photograph by Alain Desvergnes. Reprinted by permission.

well as many others—provide a complex window into the life of the writer. To be understood fully, however, we must know something of the situation of the making and the intent of the maker. Read closely, these images can provide us with a "lasting form," one Faulkner himself associated with the artistic process:

> The artist, whether or not he wishes it, discovers with the passage of time that he has come to pursue a single path, a single objective, from which he cannot deviate. That is, he must strive with all the means and all the talents he possesses—his imagination, his experience, his powers of observation—to put into more lasting form than his own frail, ephemeral instant of life . . . what he has known at firsthand during his brief period of existence.[27]

NOTES

1. FotoFolio postcard MP51, published by FotoFolio, New York, NY, n.d.

2. Henri Cartier-Bresson, quoted in Brooks Johnson, *Photography Speaks: 66 Photographers on Their Art* (New York and Norfolk, Virginia: Aperture Foundation, Inc. and The Chrysler Museum, 1989), 52.

3. William Faulkner, interview 1956. Reprinted in *Lion in the Garden: Interviews with William Faulkner, 1926–1962*, ed. James B. Meriwether and Michael Millgate (Lincoln: University of Nebraska Press, 1980), 253.

4. I have heard several variants of this story in Oxford. Richard Howorth, owner of Square Books, told me this version, the most developed one I've heard yet.

5. David Madden, "Photographs in the 1929 Version of *Sanctuary*," in *Faulkner and Popular Culture*, ed. Doreen Fowler and Ann J. Abadie (Jackson: University Press of Mississippi, 1990), 93–109.

6. Judith Sensibar, "Pop Culture Invades Jefferson: Faulkner's Real and Imaginary Photos of Desire," in ibid., 110–41.

7. J. R. Cofield, "Many Faces, Many Moods," in *William Faulkner of Oxford*, ed. James W. Webb and A. Wigfall Green (Baton Rouge: Louisiana State University Press, 1965), 109–10.

8. William Faulkner's Last Will and Testament, quoted in Louis David Brodsky and Robert W. Hamblin, *Faulkner: A Comprehensive Guide to the Brodsky Collection, Volume V: Manuscripts and Documents* (Jackson: University Press of Mississippi, 1988), 362–81.

9. Personal interview with Martin J. Dain, Carmel Valley, California, June 19, 1993.

10. J. R. Cofield, "Many Faces, Many Moods," 108–9.

11. Personal interview with Martha Cofield, Oxford, Mississippi, July 13, 1993.

12. J. R. Cofield, " 'Memoirs' of His Friend William Faulkner," an unpublished manuscript prepared for Dr. James Webb by Cofield in 1964. I have reprinted this excerpt exactly as J. R. Cofield typed it, preserving his unique use of punctuation and spelling. This manuscript was later edited into "Many Faces, Many Moods."

13. Martha Cofield, interview.

14. Martin J. Dain, interview.

15. Martin J. Dain, *Yoknapatawpha: Faulkner's County* (New York: Random House, 1964), 157.

16. Ed Meek, personal conversation, July 1993.

17. Letter from James Silver to Linton Massey, January 4, 1962, Silver Collection, University of Mississippi.

18. Letter from Martin J. Dain to James Silver, January 15, 1962, Silver Collection, University of Mississippi.

19. Joseph Blotner, *Faulkner: A Biography* (New York: Random House, 1974), 2:1813.

20. Martin J. Dain, interview.

21. Letter from William Faulkner to James W. Silver, quoted in Louis David Brodsky and Robert W. Hamblin, *Faulkner: A Comprehensive Guide to the Brodsky Collection, Volume II: The Letters* (Jackson: University Press of Mississippi, 1984), 299.

22. Letter from Martin J. Dain to James W. Silver, quoted in Brodsky and Hamblin, 302.

23. Letter from Martin J. Dain to James W. Silver, October 6, 1962, Silver Collection, University of Mississippi.

24. Alain Desvergnes, *Yoknapatawpha: The Land of William Faulkner* (NP: Marvel, 1990), n.p.

25. Ibid, n.p.

26. Noel Polk, " 'Polysyllabic and Verbless Patriotic Nonsense': Faulkner at Midcentury—His and Ours," *Faulkner and Ideology: Faulkner and Yoknapatawpha, 1992*, ed. Donald M. Kartiganer and Ann J. Abadie (Jackson: University Press of Mississippi, 1995), 297–328.

27. Willam Faulkner, Speech of Acceptance for the Andres Bello Award, Caracas, 1961, in *A Faulkner Miscellany*, ed. James B. Meriwether (Jackson: University Press of Mississippi, 1974), 165.

Uncle High Lonesome

BARRY HANNAH

They were coming toward me—this was 1949—on their horses
with their guns, dressed in leather and wool and canvas and
with different sporting hats, my father and his brothers, led by
my uncle on this his hunting lands, several hundred acres called
Tanglewood still dense in hardwoods but also opened by many
meadows, as a young boy would imagine from cavalry movies.
The meadows were thick with fall cornstalks, and the quail and
doves were plenty. So were the squirrels in the woods where I
had been let off to hunt at a stand with a thermos of chocolate
and my .28 double. At nine years old I felt very worthy for a
change even though I was a bad hunter.

But something had gone wrong. My father had put me down
in a place they were hunting toward. Their guns were coming
my way. Between me and them I knew there were several
coveys of quail to ground, frozen in front of the dogs, two setters
and a pointer, who were now all stiffening into the point. My
uncle came up first. This was my namesake, Peter Howard,
married but childless, at forty-five. I was not much concerned.
I'd seen, on another hunt, the black men who stalked for my
uncle flatten to the ground during the shooting, it was no big
thing. In fact I was excited to be receiving fire, real gunfire,
behind my tree. We had played this against Germans and
Japanese back home in my neighborhood. But now I would be
a veteran. Nobody could touch me at War.

My uncle came up alone on his horse while the others were
still hacking through the overhang behind him. He was quite a
picture. On a big red horse, he wore a yellow plaid corduroy

vest with watch chain across, over a blue broadcloth shirt. On
his bald head was a smoky brown fedora. He propped up an
engraved 16-gauge double in his left hand and bridled with his
right, caressing the horse with his thighs, over polo boots, a
high gloss tan. An unlit pipe was fixed between his teeth. There
was no doubting the man had a sort of savage grace, though I
noticed later in the decade remaining to his life that he could
also look, with his ears out, a bit common, like a Russian in the
gate of the last Cold War mob; thick in the shoulders and stocky
with a belligerence like Khrushchev. Maybe peasant nobility is
what they were, my people. Uncle Peter Howard watched the
dogs with a pleasant smile now, with the sun on his face at
midmorning. I had a long vision of him. He seemed, there on
the horse, patient and generous with his time and his lands,
waiting to flush the quail for his brothers. I saw him as a
permanent idea, always handy to reverie: the man who could
do things.

In the face he looked much like—I found out later—the
criminal writer Jean Genet, merry and Byzantine in the darks
of his eyes. Shorter and stockier than the others and bald, like
none of them, he loved to gamble. When he was dead I
discovered that he also was a killer and not a valiant one. Of all
the brothers he was the most successful and the darkest. The
distinct rings under my eyes in middle age came directly
from him.

The others, together, came up on their horses, ready at the
gun. They were a handsome clan. I was happy to see them
approach this way, enemy cavalry, gun barrels toward me. I
knew I was watching something rare, seen as God saw it, and I
was warm, almost flushed. My uncle Peter tossed a stick over
into a stalk pile and the quail came out with that fearsome
helicopter *bluttering* noise always bigger than you are ready for.
The guns tore the air. You could see sound waves and feathers
in dense blue-gray smoke. I'd got behind my big tree. The shot
ripped through all the leaves around. I adored it.

Then I stepped out into the clearing, walked toward the horses, and said hello.

My uncle Peter saw me first, and he blanched at my presence like a man visited by a ghoul in the shooting zone. He nearly fell from his horse. He waddled over on his glossy boots and knelt, then grabbed my shoulders.

"Boy? Boy? Where'd you come from? You were *there*?"

"Pete, son?" called my father, climbing down mystified. "Why didn't you call out? We could've—"

My uncle hugged me to him urgently, but I couldn't see the great concern. The tree I was behind was thick. I was a hunter, not a fool. But my uncle was shaken, and he began taking it out on my father. Maybe he was trembling, I guess now, because he'd almost shot yet another person.

"Couldn't you keep up with where your own boy was?"

"I couldn't know we'd hunted this far. I've seen you lost yourself out here."

An older cousin of mine had had his calf partially blown away in a hunting accident years ago, out squirrel hunting with his brother. Even the hint of danger would bring mothers to their throats. Also, I personally had had a rough time near death, though I hadn't counted up. My brother had nearly cut my head off with a sling blade when I walked up behind as a toddler, but a scar on the chin was all I had. A car had run me down as I crossed the street in first grade. Teaching me to swim the old way, my pa had thrown me off an ocean pier, then watched me drown, almost.

But this skit I planned, it was no trouble. I wanted them to fire my way, and I was happy there in the zone of fire.

I felt for my father, who was a good enough man. But he was a bumbler, an infant at a number of tasks, even though he was a stellar salesman. He had no grace, even though nicely dressed, black hair, pulled straight back, with always a good car and a far traveller in it around the United States, Mexico, and Canada. His real profession was an awed courtship of the North American Continent—its people, its birds, animals, and fish. I've never met such a pilgrim of his own country as my father, who had the reverence of a poet without page or pen. But a father's humility did not cut much ice with this son, although I enjoyed all the trips with him and Mother.

From that day on my uncle took more regard of me. He gathered me up as his own, and it annoyed my turkey-throated aunt when I visited, which was often. We lived only an hour and a half away, and my uncle might call me up just to hear a baseball game on the radio with him as he drove his truck around the plantation afternoons. On this vast place were all his skills and loves, and they all made money: a creosote post factory, turkey and chicken houses, cattle, a Big Dutchman farm machinery dealership; his black help in their gray weathered wrinkled houses; his lakes full of bass, crappie, bluegills, catfish, ducks, and geese, where happy customers and friends from the county were let fish and sport, in the spirit of constant obligation each to each that runs the rural South. Also there was a bevy of kin forever swarming toward the amenities, till you felt endlessly redundant in hayseed cousins. Uncle Peter had a scratchy well-deep voice in which he offered free advice to everybody except his wife. And he would demand a hug with it and be on you with those black grinding whiskered cheeks before you could grab the truck door. He was big and clumsy with love, and a bit imperial; short like Napoleon, he did a hell of a lot of just . . . surveying. Stopping the truck and eyeballing what he owned as if it were a new army at rest across the way now, then with just the flick of his hand he'd . . . turn up the radio for the St. Louis Cardinals, the South's team, the only one broadcast. I loved his high chesty grunts when one of his favorites would homer. He'd grip the steering wheel and howl: "Musial! Stan the Man!" I was no fan, a baseball dolt, but I got into it with my uncle.

If I'd known the whole truth of where he had come from, I would have been even more impressed by his plenty. I mean not only from the degrading grunting Depression, beneath broke, but before that to what must have been the most evil hangover there is, in a jail cell with murder of a human being in your mind, the marks of the chairlegs he ground in your face all over you, and the crashing truth of your sorriness in gambling and drink so loud in your head they could be popping the trapdoor for the noose over and over just outside the door. That night. From there. Before the family got to the jurors. Before the circuit judge showed up to agree that the victim was an unknown quantity from *out of town*. Before they convicted the victim of not being from here. Before he himself might have agreed on his own reasonable innocence and smiled into a faint light of the dawn, just a little rent down on any future at all. That was a far trip, and he must have enjoyed it every time we stopped and he, like Napoleon, surveyed.

He taught me to fish, to hunt, to handle dogs, to feed poultry, to stand watch at the post factory over a grown black man while he left in a truck for two hours. But this I highly resented.

"I want to see if this nigger can count. You tell me," he said, right in front of the man, who was stacking posts from the vat with no expression at all. He had heard but he didn't look at me yet, and I was afraid of when he would.

Peter Howard was hardly unusual in his treatment of black help around the farm. He healed their rifts, brought the men cartons of cigarettes. He got them medical treatment and extended credit even to children who had run away to Chicago. Sometimes he would sock a man in the jaw. I don't believe the current etiquette allowed the man to hit back. In his kitchen his favorite jest, habitual, was to say to a guest in front of their maid Elizabeth: "Lord knows, I do hate a nigger!" This brought huge guffaws from Elizabeth, and Peter was known widely as a hilarious crusty man, good to his toes. But I never thought this was funny, and I wanted my uncle to stop including me in this sport, or maybe go call a big white man a nigger.

While he was gone those two hours in the truck I burned with how mean an act this was to me and the man stacking the fence poles. I never even looked his way. I was embarrassed and could not decide what my uncle *wanted* from this episode.

Was he training me to be a leader of men? Was he squeezing this man, some special enemy, the last excruciating turn possible, with a mere skinny white boy, wearing his same name? I couldn't find an answer with a thing decent in it. I began hating Uncle Peter. When he came back I did not answer him when he wanted to tally my figure with the black man's. I said nothing at all. He looked at me in a blurred way, his eyes like glowing knots in a pig's face. He had on his nice fedora but his face was spreading and reddening, almost as in a fiend movie. I smelled medicine in the cab as from the emergency room when I was hit by that car, waking up to this smell.

"Wharoof? Did you ever answer? Didja gimme the number?"

"Have you been in an accident somewhere, Uncle Peter?"

"No. Let me tell you. I have no problem. I know you might've heard things. This—" he lifted out a pint bottle of vodka, Smirnoff "—is just another one of God's things, you understand? We can use it, or you can abuse it. It is a gift to man in his lonesomeness." To illustrate he lifted it, uncapped it, turned it up, and up came enormous bubbles from the lip as in an old water cooler. He took down more than half of the liquor. The man could drink in cowboy style, quite awesomely. I'd never heard a word about this talent before.

"I'm fessin' up. I'm a bad man. I was using you out there as an alibi for having a drink down the road there, so's your aunt wouldn't know. She has the wrong idea about it. But she knew I wouldn't drink with you along."

"You could drink right here in front of me. I wouldn't tell, anyway."

"Well. I'm glad to know it. It got to my conscience and I came back to make my peace with you about it. Everything between you and me's on the up and up, pardner."

"You mean you didn't need me counting those poles at all?"

"Oh yes I did. It was a real job. It wasn't any Roosevelt make-work."

"Don't you consider that man over there has any feelings, what you said right in front of him?"

"What's wrong with shame, boy? Didn't you ever learn by it? You're tender like your pop, you can't help it. But you're all right, too."

"Anybody ever shame you real bad, Uncle Peter?"

He looked over, his jowls even redder and gone all dark and lax, gathered-up furious eyes. "Maybe," he said. An honest answer would have been, had he come all out: "Once. And I killed him." I wonder how much of that event was in his mind as he looked at me sourly and said "Maybe."

He feared my aunt, I knew it, and he let me off at the house, driving off by himself while I gathered my stuff and waited for my folks to pick me up. I heard later he did not return home for three weeks. For months, even a year, he would not drink, not touch a drop, then he would have a nip and disappear. Uncle Peter was a binge drinker. Still, I blamed my aunt, a fastidious and abrasive country woman with a previous marriage. It was a tragedy she could give him no children and I had to stand in as his line in the family. She blundered here and there, saying wrong and hurtful things, a hag of unnecessary truth at family gatherings—a comment about somebody's weight, somebody's hair, somebody's lack of backbone. She was always correcting and scolding when I visited, and seemed to think this was the only conversation possible between the old and young, and would have been baffled, I think, had you mentioned it was an unbearable habit. I blamed her for his drinking and his insensitivity to blacks. He was doing it to show off to evil her, that's what. He was drinking because he could not stand being cruel.

The next time I saw him he had made me two fishing lures, painting them by hand in his shop. These he presented me along with a whole new Shakespeare casting reel and rod. I'd never caught a fish on an artificial lure. Here with the spring nearly on we had us a mission. His lakes were full of big healthy bass. Records were broken every summer, some of them by the grinning wives and children of his customers, so obliged to Mister Peter, Squire of Newton County. On his lands were ponds and creeks, brimful and snapping with fish, almost foreign they were so remote from the highways. You would ramble and bump down through a far pasture with black angus in it, spy a stretch of water through leaves, and as you came down to it you heard the fish in a feeding so noisy it could have been school children out for a swim. I was trembling to go out with him to one of these far ponds. It seemed forever before we could set out. Uncle Peter had real business, always, and stayed in motion constantly like a shark who is either moving or dead. Especially when he came out of a bender, paler and thinner, ashen in the face like a deacon. He hurled himself into penitential work. His clothes were plainer, like a sharecropper's more than the baron's, and it would be a few weeks before you'd see the watch chain, the fedora, or the nice boots—the cultured European scion among his vineyards.

I did not know there were women involved in these benders, but there were. Some hussy in a motel in a bad town. I'd imagine harlots of both races, something so bad it took more than a bottle a day to maintain the illusion you were in the room with your own species. He went the whole hog and seemed unable to beat the high lonesomes that came on him in other fashion. I'd have only cheered for his happiness against my aunt, whom I blamed for every misery in him.

At home my father meant very well, but he didn't know how to do things. He had no grace with utensils, tools, or equipment. We went fishing many times, never catching a thing after getting up at four and driving long distances. I think of us now fishing with the wrong bait, at the wrong depth, at the wrong time. He could make money and drive (too slowly), but the processes of life eluded him. As a golfer he scored decently, but with an ugly chopping swing. He was childlike with wonder when we traveled, and as to sports, girls, hobbies, and adventures my father remained somewhat of a baffled pupil throughout his life and I was left entirely on my own. He had no envy of his wealthy brother's skills, on the other hand, only admiration. "Old Peter knows the *way* of things, doesn't he, son?" he'd cheer. It seemed ordained that he himself was a dull and slow slob. I see my father and the men of his generation in their pinstripe suits and slicked-back hair, standing beside their new automobiles or another symbol of prosperity that was the occasion for the photograph, and these men I admire for accepting their own selves and their limits better, and without therapy. There's more peace in their looks, a more possessed fate, even with the World War around them. You got what you saw more, I'd guess, and there was plainer language then, there had to be. My father loved his brother and pitied him for having no son of his own. So he lent me to him, often.

In the worthy ledger mark my father down as no problem with temper, moodiness, or whiskey, a good man of no unpleasant surprises that way. He was sixty-five years old before he caught a bass on a spinning reel with artificial bait. He died before he had the first idea how to work the remote control for the television.

At last Uncle Peter had the time to take me out to a far pond, with a boat in the bed of the truck and his radio dialed to his Cardinals. We drove so far the flora changed and the woods got darker, full of lonesome longlegged fowl like sea birds. The temperature dropped several degrees. It was much shadier back here where nobody went. Uncle Peter told me he'd seen a snapping turtle the width of a washtub out in this pond. It was a ripe place, fed by springs, the water nearly as clear as Florida lakes.

He paddled while I threw a number of times and, in my fury to have one on, messed up again and again with a backlash, a miscast, and a wrap, my lure around a limb six feet over the water next to a water moccasin who raised its head and looked at me with low interest. I jerked the line, it snapped, and the handpainted lure of all Uncle Peter's effort was marooned in the wood. I was a wretched fool, with a rush of bile.

"Take your time, little Pete. Easy does it, get a rhythm for yourself."

I tied the other lure on. It was a bowed lure that wobbled on top of the water. I didn't think it had a prayer and was still angry about losing the good one, which looked exactly like a minnow. We were near the middle of the pond, but the middle was covered with dead tree stumps and the water was clear a long ways down.

A big bass hit the plug right after it touched the water on my second cast. It never gave the plug a chance to be inept. It was the first fish I'd ever hooked on artificial bait, and it was huge. It moved the boat. My arms were yanked forward, then my shoulders, as the thing wanted to tear the thing out of my palms on the way to the pond bottom. I held up and felt suddenly a dead awful weight and no movement. The bass had got off and left me hooked on a log down there, I knew. What a grand fish. I felt just dreadful until I looked down into the water when the thrashing had cleared.

The fish was still on the plug in ten feet of water. He was smart to try to wrap the line around the submerged log, but he was still hooked himself, and was just sitting there breathing from the gills like some big thing in an aquarium. My uncle was kneeling over the gunwale looking at the fish on the end of the line. His fedora fell in the water. He plucked it out and looked up at me in sympathy. I recall the situation drew a tender look from him such as I'd never seen.

"Too bad, little Pete. There she is, and there she'll stay. It's almost torture to look at your big fish like that, ain't it? Doesn't seem fair."

Uncle Peter didn't seem to enjoy looking in the water. Something was wrong, besides this odd predicament.

"No. I'm going down for it. I'm going to get the fish," I said.

"Why boy, you can't do that."

"Just you watch. That fish is mine."

I took off all my clothes and was in such a hurry I felt embarrassed only at the last. I was small and thin and ashamed in front of Uncle Peter, but he had something like awe on his face I didn't understand.

"That fish big as you are," he said in a foreign way. "That water so deep and snakey."

But I did swim down, pluck up the fish by its jaws, and came back to throw it in the boat. The plug stayed down there, visible, very yellow, as a monument to my boyhood dive, and I wonder what it looks like now, forty years later.

My uncle had the fish mounted for me. It stayed in our home until I began feeling sorry for it after Peter's death and gave it to a barber for his shop. The fish weighed about nine pounds, the biggest I'll ever catch.

I was not the same person to my uncle after that afternoon. I did not quite understand his regard of me until my father explained something very strange. Uncle Peter was the country squire and master of many trades, but he could not swim and he had a nightmare fear of deep water. He had wanted to join the navy, mainly for its white officers' suits, but they had got him near a deep harbor somewhere in Texas and he'd gone near psychotic. He expected great creatures to get out of the sea and come for him, too, and it was past reason, just one of those odd strands in the blood where there can be no comment or change. Since then I've talked to several country people with the same fear, one of them an All-American linebacker. They don't know where it came from and don't much want to discuss it.

When television appeared I was enamored of Howdy Doody. Some boys around the neighborhood and I began molding puppet heads from casts you could buy at the five and dime. You could have the heads of all the characters from the Howdy show in plaster of Paris. Then you'd put a skirt with arms on it and commence the shows on stage. We wrote whole plays, very violent and full of weapons and traps, all in the spirit of nuclear disaster and Revelations, with Howdy, Flubadub and Clarabelle. I couldn't get over my uncle's interest in the puppets when I brought them over and set up the show in his workshop.

The puppets seemed to worry him like a bouncing string would worry a cat. He looked at me as if I were magic, operating these little people and speaking for them. He had the stare of a studious confused infant. When I'd raise my eyes to him, he'd look ashamed, as if he been seduced into taking these toys for living creatures. He watched my mouth when I spoke in a falsetto for them.

I still don't know what in hell went on with him and the puppets, the way he watched them, then me. You'd have thought he was staring into a world he never considered possible, somewhere on another planet; something he'd missed and was very anxious about. I noticed, God help me, that he would dress *up* a little for the puppet shows. Once he wore his fedora and a red necktie as well.

For a number of years I did not see my uncle much at all. These were my teen years when I was an alien person. He remained the same, and his ways killed him. I don't know if the dead man in his past urged him toward the final DTs and heart attack, nor will I ever know how much this crime dictated his life, but he seemed to be attempting to destroy himself in episode after episode when, as he would only say afterward, the high lonesomes struck him.

The last scene I recall him whole was the summer right after I turned thirteen. We were all around the beach of Bay St. Louis, Mississippi, where we'd gathered for a six-family reunion of my father's people. The Gulf here was brown, fed by the Wolf and Jordan rivers. It provided groaning tables of oysters, shrimp, flounders, crabs, and mullet. Even the poor ate very well down here, where there were Catholics, easy liquor and gambling, bingo, Cajuns, Sicilians, and Slavs. By far it was the prettiest and most exotic of the towns where any of the families lived, and my Uncle Max and Aunt Ginny were very proud showing us around their big comfortable home, with a screened porch on three sides where all the children slept for the cool breeze from the bay. All over the house were long troughs of ice holding giant watermelons and cantaloupes and strawberries. Something was cooking all the time. This was close to heaven, and everybody knew it. You drifted off to sleep with the tales of the aunts and uncles in your ears. What a bliss. I still hear the laughter in the other rooms.

Most of us were on the beach or in the water when Uncle

Peter went bizarre, although for this I do have an interpretation. He had been watching me too intently, to the exclusion of others. He was too *around*, I could feel his eyes close while I was in the water swimming. He was enduring a sea change here at the sea, which he was supposed to be deathly afraid of. I believe he was turning more *urban*, or more cosmopolitan. He'd been to a Big Dutchman convention in Chicago. Somebody had convinced him to quit cigarettes, take up thin cigars, get a massage, and wear an Italian hat, a borsalino hat, which he now wore with sunglasses and an actual designed beach towel, he and his wife sitting there in blue canvas director's chairs. He has been dry for over a year, had lost weight, and now looked somewhat like Versace, the Italian designer. If this was our state's most European town, then Uncle Peter would show the way, leading the charge with his Italian hat high and his beach towel waving.

He was telling all of them how he was getting rid of the bags under his eyes. He was going to take up tennis. He had bought a Jaguar sedan, hunter green. Now on the beach as he sat with the other uncles and my father, watching us kids swim, he seemed rehearsed for a breakout into a new world, even if he couldn't swim, even in his pale country skin. He was in wild denial of his fear of the water. His wife, my aunt, seemed happier sitting there beside him. She'd been kinder lately, and I forgave her much. Maybe they had settled matters at home.

I'll remember him there before the next moment, loved and honored and looking ahead to a breakout, on that little beach. He could be taken for a full man of the world, interested even in puppets, even in fine fabrics. You could see him—couldn't you?—reaching out to pet the cosmos. Too long had he denied his force to the cosmos at large. Have me, have me, kindred, he might be calling. May my story be of use. I am meeting the ocean on its own terms. I am ready.

The New Orleans children were a foul-mouthed group out there in the brown water of the bay. Their parents brought them over to vacation and many of the homes on the beach were owned by New Orleans natives. The kids were precocious and street-mouthed, sounding like Brooklynites really, right out of a juvenile delinquent movie. They had utter contempt for the local crackers. The girls used rubes like me and my cousins to sharpen up their tongues. They could astound and wither you if you let them get to you. They had that Catholic voodoo around them, too, that you didn't know what to do with.

A sunbrowned girl, maybe twelve, in a two-piece swimsuit, got nudged around while we were playing, and started screaming at me.

"Hey cracker, eat me!"

"What?"

"Knockin' me with ya foot! Climb on this!" She gave me the finger.

You see? Already deep into sin, weathered like a slut at a bingo table, from a neighborhood that smelled like whisky on a hot exhaust pipe. I guess Uncle Peter saw the distress in my face, although I was probably a year older than the girl. He had heard her too. He began raving at her across the sand and water, waving both arms. He was beside himself, shouting at her to "Never say those things! Never *ever* say those things to him!"

I looked at her, and here was another complication. She had breasts and a cross dangling by a chain between them and was good-looking. Uncle Peter came up to the waterline and was looking at her too, forcing his hooked finger down for emphasis, "Don't ever!" But her body, thrust back to mock this old man, confused him and broke his effect.

Another uncle called out for him to come back, I was old enough to take care of myself, there wasn't any real problem here. But Uncle Peter hurled around and said: "There *is* a problem. There *is*!"

Then he left the beach by himself and we didn't see him the rest of the reunion. I saw my aunt sitting in their bedroom with her shoulders to me, her head forward, alone, and I understood there was huge tragedy in my uncle, regardless of anything she ever did.

A couple of the brothers went out on his trail. They said he began in a saloon near the seawall in Waveland.

Could it be simple, that my uncle saw, in his nervous rage and unnatural mood, the girl calling me down the road to sin, and he exploded? That he saw my fate coming to me in my teens, as his had, when he killed the man? Or was he needing a drink so badly that none of this matters? I don't know. After that bender he didn't much follow up on any great concern for me. Maybe he gave up on himself.

It took seven years more. My father came and got me at my apartment in the college town and told me about his death, in a hospital over in that county. My father had white hair by then, and I remember his head lowered, his arm over the shoulders of his own mother, my grandmother, with her own white-haired head bowed in grief no mother should bear. My grandmother repeated over and over the true fact that Peter was always "doing things, always his projects, always moving places." His hands were busy, his feet were swift, his wife was well-off, forever.

Back in the twenties a man came to town and started a poker game. Men gathered and drank. Peter lost his money and started a fight. The man took a chair and repeatedly ground it into his face while Peter was on the floor. Peter went out into the town, found a pistol, came back and shot the man. The brothers went about influencing the jury, noting that the victim was trash, an out-of-towner. The judge agreed. The victim was sentenced to remain dead. Peter was let go.

I've talked to my nephew about this. For years now I have dreamed I killed somebody. The body has been hidden, but certain people know I am guilty, and they show up and I know, deep within, what they are wanting, what this is all about. My nephew was nodding the whole time I was telling him this. He has dreamed this very thing, for years.

Whispers in the High Lonesome

BARRY HANNAH

Mr. Hannah, after a brief plea for indulgence, reads his story "Uncle High Lonesome."

Pass thirty minutes.

Hannah sets aside his story, mildly staggered by the errors still in it. Begin the homage.

What do *you* hear in the high lonesomes? Well, since age nineteen, I hear the sentences of Beckett and Faulkner. Maybe too much. They are to me the angels and the true voices of the century. They had not mere style but real *current* in their writings. Matter posed as on a great river angry for meaning. *Yockny patapha*. Chickasaw for "slow river runs through flat land," says Faulkner. Yes, slow sometimes, but always the river, in a rush of whispers urgent and necessary. A liquid voice inside the ear. A force of nature couples with the highest and finest erudition. Not mere diction and syntax, mere style, such as we would get from even our best "stylists" nowadays, who too often get only highly refined static dead matter, polished information. No, something closer to life itself and even sometimes to heaven.

The men were my gods. In my ears they saved me from dread and drunken times, especially in the heat of summer 1979, Tuscaloosa, when I would write a bit in a sweaty notebook, then return to Beckett and read a few sentences, just to be sane and carry on. A prayer in every sentence, a holding on, a quiet insistence that writing was supremely worth doing even through the awfullest. Thanks, gents.

When I award myself a glow by invoking these prose angels,

as if I were crucial, gathered up in a whirlwind of narcissism by namedropping and blithe association, I am cut down humble all over again. I worshipped them even before I comprehended them. In fact I'm wistful about those days: the sophomore who didn't quite know what had gone on in *The Sound and the Fury* but was nonetheless rapt over images running hard, naked, and glorious as never before. The elder child trying to find his first good words, having read a blotched copy of *Waiting for Godot* almost without a clue but with a conviction something like a rain of heavy water had passed through.

Knock knock, please let me in. I wanted into this party. I quit pre-med and the trumpet and went literary, a loose cannon on deck of the fine arts until a little training in graduate school gave me a profession. I mean writing.

My "Uncle High Lonesome" still lacks the ideal current. The current is there in the last revision in my head; the final version all of us who care have in our heads. The Flaubert version. *Le mot juste, le* current *juste.* Only I could never buy into the man seven years up in the attic writing one book about Ms. Bovary. Not for me. I bought rather the good legends like Faulkner writing my favorite *As I Lay Dying* on the back of a wheelbarrow in six weeks. In the last version of the Vintage International I see Noel Polk has stretched that mythic time to eight weeks, in truth. Very good, Dr. Polk and Dr. Blotner. But be warned, troubleshooters and revisionists. We fundamentalists may one day revolt and hurl you from the temple. We like the Old Lying Faulkner better. Inerrancy, *mon semblables*, or death. Also, I have to sell my stuff quickly like Faulkner, in this case to Versace the designer, who has turned literary with a salon book of hot new American fiction. Too much revision reminds me of the corpse of Emma Bovary, or of an impoverished dance major.

But back to the best, friends.

The necessary thing in the wind right beside your ear. The thing that speaks of another entire world next door, "a hell of a universe," as E. E. Cummings promised. As the mother advises in Padgett Powell's novel *Edisto*: something is always happening. Those long flat summer days, even in them when it seems nothing is moving. Something is going on. Certain whispers tell you. "You, Vardaman. You!" It claims the little oblivious you, as in a Faulkner country imperative.

Another writer has said the writer is the baby who never quits making up imaginary friends. Then you draw them together into this world of whispers. After some study, I have determined that the character Darl in *AILD* is Faulkner himself, his best imaginary friend. The Bundren family is so awful Mister Bill must have felt nostalgic, homesick, so he elbowed himself into the book. Enter Darl, the curious philosopher/idiot, a creature like a Bennington fine arts grad with a thesaurus around his neck, parachuted into this scratchy country. Like Father Time in Hardy. Like an omniscient peeping Tom borrowed from the last century, a not infrequent visitor to a number of Faulkner's books. They appear like berserk interior decorators when things get too slow, or not instructive enough, or adjectival enough. Such screaming flaws in a lesser's work have worked their way into sheer reverence in the canon. Darl must have been a monster to live with. "Kill the son of a bitch, kill him!" demands Jewel, a monster of equal proportion to Darl and hating him worse, as they tackle Darl in the street to be hauled off to the state asylum. Darl guilty, really, of only a little sanitary barn-burning. And through, well, *below* the novel, that little pest Vardaman runs with *his* maimed take, *his* precocious surrealism: "My mother is a fish." But all this, remember, in whispers, for this book, notwithstanding its powerful disaster-driven lunacy, is not a noisy book. Ah, the old enduring Anse with his new teeth after ripping his daughter's abortion money from her paw, the paw of that "wet seed wild in the hot blind earth." Like so many of my acquaintances in the South, Anse would be danger-ous if he had any energy. "If ere a man." Oh shut up. But never noisy, all this. The whole Dysfunction movement started here, in 1930, maybe. I call it life, groaning with laughter. Nothing is funnier than unhappiness, said Beckett.

Facts with neither of these authors just sit still. That remains the attraction of Faulkner and Beckett to me. There is no mere information, as in my story too often. There is no mere lengthed unscrolled photograph as we get in the competent Southern novel these days. Facts move in a current. These men were my principal gods when I was a first reader and remain so into middle age. Sound and fury signifying nothing. Well then what a nothing—no better description of much of Beckett's work.

Richard Howorth reminded me the other day of the priceless Beckett anecdote. Beckett walks out on a fine sunny spring day in Paris with a friend. His friend says What a fine bright wonderful day. Beckett replies Indeed it is. Then his friend says: It's the kind of day that makes a fellow glad to be alive. Beckett: Well, I wouldn't go *that* far.

He was tall and handsome, eaglelike in the face at the end. Faulkner was short and handsome, another brilliant bird in his features, although once he aspired to being a buzzard, given his druthers. Both were understudies of Joyce, both had long and terrifying experiences with drink. But Faulkner was Napoleonic in his views, owning the world in a made-up county. Beckett, built like a shining DeGaulle, grows more asthmatic and near-sighted as he ages, finally drilling a hole of vision through his own navel and down to the process of shifting bones and masses of uncertain and implausible movement. Digestion. Peristalsis. I can't go on, I can't. I go on. Both, too, were attentive to Charles Chaplin (*vide* Faulkner's own moustache), knockabout comedy, and the educated bum. In the single Faulkner recording I've heard, Faulkner reads from *AILD* in a rushed whisper as if really it is an agony to pronounce these things aloud, and in fact he was a lousy reader. You sense his not wanting to be in the room at all. Who can blame him? He knew these voices were interior symphony, never made to be voiced. It is a violation when given audiality to the simple ear. With Faulkner you listen with the whole mind, or *he* must have. I've seen photos of Faulkner utterly worn by these voices, as if wracked by the Furies, who tortured men by turning up the volume of their *own* inner voices. This is also what happens with the practicing drunkard. A doctor in the field of alcoholic treatment once told me that death comes by exhaustion to the terminal drinker, a wracking of the brain, a depletion almost as in the burning of meat. Both Beckett and Faulkner, in their long endurance of drinking bouts, suffered howling voices and visions. Some of them got on the page. But in a current, in a whisper, as close to the prayerful and to the godly in rhythm, pace, and ausculation as we are ever likely to get.

As senior writers, they were "mad, bad and dangerous to know," (said of Byron) not only because they were infectious to your style. Not just style but life. They were likely to make atheists or feverish acolytes of the Other of you—we zealots, we young, we pilgrims with hardly a clue, only big ears and eyes. We found in literary life a subreligion. So I did *not* want to drive from Jackson with my fellow beatniks in Ivy League clothes to shake hands with Faulkner. I knew the man who wrote what I had read had nothing to say to me, nor I to him. I didn't want to see my idol in street shoes, shoulders with some citizen's coat on them—this facsimile. It wouldn't be him. I was glad too that Beckett was far away and weird, an Irishman in Paris, three layers of weird around him. They were not of this earth, those whispers. I would not trivialize them by actually demanding their flesh in sight. Beckett, in fact, spooked me. I apprehended him as *all* voice, out of a low blackish cloud. Beckett was a man of legendary politeness and self-deprecation, referring to every masterpiece as "trash." Faulkner was the legendary statue of the Taciturn. Both men were recalled as . . . *away*, by social acquaintances. They were heeding the involuntary music and the dangerous currents within.

Both, when asked why they wrote, seemed baffled. They remind me of stunned angels, not quite conscious of whom they serve. It might be scriptural and accurate that "to the making of books there is no end." But the making of angels is definitely limited. Forgive me for worshipping at the altar of the great secular scribes, but my God, God, sometimes they did sound like heaven.

Contributors

Joseph Blotner, professor emeritus, University of Michigan, is the author of *Faulkner: A Biography*, published in two volumes in 1974, and in a revised one-volume edition in 1984; *Selected Letters of William Faulkner*; and *Uncollected Stories of William Faulkner*. Professor Blotner has lectured extensively in the United States and Europe on American literature and particularly the work of Faulkner. He has recently completed a literary biography of Robert Penn Warren.

Panthea Reid, professor of English at Louisiana State University, is the author of *William Faulkner: The Abstract and the Actual* and numerous essays, including several on the relations between literature and the visual arts: "The Cubist Novel: Toward Defining the Genre," "Faulkner's Cubist Novels," and "The Economy of Desire: Faulkner's Poetics, from Eroticism to Post-Impressionism." Oxford University Press will publish her *Art and Affection: A Life of Virginia Woolf* in 1996.

Susan V. Donaldson has published essays and presented papers on many Southern literary and visual artists, and is completing a book-length study entitled *Reluctant Visionaries and Southern Others: Writers and Painters of the Modern South*. Among her publications on Faulkner are "Subverting History: Women, Narrative, and Patriarchy in *Absalom, Absalom!*," "Contending Narratives: *Go Down, Moses* and the Short Story Cycle," and "Dismantling *The Saturday Evening Post* Reader: *The Unvanquished* and Changing 'Horizons of Expectations.' " Professor Donaldson teaches at the College of William and Mary.

Michel Gresset is professor of English at the Institut d'Anglais, Université de Paris VII. He is the author of *A Faulkner Chronology* and *Fascination: Faulkner's Fiction, 1919–1936*, as well as editor of the first volume of the Pléiade edition of Faulkner. His latest translation is that of *Thinking of Home: William Faulkner's Letters to His Mother and Father, 1918–1925*, edited by James G. Watson (Paris, Gallimard, 1995).

Robert W. Hamblin is professor of English and director of the Center for Faulkner Studies at Southeast Missouri State University. In addition to publishing numerous essays on Faulkner in various books and journals, he coedited *Faulkner: A Comprehensive Guide to the Brodsky Collection*, a multivolume work published by the University Press of Mississippi. He is also coeditor of the *Teaching Faulkner* newsletter.

Barry Hannah received the William Faulkner Prize for his first novel, *Geronimo Rex*, and the Arnold Gingrich Short Fiction Award for *Airships*, a collection of stories. His achievement in fiction has been honored by the American Academy of Arts and Letters. Among his ten volumes of fiction are *Ray*, *The Tennis Handsome*, *Hey Jack!*, and a recent collection of stories, *Bats Out of Hell*. He is writer in residence at the University of Mississippi.

Thomas C. Hines is professor of history and architecture at the University of California, Los Angeles. He is the author of prize-winning biographies of architects Richard Neutra and Daniel Burnham and more than fifty essays on architectural history in books, scholarly and professional journals, and popular periodicals. In 1996 the University of California Press will publish *William Faulkner and the Tangible Past: The Architecture of Yoknapatawpha*.

Martin Kreiswirth is the author of *William Faulkner: The Making of a Novelist*, as well as coeditor of *The Johns Hopkins Guide to Literary Theory and Criticism*, *Theory Between the Disciplines: Authority/ Vision/ Politics*, and *Constructive Criticism: The Human Sciences in the Age of Theory*. He is professor of English and Associate Dean of Graduate Studies at the University of Western Ontario.

Michael Lahey has recently completed his doctoral work at the University of Alberta. Among his publications are the journal articles "Women and Law in Faulkner," "Trying Emotions: Unpredictable Justice in Faulkner's 'Smoke' and 'Tomorrow,' " and the forthcoming essay "Narcissa's Love Letters: Illicit Space and the Writing of Female Identity in 'There Was a Queen.' " His dissertation is entitled " 'Constructing Justice: Faulkner and the Law.' "

Wesley Morris is the author of *Toward a New Historicism, Friday's Footprint: Structuralism and the Articulated Text*, and (with Barbara Alverson Morris) *Reading Faulkner*. His articles and reviews have appeared in *Western Humanities Review, Georgia Review, Novel, Clio*, and other journals. He is professor of English at Rice University.

Thomas Rankin is associate professor of art and Southern studies at the University of Mississippi. His photographs have appeared in numerous magazines, journals, and books and in his own collection, *Sacred Space: Photographs from the Mississippi Delta*. In 1995 he published *Deaf Maggie Lee Sayre: Photographs of a River Life*.

Candace Waid is associate professor of English and American Studies at Yale University. She is the author of *Edith Wharton's Letters from the Underworld: Fictions of Women and Writing* and coeditor of *Generations: Women in the South*, a special issue of *Southern Exposure*. Her work in progress, *Words in Flesh: Conjuring Art in Southern Literature*, examines Faulkner, among others.

Joel Williamson is the author of *The Crucible of Race: Black-White Relations in the American South Since Emancipation, A Rage for Order, New People: Miscegenation and Mulattos in the United States*, and, most recently, *William Faulkner and Southern History*. The last, Professor Williamson says, attempts "to bring Southern culture to bear upon Faulkner's life and work and simultaneously to bring that life and work to bear upon Southern culture." Fineberger Professor in the humanities at the University of North Carolina, he is currently working on a study of Elvis Presley.

Michael Zeitlin is associate professor of English at the University of British Columbia. He is the author of a number of essays on Faulkner, including "The Passion of Margaret Powers: A Psychoanalytic Reading of *Soldiers' Pay*" and "Faulkner and Psychoanalysis: The *Elmer* Case," published in *Faulkner and Psychology: Faulkner and Yoknapatawpha, 1991*.

Index

343